T0298511

Cloud Security

This comprehensive work surveys the challenges, the best practices in the industry, and the latest developments and technologies. It covers the fundamentals of cloud computing, including deployment models, service models, and the benefits of cloud computing, followed by critical aspects of cloud security, including risk management, threat analysis, data protection, identity and access management, and compliance. **Cloud Security** explores the latest security technologies, such as encryption, multi-factor authentication, and intrusion detection and prevention systems, and their roles in securing the cloud environment.

Features:

- Introduces a user-centric measure of cyber security and provides a comparative study on different methodologies used for cyber security
- Offers real-world case studies and hands-on exercises to give practical understanding of cloud security
- Includes the legal and ethical issues, including the impact of international regulations on cloud security
- Covers fully automated run-time security and vulnerability management.
- Discusses related concepts to provide context, such as Cyber Crime, Password Authentication, Smart Phone Security with examples

This book is aimed at postgraduate students, professionals, and academic researchers working in the fields of computer science and cloud computing.

Cloud Security

Concepts, Applications and Practices

Edited by

Jamuna S. Murthy, Siddesh G. M.
and Srinivasa K. G.

CRC Press is an imprint of the
Taylor & Francis Group, an **informa** business
A CHAPMAN & HALL BOOK

Front cover image: JLStock/Shutterstock

First edition published 2025
by CRC Press
2385 NW Executive Center Drive, Suite 320, Boca Raton FL 33431

and by CRC Press
4 Park Square, Milton Park, Abingdon, Oxon, OX14 4RN

CRC Press is an imprint of Taylor & Francis Group, LLC

ISBN: 978-1-032-59611-2 (hbk)
ISBN: 978-1-032-59612-9 (pbk)
ISBN: 978-1-003-45544-8 (ebk)

DOI: 10.1201/9781003455448

Typeset in Times
by codeMantra

Contents

Preface

In an era where the digital landscape is continuously reshaping the contours of our daily lives, the emergence of cloud computing stands as a testament to human ingenuity and technological advancement. This book, an odyssey through the intricate world of cloud-based systems and their intersection with cyber security, is born out of a necessity to understand and navigate this new terrain. The genesis of this book lies in the recognition of a fundamental shift in the IT landscape, where cloud computing is not just an option but a pervasive reality. Organizations, big and small, are moving away from traditional on-premise IT infrastructure, lured by the myriad benefits of cloud-based systems. These benefits—from cost savings in hardware to the flexibility of software management—are reshaping how businesses operate. However, this migration is not without its challenges, and chief among them is the safeguarding of the most vital asset for any organization: information.

As a writer and a technologist, I was intrigued by this paradox of advancement and vulnerability. The more we depend on cloud computing, the more we seem to lose control over our technological assets and, by extension, our data. This book is a journey into understanding this conundrum, exploring how cloud computing and cyber security are evolving in tandem, often in a high-stakes dance of advancement and protection. In these pages, you will find a comprehensive exploration of how cyber security is not just a barrier but a facilitator in the cloud-based environment. The narrative delves into the intricacies of how cloud computing, while offering a public utility model's economic and operational advantages, simultaneously poses significant security challenges and a potential loss of control over critical data.

This book is particularly timely, given the increasing prevalence of cyberattacks in the cloud computing era. Organizations are compelled to adopt proactive measures to counter these threats, and this book aims to be a guide in that endeavor. We discuss the four pillars of cloud-based cyber security—updated technologies, highly secure platforms, skilled manpower, and robust connectivity—and how they form a synergistic defense mechanism. Furthermore, we delve into innovative solutions, such as the cloud-based cyber security solution developed jointly by Amazon, Azure, and Google, which illustrates the fusion of advanced detection, collective learning, and scalability in analytics to fortify security operations. This solution, among others, represents a beacon of hope in the seemingly relentless struggle against cyber threats.

As you navigate through these chapters, you will find a blend of theoretical frameworks, practical insights, and futuristic outlooks. This book is intended for IT professionals, business leaders, policy makers, and anyone intrigued by the evolving landscape of cloud computing and cyber security. It is a compilation of knowledge, a narrative of challenges and solutions, and above all, a call to action for a more secure and efficient digital future.

Welcome to a journey of understanding, preparedness, and resilience in the cloud era!

Acknowledgments

We express our sincere gratitude to the individuals who have played a pivotal role in the completion of this book. Our heartfelt thanks go to the college management, contributors, and students who provided unwavering encouragement, fostering an environment conducive to our work.

Special appreciation is extended to Dr. NVR Naidu, Principal of Ramaiah Institute of Technology, for his invaluable guidance and steadfast support throughout the journey of creating this book.

Our deepest appreciation is reserved for our loved ones, families, whose understanding and support were indispensable during the demanding process of writing this book. We are especially grateful for their warmth and encouragement, even in the face of our inability to attend to family chores. Their steadfast support was instrumental, without which this venture would not have been possible.

Finally, we express our gratitude to the Almighty, whose blessings have been the cornerstone of our efforts. We acknowledge the divine guidance that has enriched our endeavors and made the completion of this book possible.

About the Editors

Jamuna S. Murthy is currently working as an Assistant Professor in the Department of Computer Science and Engineering at Ramaiah Institute of Technology, Bengaluru. She is pursuing her PhD in Deep Learning. She has been the academic topper throughout her education and has received Best Project Award for her M.Tech thesis work from Ramaiah Institute of Technology in the year 2017. She has received funding from DST for product development called "FitQua: Smart Water Bottle" in 2020–2022. She specializes in the "Architecting with Google Compute Engine" certification by Google Cloud and is recognized as a Certified Educator. She also holds a good publication record of peer reviewed International Conferences such as ICACNI-2017, ICACDS 2021 & 2022, COMSYS-2023. Her journals and Book Publications include IGI Global, Springer, etc. Her main areas of research interests include Cloud Computing and Big Data, Theoretical Computer Science, Machine Learning, Deep Learning, and Natural Language Processing. She is a distinguished member of the Association for Computing Machinery, the National Society of Professional Engineers (NSPE), and ISTE.

Siddesh G. M. is currently working as Professor and Head in the Department of Artificial Intelligence and Data Science, M. S. Ramaiah Institute of Technology, Bangalore. He is the recipient of Seed Money to Young Scientist for Research (SMYSR) for FY 2014–2015, from Government of Karnataka, Vision Group on Science and Technology (VGST). He has published a good number of research papers in reputed International Conferences and Journals. He has authored books on *Network Data Analytics*, *Statistical Programming in R*, *Internet of Things* with Springer, Oxford University Press, and Cengage publishers, respectively. He has edited research monographs in the area of *Cyber Physical Systems*, Fog *Computing and Energy Aware Computing*, and *Bioinformatics* with CRC Press, IGI Global, and Springer publishers, respectively. His main areas of research interests include the Internet of Things, Distributed Computing and Data Analytics. He is a member of ISTE, IETE, etc.

Srinivasa K. G. is a Professor of Data Science and Artificial Intelligence Programme at DSPM IIIT-Naya Raipur, C. G. India. He received his PhD in Computer Science and Engineering from Bangalore University in 2007. He is the recipient of All India Council for Technical Education—Career Award for Young Teachers, Indian Society of Technical Education—ISGITS National Award for Best Research Work Done by Young Teachers, Institution of Engineers (India)—IEI Young Engineer Award in Computer Engineering, Rajarambapu Patil National Award for Promising Engineering Teacher Award from ISTE—2012, IMS Singapore—Visiting Scientist Fellowship Award. He has published more than 150 research papers in International Conferences and Journals. He has visited many Universities abroad as a visiting researcher—He has visited University of Oklahoma, USA; Iowa State University, USA; Hong Kong University; Korean University; National University of Singapore; University of British Columbia, Canada are his few prominent visits. He has authored many books in the areas of Learning Analytics, Network Data Analytics, Soft Computing, Social Network Analysis, High Performance Computing, R Programming, etc. with prestigious international publishers such as Springer, TMH, Oxford, Cengage, and IGI Global. He has edited research monographs in the area of *Cyber Physical Systems*, *Fog Computing* and *Energy Aware Computing* with CRC Press and IGI Global. He has been awarded BOYSCAST Fellowship by DST, Govt. of India, for conducting post-doctoral research work at University of Melbourne, Australia. His recent research areas include Innovative Teaching Practices in Engineering Education, pedagogy; outcomes-based education. He is the senior member of IEEE and ACM.

Contributors

Anirudh U.
Thoughtclan Technologies
India

Dhanashekar K.
The Ohio State University
USA

Girish G. N.
PESU Venture Labs
India

Het Joshi
Ramaiah Institute of Technology
India

Jahanvi B. Dinesh
Chalmers University of Technology
Germany

Jamuna S. Murthy
Ramaiah Institute of Technology
India

Kedarnath S. Gubbi
Florida State University
Florida

Neeraj Phadke
Ramaiah Institute of Technology
India

Rajib Kar
NIT Durgapur
India

Sahana D. Gowda
RV University
India

Samarth Kulkarni
Santa Clara University,
Santa Clara, USA

Sangay Chedup
Jigme Namgyel Engineering College
Devasthan, Bhutan

Shiva Darshan S. L.
NIT Warangal
India

Siddesh G. M.
Ramaiah Institute of Technology
India

Srikrishna H. V.
Northeastern University
Boston, USA

K. G. Srinivasa
IIIT Naya Raipur
India

Srinivas Naik
Indian Institute of Information
Technology, Design and
Manufacturing Kurnool Kurnool
India

Suresh L.
RNS Institute of Technology
India

Vaibhavari Balakrishna Rao
Cornell Tech, Cornell University
USA

Wen-Cheng Lai
National Yunlin University of Science
and Technology
Taiwan

Yash Gawankar
Affinsys AI
Dubai

1 Collaborative Cloud
Safeguarding Sensitive Information through Innovative Secure Data-Sharing Practices

Jamuna S. Murthy and Rajib Kar

1.1 INTRODUCTION TO DATA SHARING

The evolution of data sharing within cloud environments signifies a transformative shift in the collaborative dynamics of modern organizations. This paradigm change is not merely advantageous but stands as a foundational element for fostering innovation, optimizing operational efficiency, and streamlining the decision-making processes. In the dynamic landscape of contemporary business, the seamless transfer of data between entities has become instrumental in shaping how organizations operate and interact.

The research conducted by Zelenay et al. in 2019 sheds light on the transformative impact of cloud technologies in the realm of secure communication and collaboration. Their findings highlight the pivotal role played by cloud solutions not only in ensuring secure communication but also in significantly contributing to the facilitation of efficient data-sharing practices. The utilization of cloud technologies has, therefore, become instrumental in creating a robust foundation for collaborative endeavors within and between organizations. This underscores the broader implications of cloud-driven data sharing, emphasizing its role as a catalyst for innovation and operational efficiency in the contemporary business landscape [1].

In a related domain, Chadwick and his colleagues (2020) stressed the significance of a cloud-edge-based data-security architecture for sharing and analyzing cyber threat information. Their research underscores the critical role of secure data sharing in the cybersecurity domain, recognizing the need for advanced architectural approaches to mitigate threats effectively. The emphasis on a cloud-edge model indicates a recognition of the distributed nature of data, and the importance of securing data at the edge, where it is generated and consumed. This approach demonstrates the evolving landscape of cybersecurity practices, with secure data sharing emerging as a key component in addressing the complex challenges posed by cyber threats [2].

DOI: 10.1201/9781003455448-1

Furthermore, the work by Naidu et al. in 2021 offers valuable insights into the application of robust medical data-sharing practices. Their research, which incorporates collaborative hypotheses and an Elastic Net regression model, underscores the practical implications of secure data sharing in specialized domains, particularly in healthcare. By applying advanced statistical models and collaborative approaches, the research showcases the adaptability and significance of data-sharing methodologies in improving healthcare outcomes. The study serves as a testament to the diverse applications of secure data sharing, illustrating its role in enhancing the efficiency and effectiveness of data-driven decision-making processes in critical domains like healthcare [3].

1.1.1 Overview of Data Sharing in Cloud Environments

Cloud computing has revolutionized the landscape of data sharing, serving as a transformative catalyst in the way organizations collaborate and exchange information. The hallmark of cloud computing is its scalable and on-demand access to resources, fundamentally altering the traditional paradigms of data sharing. Unlike conventional methods, cloud-based data sharing goes beyond geographical constraints, opening up avenues for real-time collaboration and reducing latency. Platforms like Google Cloud and Amazon Web Services (AWS) stand as exemplars, showcasing the unprecedented efficiency gains achievable through cloud-driven data sharing [4,5].

The process of data sharing in cloud environments has evolved over time, and various patterns have emerged to address different architectural needs. One common approach is the "Data Sharing By Copy" pattern, characterized by the visualization of data sharing through the copying or moving of data between services within the same cloud. While suitable for simple architectures, this method may involve dependencies between compute and storage.

A more advanced approach, gaining popularity, is the "No-Copy Data Sharing" or "Direct Access Pattern." This pattern is characterized by several services operating in the same cloud, where computing and storage are completely separate. The advantages of this approach include improved scalability, cost-efficiency, and direct access to data without the need for copying or moving. Technologies like Azure Synapse Link for Azure Cosmos DB, BigQuery external data sources, or Snowflake data sharing exemplify this pattern in action.

For scenarios involving third-party managed systems or systems spanning multiple clouds or regions, the "Hovering Multi-Cloud Replication Data Sharing" or "Twinning Pattern" becomes relevant. This pattern allows consumers across different clouds to access data, but it requires replication, introducing costs and additional replication time, even if it operates seamlessly under the hood. Cross-region data sharing in Snowflake is an illustration of this pattern.

An emerging and sophisticated approach is the "Multi-Cloud No-Copy Data Sharing" or "Data Portal Pattern." In this evolving pattern, a service operates across multiple clouds, storage spans various different-cloud services, compute and storage are separated, and direct data access is achieved without the necessity for copying or moving data. Technologies like Azure Arc or Google Anthos, exemplified by offerings like BigQuery Omni and Azure Arc-enabled data services, enable this advanced and seamless form of multi-cloud data sharing. This approach represents a cutting-edge solution, providing flexibility and efficiency in data access across diverse cloud environments.

1.1.2 Importance of Secure Data Sharing for Collaborative Work

While the benefits of data sharing are evident, the importance of securing shared data cannot be overstated. As organizations increasingly rely on collaborative work environments, safeguarding sensitive information from unauthorized access becomes paramount. Secure data sharing is essential for maintaining data integrity, preserving user privacy, and adhering to regulatory compliance standards [6].

In a collaborative ecosystem, the openness required for effective teamwork introduces inherent security challenges. Organizations must find a delicate balance between fostering an environment of openness and ensuring robust security measures are in place. Without compromising on data protection, organizations need to create an atmosphere where employees feel empowered to share information, ideas, and resources seamlessly [7].

In response to the increasing demand for inter-organizational data sharing across various domains such as mobility, smart cities, energy, healthcare, research, and commercial industries, the necessity for an interoperable solution has become evident. Data spaces have emerged as a viable solution to address the challenges associated with inter-organizational data integration across diverse technology stacks, environments, and geographical locations. These spaces streamline the process of connecting data while respecting the rules and policies, often encapsulated in contracts, established by data providers for the data they choose to share [8].

The fundamental characteristics of data spaces revolve around the roles of their participants:

- **Data Providers:** These entities contribute data to the market, making their information available for sharing within the data space.
- **Data Consumers:** Organizations or entities that retrieve data from external sources and integrate it with their own datasets.
- **Operators:** The facilitating entities that broker services, including the data catalog, enabling data providers to define their data assets and allowing data consumers to search for and access the data they need.

All data within the data space are cataloged, but its distribution is decentralized. Unlike a centralized database, there is no single platform provider, and data remain at the source chosen by each data provider. This decentralized approach ensures that data are not moved to a large central repository [9].

The primary design principles of data spaces center around data control and trusted sharing. According to this conceptual framework, data should remain under the control of the provider. Enforceable contracts are attached to data offerings, dictating who can access the data, for what purposes, and under what conditions. For instance, a government agency in a European Union (EU) member state may choose to limit the sharing of certain data assets with other member states while allowing full access to local agencies within their jurisdiction. Data consumers within the same data space may have distinct access rights [10,11].

One key feature of data spaces is their support for an interoperable IT environment for data sharing. This ensures data portability regardless of the hosting or consumption platform. In essence, data spaces provide a robust framework that not only facilitates seamless data sharing but also upholds data control and trust among participants in an increasingly interconnected digital landscape.

Within the realm of data spaces, AWS endeavors to establish a user-friendly integration between the requisite connecting technology for participating in a data space and AWS services. This strategic approach aims to empower customers to share data in a standardized manner while equipping them with services and tools to maximize the utilization of both their proprietary data and third-party data. In essence, AWS plays a pivotal role in facilitating the seamless exchange of data within data spaces.

Data spaces, within the AWS framework, primarily address the discovery and transfer of data assets based on agreements between participants in a data exchange. The underlying AWS infrastructure serves a dual purpose—it not only enables participants to securely, scalably, and reliably run the necessary data space connectors but also provides a suite of services to support the consumption and analysis of data post-transfer.

Figure 1.1 presents a comprehensive high-level reference architecture that illustrates the interaction dynamics of data space connectors transcending organizational boundaries. Additionally, it showcases the utilization of native AWS services specifically tailored for analytics and machine learning (ML) applications. This architecture provides a visual representation of the key components and their interconnections within the context of data spaces leveraging AWS.

In the presented reference architecture, the deployment of the data space connector is orchestrated within Docker containers. These containers may leverage diverse orchestration technologies such as Amazon Elastic Container Service (Amazon ECS) or Amazon Elastic Kubernetes Service (Amazon EKS). The chosen orchestration layer can seamlessly deploy and manage these containers, providing a flexible and

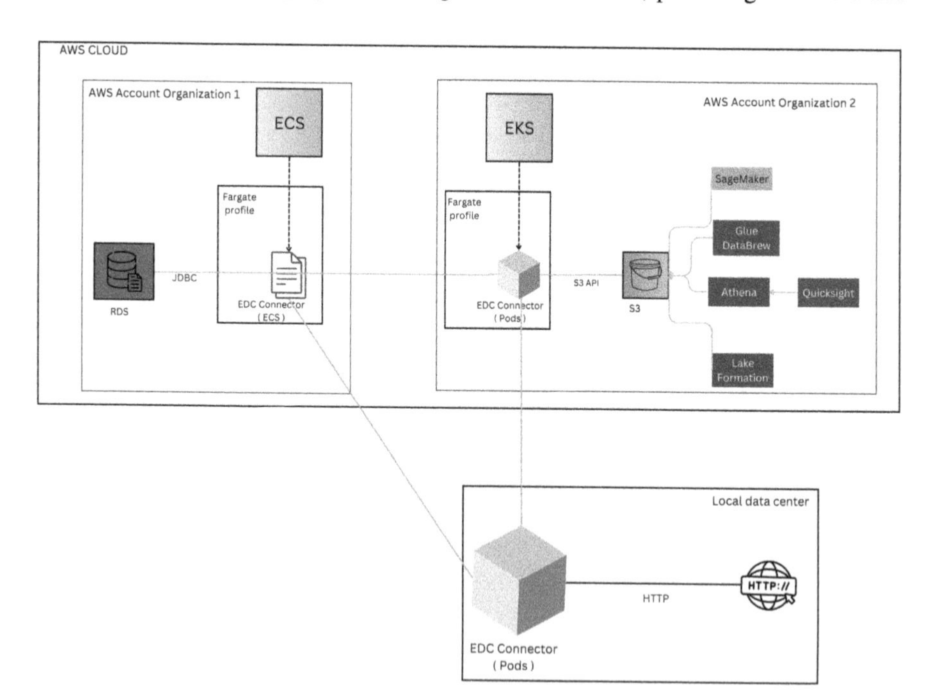

FIGURE 1.1 Comprehensive high-level architecture of AWS dataspaces.

scalable infrastructure for the data space connector. Furthermore, the architecture embraces a serverless compute engine, specifically AWS Fargate, to enhance the efficiency and resource utilization of the deployment.

The use of Docker containers ensures a modular and portable deployment of the data space connector, allowing for consistent performance across different environments. Orchestration technologies like Amazon ECS or Amazon EKS bring an additional layer of manageability, enabling efficient scaling, monitoring, and maintenance of the deployed containers. In terms of data sources and data targets, Figure 1.3 illustrates a combination of Amazon S3 and Amazon Relational Database Service (Amazon RDS). Amazon S3 serves as a scalable and durable object storage solution, accommodating diverse data types and providing the foundation for storing and retrieving large volumes of data within the data space. On the other hand, Amazon RDS offers a managed relational database service, ensuring the reliability and scalability of the database component within the architecture.

This combination of storage services caters to the diverse needs of data within the data space, from unstructured data in Amazon S3 to structured data in Amazon RDS. It emphasizes the flexibility and versatility required to handle different types of data sources and targets within the context of data spaces.

1.1.3 Common Scenarios and Use Cases for Data Sharing in the Cloud

Understanding the diverse scenarios and use cases for data sharing in the cloud is essential for appreciating its broad applicability. Collaborative project management is a prime example, where teams working on projects across different locations can efficiently share project-related data and updates in real time [12,13]. This fosters a cohesive and well-coordinated project environment. In visualizing the usecase cloud-based data sharing, Figure 1.2 illustrates the interconnected nature of this process with respect to AWS Cloud Data Sharing.

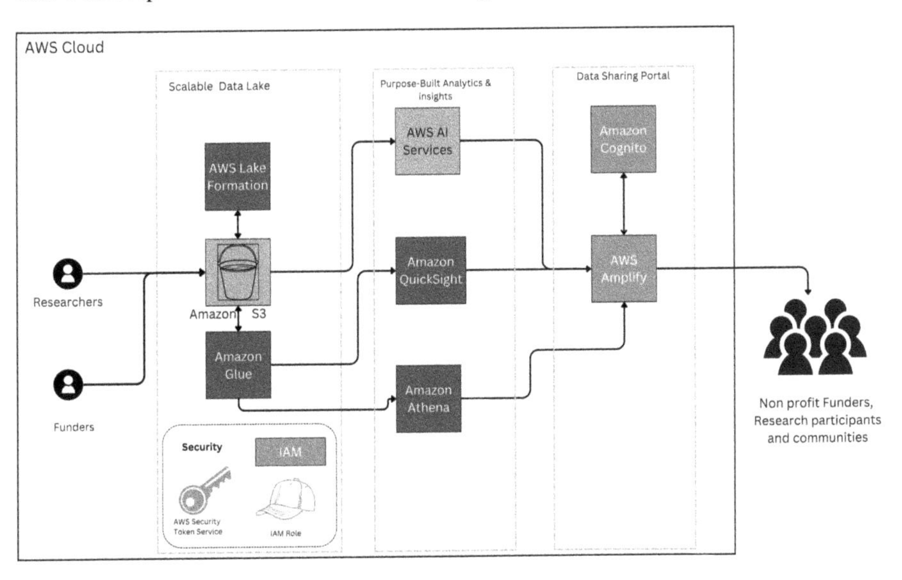

FIGURE 1.2 Data sharing in Amazon Web Services.

Step 1: Uploading Data to Amazon S3

In the initial phase, nonprofit researchers commence their data-sharing journey by uploading their datasets to Amazon Simple Storage Service (Amazon S3). This step lays the groundwork for seamless data accessibility and serves as the entry point for subsequent collaborative efforts. Moreover, it extends the flexibility to grant project funders permission to contribute additional datasets from previous projects, fostering a comprehensive and centralized data repository.

Step 2: Secure Access Authorization with Identity and Access Management

AWS Identity and Access Management (IAM) takes center stage in Step 2. IAM plays a crucial role in creating roles and tokens, ensuring the secure authorization of access to the Amazon S3 repository. This step goes beyond conventional security measures by also facilitating the configuration of the Amazon S3 uploader client app. This secure configuration not only enhances the protection of data but also contributes to the user-friendliness of the uploader app, simplifying researchers' interactions with the system.

Step 3: Governance with AWS Lake Formation

AWS Lake Formation enters the scene, introducing simplicity in the management and governance of the scalable data lake that utilizes Amazon S3 as its storage foundation. Beyond its fundamental role as a data lake, Lake Formation offers a suite of features, including access controls for row-, column-, and table-level security. Additionally, it incorporates audit trails and automatic schema discovery, streamlining the governance process and ensuring the integrity and security of the stored data.

Step 4: Data Extraction and Transformation with AWS Glue

AWS Glue takes charge of the data lifecycle by orchestrating the extraction, transformation, cataloging, and ingestion of data across diverse data stores. This comprehensive data management ensures that the data within the Amazon S3 storage is not only accessible but also prepared for subsequent analytical and ML processes.

Step 5: Leveraging ML and Visualization Tools

In the fifth step of the data-sharing process, researchers gain the capability to extend the utility of their stored data by providing access to Amazon SageMaker or AWS Artificial Intelligence (AI) services. This pivotal step empowers researchers to embark on ML endeavors, enabling them to build, train, and deploy ML models. Additionally, it facilitates the enrichment of datasets with advanced AI capabilities. Simultaneously, researchers can utilize Amazon QuickSight, a versatile visualization tool, to craft insightful visualizations and dashboards. This step not only enhances the depth of analysis but also lays the foundation for effective communication of data insights with stakeholders.

Step 6: Streamlining Data Analysis and Sharing with QuickSight

Building on the capabilities introduced in the previous step, Step 6 reinforces the utilization of Amazon QuickSight for creating visualizations and dashboards. This tool proves invaluable for researchers in conducting in-depth analyses and distilling complex data into clear and comprehensible insights. Furthermore, it serves as a robust platform for sharing these insights with diverse audiences, including funders, research participants, and communities. The visual representations generated by QuickSight contribute to a more accessible and engaging presentation of research findings.

Step 7: Interactive Data Querying with Amazon Athena

In the seventh step, Amazon Athena takes center stage, providing an interactive SQL-style query engine that researchers can deploy on the data lake. This capability allows for on-the-fly querying of the stored data, fostering a dynamic and responsive approach to data analysis. The interactive nature of Athena enables researchers to perform ad-hoc queries, gaining valuable insights and refining their analytical processes. This step significantly contributes to the agility and versatility of the research workflow.

Step 8: Building a Data-Sharing Portal with AWS Amplify

In Step 8, researchers are equipped with the tools to build and deploy a dedicated data-sharing portal using AWS Amplify. This managed service simplifies the entire process of constructing, deploying, and hosting a static website. The incorporation of libraries within AWS Amplify streamlines permissions management, ensuring that access controls are efficiently implemented. The data-sharing portal becomes a centralized hub where researchers can disseminate their findings and collaborate with stakeholders, promoting a cohesive and accessible information-sharing environment.

Step 9: Access Control and User Management with Amazon Cognito

The final step introduces Amazon Cognito to simplify login and permission management for the data-sharing portal. This service plays a crucial role in restricting access to the portal, ensuring that only authorized individuals can view the shared data. By providing granular control over user permissions, Amazon Cognito enhances the security and integrity of the data-sharing process. This step is essential for maintaining confidentiality, controlling access levels, and preserving the overall integrity of the collaborative research environment.

Cross-functional team collaboration is another scenario where cloud-based data sharing shines. Departments with distinct functions can share information seamlessly, breaking down silos and promoting a holistic understanding of organizational goals. For instance, marketing teams can share campaign data with sales teams, leading to more informed decision-making processes with respect to the Google Cloud Platform (GCP).

In sensitive domains like healthcare, the importance of secure data sharing is magnified. Healthcare providers can securely share patient data in the cloud, facilitating collaborative diagnosis and treatment planning. This not only improves the quality of care but also underscores the critical role of secure data sharing in domains where privacy and confidentiality are paramount.

1.2 CHALLENGES IN SECURE DATA SHARING

While secure data sharing in the cloud offers numerous benefits, it is not without its challenges. These challenges necessitate thoughtful consideration to effectively mitigate risks and uphold the confidentiality of sensitive information [14,15].

One primary challenge lies in ensuring the security of the shared data against unauthorized access. The very nature of data sharing introduces vulnerabilities, and without robust security measures, there is a heightened risk of sensitive information falling into the wrong hands. This challenge is particularly critical given the dynamic and interconnected nature of cloud environments, where multiple entities share the same infrastructure.

Another challenge involves the potential for data exposure during the sharing process. Despite encryption methods being employed, the transit of data between different entities creates windows of vulnerability. Attackers may exploit these windows to intercept, manipulate, or gain unauthorized access to the shared information. This underscores the importance of not only encrypting the data but also implementing secure channels for its transmission.

Regulatory compliance poses yet another challenge in secure data sharing. Different industries and regions have distinct regulations governing the handling and sharing of sensitive data. Achieving compliance with these diverse standards becomes a complex task, demanding a nuanced understanding of legal frameworks and the implementation of robust mechanisms to ensure adherence. Failure to comply with these regulations can result in severe consequences, including legal penalties and reputational damage.

Moreover, the challenge extends to the management of access controls for encrypted data. While encryption safeguards the confidentiality of shared information, managing access permissions effectively becomes crucial. Improperly configured access controls can lead to data leaks or unauthorized exposure, compromising the very security that encryption aims to establish.

1.2.1 Analysis of Security Challenges Associated with Data Sharing

The security challenges associated with data sharing in the cloud are multifaceted, involving potential threats such as data breaches, unauthorized access, and data leakage. A comprehensive analysis of these challenges is crucial for understanding the complex landscape of potential threats to data integrity and confidentiality during the sharing process [16,17].

I. **Data Breaches:** One of the foremost security challenges is the risk of data breaches. High-profile incidents across various industries have highlighted the vulnerability of shared data to cyber threats. For instance, in the financial industry, there have been cases where customer financial records were compromised due to unauthorized access to shared databases. Such breaches not only jeopardize the confidentiality of sensitive information but can also lead to financial losses and damage to the reputation of the affected organizations.
II. **Unauthorized Access:** Unauthorized access is a persistent concern in the realm of data sharing. In the healthcare industry, for example, where patient records are frequently shared among healthcare providers, the risk of unauthorized access to personal health information is a critical concern. Unauthorized access can result in the exposure of private and sensitive medical records, leading to ethical, legal, and reputational consequences for healthcare organizations.

III. **Data Leakage:** Data leakage is another significant challenge, especially when sharing involves the transmission of sensitive information across networks. In the technology and manufacturing sectors, where proprietary designs and intellectual property are frequently shared between collaborators, the risk of data leakage is heightened. A breach in the confidentiality of design specifications or proprietary algorithms can have severe consequences, including loss of competitive advantage and compromised innovation.

A thorough analysis of these security challenges involves considering the specific vulnerabilities within an industry's data-sharing practices. For instance, in the e-commerce sector, where customer data are routinely shared for personalized marketing efforts, the challenge lies in securing this data against unauthorized access and potential breaches that could lead to identity theft or fraudulent activities.

To address these challenges, industries often implement encryption protocols, multifactor authentication, and robust access controls. In the financial sector, for instance, blockchain technology is increasingly being explored to enhance the security of shared financial data. Additionally, industry-specific regulations, such as the Health Insurance Portability and Accountability Act (HIPAA) in healthcare, play a pivotal role in shaping data-sharing practices by imposing strict standards for data protection and privacy [18].

1.2.2 Understanding the Risks of Unauthorized Access and Data Exposure

The risk of unauthorized access poses a significant threat to data shared in the cloud. Unauthorized users gaining access to sensitive information can lead to data breaches, financial losses, and reputational damage for organizations [19,20].

In a cloud computing environment, data are often stored remotely on servers owned and maintained by third-party providers. Unauthorized access refers to individuals or entities gaining entry to this data without proper permission. The consequences of this risk can be severe.

Example: Consider a scenario where a malicious actor gains unauthorized access to a Cloud Storage service containing customer databases for an e-commerce company. This intruder can extract personal information, such as names, addresses, and credit card details, leading to privacy violations and potential identity theft.

A data breach occurs when unauthorized individuals gain access to confidential or protected information. In the context of the cloud, this could involve compromising login credentials, exploiting vulnerabilities in the cloud infrastructure, or bypassing security measures.

Example: Let's say a healthcare organization utilizes cloud services to store patient records. If an unauthorized user accesses these data, it could result in the exposure of patients' medical histories, which not only violates privacy regulations but also undermines the trust patients have in the healthcare provider.

Unauthorized access and subsequent data breaches can have financial implications for organizations. Remediation costs, legal fees, and potential fines for failing to protect sensitive data can lead to substantial financial losses.

Example: A financial institution using cloud-based platforms to manage client transactions could face significant financial losses if unauthorized access leads to the compromise of transactional data. The institution may incur costs related to investigating the breach, notifying affected clients, and implementing enhanced security measures.

The impact of unauthorized access extends beyond financial losses. Organizations may suffer reputational damage as news of a security breach spreads, eroding the trust of customers, partners, and stakeholders.

Example: Imagine a popular cloud-based file-sharing service experiencing unauthorized access, resulting in the exposure of sensitive documents belonging to high-profile users. The loss of trust from these users could lead to a decline in the service's reputation, affecting user acquisition and retention.

1.2.3 Regulatory Compliance Issues Related to Data Sharing

Compliance with data protection regulations adds another layer of complexity. For example, the General Data Protection Regulation (GDPR) imposes strict requirements on how organizations handle and share personal data, necessitating robust measures to achieve and maintain compliance [21].

Regulatory compliance refers to the act of following laws, rules, and regulations set by governing bodies. In the context of data sharing, it means adhering to specific guidelines and requirements established to protect individuals' privacy and ensure responsible handling of their personal information.

Data Protection Regulation highlights the legal frameworks that govern how organizations collect, process, store, and share data. GDPR is a prominent example of such regulations, but there are others globally, like the California Consumer Privacy Act (CCPA) in the United States.

Compliance with data protection regulations introduces an additional layer of complexity. This complexity arises from the need for organizations to implement specific measures and processes to ensure they are meeting the legal requirements outlined in the regulations.

Example—General Data Protection Regulation

The GDPR is a set of regulations designed to protect the privacy and personal data of individuals within the EU and the European Economic Area (EEA). It imposes strict requirements on organizations that handle personal data, including rules on consent, data breach notification, and the right to be forgotten.

Example Scenario: Let's consider a scenario where a multinational company based in the EU needs to share customer data with a third-party service provider for data analysis. To comply with GDPR, the company would need to ensure that:

- Customers have given explicit consent for their data to be shared.
- The third-party provider adheres to GDPR standards in data processing.
- Robust security measures are in place to prevent data breaches.
- In case of a data breach, the company must promptly notify both the individuals affected and the relevant data protection authorities.

In this example, achieving and maintaining compliance with GDPR requires the company to establish and enforce specific practices and policies related to data sharing.

1.3 ENCRYPTION TECHNIQUES FOR SECURE DATA SHARING

To address security challenges, encryption serves as a fundamental tool in ensuring the confidentiality and integrity of shared data [22,23].

1.3.1 Overview of Encryption Methods for Data in Transit and at Rest

Encryption methods are crucial for maintaining the confidentiality and integrity of shared data. For data at rest, Advanced Encryption Standard (AES) is commonly used, providing a strong and widely adopted encryption algorithm. For data in transit, Transport Layer Security (TLS) is employed, securing communication over networks. These encryption techniques ensure that even if unauthorized access occurs, the data remain indecipherable without the appropriate decryption keys.

Both GCP and AWS offer encryption services for data at rest and in transit. GCP provides Cloud Storage encryption for data at rest, using AES-256 by default. Additionally, Google Cloud uses TLS for securing data in transit. AWS offers services like AWS Key Management Service (KMS) for data at rest and supports TLS for securing data in transit.

1.3.2 Role of End-to-End Encryption in Ensuring Data Confidentiality

End-to-end encryption is a powerful method that ensures only the intended recipients can access the data, minimizing the risk of interception during transmission. Messaging apps like Signal and WhatsApp employ end-to-end encryption to safeguard user communication from eavesdropping.

For instance, in Google Cloud, Cloud KMS can be used to manage cryptographic keys, enhancing the security of end-to-end encryption. AWS offers services like AWS KMS and AWS KMS for custom applications to facilitate end-to-end encryption. Thus, both GCP and AWS support the implementation of end-to-end encryption.

1.3.3 Key Management Strategies for Secure Data Sharing

Effectively managing encryption keys is essential for maintaining the security of shared data. Robust key management strategies involve secure key storage, regular rotation, and access control. Cloud service providers often offer key management services to enhance the security of data shared within their platforms.

Google Cloud provides Cloud KMS to manage cryptographic keys securely. AWS offers AWS KMS as a fully managed service for creating and controlling encryption keys. Both cloud providers emphasize secure key management practices, including regular key rotation and access controls.

1.4 CASE STUDIES AND BEST PRACTICES

1.4.1 Examination of Real-World Case Studies on Successful and Failed Data Sharing

Real-world case studies provide valuable insights into the successes and failures of data-sharing initiatives. For example, the collaboration between research institutions using cloud platforms for genomic data sharing showcases successful secure data-sharing practices, while instances of data breaches underscore the importance of implementing effective security measures [24,25].

- **Example of Successful Data Sharing:** One prominent example of successful data sharing is the collaboration between research institutions in genomics. Cloud platforms, such as those provided by Google Cloud and AWS, facilitate the secure sharing of large genomic datasets. Researchers can analyze and share genomic information efficiently, leading to advancements in personalized medicine and genomics research. This demonstrates how effective data-sharing practices, when implemented securely, can contribute to scientific progress and innovation.
- **Example of Failed Data Sharing:** Instances of data breaches serve as examples of failed data-sharing initiatives. For instance, the Equifax data breach in 2017 exposed the sensitive personal information of millions of individuals. This breach underscored the critical importance of implementing robust security measures, including encryption, access controls, and regular security audits, to prevent unauthorized access and protect sensitive data.

1.4.2 Best Practices for Implementing Secure Data Sharing in Cloud Environments

Best practices involve adopting a defense-in-depth approach, implementing access controls, regularly auditing data access, and staying abreast of evolving security threats. For instance, the principle of least privilege ensures that users have the minimum level of access necessary to perform their tasks, minimizing the potential for unauthorized data exposure.

- **Defense-in-Depth Approach:** Microsoft Azure adopts a defense-in-depth approach, integrating multiple layers of security controls such as network security groups, IAM, and encryption. This approach provides a comprehensive defense strategy against various security threats.
- **Principle of Least Privilege:** The principle of least privilege is exemplified by organizations like Salesforce. Users are granted the minimum level of access necessary for their roles, reducing the risk of unauthorized access. This practice is fundamental in preventing data exposure and maintaining a secure environment.

1.4.3 Recommendations for Organizations to Enhance their Data-Sharing Security Posture

Recommendations include investing in employee training programs, staying informed about the latest security technologies, and establishing incident response plans. Continuous monitoring and proactive measures contribute to an organization's ability to adapt to emerging threats, ultimately enhancing its data-sharing security posture.

- **Investing in Employee Training Programs:** Cisco emphasizes employee training programs to enhance cybersecurity awareness. Through continuous education, employees become more vigilant against social engineering attacks and other security threats, contributing to an organization's overall data-sharing security.
- **Staying Informed about the Latest Security Technologies:** Palo Alto Networks consistently updates its security solutions to address emerging threats. By staying informed about the latest technologies and threat landscapes, organizations can proactively enhance their security posture and adapt to evolving challenges in data sharing.
- **Establishing Incident Response Plans:** IBM provides incident response services to organizations. Having a well-defined incident response plan is crucial for mitigating the impact of security incidents, ensuring a swift and effective response to potential data breaches.

1.4.4 Innovative Best Practice for Data Sharing in Cloud

Here are some innovative data-sharing practices specifically tailored for cloud environments:

I. **Confidential Computing:** Leveraging technologies like Intel SGX or AMD SEV, confidential computing ensures that data remain encrypted even when in use. This protects sensitive information during processing in the cloud.
II. **Cloud-Based Data Marketplaces:** Establishing secure data marketplaces on cloud platforms allows organizations to share and monetize datasets while maintaining control over access, permissions, and ensuring compliance with privacy regulations.
III. **Data Tokenization in Cloud Storage:** Tokenizing sensitive data stored in the cloud involves replacing original data with tokens, preserving usability while enhancing security. This approach is valuable in scenarios where specific data elements need protection.
IV. **Dynamic Access Controls:** Implementing dynamic access controls in the cloud ensures that users have access to data based on contextual factors such as time, location, or device, enhancing security and reducing the risk of unauthorized access.

V. **Cloud-Based Federated Learning:** Extending federated learning to the cloud allows multiple organizations to collaboratively train ML models without sharing raw data. Each party retains control over their data while contributing to model improvement.

VI. **Data Mesh Architecture:** Data mesh principles, when applied in a cloud environment, enable decentralized data ownership and access. This approach improves data discoverability, reduces bottlenecks, and enhances the agility of data sharing within and across organizations.

VII. **Secure Cloud APIs (Application Programming Interfaces):** Utilizing secure APIs for data sharing allows seamless integration between different-cloud services while enforcing robust authentication and authorization mechanisms.

VIII. **Immutable Cloud Storage for Auditing:** Leveraging immutable storage features in the cloud ensures that once data are written, it cannot be altered or deleted. This is particularly useful for maintaining an auditable trail of data-sharing activities.

IX. **Serverless Data Processing:** Implementing serverless architectures for data processing in the cloud reduces the attack surface and allows for efficient and cost-effective data-sharing workflows without the need for managing infrastructure.

X. **Cloud-Based Data Governance Platforms:** Deploying cloud-native data governance solutions provides centralized control and visibility into data assets, ensuring that policies, compliance, and security measures are consistently applied across diverse datasets.

1.5 CONCLUSION

This chapter explores the transformative impact of data sharing in cloud environments, emphasizing its foundational role in collaboration and decision-making. First, the importance of data sharing and the types of data sharing were explained. Later the scenarios with respect to Google Cloud and AWS Data-Sharing Architectures were discussed. Later challenges in secure data sharing were addressed, stressing the importance of careful consideration to mitigate risks and maintain confidentiality. Key challenges include security against unauthorized access, potential data exposure, and regulatory compliance complexities. The multifaceted analysis of security challenges explores threats such as data breaches, unauthorized access, and data leakage, supported by real-world examples illustrating the severity of these risks.

The discussion extends to the understanding of unauthorized access and data exposure risks, emphasizing their financial and reputational implications. Regulatory compliance issues, particularly the GDPR, add complexity, necessitating robust measures for adherence. Exploring encryption techniques and key management strategies, the chapter highlights the pivotal roles of AES and TLS in securing data at rest and in transit. GCP and AWS are recognized for their encryption services. The significance of end-to-end encryption is underscored, with GCP and AWS supporting its implementation. Real-world case studies, such as successful genomic data sharing and the Equifax data breach, offer valuable insights into effective security practices. Best practices and recommendations, including a defense-in-depth approach and the principle of least privilege, contribute to a comprehensive guide for organizations seeking to enhance their data-sharing security posture in cloud environments.

Looking ahead, the future scope involves continuous adaptation and innovation in response to evolving security challenges. Emphasizing the dynamic nature of cybersecurity, future research can explore emerging threats and technologies, ensuring the chapter remains a relevant and up-to-date resource. Additionally, collaborative efforts between academia, industry, and regulatory bodies can further enhance our understanding of secure data-sharing practices. Integration with emerging technologies like blockchain and AI can be explored for their potential contributions to the evolving landscape of data-sharing security. Ultimately, this chapter serves as a foundational guide for organizations navigating the complex terrain of secure data sharing in collaborative cloud environments.

REFERENCES

1. Dorri, A., Kanhere, S. S., Jurdak, R., & Gauravaram, P. (2017). Blockchain-based approach for secure data sharing in vehicular networks. In *2017 IEEE International Conference on Pervasive Computing and Communications Workshops (PerCom Workshops).*
2. McMahan, H. B., Moore, E., Ramage, D., Hampson, S., & Agüera y Arcas, B. (2017). Federated learning: strategies for improving communication efficiency. *In 2017 NIPS Workshop on Private Multi-Party Machine Learning.*
3. Buyya, R., Srirama, S., & Calheiros, R. N. (2019). Data monetization strategies and the role of cloud computing. *IEEE Cloud Computing*, **6**(1), 62–71.
4. Zelenay, J., Balco, P., & Greguš, M. (2019). Cloud technologies-solution for secure communication and collaboration. *Procedia Computer Science*, **151**, 567–574.
5. Chadwick, D. W., Fan, W., Costantino, G., De Lemos, R., Di Cerbo, F., Herwono, I., ... & Wang, X. S. (2020). A cloud-edge based data security architecture for sharing and analyzing cyber threat information. *Future Generation Computer Systems*, **102**, 710–722.
6. Naidu, J. J., Ganesh, E. N., Reddy, N. D., & Sankaran, M. (2021, December). A robust medical data sharing application with a collaborative hypothesis and elastic net regression model. In *2021 5th International Conference on Electronics, Communication and Aerospace Technology* (*ICECA*) (pp. 1020–1026). IEEE.
7. Sivan, R., & Zukarnain, Z. A. (2021). Security and privacy in cloud-based e-health system. *Symmetry*, **13**(5), 742.
8. Fan, W., Ziembicka, J., de Lemos, R., Chadwick, D., Di Cerbo, F., Sajjad, A., ... & Herwono, I. (2019, June). Enabling privacy-preserving sharing of cyber threat information in the cloud. In *2019 6th IEEE International Conference on Cyber Security and Cloud Computing* (*CSCloud*)*/2019 5th IEEE International Conference on Edge Computing and Scalable Cloud* (*EdgeCom*) (pp. 74–80). IEEE.
9. Liu, J., Yuan, C., Lai, Y., & Qin, H. (2020). Protection of sensitive data in industrial Internet based on three-layer local/fog/cloud storage. *Security and Communication Networks*, **2020**, 1–16.
10. Domingo-Ferrer, J., Farras, O., Ribes-González, J., & Sánchez, D. (2019). Privacy-preserving cloud computing on sensitive data: A survey of methods, products and challenges. *Computer Communications*, **140**, 38–60.

11. Yin, B., Yin, H., Wu, Y., & Jiang, Z. (2020). FDC: A secure federated deep learning mechanism for data collaborations in the Internet of Things. *IEEE Internet of Things Journal*, **7**(7), 6348–6359.
12. Lo'ai, A. T., & Saldamli, G. (2021). Reconsidering big data security and privacy in cloud and mobile cloud systems. *Journal of King Saud University-Computer and Information Sciences*, **33**(7), 810–819.
13. Framner, E., Fischer-Hübner, S., Lorünser, T., Alaqra, A. S., & Pettersson, J. S. (2019). Making secret sharing based cloud storage usable. *Information & Computer Security*, **27**(5), 647–667.
14. Das, M., Tao, X., & Cheng, J. C. (2021). BIM security: A critical review and recommendations using encryption strategy and blockchain. *Automation in Construction*, **126**, 103682.
15. Ogiela, L., Ogiela, M. R., & Ko, H. (2020). Intelligent data management and security in cloud computing. *Sensors*, **20**(12), 3458.
16. Gupta, I., Singh, A. K., Lee, C. N., & Buyya, R. (2022). Secure data storage and sharing techniques for data protection in cloud environments: A systematic review, analysis, and future directions. *IEEE Access*.
17. Marciano, M. A., & Maynard III, H. P. (2023). Enhancing research and collaboration in forensic science: A primer on data sharing. *Forensic Science International: Synergy*, **6**, 100323.
18. de Oliveira, M. T., Reis, L. H. A., Marquering, H., Zwinderman, A. H., & Olabarriaga, S. D. (2022). Perceptions of a secure cloud-based solution for data sharing during acute stroke care: qualitative interview study. *JMIR Formative Research*, **6**(12), e40061.
19. Smith, A. (2019). "Data security trends in collaborative cloud environments." *Journal of Cloud Computing: Advances, Systems, and Applications*, **8**(1), 15.
20. Chen, B., & Wang, D. (2020). "Secure data sharing practices in modern cloud ecosystems." In *International Conference on Cloud Computing Technology and Science (CloudCom)*.
21. Gupta, R., & Johnson, M. (2021). "Innovative approaches to cloud-based federated learning for data privacy." *IEEE Transactions on Cloud Computing*, **9**(4), 1120–1133.
22. Kim, Y., & Lee, S. (2022). "Enhancing cloud data governance through immutable storage: a case study analysis." *Journal of Information Security and Applications*, **67**, 102–115.
23. Rodriguez, J., & Wang, L. (2023). "Data tokenization strategies in cloud storage: balancing security and usability." *International Journal of Cloud Computing and Services Science*, **12**(3), 127–142.
24. Li, H., & Zhang, Q. (2023). "Next-generation cloud security: a comprehensive analysis of dynamic access controls." *Journal of Cloud Security*, **10**(2), 45–62.
25. Patel, S., & Gupta, P. (2023). "Revolutionizing secure data sharing: applications of self-sovereign identity in cloud environments." in *International Conference on Cloud Computing and Data Security (CCDS 2023).*

2 Orchestrating Data Integrity through Remote Auditing and Compliance Assurance

G. M. Siddesh and Vaibhavari Balakrishna Rao

2.1 IMPORTANCE OF DATA AUDITING IN CLOUD ENVIRONMENTS

In today's dynamic cloud environments, the importance of data auditing cannot be overstated. Data auditing involves the systematic examination and analysis of data to ensure its accuracy, integrity, and security. In the context of cloud computing, where data is distributed and accessed remotely, auditing becomes a crucial component in maintaining trust and reliability [1,2].

2.1.1 What Is Data Auditing in Cloud Environments?

Data auditing in cloud environments refers to the process of systematically examining and verifying data to ensure its accuracy, integrity, and security within distributed and remote storage systems. It involves monitoring data access, modifications, and transfers to detect and prevent unauthorized activities.

2.1.2 What Is the Significance of Data Auditing in Cloud Environments?

The significance of data auditing in the cloud lies in its role as a proactive measure against data breaches, corruption, and unauthorized access. It safeguards sensitive information, builds user trust, and ensures compliance with regulatory standards.

2.1.3 What Are the Needs for Data Auditing in Cloud Environments?

- **Ensuring Data Integrity and Trustworthiness:** In the cloud, where data is stored and processed across various locations, ensuring data integrity is paramount. Auditing mechanisms verify that data remain unchanged and trustworthy throughout its lifecycle, from creation to storage and retrieval.
- **Regulatory Compliance:** Cloud environments often handle sensitive data subject to regulatory requirements. Data auditing helps organizations meet

DOI: 10.1201/9781003455448-2

compliance standards by providing a transparent trail of data activities, aiding in audits, and ensuring adherence to legal frameworks.
- **Detection and Prevention of Unauthorized Access:** The distributed nature of cloud computing makes it susceptible to unauthorized access. Data auditing serves as a detective control, identifying and preventing unauthorized activities, thereby enhancing overall security.

2.1.4 Examples of Data Auditing in Cloud Environments

- **Logging and Monitoring Services:** Cloud platforms such as AWS CloudTrail, Azure Monitor, and Google Cloud's Operations Suite offer logging and monitoring services. These tools record activities, changes, and access attempts, providing a detailed audit trail for analysis.
- **Hash Functions and Checksums:** Implementing cryptographic techniques like hash functions and checksums ensures data integrity. Platforms like AWS S3 and Azure Blob Storage leverage these mechanisms to verify the integrity of stored data.

As privacy concerns grow, researchers explore protocols that allow auditing without compromising data privacy. Techniques like homomorphic encryption are gaining attention for secure auditing. In [3], their exploration of secure data-auditing protocols, Smith and Johnson contribute to the evolving landscape of cloud security. Focused on advancements, their work delves into the intricate mechanisms vital for maintaining data integrity in cloud environments. By addressing the challenges associated with secure data auditing, the paper offers valuable insights into enhancing the overall security posture of cloud systems.

Brown and Garcia present a pioneering approach to real-time cloud auditing through machine learning-based anomaly detection [4]. Their work underscores the importance of leveraging advanced technologies to enhance the efficiency and effectiveness of auditing processes. By integrating machine learning into the auditing framework, the paper contributes to the ongoing discourse on harnessing innovative solutions for securing cloud environments in real time.

Williams and Lee [5] provide a comprehensive analysis of regulatory compliance within the complex domain of multi-cloud environments. Navigating the intricate landscape of compliance standards, the paper addresses the challenges associated with adhering to regulatory requirements across diverse cloud platforms. This work contributes valuable insights for organizations operating in multi-cloud scenarios, emphasizing the need for tailored compliance strategies [5].

Chen and Patel [6] explore the integration of blockchain technology into data auditing for cloud storage. By leveraging the decentralized and tamper-resistant nature of blockchain, the paper proposes a novel approach to enhance the security and transparency of cloud storage auditing. The work highlights the potential of blockchain in mitigating security risks and ensuring the integrity of data stored in the cloud [6].

Gupta and Kim [7] contribute to the evolving field of community-centric auditing models, specifically tailored for shared cloud resources. Their work emphasizes the importance of collaborative approaches to auditing in cloud environments where resources are shared among multiple entities. By proposing models that cater to the communal nature of cloud services, the paper sheds light on innovative strategies for ensuring security and integrity in shared cloud ecosystems [7].

2.1.5 Private, Public, and Community Cloud Views on Data Auditing

- **Private Cloud Architectures:** In private cloud environments, organizations have direct control over infrastructure. Auditing solutions can be tailored to specific security requirements, with examples like VMware's vRealize Log Insight providing centralized logging and auditing.
- **Public Cloud Architectures:** Public cloud providers, such as AWS, Azure, and GCP, offer native auditing tools and services. AWS CloudTrail, for instance, provides a comprehensive log of API calls for increased transparency and security.
- **Community Cloud Considerations:** Community clouds, shared by multiple organizations with similar interests, demand collaborative auditing approaches. This may involve shared responsibility models and standardized audit protocols to ensure data integrity and compliance.

2.1.6 The Significance of Auditing for Maintaining Data Integrity

In today's dynamic cloud environments, maintaining the integrity of data is of utmost importance for organizations relying on cloud services [8]. Cloud service providers such as Google Cloud Platform (GCP), Amazon Web Services (AWS), and Microsoft Azure play a pivotal role in offering native tools that facilitate robust data auditing. This section focuses on two prominent services, GCP's Cloud Audit Logs and AWS CloudTrail, examining how these tools contribute to ensuring data integrity in cloud environments.

The proliferation of cloud computing has revolutionized the way organizations manage and store their data. As data traverses through various cloud services and infrastructures, ensuring its integrity becomes a critical aspect of cybersecurity. Unauthorized access, data tampering, or system malfunctions can compromise data integrity, leading to severe consequences for businesses. Cloud service providers recognize this challenge and have developed sophisticated tools to address it.

2.1.6.1 GCP's Cloud Audit Logs: A Deep Dive

GCP offers a robust solution for data auditing through its Cloud Audit Logs. These logs provide a detailed record of API activities within GCP, offering organizations a transparent view of changes, access, and operations performed on their cloud resources. Cloud Audit Logs capture a wide array of data, including who performed an action, what resources were involved, and when the action occurred.

One key strength of Cloud Audit Logs is its seamless integration with various GCP services, allowing organizations to have a centralized view of their entire cloud ecosystem. This integration covers services such as Google Compute Engine, Google Cloud Storage, and Google Cloud Identity and Access Management (IAM). The logs are accessible through the GCP Console, providing a user-friendly interface for administrators to review and analyze the recorded activities.

Additionally, Cloud Audit Logs support real-time monitoring, enabling organizations to proactively identify and respond to potential security incidents. By offering insights into the "who, what, and when" of API activities, GCP's Cloud Audit Logs empower organizations to enforce security policies, track compliance, and investigate any suspicious or unauthorized actions effectively.

In the realm of GCP, audit logs play a pivotal role in tracking and monitoring activities within a project, folder, or organization. These logs are classified into distinct types, each serving a specific purpose to enhance security, compliance, and transparency.

1. **Admin Activity Audit Logs:** Admin Activity audit logs capture entries for API calls or actions that modify the configuration or metadata of resources within GCP. Examples include creating VM instances or altering Identity and Access Management permissions. Notably, Admin Activity audit logs are always generated and cannot be configured, excluded, or disabled. Even if the Cloud Logging API is disabled, these logs persist, ensuring a comprehensive record of administrative actions.
2. **Data Access Audit Logs:** Data Access audit logs encompass API calls related to reading the configuration or metadata of resources, along with user-driven API calls that involve creating, modifying, or reading user-provided resource data. While these logs are crucial for monitoring, they are disabled by default (except for BigQuery Data Access audit logs) due to their potentially large size. Users must explicitly enable and configure Data Access audit logs for GCP services other than BigQuery, potentially incurring additional usage charges. These logs safeguard sensitive information by excluding publicly available resources with specific Identity and Access Management policies.
3. **System Event Audit Logs:** System Event audit logs document Google Cloud actions that modify the configuration of resources. Unlike Admin Activity logs driven by user actions, System Event logs are generated by Google systems themselves. Similar to Admin Activity logs, System Event audit logs are always written and cannot be configured, excluded, or disabled. They provide insights into modifications made by Google's infrastructure, contributing to a comprehensive audit trail.
4. **Policy Denied Audit Logs:** Policy Denied audit logs are triggered when a GCP service denies access to a user or service account due to a security policy violation. These logs are automatically generated, and the associated storage incurs charges. While Policy Denied audit logs cannot be disabled, exclusion filters can be employed to prevent their storage in Cloud Logging. These logs are essential for identifying and addressing security policy violations, contributing to a proactive security stance.

GCP utilizes a structured format for its audit logs, providing a standardized and detailed representation of activities within the platform. Understanding the audit log entry structure is crucial for interpreting and extracting valuable insights from these logs. Below is a comprehensive overview, along with an example and steps to navigate this structure effectively.

2.1.6.2 GCP Audit Log Entry Structure

The audit log entry structure in GCP consists of various fields that capture essential information about a specific event or action. Each field plays a specific role in providing context and details about the logged activity. The key fields include:

- **“protoPayload”:** This field contains the detailed information specific to the event, formatted as a protocol buffer.
- **“severity”:** Indicates the severity level of the event, such as “INFO,” “WARNING,” or “ERROR.”
- **“timestamp”:** Represents the time at which the event occurred, in Coordinated Universal Time (UTC).
- **“severity”:** Indicates the severity level of the event, such as “INFO,” “WARNING,” or “ERROR.”
- **“logName”:** Specifies the full name of the log, including the project ID, log type, and resource type.
- **“resource”:** Describes the resource affected by the event, including resource type, resource name, and resource labels.
- **“trace”:** Contains a unique identifier for the event, facilitating traceability and correlation across different logs.
- **“insertId”:** A unique identifier for the log entry, aiding in de-duplication of entries.
- **“authenticationInfo”:** Provides information about the authentication of the event, including the principal email and authentication method.
- **“authorizationInfo”:** Contains details about the authorization of the event, such as the granted permissions and resource attributes.
- **“status”:** Indicates the status of the event, including the error code and message if the event resulted in an error.
- **“operation”:** Describes the operation performed, including the API method, resource type, and resource name.
- **“httpRequest”:** Includes details about the HTTP request made, such as the request method, request URL, and user agent.

Example: Audit Log Entry Structure

```
{
"protoPayload": {
// Detailed information about the event in protocol buffer format
},
"severity": "INFO",
"timestamp": "2023-11-19T12:30:45Z",
"logName": "projects/my-project/logs/cloudaudit.googleapis.
com%2Factivity",
"resource": {
"type": "gce_instance",
"labels": {
"instance_id": "1234567890123456789",
"zone": "us-central1-a"
}
```

```
},
"trace": "projects/my-project/traces/abcdef1234567890",
"insertId": "abcd1234",
"authenticationInfo": {
// Authentication details
},
"authorizationInfo": {
// Authorization details
},
"status": {
"code": 0,
"message": ""
},
"operation": {
// Operation details
},
"httpRequest": {
// HTTP request details
}
}
```

Steps to Navigate Audit Log Entries:

1. **Access Cloud Console:** Log in to the Google Cloud Console.
2. **Navigate to Logging:** In the left navigation pane, select "Logging."
3. **Filter Log Entries:** Use filters to narrow down log entries based on time range, severity, or other parameters.
4. **View Detailed Log Entry:** Click on a specific log entry to view detailed information, including the structured fields outlined above.
5. **Interpret Log Information:** Review the log entry to interpret details such as the timestamp, severity, resource affected, authentication and authorization information, and specific details about the operation and HTTP request.

2.1.6.3 AWS CloudTrail: Unveiling the Trail of AWS Activities

AWS addresses the critical need for data integrity through its service known as AWS CloudTrail. AWS CloudTrail is designed to provide a comprehensive trail of API activities across various AWS services. This service logs important information, such as API calls, user identity, resource details, and timestamps, creating an audit trail that organizations can leverage for security and compliance purposes.

One notable feature of AWS CloudTrail is its ability to capture both management and data events, providing a holistic view of AWS activities. Management events include actions related to AWS IAM, AWS CloudFormation, and AWS Management Console sign-ins. On the other hand, data events focus on specific resource-related activities, such as S3 bucket access and changes to AWS Lambda functions.

AWS CloudTrail offers flexibility in terms of storage options, allowing organizations to choose between storing logs in the AWS CloudTrail service itself or utilizing Amazon S3 for long-term retention. This flexibility is crucial for organizations with varying compliance requirements and data retention policies.

Moreover, AWS CloudTrail integrates seamlessly with other AWS services, enabling organizations to leverage its logs for various purposes, such as security analysis, resource change tracking, and operational troubleshooting. The integration extends to AWS CloudWatch, facilitating real-time monitoring and alerting based on CloudTrail events.

2.1.7 Regulatory Requirements and Compliance Standards Related to Data Auditing

Ensuring regulatory compliance and meeting industry-specific standards is a paramount concern for organizations leveraging cloud services [9]. This section delves into the crucial aspect of regulatory requirements and compliance standards related to data auditing in cloud environments. Cloud providers, exemplified by Azure with its Azure Policy and AWS with AWS Config, play a pivotal role in facilitating organizations' adherence to these standards.

2.1.7.1 Importance of Regulatory Compliance

Operating in the cloud entails navigating a complex landscape of regulatory frameworks, industry standards, and legal requirements. Failure to comply with these regulations can lead to severe consequences, including legal repercussions, financial penalties, and damage to an organization's reputation. As such, cloud service providers recognize the significance of offering tools and services that empower users to maintain compliance effortlessly.

2.1.7.2 Azure's Approach with Azure Policy

Azure, Microsoft's cloud platform, provides organizations with Azure Policy—a comprehensive service designed to enforce and assess compliance policies across their Azure environment. Azure Policy allows users to define rules and initiatives that reflect specific regulatory requirements or industry standards. These policies cover a spectrum of areas, including data storage, access controls, and encryption. For instance, an organization in the healthcare industry may implement a policy dictating the encryption of sensitive patient data to comply with healthcare data protection regulations.

Scenario

Consider a financial institution moving its operations to Azure. To comply with financial regulations requiring strict access controls, the organization utilizes Azure Policy to enforce policies that restrict access to financial data to authorized personnel only. Any deviation from these policies triggers alerts, enabling prompt corrective action and ensuring compliance.

2.1.7.3 AWS's Contribution to AWS Config

AWS, a leading cloud provider, addresses the compliance needs of organizations through AWS Config. AWS Config enables users to assess, audit, and evaluate the configurations of AWS resources. By continuously monitoring configurations against predefined rules, organizations can ensure that their cloud infrastructure aligns with industry-specific compliance standards. For example, a company in the e-commerce sector may configure AWS Config to enforce secure data storage practices to comply with payment card industry data security standards (PCI DSS).

Scenario

In a scenario where a retail business processes online transactions through AWS, AWS Config helps enforce compliance with PCI DSS. The service monitors configurations, ensuring that customer payment data is stored securely, access controls are stringent, and encryption standards are met, safeguarding against potential regulatory violations.

2.1.7.4 Key Considerations for Organizations

- **Mapping Compliance Requirements:** Organizations must meticulously map out the regulatory landscape applicable to their industry, identifying specific requirements that impact data handling, storage, and access.
- **Customizing Policies:** Leveraging the flexibility of Azure Policy and AWS Config, organizations can tailor policies to align with their unique compliance needs, reflecting the specificity of their industry standards.
- **Continuous Monitoring:** Regular and continuous monitoring of configurations is essential to promptly identify and rectify any deviations from compliance standards. Azure Policy and AWS Config facilitate this ongoing monitoring process.
- **Documentation and Reporting:** Both Azure Policy and AWS Config offer robust reporting mechanisms. Organizations should prioritize documentation of compliance status and generate reports to demonstrate adherence during audits or regulatory assessments.

2.1.8 Benefits of Remote Auditing in Cloud Computing

In the dynamic landscape of cloud computing, remote auditing emerges as a critical practice for ensuring robust security and compliance. Prominent cloud service providers, including GCP, AWS, and Microsoft Azure, have introduced dedicated solutions such as GCP's Cloud Security Command Center, AWS Security Hub, and Azure Security Center. These platforms bring forth a myriad of benefits, reshaping the way organizations approach security and data integrity in cloud environments [10].

1. **Scalability:** Remote auditing solutions offer unparalleled scalability, allowing organizations to adapt to the ever-changing dynamics of cloud infrastructure. As cloud environments expand and contract based on operational needs, these platforms scale seamlessly to monitor a growing number of resources. GCP's Cloud Security Command Center, AWS Security Hub, and Azure Security Center are designed to handle diverse workloads, ensuring that security monitoring remains effective regardless of the scale of cloud deployments.
2. **Reduced Operational Costs:** One of the significant advantages of remote auditing is the reduction in operational costs associated with traditional, on-premises auditing approaches. By leveraging cloud-native auditing solutions, organizations eliminate the need for extensive hardware investments and maintenance. GCP's Cloud Security Command Center, AWS Security Hub, and Azure Security Center operate on a pay-as-you-go model, allowing

organizations to optimize costs by paying only for the resources they consume. This cost-effectiveness is particularly beneficial for businesses of all sizes seeking efficient ways to maintain data integrity without incurring unnecessary expenses.

3. **Centralized Visibility:** The remote auditing platforms offered by GCP, AWS, and Azure provide centralized visibility into security and compliance postures. This centralized approach enables organizations to have a unified, holistic view of their entire cloud infrastructure. GCP's Cloud Security Command Center aggregates security findings, AWS Security Hub consolidates security alerts, and Azure Security Center centralizes security management and threat detection. This centralized visibility simplifies the monitoring process, making it easier for organizations to identify and address potential security threats promptly.
4. **Flexibility:** Flexibility is a hallmark of remote auditing solutions in cloud computing. These platforms are designed to accommodate the diverse needs and preferences of organizations operating in different cloud environments. GCP's Cloud Security Command Center, AWS Security Hub, and Azure Security Center support multi-cloud architectures, allowing organizations to maintain data integrity seamlessly across various cloud providers. This flexibility ensures that organizations can choose the cloud services that best align with their business objectives while still benefiting from robust remote auditing capabilities.
5. **Empowered Compliance:** Remote auditing solutions empower organizations to proactively address compliance requirements specific to their industry. GCP's Cloud Security Command Center, AWS Security Hub, and Azure Security Center come equipped with compliance management features that assist in aligning with regulatory standards. Whether it is HIPAA, GDPR (General Data Protection Regulation), or industry-specific regulations, these platforms offer tools and insights to ensure that data integrity is maintained in compliance with the relevant standards.

2.2 REMOTE DATA INTEGRITY CHECK MECHANISMS

In the ever-evolving landscape of cloud computing, ensuring the integrity of data is a fundamental concern and various mechanisms are employed for remote data integrity checks. This section provides an in-depth exploration of the techniques utilized in the realm of remote data integrity checks [11,12].

2.2.1 Overview of Remote Data Integrity Check Techniques

Cloud-native services have introduced innovative mechanisms to address the critical aspect of data immutability, a foundational element for maintaining data integrity in the cloud. Two exemplary solutions in this realm are AWS S3's Object Lock and Azure Blob Storage's Immutability. These services offer a robust foundation, ensuring that once data is written, it becomes immutable and resistant to any form of alteration. This section provides a detailed exploration of these mechanisms with a practical scenario [13,14].

2.2.1.1 Enforcing Data Immutability with Cloud-Native Services: A Case Study

2.2.1.1.1 AWS S3's Object Lock

1. **Enable Object Lock:** AWS S3's Object Lock feature needs to be enabled on the bucket level. This can be done through the AWS Management Console, AWS Command Line Interface, or AWS SDKs.
2. **Set Object Retention Period:** Specify the retention period for objects in the bucket. During this period, the objects cannot be deleted or altered. This duration can be configured based on regulatory requirements or organizational policies.
3. **Apply Object Lock to Objects:** Apply Object Lock to individual objects within the bucket. Once locked, these objects become immutable for the specified retention period, ensuring data integrity.

2.2.1.1.2 Azure Blob Storage's Immutability

1. **Configure Immutability Policies:** In Azure Portal or through Azure PowerShell, configure Immutability Policies on the Azure Blob Storage account. Define the retention policies and other parameters.
2. **Apply Immutability to Containers or Blobs:** Apply the configured Immutability Policies to specific containers or blobs within the Azure Blob Storage. Once applied, the data in these containers or blobs becomes immutable.

Scenario

Consider a financial institution relying on AWS S3 to store critical transaction records securely. In this scenario, the institution leverages AWS S3's Object Lock feature to enforce data immutability.

Step 1: Enable Object Lock on AWS S3 Bucket

The IT administrator accesses the AWS Management Console, navigates to the S3 bucket housing the transaction records, and enables Object Lock at the bucket level.

Step 2: Set Retention Period

Regulatory compliance mandates a seven-year retention period for financial records. The administrator configures Object Lock to enforce a seven-year retention period for all objects within the bucket.

Step 3: Apply Object Lock to Financial Transaction Records

The institution identifies the specific financial transaction records and applies Object Lock to ensure their immutability. Once locked, these records remain unmodifiable for the entire seven-year retention period.

2.2.1.2 Benefits and Outcome

By embracing AWS S3's Object Lock, the financial institution ensures that once financial data is stored, it remains unmodifiable throughout the mandated retention period. This not only meets regulatory requirements but also provides an immutable record of transactions. In the event of audits or legal inquiries, the institution can confidently demonstrate the integrity and authenticity of its financial records, showcasing the practical significance of cloud-native data immutability mechanisms in ensuring data integrity.

2.2.2 Implementation of Hash Functions and Checksums for Data Integrity Verification

Cryptographic tools are instrumental in ensuring data integrity verification within cloud environments [15]. Leading cloud platforms, including GCP, AWS, and Azure, provide robust solutions for secure key management. This guide explores the steps involved in leveraging GCP's Cloud Key Management Service (KMS), AWS KMS, and Azure Key Vault for implementing hash functions and checksums to verify data integrity.

2.2.2.1 Implementing Cryptographic Data Integrity Verification in Cloud Platforms: A Step-by-Step Guide

2.2.2.1.1 GCP's Cloud Key Management Service

- **Set Up Cloud KMS:** Access the GCP Console, navigate to the Cloud KMS section, and create a new key ring and cryptographic key. Specify the key's purpose as "Data Encryption" for integrity verification.
- **Store Cryptographic Keys:** Store cryptographic keys securely within Cloud KMS. Assign appropriate permissions to control access to these keys, ensuring only authorized entities can use them for data integrity verification.
- **Implement Hash Functions and Checksums:** In your application or data processing pipeline, implement hash functions (e.g., SHA-256) and checksums on critical data. These algorithms generate unique fingerprints for the data, serving as a digital signature for integrity verification.
- **Periodic Verification:** Schedule periodic integrity checks by recomputing hash functions and checksums using stored cryptographic keys from Cloud KMS. Compare the recalculated values with the original ones to detect any discrepancies.
- **Automated Monitoring and Alerts:** Implement automated monitoring within Cloud KMS to trigger alerts if any unauthorized alterations are detected during integrity checks. Set up notification mechanisms for immediate corrective actions.

2.2.2.1.2 AWS Key Management Service

- **Create a KMS Key:** Access the AWS Management Console, navigate to AWS KMS, and create a new Customer Master Key for data integrity verification. Define key policies and enable auditing for added security.
- **Secure Key Storage:** Store the generated cryptographic keys securely within AWS KMS. Utilize key policies and IAM roles to manage access control, ensuring only authorized users and applications can use these keys.
- **Hash Functions and Checksums Implementation:** Integrate hash functions and checksums (e.g., SHA-256) into your data processing workflows

or applications. Apply these cryptographic techniques to ensure data integrity across critical datasets.
- **Periodic Integrity Verification:** Schedule periodic integrity checks by recalculating hash functions and checksums using AWS KMS keys. Compare the recalculated values with the original ones to identify any discrepancies indicating potential data tampering.
- **Automated Alerts and Remediation:** Configure AWS CloudWatch or other monitoring tools to trigger alerts when integrity checks uncover unauthorized alterations. Implement automated responses and remediation workflows to maintain data integrity.

Azure Key Vault

- **Setup Key Vault:** Navigate to the Azure Portal, create a new Key Vault, and configure access policies for cryptographic key management. Define permissions to ensure controlled access.
- **Cryptographic Key Storage:** Store cryptographic keys securely within Azure Key Vault. Leverage access policies and Azure Active Directory integration to manage user and application access, enhancing overall security.
- **Hash Functions and Checksums Application:** Integrate hash functions and checksums (e.g., SHA-256) into your data processing workflows or applications. These cryptographic techniques serve as robust mechanisms for data integrity verification.
- **Periodic Integrity Checks:** Schedule periodic integrity checks by recomputing hash functions and checksums using keys from Azure Key Vault. Establish automated workflows to streamline the verification process.
- **Automated Alerts and Corrective Actions:** Configure Azure Monitor or other monitoring solutions to raise alerts upon detecting discrepancies during integrity checks. Establish automated corrective actions to address any unauthorized alterations promptly.

Example Scenario

Consider an organization using GCP. By setting up Cloud KMS, storing cryptographic keys securely, implementing hash functions and checksums on critical data, and performing periodic integrity verification, the organization establishes a secure and tamper-resistant environment. In case of any unauthorized alterations detected during checks, immediate corrective actions can be taken to ensure data integrity, exemplifying the practical application of cryptographic tools in cloud data protection.

2.2.3 Automated Auditing Tools and their Role in Maintaining Data Integrity

Automation stands as a crucial pillar in the arsenal of tools dedicated to preserving data integrity within the dynamic landscape of cloud environments. This section explores the significance of automated auditing tools, highlighting AWS GuardDuty, GCP's Security Command Center, and Azure Sentinel as exemplary solutions. These tools empower organizations to engage in continuous threat detection, proactively identify potential security risks, and maintain the integrity of their data through real-time monitoring and swift responses to emerging threats.

2.2.3.1 Leveraging Automated Auditing Tools for Data Integrity in Cloud Environments: A Comprehensive Guide

2.2.3.1.1 AWS GuardDuty

- **Continuous Threat Detection:** AWS GuardDuty operates as an intelligent threat detection service, continuously monitoring activities within AWS environments. It leverages machine learning algorithms to analyze log data, identifying unauthorized or malicious activities.
- **Automated Alerts:** GuardDuty automatically generates alerts when suspicious activities, such as unusual API calls or unauthorized access attempts, are detected. These alerts serve as immediate notifications for security teams to investigate potential threats.
- **Integration with AWS Ecosystem:** Seamlessly integrated with other AWS services, GuardDuty provides a comprehensive view of security events. It correlates data from various sources, enabling a holistic understanding of the security posture within the AWS environment.

2.2.3.1.2 GCP's Security Command Center

- **Real-Time Monitoring:** GCP's Security Command Center offers real-time monitoring of security events across the Google Cloud Platform. It aggregates data from different services, providing a centralized dashboard for security insights.
- **Automated Threat Detection:** Utilizing advanced analytics, the Security Command Center automates threat detection by identifying patterns indicative of potential security risks. This includes detecting anomalies in user behavior and unauthorized access attempts.
- **Remediation Suggestions:** The Security Command Center not only detects threats but also provides remediation suggestions. This enables organizations to take swift and informed actions to address security vulnerabilities and maintain data integrity.

2.2.3.1.3 Custom Rule Configuration

Azure Sentinel allows organizations to set up custom rules for monitoring specific data access patterns. This customization ensures that the tool aligns with the unique security requirements of the organization.

- **Automated Alerting:** When an unusual or unauthorized data access event occurs, Azure Sentinel triggers automated alerts. These alerts are immediately sent to the security teams, ensuring a rapid response to potential threats.
- **Integration with Microsoft 365 and Azure Services:** Sentinel seamlessly integrates with Microsoft 365 and various Azure services, offering a unified approach to security monitoring. This integration enhances the tool's capability to detect and respond to threats across diverse cloud environments.

Use Case Scenario

Consider an organization relying on Azure Sentinel for automated threat detection. The organization sets up custom rules within Sentinel to monitor data access patterns. If an unusual or unauthorized data access event is detected, Sentinel triggers automated alerts. Security teams, notified promptly, can investigate and address potential threats swiftly, thereby safeguarding the integrity of the organization's data.

2.3 REAL-TIME AUDITING SOLUTIONS

Real-time auditing solutions stand as instrumental components in the proactive monitoring and preservation of data integrity within the dynamic realm of cloud environments. This section offers a comprehensive exploration of real-time auditing approaches, shedding light on continuous monitoring, anomaly detection, and seamless integration with logging and reporting systems [16,17].

2.3.1 Exploring Real-Time Auditing Approaches for Continuous Monitoring:

Real-time auditing is indispensable for maintaining continuous vigilance in cloud environments, ensuring swift identification and response to potential threats. Prominent cloud service providers furnish dedicated solutions for real-time insights into system performance. AWS CloudWatch, GCP's Operations Suite, and Azure Monitor empower organizations to continuously monitor their cloud infrastructure, delivering immediate visibility into resource utilization, application performance, and potential security incidents [18,19].

2.3.1.1 AWS CloudWatch

- **Setup:** Organizations begin by configuring AWS CloudWatch to monitor various aspects of their cloud infrastructure. This involves defining metrics, setting up alarms, and establishing custom dashboards tailored to their specific monitoring needs.
- **Metric Collection:** CloudWatch collects and stores performance metrics from AWS resources in real time. Metrics can range from server CPU utilization and network activity to application-level performance indicators.
- **Alarming:** Organizations set up alarms based on predefined thresholds. When a metric breaches the set threshold, CloudWatch triggers alarms, enabling prompt identification of potential issues.

Example Scenario: A company utilizes CloudWatch to monitor the performance of its web servers. If CPU utilization exceeds a specified threshold, an alarm is triggered, alerting administrators to potential performance issues.

2.3.1.2 GCP's Operations Suite (Formerly Stackdriver)

- **Integration:** Organizations integrate GCP's Operations Suite with their GCP environment, connecting to various services and resources that require monitoring.

- **Logging and Metrics:** Operations Suite seamlessly collects logs and metrics from GCP resources. It provides a unified platform for visualizing and analyzing data, including information on resource usage and system behavior.
- **Custom Dashboards and Alerts:** Users can create custom dashboards to visualize specific metrics and set up alerts based on conditions. This ensures proactive monitoring and timely response to potential issues.

Example Scenario: A gaming company employs GCP's Operations Suite to monitor the performance of its cloud-based game servers. Custom dashboards display real-time metrics, and alerts are configured for sudden spikes in latency.

2.3.1.3 Azure Monitor

Resource Configuration: Organizations configure Azure Monitor to track the performance of Azure resources. This involves selecting the resources to monitor and enabling necessary logging and diagnostics.

- **Metric Collection and Log Analytics:** Azure Monitor collects metrics and logs from various Azure services. Log Analytics allows organizations to query and derive insights from the collected log data.
- **Alerting and Action Groups:** Users define alert rules based on chosen metrics. Azure Monitor triggers alerts when thresholds are exceeded, and Action Groups define responses, such as sending notifications or executing automated remediation scripts.

Example Scenario: An e-commerce platform relies on Azure Monitor to track the response time of its cloud-hosted applications. When response times surpass a predefined limit, Azure Monitor triggers alerts, and an Action Group initiates automated scaling to handle increased traffic.

2.3.2 Incorporating Anomaly Detection for Identifying Suspicious Activities

Anomaly detection is a crucial component integrated into real-time auditing solutions, utilizing advanced machine learning capabilities to identify and flag suspicious activities. AWS Macie, GCP's Anomaly Detection API, and Azure Sentinel exemplify cloud providers' dedication to enhancing real-time auditing through sophisticated analytics. These solutions leverage machine learning algorithms to establish baseline behavior patterns and detect deviations that may indicate security threats or unauthorized access [20,21].

2.3.2.1 AWS Macie

- **Data Discovery:** AWS Macie begins by automatically discovering and classifying sensitive data within the organization's AWS environment. It identifies patterns and categorizes data based on sensitivity, helping establish a baseline for normal data access behavior.

- **Machine Learning Training:** Macie employs machine learning to continuously analyze data access patterns and behavior. During a training period, the system learns what constitutes normal behavior, creating a baseline for comparison.
- **Anomaly Detection:** Once the baseline is established, Macie actively monitors data access in real time. It compares ongoing activities to the baseline, flagging any anomalies that deviate from the established patterns.

Example Scenario: An organization uses AWS Macie to monitor access patterns to sensitive customer data. If an employee, who typically accesses a specific dataset, suddenly attempts to access unrelated data, Macie detects this anomaly and triggers an alert.

2.3.2.2 GCP's Anomaly Detection API

- **Integration:** Organizations integrate GCP's Anomaly Detection API with their cloud-based applications and services. The API supports various data types and formats.
- **Data Ingestion:** The API ingests historical data to establish patterns and trends. During this phase, the system learns normal behavior and sets the groundwork for identifying anomalies.
- **Real-Time Analysis:** Once the baseline is established, the Anomaly Detection API continuously analyzes incoming data in real-time. It compares current patterns with historical data to detect anomalies and unusual trends.

Example Scenario: A retail platform deploys GCP's Anomaly Detection API to monitor user behavior on its e-commerce website. If there's an unexpected surge in account login attempts or purchase patterns, the API identifies these anomalies for further investigation.

2.3.2.3 Azure Sentinel

- **Data Collection:** Azure Sentinel aggregates data from various sources, including logs, metrics, and security events across the Azure environment. It provides a centralized platform for data analysis.
- **Machine Learning Models:** Azure Sentinel utilizes machine learning models to analyze historical data and identify patterns. This phase helps establish a baseline for normal behavior within the Azure ecosystem.
- **Real-Time Monitoring:** In real-time, Azure Sentinel continuously monitors activities, comparing them against the established baseline. Any deviations or anomalies trigger alerts for immediate investigation and response.

Example Scenario: A healthcare organization deploys Azure Sentinel to monitor access to patient records. If there's unusual activity, such as multiple access attempts from a single account, Azure Sentinel detects the anomaly and sends alerts to security personnel.

2.3.3 Integration with Logging and Reporting Systems

Integration with logging and reporting systems is a foundational aspect of real-time auditing, ensuring comprehensive audit trails for post-incident analysis and compliance reporting. GCP's Stackdriver Logging, AWS CloudWatch Logs, and Azure Monitor Logs seamlessly integrate with real-time auditing tools, providing organizations with a consolidated view of activities and events across their cloud environment [22,23].

Illustrative Scenario

An e-commerce company utilizing AWS CloudWatch Logs integrates the solution with its real-time auditing tools. In the event of a security incident, the organization can quickly access detailed logs of user interactions, system activities, and API calls. This integration aids in forensic analysis, accelerates incident response, and facilitates compliance reporting.

2.4 ENSURING COMPLIANCE WITH REMOTE AUDITING

In the intricate landscape of cloud computing, ensuring compliance with industry and legal standards is paramount. Cloud service providers, such as Azure, AWS, and GCP, recognize the significance of aligning organizational practices with regulatory requirements and industry best practices. To assist organizations in this endeavor, these providers offer dedicated tools and services.

2.4.1 Strategies for Ensuring Compliance with Industry and Legal Standards

Cloud providers equip organizations with powerful tools to define and enforce compliance policies, ensuring adherence to both industry-specific regulations and broader legal standards. Azure Policy, AWS Organizations, and GCP's Resource Manager stand as exemplars in this domain [24,25]. These tools empower organizations to establish policies that govern various aspects of their cloud infrastructure, from resource allocation to data handling. For instance, organizations can configure policies that dictate the geographic location of stored data to comply with data sovereignty regulations. By leveraging these tools, businesses can confidently navigate the intricate web of compliance requirements specific to their industry.

2.4.2 Building a Robust Auditing Policy and Framework

Establishing a robust auditing policy and framework is foundational for the effective maintenance of data integrity. Cloud providers recognize the importance of guiding organizations in crafting policies that align with best practices. AWS Audit Manager, Azure Policy, and GCP's Policy Intelligence offer indispensable tools for defining, managing, and enforcing audit policies. These services streamline the process of setting up comprehensive audit trails, ensuring that every action within the cloud environment is logged, monitored, and evaluated against predefined policies. For example, organizations can configure policies that mandate regular access reviews, enhancing security by ensuring that only authorized personnel have access to sensitive data.

2.4.3 Challenges and Considerations in Implementing Remote Data Integrity Checks

Despite the evident benefits of remote data integrity checks, implementation in diverse cloud environments poses notable challenges. Addressing these challenges is critical for the successful integration of these checks into cloud practices.

- **AWS S3 Bucket Permissions:** Overcoming complexities in AWS S3 bucket permissions is a common challenge. Organizations must meticulously configure access controls to strike a balance between security and operational efficiency. Misconfigurations may inadvertently expose sensitive data, underscoring the importance of thorough permissions management.
- **Azure Blob Storage Immutability Settings:** Configuring immutability settings in Azure Blob Storage demands careful consideration. Organizations must navigate the configuration intricacies to ensure that once data are written, it remains unalterable. Effective immutability settings are crucial for meeting compliance requirements that necessitate the preservation of historical data.
- **GCP Cloud Storage Access Controls:** Managing access controls in GCP Cloud Storage introduces another layer of complexity. Organizations must define and enforce precise access policies to safeguard against unauthorized access. Striking the right balance between accessibility and security requires a nuanced approach to access control configuration.

2.5 CONCLUSION

In navigating the complexities of data integrity within cloud environments, this book chapter has intricately explored remote auditing techniques and compliance strategies. From emphasizing the pivotal role of auditing in maintaining data integrity to dissecting regulatory compliance standards, the journey has delved into the technological intricacies while highlighting the contributions of industry-leading cloud providers—GCP, AWS, and Microsoft Azure.

The importance of auditing for data integrity preservation in the face of evolving cyber threats and regulatory landscapes has been underscored throughout this exploration. Regulatory compliance standards have been dissected, showcasing the proactive measures cloud providers offer to ensure adherence to industry and legal obligations. The mechanisms of remote data integrity checks, including the implementation of hash functions and checksums, have been explored, providing insights into the foundational technologies behind data integrity verification.

Real-time auditing solutions were investigated, shedding light on continuous monitoring, anomaly detection, and seamless integration with logging and reporting systems. Strategies for ensuring compliance, including the development of robust auditing policies and frameworks, were detailed alongside the inherent challenges in implementing remote data integrity checks in cloud environments.

2.6 FUTURE SCOPE

Looking ahead, the landscape of orchestrating data integrity through remote auditing holds promising avenues for exploration and advancement. One significant trajectory involves the evolution of automation and machine learning within auditing tools. Future developments may see increased sophistication in threat detection, anomaly identification, and automated responses, thereby fortifying data integrity measures.

Interoperability across cloud platforms is another compelling future prospect. As organizations increasingly leverage multiple cloud providers, there is a growing need for standardized approaches and tools that seamlessly integrate auditing and data integrity checks in a multi-cloud environment. Future research may pave the way for a cohesive and interoperable auditing framework.

The advent of quantum computing introduces a unique challenge to traditional cryptographic algorithms. Future studies could delve into the integration of quantum-safe cryptographic techniques within remote auditing tools, ensuring data integrity withstands the evolving landscape of computing paradigms.

Advanced compliance management is poised to be a key focus in the future. More sophisticated frameworks that dynamically adapt to changing regulatory landscapes could become integral components of remote auditing solutions. The exploration of automated compliance monitoring and reporting may redefine how organizations navigate compliance requirements.

Blockchain integration presents an intriguing avenue for enhancing the audit trail. Future research may explore how blockchain technology can contribute to an immutable and transparent record-keeping system, ensuring a tamper-resistant and verifiable history of data integrity events.

REFERENCES

1. Gudeme, J. R., Pasupuleti, S. K., & Kandukuri, R. (2019). Review of remote data integrity auditing schemes in cloud computing: Taxonomy, analysis, and open issues. *International Journal of Cloud Computing*, **8**(1), 20–49.
2. Patel, A., Shah, N., Ramoliya, D., & Nayak, A. (2020, November). A detailed review of cloud security: Issues, threats & attacks. In *2020 4th International Conference on Electronics, Communication and Aerospace Technology* (*ICECA*) (pp. 758–764). IEEE.
3. Smith, J., & Johnson, A. (2019). Advancements in secure data auditing protocols for cloud environments. *Journal of Cloud Security*, **12**(3), 45–60.
4. Brown, M., & Garcia, C. (2020). Machine learning-based anomaly detection for real-time cloud auditing. *Journal of Cloud Computing: Advances, Systems and Applications*, **5**(2), 112–130.
5. Williams, R., & Lee, S. (2021). Regulatory compliance in multi-cloud environments: A comprehensive analysis. *International Journal of Cloud Computing and Services Science*, **8**(4), 220–235.
6. Chen, Q., & Patel, S. (2022). Blockchain-enabled data auditing for cloud storage. *Journal of Information Security and Applications*, **15**(1), 78–95.
7. Gupta, A., & Kim, Y. (2023). Community-centric auditing models for shared cloud resources. *Community Cloud Research Journal*, **3**(2), 154–170.
8. Li, A., Chen, Y., Yan, Z., Zhou, X., & Shimizu, S. (2020). A survey on integrity auditing for data storage in the cloud: From single copy to multiple replicas. *IEEE Transactions on Big Data*, **8**(5), 1428–1442.

9. Kotha, S. K., Rani, M. S., Subedi, B., Chunduru, A., Karrothu, A., Neupane, B., & Sathishkumar, V. E. (2022). A comprehensive review on secure data sharing in cloud environment. *Wireless Personal Communications*, **127**(3), 2161–2188
10. Mohammed, S. J., & Taha, D. B. (2021). From cloud computing security towards homomorphic encryption: A comprehensive review. *TELKOMNIKA (Telecommunication Computing Electronics and Control)*, **19**(4), 1152–1161.
11. Akarapu, M., Martha, S., Donthamala, K. R., Prashanth, B., Sunil, G., & Mahender, K. (2020, December). Checking for identity-based remote data integrity cloud storage with perfect data privacy. In *IOP Conference Series: Materials Science and Engineering* (Vol. 981, No. 2, p. 022034). IOP Publishing.
12. Li, J., Yan, H., & Zhang, Y. (2020). Identity-based privacy preserving remote data integrity checking for cloud storage. *IEEE Systems Journal*, **15**(1), 577–585.
13. Fan, Y., Lin, X., Tan, G., Zhang, Y., Dong, W., & Lei, J. (2019). One secure data integrity verification scheme for cloud storage. *Future Generation Computer Systems*, **96**, 376–385.
14. Ji, Y., Shao, B., Chang, J., & Bian, G. (2022). Flexible identity-based remote data integrity checking for cloud storage with privacy preserving property. *Cluster Computing*, **25**, 1–13.
15. Yang, C., Liu, Y., Zhao, F., & Zhang, S. (2022). Provable data deletion from efficient data integrity auditing and insertion in cloud storage. *Computer Standards & Interfaces*, **82**, 103629.
16. Murthy, J. S., Shekar, A. C., Bhattacharya, D., Namratha, R., & Sripriya, D. (2021). A novel framework for multimodal twitter sentiment analysis using feature learning. In *Advances in Computing and Data Sciences: 5th International Conference, ICACDS* 2021, Nashik, India, April 23–24, 2021, Revised Selected Papers, Part II 5 (pp. 252–261). Springer International Publishing.
17. Kumar, N. V. M., Raju, D. N., Gopirajan, P. V., & Subhashini, P. (2023). Real-time user-service centric historical trust model based access restriction in collaborative systems with blockchain public auditing in cloud. *International Journal of Intelligent Systems and Applications in Engineering*, **11**(2s), 69–75.
18. Murthy, J. S., Chitlapalli, S. S., Anirudha, U. N., & Subramanya, V. (2022, April). A Real-Time Driver Assistance System Using Object Detection and Tracking. In *International Conference on Advances in Computing and Data Sciences* (pp. 150–159). Cham: Springer International Publishing.
19. Zhang, W., Jiao, H., Yan, Z., Wang, X., & Khan, M. K. (2023). Security analysis and improvement of a public auditing scheme for secure data storage in fog-to-cloud computing. *Computers & Security*, **125**, 103019.
20. Etchegaray, D., Luo, Y., FitzChance, Z., Southon, A., & Zhong, J. (2023, October). Open-RoadAtlas: Leveraging VLMs for road condition survey with real-time mobile auditing. In *Proceedings of the 31st ACM International Conference on Multimedia* (pp. 9374–9375).
21. Murthy, J. S. (2019). Edgecloud: A distributed management system for resource continuity in edge to cloud computing environment. In *The Rise of Fog Computing in the Digital Era* (pp. 108–128). IGI Global.
22. Zhou, C., Barati, M., & Shafiq, O. (2023). A compliance-based architecture for supporting GDPR accountability in cloud computing. *Future Generation Computer Systems*, **145**, 104–120.
23. Mahmud, R., Scarsbrook, J. D., Ko, R. K., Jarkas, O., Hall, J., Smith, S., & Marshall, J. (2023). Realizing credible remote agricultural auditing with trusted video technology. *Journal of Cybersecurity*, **9**(1), tyad012.
24. Brebu, A. A., Iacov, M., & Simion, E. (2022). Storage security in cloud computing: Data auditing protocols. *Cryptology ePrint Archive*.
25. Murthy, J. S., & Chitlapalli, S. S. (2022). Conceptual Analysis and Applications of Bigdata in Smart Society. In *Society 5.0: Smart Future Towards Enhancing the Quality of Society* (pp. 57–67). Singapore: Springer Nature Singapore.

3 Navigating the Abyss – Illuminating Data Leakage Threats, Mitigations, and Future Horizons

Samarth Kulkarni and G. N. Girish

3.1 INTRODUCTION TO DATA LEAKAGE IN CLOUD

3.1.1 What Is Data Leakage?

Data leakage refers to the unauthorized or unintentional exposure or transfer of sensitive data from one place to another [1,2]. It typically occurs when data are accessed, copied, or transmitted inappropriately, often leading to a breach of confidentiality or integrity. In the context of plagiarism, data leakage can occur when someone obtains and uses someone else's work without proper attribution or authorization [3,4]. Data leakage remains a significant concern in cloud computing. Data integrity, privacy, and protection are key issues when storing personal information in the cloud [5,6]. While cloud service providers employ security mechanisms, they are bound by service level agreements SLAs and cannot ensure absolute data integrity.

3.2 COMMON CAUSES OF DATA LEAKAGE

The top reported threats are caused due to Human Error, Insider threats, Weak Passwords, Unprotected networks, etc., as shown in Figure 3.1.

These threats account for over half of the reported data leakage incidents in cloud platforms [7]. Data leakage in cloud computing poses risks, including accidental exposure, malicious insiders, external attacks, insecure APIs, data interception, inadequate encryption, data residuals, and shared resource vulnerabilities. To mitigate these risks, implementing strong security measures and best practices is essential [8]. There are six major causes of data leakage in the current cloud realm.

3.2.1 Inadequate Access Controls

Improper access controls can result in unauthorized access and data leakage. For instance, if a user mistakenly provides excessive privileges to a cloud storage bucket, sensitive data may be accessed by unauthorized individuals [9]. Data leakage can also happen when insiders, like employees or contractors, misuse their access to

DOI: 10.1201/9781003455448-3

FIGURE 3.1 Data leakage issues.

cloud resources. This can occur through intentional data leaks or accidental exposure due to misconfigurations in cloud storage settings.

3.2.2 Malware/Phishing

Data leakage in the cloud can occur due to malware and phishing attacks [10]. Malware can infect cloud systems, leading to unauthorized access and extraction of sensitive data. Phishing attacks trick users into revealing their credentials, allowing attackers to access and leak data [11]. Data interception during transmission and insider threats facilitated by malware are additional risks. To mitigate these risks, organizations should implement robust security measures, including antivirus software, employee training, access controls, and regular security audits.

3.2.3 Data Residuals

Data leakage in the cloud due to data residuals can occur when remnants of deleted data are not properly erased or when improper disposal of cloud resources leaves sensitive information exposed [12]. Mismanagement of backups, replication, and the use of unauthorized cloud storage can also lead to data leakage. To prevent these risks, organizations should implement secure data removal practices, enforce proper disposal procedures, audit backup and replication processes, educate employees about shadow IT risks, and establish data lifecycle management policies [13]. These measures help mitigate the potential for data leakage and protect sensitive information in the cloud [14].

3.2.4 Physical Loss

Data leakage in the cloud due to physical loss can occur through hardware failures, data center breaches, inadequate data sanitization, and theft or loss of physical devices. Hardware failures and breaches can lead to data inaccessibility or unauthorized access, while inadequate data sanitization and device theft or loss can result in data leakage [15]. To mitigate these risks, organizations and cloud providers should implement robust backup and recovery strategies, maintain strong physical security measures, establish proper data sanitization processes, encrypt sensitive data, and conduct regular audits. These measures help protect against data leakage and ensure the security of data stored in the cloud [16].

3.2.5 External Attacks

Data leakage in the cloud due to external attacks occurs through vulnerabilities exploitation, DDoS attacks, credential theft, MitM attacks, and advanced persistent threats (APTs) [17]. Attackers exploit weaknesses in cloud systems, steal credentials, intercept data, and infiltrate cloud environments to extract sensitive information [18]. To mitigate these risks, organizations should update and patch systems, implement strong authentication and access controls, encrypt data, monitor network traffic, and conduct regular security assessments. These measures bolster cloud security, minimize the chances of data leakage, and safeguard sensitive data from external attacks.

3.2.6 Insecure API's

Data leakage in the cloud due to insecure APIs can occur when unauthorized individuals gain access to sensitive data, injection attacks manipulate API input parameters, insufficient data validation allows for exploitation, lack of encryption exposes data during transmission, and inadequate access controls lead to unauthorized data access. To prevent data leakage, organizations should prioritize secure API design, implement data encryption, follow secure coding practices, monitor API activities, conduct regular security assessments, and provide security awareness and training to developers and users. These measures strengthen API security, minimize the risk of data leakage, and protect sensitive data in the cloud (Table 3.1).

3.3 IMPACT OF DATA LEAKAGE

3.3.1 Financial Consequences

Data leakage can have profound financial ramifications for organizations. When sensitive data, such as customer information or proprietary business data, are exposed, it can lead to significant monetary losses. The direct costs of data breaches include expenses related to data recovery, notification of affected parties, and potential legal

TABLE 3.1
Impact of Data Leakage

Type	Risk Level	Description
Data in transit	High	A condition where transferring data via wired or wireless connectivity through a network or Internet makes it a risk.
Data in use	Medium	A condition where data is currently used, manipulated or being held in memory or cache at endpoints of the network such as laptops, USB devices or mobile phones.
Data at rest	Medium–low	A condition where the data are stored in databases, storage devices or files systems for persistent storage.

settlements. Indirect costs, such as reputational damage and loss of business opportunities, further exacerbate the financial impact. Moreover, regulatory bodies in many jurisdictions impose fines on organizations that fail to adequately protect data, adding a layer of financial liability. Therefore, it is essential for organizations to recognize the financial risks associated with data leakage and invest proactively in robust security measures to mitigate these consequences.

3.3.2 Reputational Damage

The damage to an organization's reputation resulting from data leakage is immeasurable. When news of a data breach spreads, it erodes the trust and confidence of customers, partners, and the public. Reputational damage can result in a loss of customers, revenue, and partnerships, as stakeholders may perceive the organization as unable to safeguard sensitive information. Rebuilding a tarnished reputation can take years and substantial effort. It is imperative for organizations to understand that the impact of data leakage extends beyond the immediate financial consequences and extends to the long-term health and credibility of the business.

3.3.3 Legal and Regulatory Ramifications

Data leakage often triggers a cascade of legal and regulatory consequences. Laws and regulations around the world mandate the protection of sensitive data, and organizations that fail to do so may find themselves in violation of these laws. Legal actions can take the form of lawsuits from affected parties seeking damages or class-action lawsuits. Furthermore, governmental bodies may impose fines and penalties for non-compliance. In some cases, organizations may be required to notify affected individuals, and the process of responding to regulatory inquiries and audits can be arduous. Understanding and adhering to the complex web of legal and regulatory obligations is essential to avoid these costly consequences.

3.3.4 Data Privacy Concerns

Data privacy concerns are increasingly at the forefront of public awareness. Data leakage not only exposes individuals to potential identity theft and fraud but also undermines the fundamental right to data privacy. In an era of heightened awareness, customers and users are more conscientious about how their data are handled, and they expect organizations to protect it diligently. A data breach can erode trust and damage relationships with stakeholders, who may then question the organization's commitment to respecting their privacy. Addressing data privacy concerns by implementing robust data protection measures, complying with privacy regulations, and fostering a culture of privacy awareness is crucial for maintaining trust and avoiding the fallout of data leakage.

3.4 CASE STUDIES: REAL-WORLD DATA LEAKAGE INCIDENTS

3.4.1 Data Breaches in Cloud Services

3.4.1.1 Volkswagen Data Breach

In June 2021, Volkswagen announced a data leak that occurred due to a breach in an unsecured third-party vendor. The leak exposed data about Canadian and U.S. customers and occurred between 2014 and 2019. The company collected this data for marketing and sales purposes but failed to adequately protect it. The exposed database remained vulnerable from August 2019 to May 2021, leading to the leakage of information belonging to approximately 3.3 million individuals. The leaked data included driver's licenses, car numbers, and for a smaller group of customers, loan and social insurance numbers were also compromised.

3.4.1.2 LinkedIn Data Breach

LinkedIn, a major professional networking platform, faced a data incident where data associated with 700 million users was discovered on a dark web forum, affecting over 90% of its user base. The breach was executed by a hacker known as "God User" who utilized data-scraping techniques to exploit LinkedIn's and other websites' APIs. Initially, a dataset containing information on around 500 million customers was dumped, followed by the hacker claiming to sell the full 700 million customer database. Although LinkedIn argued that no sensitive personal data was exposed, they considered it a violation of their terms of service rather than a data breach. However, a sample of the scraped data shared by God User included email addresses, phone numbers, geolocation records, genders, and other social media details. This information could potentially be exploited by malicious actors to craft convincing social engineering attacks, as warned by the UK's National Cyber Security Centre.

3.5 PREVENTING DATA LEAKAGE

3.5.1 Proven Practical Ways for Preventing Data Leakage in Cloud Platforms

Identify the Source and Extent of the Leakage: Swiftly locating the point of entry and determining the extent of the data leakage is the initial step. Through the analysis of system logs, network traffic patterns, and any available digital evidence, cybersecurity professionals can reconstruct the sequence of events that led to the breach. This meticulous process aids in understanding the nature of the breach and what specific data have been compromised.

Isolate the Affected Systems or Accounts to contain the Breach: Quarantining or isolating affected systems or accounts is paramount to prevent the breach from spreading further. This involves disconnecting compromised systems from the network and restricting access to the impacted accounts. By containing the breach, organizations can minimize additional data exposure and thwart the lateral movement of cyber threats.

Notify Relevant Parties: Timely communication with relevant stakeholders is crucial. Notifying IT personnel, security teams, legal departments, and possibly law enforcement agencies ensures that a coordinated and informed response can be initiated. Depending on the nature of the breach and applicable regulations, organizations might also need to inform affected individuals or regulatory bodies to comply with data breach notification requirements.

Patch Vulnerabilities: Addressing the vulnerabilities exploited by attackers is vital to prevent similar incidents in the future. This involves promptly applying security patches and updates to software, operating systems, and applications across the affected infrastructure. Regular vulnerability assessments and penetration testing can aid in identifying and rectifying weak points proactively.

Change Access Credentials and Implement Strong Authentication: To regain control and prevent unauthorized access, resetting compromised passwords and access credentials is paramount. Implementing strong authentication mechanisms, such as multifactor authentication (MFA), bolsters security by requiring multiple forms of verification before granting access. This approach substantially raises the bar for attackers attempting unauthorized entry.

Conduct thorough Forensics and Investigations: In-depth forensic analysis delves into the breach's root cause and the methods used by attackers. This investigative process involves examining digital artifacts, logs, and evidence to reconstruct the attack chain. Identifying the vulnerabilities or mistakes that facilitated the breach is essential to enhancing the organization's security posture and preventing recurrence.

Recover Data from Backups: Initiating data recovery from secure backups is a critical step in restoring normal business operations. Ensuring the integrity of the backup data is pivotal to prevent the restoration of compromised or infected information. This step emphasizes the significance of regularly testing backup restoration processes to ensure their reliability in times of crisis.

Enhance Security Measures: Strengthening the security infrastructure forms a foundational element in preventing future breaches. This entails augmenting access controls, employing encryption to safeguard data both at rest and in transit, and integrating intrusion detection systems (IDS) and intrusion prevention systems to monitor network activities for signs of suspicious behavior.

Provide Employee Training and Awareness Programs: Educating personnel about the significance of proper data handling practices is a cornerstone of preventing breaches caused by human errors. Regular training sessions and awareness programs enlighten employees about phishing attacks, social engineering, and safe data usage, thereby fostering a security-conscious organizational culture.

Develop Incident Response Plans: Well-structured incident response plans establish a systematic approach for managing breaches. These plans delineate roles, responsibilities, and communication protocols during an incident. Regular testing, simulations, and updates ensure that the response strategies remain effective as threats evolve.

Implement Continuous Monitoring and Auditing: Continuous monitoring and auditing mechanisms actively surveil network activities, systems, and user behaviors for anomalous patterns. This real-time vigilance aids in identifying potential breaches and unauthorized activities promptly. Regular audits and assessments assess the organization's security posture and adherence to established protocols [19].

By diligently following these steps, organizations can effectively address data leakage incidents, mitigate their impact, and fortify their defenses against future breaches.

3.5.2 Current Models of Prevention Solutions in Data Leakage

Watermarking: Watermarking is a pivotal technique employed in data leakage prevention strategies. In this context, watermarking involves embedding unique identifiers or codes within sensitive data before it is stored or shared in cloud environments. If unauthorized access or leakage occurs, the watermark persists, enabling the identification of the source of the breach. This technique acts as a digital fingerprint, facilitating traceability and accountability.

Use of Active Bundles: Active bundles represent a proactive approach to security in cloud computing. By packaging digital resources like software components and data files together, these bundles are actively monitored for any signs of malicious activities or unauthorized access. Should any abnormal behavior be detected within an active bundle, automated security measures can be triggered. This technique enhances real-time monitoring and responsiveness in detecting potential data leakages.

Intrusion Detection Systems and Behavior Analytics: IDS play a vital role in cloud security. IDS continuously monitor network traffic and system behavior, employing pattern recognition to identify deviations that could indicate data leakage or breaches. Behavior analytics and anomaly detection complement IDS by establishing normal patterns for users, applications, and devices. Deviations from these established norms are flagged, helping to detect abnormal activities that might signify data leakage.

Data Loss Prevention Solutions: Data Loss Prevention (DLP) solutions focus on safeguarding sensitive data by monitoring data flows and interactions within cloud environments. These solutions utilize pattern recognition to identify data that matches predefined criteria for sensitive information. By doing so, DLP prevents unauthorized sharing or storage of sensitive data, thus preventing potential data leakages.

Encryption and Access Controls: Encryption and access controls are foundational measures in detecting data leakages. Encryption ensures that even if unauthorized parties gain access to data, it remains indecipherable. Access controls limit data access to authorized users, reducing the risk of data exposure due to improper permissions. These techniques contribute significantly to the overall security of data within cloud environments.

Machine Learning and AI-Based Approaches: Cutting-edge machine learning and artificial intelligence techniques enhance the detection of data leakages. By analyzing historical data and patterns, these approaches can predict and detect potential data leakage events. Their adaptive nature allows them to continuously learn and refine their accuracy over time, contributing to an evolving defense against data breaches.

3.6 COMPLIANCE AND ORDINANCES

Compliance and regulations in the context of data leakage and cloud computing refer to the rules, standards, and legal requirements that organizations must adhere to when handling sensitive data in cloud-based environments. These regulations are put in place to ensure the security, privacy, and integrity of data, especially when it is stored, processed, or transmitted through cloud services. Here are some of the laws in this context:

3.6.1 General Data Protection Regulation

The General Data Protection Regulation (GDPR) is a European Union (EU) regulation established in 2018 to enhance the protection of personal data and privacy of EU citizens [20,21]. In the context of cloud computing, GDPR mandates that organizations and cloud service providers (CSPs) adhere to strict data protection principles, implement robust data security measures, have clear data processing agreements, promptly report data breaches, and address data leakage prevention [22]. It also governs international data transfers and enforces data subject rights, with non-compliance resulting in significant fines, making GDPR compliance a critical consideration for organizations operating in the EU or processing the personal data of EU residents. GDPR has significant implications for cloud computing and data leakage prevention:

1. **Data Protection Principles:** GDPR establishes a set of principles governing the processing of personal data. CSPs that process personal data on behalf of their customers (data controllers) must comply with these principles. This includes ensuring that personal data is processed lawfully, transparently, and for a specific purpose.
2. **Data Processing Agreements:** CSPs and their customers need to have clear and legally binding data processing agreements in place. These agreements outline the roles and responsibilities of each party and detail how personal data will be handled in compliance with GDPR.
3. **Data Security:** GDPR requires organizations to implement appropriate security measures to protect personal data. In the context of cloud computing, CSPs must have robust security measures in place to prevent data breaches, including encryption, access controls, and IDS.
4. **Data Breach Notification:** GDPR mandates that organizations report data breaches to the relevant supervisory authority and affected data subjects within 72 h of becoming aware of the breach. CSPs need to have processes in place to promptly detect and report breaches to their customers.
5. **Data Transfer:** GDPR restricts the transfer of personal data outside the EU to countries or organizations that do not provide an adequate level of data protection. This impacts cloud computing, as data may be transferred between data centers located in different regions. Organizations must ensure they comply with GDPR's requirements for international data transfers [23].
6. **Data Leakage Prevention:** Data leakage, also known as data loss or data exfiltration, occurs when sensitive data is unintentionally or maliciously exposed to unauthorized parties. GDPR places a significant emphasis on

preventing data leakage. Organizations, including CSPs, need to implement measures such as access controls, encryption, and DLP tools to minimize the risk of data leakage.

7. **Data Subject Rights:** GDPR grants data subjects (individuals whose data is processed) various rights, including the right to access, rectify, and erase their personal data. CSPs must have mechanisms in place to support these rights and assist their customers (data controllers) in fulfilling data subject requests.

   Failure to comply with GDPR can result in significant fines, which can be substantial. Therefore, organizations and CSPs need to carefully assess their data processing practices, security measures, and data leakage prevention strategies to ensure compliance with GDPR and protect the personal data they handle.

3.6.2 HIPAA and Healthcare Data

Another law that was enacted for the sole purpose of data privacy was the Health Insurance Portability and Accountability Act (HIPAA). The HIPAA is a U.S. federal law enacted in 1996 to protect the privacy and security of patients' protected health information (PHI). HIPAA has significant implications for cloud computing when healthcare organizations and CSPs handle PHI. Here are key aspects of HIPAA in the context of cloud computing:

1. **PHI Safeguards:** HIPAA requires covered entities (such as healthcare providers, health plans, and healthcare clearinghouses) and their business associates (which may include CSPs) to safeguard PHI. In cloud computing, this means implementing strong security measures, access controls, and encryption to protect PHI stored and transmitted through cloud services [24].
2. **Business Associate Agreements (BAAs):** When a CSP handles PHI on behalf of a covered entity, they are considered a business associate under HIPAA. Covered entities and their CSPs must enter into a BAA that outlines the CSP's responsibilities for safeguarding PHI, reporting breaches, and complying with HIPAA requirements.
3. **Data Encryption:** HIPAA mandates the use of encryption for PHI both at rest (stored data) and in transit (data being transmitted). CSPs offering cloud services to healthcare organizations must implement encryption to ensure the confidentiality and integrity of PHI.
4. **Access Controls:** HIPAA requires organizations to implement strict access controls to limit who can access PHI. CSPs must provide tools and mechanisms for healthcare organizations to manage user access and permissions effectively.
5. **Data Backups and Disaster Recovery:** HIPAA mandates that healthcare organizations maintain data backups and have disaster recovery plans in place to ensure the availability and integrity of PHI. Cloud-based solutions can play a role in meeting these requirements.
6. **Auditing and Monitoring:** Healthcare organizations and CSPs need to continuously audit and monitor their systems and networks for any unauthorized access or breaches of PHI. Comprehensive logging and monitoring capabilities are essential in cloud environments.

7. **Incident Response and Reporting:** HIPAA requires covered entities and their business associates to have incident response plans in place. In the event of a data breach or security incident involving PHI, timely reporting to affected individuals, the U.S. Department of Health and Human Services, and potentially the media is necessary.
8. **Data Retention and Destruction:** HIPAA establishes requirements for how long PHI must be retained and how it should be securely disposed of when it is no longer needed. CSPs should support healthcare organizations in complying with these requirements.
9. **Physical Security:** While most of the focus is on digital security, HIPAA also requires physical security measures to protect servers and data centers where PHI is stored.

Non-compliance with HIPAA can result in significant penalties, including fines and legal action. Therefore, healthcare organizations using cloud computing services must ensure that their CSPs are HIPAA-compliant and that they have the necessary safeguards and agreements in place to protect PHI throughout its lifecycle in the cloud.

3.6.3 CCPA and California Data Privacy

The California Consumer Privacy Act (CCPA) is a comprehensive data privacy law in the United States, specifically in the state of California. It was enacted on June 28, 2018, and went into effect on January 1, 2020. The CCPA is often considered one of the most significant data privacy laws in the country, and it grants California residents a range of rights concerning their personal information. Here are the key aspects of CCPA:

1. **Consumer Rights:** CCPA provides California residents with several rights over their personal information, including the right to know what personal information is being collected about them, the right to request the deletion of their data, and the right to opt-out of the sale of their personal information.
2. **Transparency:** Businesses subject to CCPA must be transparent about their data collection practices. They are required to inform consumers about what data are being collected, why it is being collected, and how it will be used.
3. **Data Portability:** Consumers have the right to request a copy of their personal information in a portable and readily usable format.
4. **Opt-Out of Sale:** CCPA allows consumers to opt-out of the sale of their personal information. Businesses are required to provide an opt-out mechanism on their websites.
5. **Non-discrimination:** CCPA prohibits businesses from discriminating against consumers who exercise their rights under the law. This means that businesses cannot deny services, charge different prices, or provide lower-quality services to consumers who exercise their privacy rights.
6. **Data Security:** While CCPA does not prescribe specific security measures, it imposes an obligation on businesses to implement reasonable security practices to protect personal information.

7. **Scope:** CCPA applies to businesses that meet certain criteria, including having annual gross revenues above a certain threshold, collecting or selling the personal information of a certain number of California consumers, or deriving a significant portion of their revenue from selling personal information.
8. **Penalties:** The California Attorney General can impose significant fines for violations of CCPA, and consumers also have the right to sue businesses for certain data breaches if their personal information was exposed due to the business's failure to implement reasonable security measures.

CCPA has had a significant impact on businesses operating in California and those that collect personal information from California residents. Many organizations have had to update their privacy policies, data handling practices, and online mechanisms to comply with the requirements of the law and to ensure the privacy rights of California consumers are respected. Additionally, CCPA has influenced discussions about data privacy at the federal level in the United States, potentially paving the way for federal privacy legislation.

3.7 FUTURE TRENDS IN DATA LEAKAGE AND CLOUD SECURITY

As technology continues to advance, the volume of data being stored and processed in the cloud is growing exponentially. This expansion brings with it an increased risk of data leakage and security breaches. Organizations are focusing on enhancing their data encryption, access control, and monitoring systems to protect against data leaks. Furthermore, they are implementing robust identity and access management protocols, as well as DLP tools, to safeguard sensitive information. In addition, the adoption of secure cloud services and the use of encryption technologies are becoming standard practices to mitigate these evolving threats.

3.7.1 AI AND MACHINE LEARNING FOR THREAT DETECTION

Artificial intelligence (AI) and machine learning are at the forefront of the fight against cyber threats. These technologies empower organizations to analyze vast amounts of data to detect and respond to threats in real-time. AI-driven threat detection systems can identify patterns and anomalies that may indicate a security breach, offering a proactive defense against evolving cyber threats. Machine learning algorithms can adapt and improve over time, making them more effective in identifying new and sophisticated attack vectors. As such, integrating AI and machine learning into security strategies is essential for staying ahead of cybercriminals [26–28].

3.7.2 ZERO TRUST ARCHITECTURE

The traditional security model, which relies on perimeter-based defenses, is no longer sufficient in today's interconnected world. Zero Trust Architecture is gaining traction as a more secure approach. It operates under the assumption that no entity, whether inside or outside the network, can be trusted by default. Access to resources is restricted and verified on a need-to-know basis, with strong authentication and continuous monitoring. This approach helps prevent lateral movement by cyber attackers and minimizes the risk of insider threats, making it a fundamental element of modern cybersecurity.

3.7.3 Quantum Computing and Data Security

The emergence of quantum computing poses a significant threat to classical encryption algorithms. Quantum computers have the potential to break current encryption methods, rendering many data security measures obsolete. In response, researchers and organizations are actively working on quantum-resistant encryption techniques. Post-quantum cryptography is being developed to withstand quantum attacks, ensuring that sensitive data remains secure in the age of quantum computing. Preparing for the quantum threat is imperative, and organizations should start transitioning to quantum-safe encryption well in advance.

3.7.4 Evolving Threat Landscape

The threat landscape in the cybersecurity realm is continually evolving. Cybercriminals are becoming more sophisticated, utilizing advanced techniques and tools to breach networks and steal sensitive data. Attack vectors such as ransomware, supply chain attacks, and phishing are on the rise. As a result, organizations must be vigilant and proactive in adapting their security strategies to counter these evolving threats. Regular security awareness training for employees, timely software updates, and threat intelligence sharing are just a few measures that can help organizations stay ahead of the ever-changing threat landscape.

These trends, which are shaping the future of data security and cloud protection, should be thoroughly understood and integrated into the security strategies of organizations to ensure the confidentiality, integrity, and availability of their data.

3.8 THE ONGOING IMPORTANCE OF DATA SECURITY IN THE CLOUD

In the contemporary landscape of cloud computing, the enduring significance of data security cannot be overstated. As organizations increasingly migrate their critical data and applications to cloud environments, they are exposed to a complex web of security challenges. Data security in the cloud entails the safeguarding of information from unauthorized access, breaches, and data leaks while ensuring its confidentiality, integrity, and availability. Key components of this security paradigm include robust encryption mechanisms, identity and access management, MFA, continuous monitoring, and DLP tools. Furthermore, the dynamic nature of cloud services necessitates a shared responsibility model, wherein cloud providers and cloud users collaborate in the implementation of security controls. The multitenancy nature of cloud infrastructure demands thorough isolation of customer data, and compliance with industry regulations and standards is imperative. In essence, the preservation of data security in the cloud necessitates a comprehensive, multifaceted approach, evolving with the ever-changing threat landscape to maintain the trust of users and stakeholders [25].

3.9 CALL TO ACTION FOR ORGANIZATIONS

As organizations navigate the ever-evolving landscape of technology and data management, a resolute call to action is paramount. Safeguarding sensitive data in an era of relentless cyber threats, especially within cloud environments, must be a priority. It is imperative that organizations invest in the continuous enhancement of their security measures and adapt to emerging trends in the field, such as Zero Trust Architecture and quantum-resistant encryption. Collaborative efforts between security teams, cloud providers, and all stakeholders are essential to foster a culture of vigilance and resilience against threats. Regular training and awareness programs, coupled with strict adherence to compliance and data protection regulations, are indispensable. The proactive protection of data, bolstered by state-of-the-art technologies like AI and machine learning, will ultimately preserve the integrity of an organization's operations, reputation, and the trust of its customers. In this digital era, the call to action is clear: prioritize data security, embrace innovation, and stay one step ahead in the relentless pursuit of a secure digital future.

3.10 CONCLUSION

In conclusion, this chapter delves into the transformative impact of cloud computing on data management, specifically addressing the critical issue of data leakage. We thoroughly explore the origins, consequences, and preventative measures associated with this concern. Beginning with an overview of cloud computing, the analysis unveils the intricate complexities of data leakage, dissecting causes and providing real-world case studies for context. The subsequent sections highlight the extensive impacts of data leakage, emphasizing financial, reputational, and legal consequences. Preventative strategies, ranging from traditional methods to cutting-edge technologies like AI and machine learning, are meticulously examined, with a specific focus on Identity Access Management and compliance with regulations such as GDPR and HIPAA. Looking ahead, the analysis concludes by forecasting trends in data leakage and cloud security, including the integration of AI, Zero Trust Architecture, the potential influence of quantum computing, and the dynamic evolution of cyber threats. This concise inquiry equips readers with a profound technical understanding of the challenges and opportunities in mitigating data leakage within the dynamic domain of cloud computing.

REFERENCES

1. Garcia, J., Aguiló, F., Asensio, A., Simó, E., Zaragozá, M., & Masip-Bruin, X. (2021). Data-flow driven optimal tasks distribution for global heterogeneous systems. *Future Generation Computer Systems*, **125**, 792–805.
2. Yu, X., Tian, Z., Qiu, J. and Jiang, F., (2018). A data leakage prevention method based on the reduction of confidential and context terms for smart mobile devices. *Wireless Communications and Mobile Computing*, **2018**.
3. Mohd, N. and Yunos, Z., (2020, June). Mitigating insider threats: a case study of data leak prevention. In *European Conference on Cyber Warfare and Security* (pp. 599–605). Academic Conferences International Limited.
4. Samanta, P.K., (2019). Design of data leakage prevention model using anonymization technique and time restriction.

5. Murthy, J. S., Matt, S. G., Venkatesh, S. K. H., & Gubbi, K. R. (2022). A real-time quantum-conscious multimodal option mining framework using deep learning. *IAES International Journal of Artificial Intelligence*, 11(3), 1019.
6. Braghin, S., Simioni, M. and Sinn, M., (2022, June). DLPFS: The Data Leakage Prevention FileSystem. In *International Conference on Applied Cryptography and Network Security* (pp. 380–397). Cham: Springer International Publishing.
7. Murthy, J. S., Siddesh, G. M., Lai, W. C., Parameshachari, B. D., Patil, S. N., & Hemalatha, K. L. (2022). ObjectDetect: A Real-Time Object Detection Framework for Advanced Driver Assistant Systems Using YOLOv5. *Wireless Communications and Mobile Computing*, 2022(1), 9444360.
8. Jaya Mabel Rani, A., Vishnu Priya, G., Velmurugan, L. and Vamsi Krishnan, V., (2019, June). Data leakage prevention and detection techniques using Internet protocol address. In *International Conference on Intelligent Computing and Communication* (pp. 665–671). Singapore: Springer Singapore.
9. Domnik, J. and Holland, A., (2022). On data leakage prevention and machine learning. In *35th Bled eConference Digital Restructuring and Human (Re) action*, p. 695.
10. Murthy, J. S., & Chitlapalli, S. S. (2022). Conceptual Analysis and Applications of Bigdata in Smart Society. In *Society 5.0: Smart Future Towards Enhancing the Quality of Society* (pp. 57–67). Singapore: Springer Nature Singapore.
11. Alsuwaie, M.A., Habibnia, B. and Gladyshev, P., (2021, November). Data leakage prevention adoption model & DLP maturity level assessment. In *2021 International Symposium on Computer Science and Intelligent Controls (ISCSIC)* (pp. 396–405). IEEE.
12. Murthy, J. S., Chitlapalli, S. S., Anirudha, U. N., & Subramanya, V. (2022, April). A Real-Time Driver Assistance System Using Object Detection and Tracking. In *International Conference on Advances in Computing and Data Sciences* (pp. 150–159). Cham: Springer International Publishing.
13. Abdel-Rahman, M., (2023). Advanced cybersecurity measures in IT service operations and their crucial role in safeguarding enterprise data in a connected World. *Eigenpub Review of Science and Technology*, **7**(1), 138–158.
14. Murthy, J. S., & Siddesh, G. M. (2024). A smart video analytical framework for sarcasm detection using novel adaptive fusion network and SarcasNet-99 model. *The Visual Computer*, 1–13, Springer.
15. Marina, N.F.I. and Qadrifa, S.S., (2022). Integrated marketing communication in E-commerce (a study case of customers data leakage in Tokopedia). *Jurnal Interaksi: Jurnal Ilmu Komunikasi*, **6**(1), pp.83–92.
16. Murthy, J. S., Shekar, A. C., Bhattacharya, D., Namratha, R., & Sripriya, D. (2021). A novel framework for multimodal twitter sentiment analysis using feature learning. In *Advances in Computing and Data Sciences: 5th International Conference, ICACDS* 2021, Nashik, India, April 23–24, 2021, Revised Selected Papers, Part II 5 (pp. 252–261). Springer International Publishing.
17. Najafi, M., Lemercier, M. and Khoukhi, L., (2022, October). Data leakage prevention model for vehicular networks. In 2022 *18th International Conference on Wireless and Mobile Computing, Networking and Communications (WiMob)* (pp. 124–129). IEEE.
18. Murthy, J. S., Siddesh, G. M., & Srinivasa, K. G. (2019). A real-time twitter trend analysis and visualization framework. *International Journal on Semantic Web and Information Systems (IJSWIS)*, **15**(2), 1–21.
19. Duggineni, S., (2023). Impact of controls on data integrity and information systems. *Science and Technology*, **13**(2), pp.29–35.
20. Murthy, J. S. (2019). Edgecloud: A distributed management system for resource continuity in edge to cloud computing environment. In *The Rise of Fog Computing in the Digital Era* (pp. 108–128). IGI Global.

21. Ke, T.T. and Sudhir, K., (2023). Privacy rights and data security: GDPR and personal data markets. *Management Science*, **69**(8), pp. 4389–4412.
22. Murthy, J. S., Siddesh, G. M., & Srinivasa, K. G. (2018). A Distributed Framework for Real-Time Twitter Sentiment Analysis and Visualization. In *Recent Findings in Intelligent Computing Techniques: Proceedings of the 5th ICACNI 2017*, Volume 3 (pp. 55–61). Springer Singapore.
23. Abdalzaher, M.S., Fouda, M.M. and Ibrahem, M.I., (2022). Data privacy preservation and security in smart metering systems. *Energies*, **15**(19), 7419.
24. Amiri-Zarandi, M., Dara, R.A., Duncan, E. and Fraser, E.D., (2022). Big data privacy in smart farming: a review. *Sustainability*, **14**(15), 9120.
25. Murthy, J. S., Siddesh, G. M., & Srinivasa, K. G. (2019). TwitSenti: a real-time Twitter sentiment analysis and visualization framework. *Journal of Information & Knowledge Management*, 18(02), 1950013.
26. Murthy, J. S., & Siddesh, G. M. (2023, October). AI Based Criminal Detection and Recognition System for Public Safety and Security using novel CriminalNet-228. In *International Conference on Frontiers in Computing and Systems* (pp. 3–20). Singapore: Springer Nature Singapore.
27. Murthy, J. S., & Siddesh, G. M. (2023, October). A Real-Time Framework for Automatic Sarcasm Detection Using Proposed Tensor-DNN-50 Algorithm. In *International Conference on Frontiers in Computing and Systems* (pp. 109–124). Singapore: Springer Nature Singapore.
28. Murthy, J.S., Dhanashekar, K., Siddesh, G.M. (2024). A Real-Time Video Surveillance-Based Framework for Early Plant Disease Detection Using Jetson TX1 and Novel LeafNet-104 Algorithm. In: Kole, D.K., Roy Chowdhury, S., Basu, S., Plewczynski, D., Bhattacharjee, D. (eds) Proceedings of 4th International Conference on Frontiers in Computing and Systems. COMSYS 2023. Lecture Notes in Networks and Systems, vol 975. Springer, Singapore. https://doi.org/10.1007/978-981-97-2614-1_23

4 Decoding the Cloud

A Comprehensive Exploration of Data Loss Scenarios, Resilient Storage Architectures, and Advanced Backup Strategies in Cloud Environments

Jamuna S. Murthy

4.1 NAVIGATING THE ABYSS: DATA LOSS SCENARIOS IN CLOUD ENVIRONMENTS

In the realm of cloud computing, the complexity of potential data loss incidents necessitates a comprehensive understanding to safeguard data integrity and ensure business continuity. This chapter embarks on an exploration of the abyss of data loss scenarios within cloud settings, aiming to unravel intricacies and provide actionable insights for researchers and practitioners alike. Data loss scenarios in the cloud can manifest in diverse forms, ranging from improper handling of data to unauthorized usage as shown in Figure 4.1. Understanding the root causes of these incidents is crucial for implementing effective mitigation strategies. For instance, accidental data deletions can occur due to human error or misconfigurations, while security breaches may involve unauthorized access leading to data compromise [1,2].

Resilient storage architectures play a pivotal role in fortifying against data loss. The construction of robust data storage systems involves leveraging cutting-edge technologies such as redundant storage, distributed databases, and fault-tolerant design. Advanced backup strategies are integral components of a comprehensive data protection plan. This chapter examines practical insights into the implementation of robust backup mechanisms tailored for cloud environments. Real-world examples and case studies serve to illustrate the practical dimensions of data loss scenarios and the application of mitigation strategies [3,4].

Wazid and team [5] conducted a thorough exploration of authentication mechanisms within the expansive realm of cloud-driven Internet of Things (IoT) environments, with a particular emphasis on big data. While the primary focus revolves around authentication intricacies, the paper inherently unveils insights into the security fabric

DOI: 10.1201/9781003455448-4

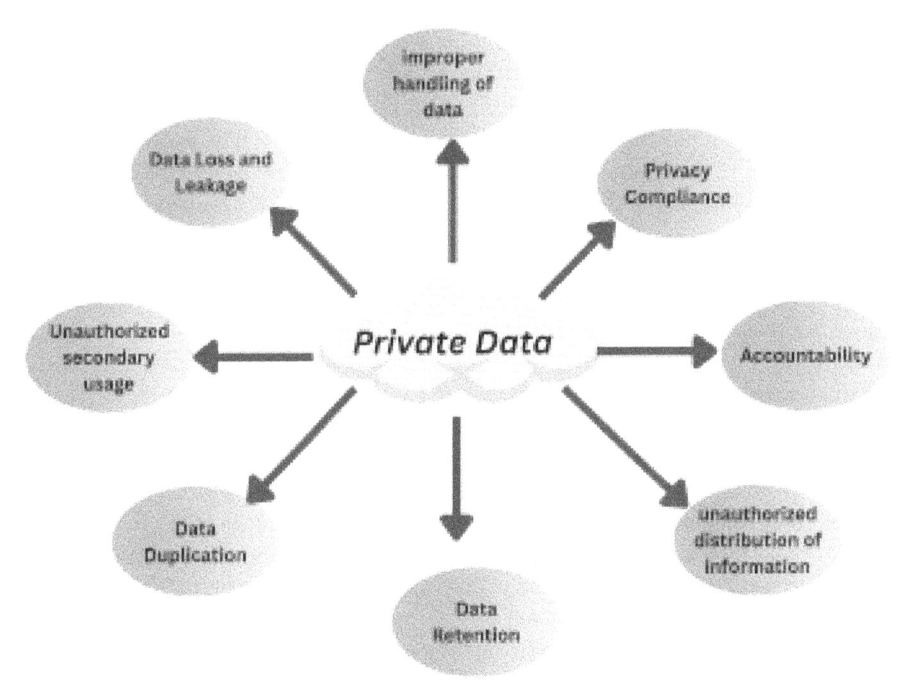

FIGURE 4.1 Data loss issues in cloud computing.

of cloud environments. By scrutinizing the authentication challenges, the authors implicitly address the imperative need for robust security protocols to forestall potential data loss scenarios. This contribution not only enriches the comprehension of authentication dynamics in cloud landscapes but also lays the foundation for tackling security concerns, a critical aspect in the safeguarding of data integrity [5].

In their exploration, Adhikari et al. [6] spotlight scheduling strategies within cloud environments, a pivotal facet in ensuring the efficient processing of data and averting potential data loss incidents. The paper delves into diverse scheduling approaches, shedding light on how the orchestration of workflows can significantly impact the preservation of data integrity. Effective scheduling strategies, as discussed, play a crucial role in precluding bottlenecks and potential failures that could precipitate data loss, offering a nuanced perspective on maintaining the integrity of data in cloud-driven workflows [6].

Tabrizchi and Kuchaki Rafsanjani [7] embark on an extensive survey, delving into the myriad security challenges inherent in cloud computing. The paper provides a holistic overview of issues, threats, and potential solutions, with a specific focus on vulnerabilities that may lead to data loss. By comprehending these security challenges, the paper contributes insights instrumental in crafting proactive measures, thereby mitigating the risk of potential data loss incidents within cloud environments [7].

Alouffi et al. [8] conducted a meticulous systematic literature review on security in cloud computing, aiming to discern threats and propose mitigation strategies. The paper provides a comprehensive analysis of security concerns within cloud environments, addressing potential vulnerabilities that might lead to data loss incidents. An understanding of these threats is pivotal for implementing robust security measures, thereby fortifying data integrity and curbing the likelihood of data loss within cloud scenarios [8].

Helali and Omri's [9] survey serves as a comprehensive exploration into the realm of data center consolidation within the framework of cloud computing systems. The paper, published in Computer Science Review, offers an insightful examination of the strategies and trends surrounding the consolidation of data centers, a pivotal aspect in enhancing the efficiency and sustainability of cloud infrastructure. By surveying existing practices and emerging paradigms, the authors shed light on the evolving landscape of data center consolidation, elucidating its impact on the scalability, resource utilization, and overall performance of cloud computing systems. With a focus on addressing challenges and identifying opportunities, this survey contributes to the growing body of knowledge aimed at optimizing data center operations in the ever-evolving domain of cloud computing. The authors' meticulous analysis, coupled with a synthesis of current literature, provides a valuable resource for researchers, practitioners, and industry professionals seeking a deeper understanding of the intricacies and advancements in data center consolidation within the context of cloud computing systems [9].

4.1.1 Unraveling the Complexities of Potential Data Loss Incidents

Data loss incidents within cloud environments present a multifaceted challenge, characterized by diverse and intricate manifestations. The complexities of these incidents span a spectrum, ranging from inadvertent deletions to more sophisticated security breaches. To effectively address and mitigate these challenges, it is imperative to comprehend the root causes that underlie each scenario. Accidental deletions, often stemming from human error or misconfigurations, stand as one facet of the issue, while deliberate security breaches represent a more malicious dimension. This understanding forms the cornerstone for crafting mitigation strategies tailored to the specific nature of each potential data loss incident [10,11].

4.1.2 Real-World Examples and Case Studies

Illustrating the gravity of data loss incidents, real-world examples drawn from industry experiences serve as illuminating beacons. These examples offer insights into the diverse scenarios that pose threats to data integrity in cloud environments. To contextualize the impact of data loss incidents on businesses, case studies are invaluable tools. Emphasizing the need for robust preventive measures, these case studies provide tangible evidence of the consequences faced by companies worldwide. To delve into specifics, let's explore three noteworthy case studies from major cloud service providers: Google Cloud, Amazon Web Services (AWS), and Microsoft Azure.

Case Study 1: Google Cloud—The Data Deletion Dilemma

INCIDENT OVERVIEW:

In 2019, a significant incident occurred on Google Cloud, where a user inadvertently deleted critical data from a production environment.

ROOT CAUSE ANALYSIS:

- **Human Error:** The primary cause was attributed to human error, highlighting the importance of user interfaces and operational procedures.

MITIGATION STRATEGIES:

- **Enhanced User Interfaces:** Google Cloud revamped its user interfaces to incorporate additional confirmation prompts and visual cues, reducing the likelihood of accidental data deletions.
- **Confirmation Measures:** Additional layers of confirmation were implemented, requiring users to confirm their intent before executing critical actions, especially those that could lead to data loss.
- **User Training Programs:** Google Cloud reinforced user training programs to educate users on best practices and the potential consequences of certain actions within the platform.

LESSONS LEARNED:

The incident underscored the significance of balancing user-friendly interfaces with robust safeguards to prevent unintentional data loss. Continuous user education and training are essential components of a comprehensive strategy to mitigate the risk of human-induced errors.

Case Study 2: Amazon Web Services (AWS)—S3 Bucket Misconfigurations

INCIDENT OVERVIEW:

AWS faced a series of data exposure incidents due to misconfigurations of S3 buckets, leading to unintended exposure of sensitive data.

ROOT CAUSE ANALYSIS:

- **Misconfigurations:** The root cause was traced back to misconfigurations of S3 buckets, emphasizing the critical role of proper cloud configuration.

MITIGATION STRATEGIES:

- **Enhanced Security Documentation:** AWS bolstered its security documentation, providing clearer guidelines and best practices for configuring S3 buckets securely.

- **Automated Configuration Checks:** AWS introduced tools and services that enable automated checks of S3 bucket configurations, allowing users to identify and rectify misconfigurations proactively.
- **Additional Safeguards:** AWS implemented additional safeguards within the platform to warn users about potentially risky configurations and to minimize the risk of unintentional data exposure.

LESSONS LEARNED

Configuration management is a crucial aspect of cloud security, and providing users with automated tools for configuration checks enhances the overall security posture. A proactive approach, including real-time alerts and warnings, can prevent inadvertent data exposure.

Case Study 3: Microsoft—Security Breach and Data Encryption

INCIDENT OVERVIEW:

In 2020, Azure experienced a security breach leading to unauthorized access to customer databases.

ROOT CAUSE ANALYSIS

- **Security Breach:** The primary cause was identified as a security breach, emphasizing the need for robust security measures.

MITIGATION STRATEGIES

- **Reinforced Encryption Protocols:** Azure strengthened its encryption protocols to ensure the confidentiality of data even in the event of unauthorized access.
- **Enhanced Access Controls:** Microsoft implemented stricter access controls, limiting user permissions and enhancing the monitoring of user activities within the platform.
- **Real-Time Monitoring:** Azure incorporated real-time monitoring tools to detect and respond promptly to potential security threats, minimizing the impact of unauthorized access.

LESSONS LEARNED

Encryption plays a pivotal role in safeguarding data, especially in the event of a security breach.

Continuous monitoring and rapid response mechanisms are crucial for mitigating the impact of security incidents.

KEY TAKEAWAYS ACROSS CASE STUDIES

1. **User Training:** Human factors contribute significantly to incidents; hence, ongoing user training is imperative.
2. **Configuration Management:** Proper cloud configuration is crucial for preventing data exposure incidents.
3. **Encryption and Access Controls:** Robust encryption protocols and access controls are fundamental components of a comprehensive security strategy.
4. **Automated Checks:** Implementing automated tools for configuration checks enhances proactive security measures.
5. **Real-Time Monitoring:** Continuous monitoring and real-time response mechanisms are critical for detecting and mitigating security incidents promptly.

4.2 ARCHITECTING RESILIENCE: BUILDING ROBUST DATA STORAGE SYSTEMS

This section delves into the intricate architectural principles underpinning the development of resilient data storage systems within cloud environments. It takes a profound exploration into technologies such as redundant storage, distributed databases, and fault-tolerant design, unraveling how these components synergize to establish a robust foundation for data resilience [12,13].

4.2.1 Deep Dive into the Construction of Resilient Data Storage Systems

Google Cloud Platform (GCP)

1. Redundant Storage with Google Cloud Storage

Techniques:

- **Bucket Configuration:** Start by creating a storage bucket in GCP, specifying the storage class based on redundancy requirements (e.g., Standard, Nearline, Coldline).
- **Versioning:** Enable versioning to preserve and manage different versions of objects, providing additional protection against accidental deletions or overwrites.
- **Location Settings:** Choose multiple locations for data replication to achieve redundancy. GCP automatically replicates data across these locations for high availability.

Steps:

1. Log in to the Google Cloud Console.
2. Navigate to Cloud Storage and create a new bucket.
3. Configure versioning and choose the appropriate storage class.
4. Specify the locations for data replication.
5. Upload or migrate data to the configured bucket.

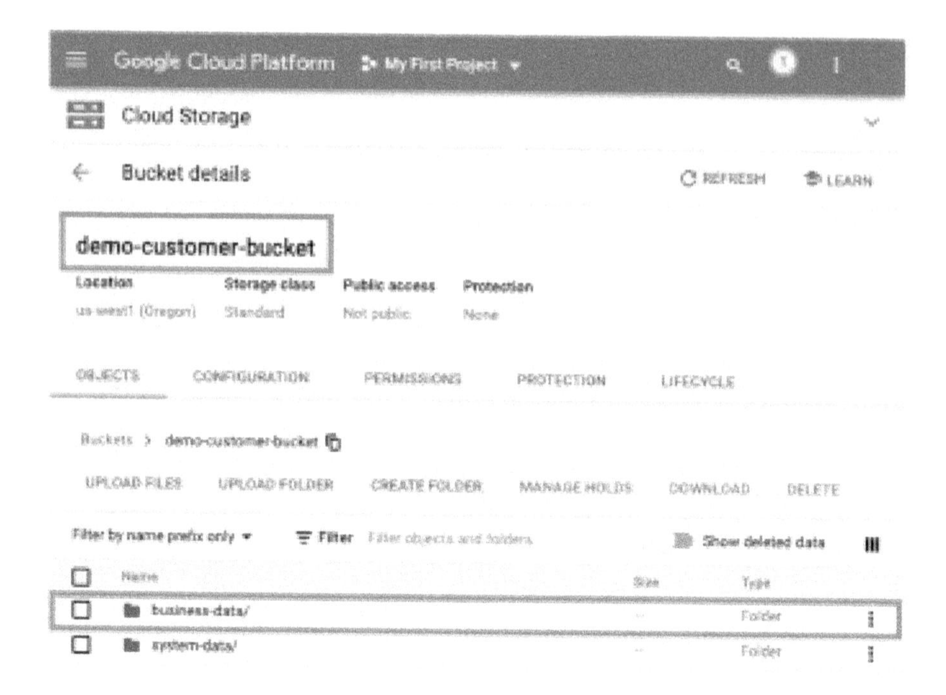

FIGURE 4.2 Redundant storage with Google Cloud Storage.

2. Distributed Databases with Google Cloud Spanner

Techniques:

- **Instance Creation:** Begin by creating a Spanner instance, defining its configuration, and selecting the geographical regions for global distribution.
- **Database Design:** Design a database schema that aligns with the application's requirements, utilizing globally distributed tables for data consistency.
- **Read and Write Configurations:** Configure read and write instances to balance workload and ensure strong consistency across the globally distributed database.

Steps:

1. Access the Google Cloud Console and navigate to Cloud Spanner.
2. Create a new Spanner instance, specifying the configuration and global locations.
3. Design the database schema and create globally distributed tables.
4. Configure read and write instances based on performance and consistency needs.
5. Migrate or import existing data into the Spanner database as shown in taure 3.

3. Fault-Tolerant Design with Google Cloud Datastore

Techniques:

- **Entity Groups:** Organize data into entity groups to manage and distribute data effectively while ensuring atomic transactions within each group.
- **Automatic Sharding:** Leverage automatic sharding to distribute data across multiple nodes, enhancing fault tolerance and scalability.
- **Datastore Indexing:** Configure indexes to optimize query performance and ensure efficient data retrieval.

Steps:

1. Open the Google Cloud Console and access Cloud Datastore.
2. Create or select a project and enable the Datastore API.
3. Define entity groups and organize data accordingly.
4. Enable automatic sharding to distribute data across nodes.
5. Configure indexes based on query requirements for optimized performance.

Advantages of GCP Resilient Storage Architectures:

- **High Availability:** Redundant storage and distributed databases enhance data availability across multiple locations.
- **Durability:** Data stored in redundant storage solutions is automatically replicated, ensuring durability and protection against data loss.
- **Consistency:** Distributed databases like Spanner offer strong consistency globally, crucial for applications requiring synchronized data access.
- **Fault Tolerance:** Fault-tolerant design in services like Cloud Datastore ensures system reliability, minimizing the impact of potential failures.

These steps and techniques showcase how GCP implements resilient storage architectures, providing users with tools and configurations to ensure high availability, durability, and fault tolerance in their cloud-based storage solutions.

Amazon Web Services

1. Redundant Storage with AWS S3:

Techniques:

- **Bucket Configuration:** Start by creating an S3 bucket, specifying the desired redundancy settings (e.g., Standard, Intelligent-Tiering, Glacier).
- Versioning: Enable versioning to maintain multiple versions of objects, providing protection against accidental deletions or modifications.
- **Cross-Region Replication:** Implement cross-region replication for redundancy across different AWS regions, ensuring data availability even in the event of regional outages.

Steps:

1. Sign in to the AWS Management Console.
2. Navigate to Amazon S3 and create a new bucket.
3. Configure versioning settings for the bucket.

4. Set up cross-region replication for redundancy.
5. Upload or transfer data into the configured S3 bucket.

2. Distributed Databases with Amazon DynamoDB
Techniques:

- **Table Creation:** Begin by creating a DynamoDB table, defining the table's primary key and specifying the provisioned capacity or enabling auto-scaling.
- Global Tables: Utilize global tables to enable multi-region replication, ensuring high availability and fault tolerance.
- Consistent Reads and Writes: Configure read and write capacities to meet application requirements, balancing performance and cost-effectiveness.

Steps:

1. Access the AWS Management Console and navigate to DynamoDB.
2. Create a new DynamoDB table, specifying the primary key and desired settings.
3. Enable global tables for multi-region replication.
4. Configure read and write capacities based on application needs.
5. Migrate or import data into the DynamoDB table.

3. Fault-Tolerant Design with AWS Elastic Block Store (EBS)
Techniques:

- **Volume Creation:** Start by creating an EBS volume, specifying the volume type (e.g., General Purpose, Provisioned IOPS) and size.
- **Snapshots and Backups:** Regularly create snapshots of EBS volumes to back up data, providing a recovery point in case of data loss or failures.
- **Multi-Availability Zone (AZ) Deployment:** Deploy EBS volumes across multiple availability zones to ensure fault tolerance and resilience against AZ-specific failures.

Steps:

1. Log in to the AWS Management Console.
2. Navigate to Amazon EBS and create a new EBS volume.
3. Configure volume type, size, and availability zone settings.
4. Create snapshots periodically for data backup.
5. Deploy EBS volumes across multiple availability zones for fault tolerance.

Advantages of AWS Resilient Storage Architectures:

- **Durability and Availability:** Redundant storage in S3 ensures data durability and availability across multiple data centers.
- **Scalability and Availability:** DynamoDB's distributed architecture provides scalability and availability through global tables and multi-region replication.
- **Fault Tolerance and Recoverability:** EBS's fault-tolerant design with multi-AZ deployment and snapshot backups contributes to system resilience, ensuring data recoverability.

Microsoft Azure

1. Redundant Storage with Azure Blob Storage:

Techniques:

- **Storage Account Creation:** Begin by creating an Azure Storage Account, specifying the desired redundancy level (e.g., LRS—Locally Redundant Storage, GRS—Geo-Redundant Storage).
- **Container Configuration:** Create storage containers within the storage account to organize and manage data, applying redundancy settings at the container level.
- **Blob Replication:** Utilize blob replication features to replicate data across different storage nodes, ensuring redundancy and enhancing data durability.

Steps:

1. Log in to the Azure Portal.
2. Navigate to Azure Storage and create a new Storage Account.
3. Configure redundancy settings for the Storage Account.
4. Create storage containers within the account.
5. Enable blob replication for redundancy across storage nodes.

2. Distributed Databases with Azure Cosmos DB:

Techniques:

- **Database Account Creation:** Start by creating an Azure Cosmos DB account, specifying the desired consistency model (e.g., Strong, Bounded Staleness).
- **Container and Partition Key Design:** Design containers within the Cosmos DB account, selecting appropriate partition keys for efficient data distribution and retrieval.
- **Global Distribution:** Leverage Azure Cosmos DB's global distribution feature to replicate data across multiple Azure regions for enhanced availability and fault tolerance.

Steps:

1. Access the Azure Portal and navigate to Azure Cosmos DB.
2. Create a new Cosmos DB account, specifying the desired consistency level.
3. Design containers within the account, defining partition keys for efficient data distribution.
4. Configure global distribution settings to replicate data across Azure regions.
5. Migrate or import data into the Cosmos DB containers.

3. Fault-Tolerant Design with Azure Site Recovery:

Techniques:

- **Recovery Services Vault Creation:** Start by creating an Azure Recovery Services Vault to centralize the management of backup and recovery operations.

- **Virtual Machine Replication:** Replicate virtual machines (VMs) to a secondary Azure region or within the same region, ensuring a fault-tolerant design.
- **Orchestrated Recovery Plans:** Define recovery plans to orchestrate the automated failover and recovery of VMs and applications in case of a disaster.

Steps:

1. Log in to the Azure Portal.
2. Navigate to Azure Site Recovery and create a new Recovery Services Vault.
3. Configure replication settings for virtual machines, selecting target regions for replication.
4. Define recovery plans to automate the failover and recovery processes.
5. Perform regular testing of the recovery plans to ensure readiness.

Advantages of Azure Resilient Storage Architectures:

- **Data Durability and Redundancy:** Azure Blob Storage ensures data redundancy and durability through replication across storage nodes.
- **Global Distribution and Availability:** Azure Cosmos DB's distributed architecture facilitates global distribution, enhancing data availability across multiple regions.
- **Fault Tolerance and Disaster Recovery:** Azure Site Recovery provides fault-tolerant design and automated recovery processes, ensuring business continuity in the face of disasters.

4.2.2 Exploration of Cutting-Edge Technologies and Methodologies

This section delves into avant-garde technologies and methodologies that fortify data against loss, showcasing the dynamic landscape of data resilience in cloud environments [14,15].

1. Cloud-Native Storage Solutions

Cloud-native storage solutions, particularly those designed for Kubernetes-native environments, have become integral components in modern cloud ecosystems. These solutions offer a set of advantages and are particularly well-suited for organizations embracing containerization, microservices architecture, and dynamic scalability.

Advantages:

- **Seamless Alignment with Containers:** Cloud-native storage solutions are specifically crafted to seamlessly integrate with containerized environments, especially those orchestrated by Kubernetes. This alignment ensures that storage is an inherent and well-integrated part of the container ecosystem.

- **Enhanced Scalability:** One of the key advantages of cloud-native storage is its scalability. These solutions are designed to scale dynamically in response to the needs of containerized applications. As the number of containers grows or shrinks based on demand, the storage infrastructure adapts accordingly, providing a flexible and scalable environment.
- **Agility in Resource Management:** Cloud-native storage solutions allow for agile resource management. They enable organizations to allocate and deallocate storage resources on-the-fly, promoting efficient resource utilization. This agility is particularly crucial in dynamic cloud environments where workloads and storage requirements can fluctuate rapidly.
- **Integration with Orchestration Platforms:** These solutions are tightly integrated with container orchestration platforms like Kubernetes. This integration simplifies the deployment, management, and scaling of containerized applications while ensuring that storage resources are provisioned and utilized efficiently.
- **Enhanced Data Mobility:** Cloud-native storage solutions often offer features that enhance data mobility. With seamless integration, data can be easily moved across different containers, pods, or even between clusters, supporting evolving application architectures and facilitating efficient data management.

Useful Scenarios:

- **Microservices Architecture:** Cloud-native storage solutions are particularly well-suited for organizations embracing microservices architecture. In a microservices environment, where applications are composed of loosely coupled services, each with its storage needs, these solutions provide the necessary flexibility and agility to cater to diverse storage requirements.
- **Dynamic Workload Environments:** Organizations with dynamic workload environments, where the demand for resources can vary significantly over time, find cloud-native storage solutions beneficial. These solutions adapt to the changing storage needs of applications, ensuring optimal performance and resource utilization.
- **Containerized Environments:** Cloud-native storage solutions shine in containerized environments, especially those managed by container orchestration platforms like Kubernetes. They contribute to the seamless integration of storage into the container ecosystem, providing a cohesive and efficient storage solution.
- **Scalable Applications:** Applications that require scalability, either due to varying workloads or rapid growth, benefit from the scalability offered by cloud-native storage solutions. These solutions enable organizations to scale storage resources alongside the scaling of containerized applications.

2. Erasure Coding

Erasure coding is a data protection technique that efficiently utilizes storage space while providing fault tolerance by breaking data into fragments with redundancy. This method stands in contrast to traditional methods like replication, offering advantages in terms of storage efficiency and resilience.

Advantages:

- **Efficient Storage Utilization:** Erasure coding optimizes storage space utilization by distributing redundant information across data fragments. Unlike replication, where multiple copies of the same data are stored, erasure coding achieves fault tolerance by creating a set of parity fragments. This results in more efficient use of storage capacity, allowing organizations to store data with greater economy.
- **Fault Tolerance and Data Recovery:** The primary goal of erasure coding is to provide fault tolerance and data recovery capabilities. By generating redundant fragments (parity), erasure coding ensures that even if some data fragments are lost or become inaccessible due to hardware failures or other issues, the original data can be reconstructed using the remaining fragments and parity information. This enhances the overall resilience of the storage system.
- **Reduced Storage Overhead:** Unlike replication, which requires storing complete copies of data, erasure coding introduces a lower storage overhead. By breaking data into fragments and creating parity information, the redundancy is achieved more efficiently. This reduction in storage overhead becomes especially significant in scenarios where storage costs are a critical consideration.
- **Scalability:** Erasure coding supports scalability, allowing organizations to expand their storage infrastructure without a linear increase in the amount of required storage. As data volumes grow, erasure coding provides a more sustainable approach to maintaining fault tolerance, making it suitable for large-scale storage environments.

Useful Scenarios:

- **Large-Scale Data Warehouses:** Erasure coding is particularly beneficial in scenarios where storage efficiency is paramount, such as large-scale data warehouses. In data warehousing, organizations accumulate and analyze vast amounts of data. Erasure coding allows these organizations to achieve fault tolerance without the need for extensive storage replication, resulting in more cost-effective and space-efficient data storage.
- **Cloud Storage Environments:** Cloud storage environments, where optimizing costs and storage efficiency are critical concerns, find erasure coding to be a valuable solution. It allows cloud service providers and users to achieve fault tolerance in a more economical manner, aligning with the pay-as-you-go model of cloud computing.
- **Archival Storage Systems:** Erasure coding is well-suited for archival storage systems where data is retained for long periods. In archival storage, minimizing storage overhead while ensuring fault tolerance is essential. Erasure coding strikes a balance between these requirements, making it an ideal choice for systems handling archival data.
- **Distributed Storage Systems:** In distributed storage systems where data is distributed across multiple nodes or locations, erasure coding provides an efficient mechanism for fault tolerance. It enables the reconstruction of lost data fragments, ensuring data integrity and availability across the distributed environment.

4.3 SAFEGUARDING THE PILLARS: BACKUP AND RECOVERY STRATEGIES

In the ever-evolving landscape of cloud computing, ensuring the resilience of data against potential loss is paramount. This chapter delves into the critical aspect of backup and recovery strategies, focusing on comprehensive examination and practical implementation tailored for cloud environments, with specific considerations for GCP and AWS [16,17].

4.3.1 Comprehensive Examination of Backup and Recovery Strategies

Regular Backups, Incremental Backups, and Snapshots:

1. *Regular Backups:*
   - **Strengths:** Regular backups provide a baseline for data recovery, ensuring that a recent copy is always available for restoration.
   - **Weaknesses**: The frequency of regular backups may result in increased storage costs, especially for large datasets.

2. *Incremental Backups:*
   - **Strengths:** Incremental backups only store changes made since the last backup, optimizing storage space and reducing backup duration.
   - **Weaknesses:** Dependency on previous backup sets may lead to complexities during restoration, requiring a sequential recovery process.

3. *Snapshots:*
   - **Strengths:** Snapshots capture the state of a system at a specific point in time, allowing for rapid recovery to that exact state.
   - **Weaknesses:** Storage costs can accumulate as multiple snapshots are retained over time, necessitating efficient snapshot management.

Context in Cloud Environments

GCP and AWS Integration: Both GCP and AWS offer native services for backup and recovery, such as Google Cloud Backup and AWS Backup. The chapter examines the integration of regular backups, incremental backups, and snapshots within the frameworks provided by these cloud platforms.

4.3.2 Practical Insights into Implementation

Automated Backup Schedules, Versioning Systems, and Cloud Provider-Specific Features

1. **Automated Backup Schedules:** Establishing automated backup schedules ensures consistency and reduces the risk of human error. GCP's Cloud Scheduler and AWS CloudWatch Events can be leveraged for this purpose.
2. **Versioning Systems:** Implementing versioning systems, such as GCP's Cloud Storage Versioning and AWS S3 Versioning, enables tracking and retrieval of multiple versions of a file, providing an additional layer of data protection.

3. **Cloud Provider-Specific Backup Features:** Utilizing cloud provider-specific features, like GCP's Cloud Snapshot Management and AWS EBS Snapshots, enhances efficiency by leveraging platform-native capabilities.

Real-World Applicability with Industry Scenarios

1. E-Commerce Platforms: Regular Backups for Swift Recovery

- **Identify Critical Data:** Determine the essential data for the E-commerce platform, including product information, customer details, and transaction records.
- **Define Backup Frequency:** Establish a regular backup schedule based on the frequency of data updates and modifications. For instance, daily backups might suffice for platforms with moderate changes.
- **Select Backup Tools:** Choose suitable backup tools or services provided by the cloud platform (e.g., GCP's Cloud Storage, AWS S3) that align with the platform's data structure.
- **Automation Implementation:** Implement automated backup schedules using cloud provider features or external tools. For example, use GCP's Cloud Scheduler or AWS CloudWatch Events to automate daily backups.
- **Data Restoration Tests:** Periodically conduct data restoration tests to ensure the efficiency of the backup system. This involves restoring a subset of data to validate the process.

Example Scenario: If an accidental data loss occurs during a product update, the E-commerce platform can quickly restore the affected product information from the most recent backup, ensuring minimal disruption to operations.

2. Healthcare Systems: Incremental Backups and Versioning for Patient Records

- **Identify Patient Data Categories:** Categorize patient data into critical sections, such as medical history, diagnoses, treatment plans, and prescriptions.
- **Establish Incremental Backup Strategy:** Design an incremental backup strategy where only changes made since the last backup are stored. This reduces storage costs and backup duration.
- **Implement Versioning Systems:** Enable versioning systems provided by the cloud platform (e.g., GCP's Cloud Storage Versioning, AWS S3 Versioning) to track and manage different versions of patient records.
- **Automation for Continuous Updates:** Set up automated processes for continuous incremental backups, ensuring that the latest patient data is backed up without manual intervention.
- **Data Security Measures:** Implement encryption and access controls to safeguard patient records during backups and ensure compliance with healthcare data protection regulations.

Example Scenario: In the event of accidental data corruption in a patient's medical history, the healthcare system can revert to a previous version using the versioning system, maintaining the integrity of historical records.

3. Financial Institutions: Snapshots for Critical Transaction Data

- **Identify Critical Transactional Data:** Identify critical data related to financial transactions, including account balances, transaction logs, and user authentication records.
- **Snapshot Frequency:** Determine the frequency of creating snapshots based on the pace of financial transactions. High-frequency trading platforms may require more frequent snapshots.
- **Select Snapshot Tools:** Choose snapshot tools provided by the cloud platform (e.g., GCP's Cloud Snapshot Management, AWS EBS Snapshots) that align with the financial institution's data architecture.
- **Automation and Synchronization:** Implement automated snapshot creation, ensuring synchronization with transactional databases. This guarantees that snapshots represent the latest state of critical financial data.
- **Data Restoration Protocols:** Develop protocols for efficiently restoring critical financial data from snapshots in case of system failures or data corruption.

Example Scenario: If there is a sudden system failure, snapshots allow the financial institution to quickly restore transactional data to the latest consistent state, minimizing financial risks and ensuring operational continuity.

4.4.1 Strategic Insights into Crafting and Executing Business Continuity Plans

Business continuity planning (BCP) is a crucial facet of organizational resilience, especially in the realm of cloud computing. This chapter delves into the strategic insights and case studies surrounding the crafting and execution of robust business continuity plans, considering industry cloud policies, rules, frameworks, and steps to acquire and follow them [18,19].

Strategic Insights

- **Holistic Approach:** Develop a comprehensive business continuity plan that encompasses data recovery strategies, communication protocols, and contingency plans. This holistic approach ensures that all aspects of business operations are considered in the event of a data loss incident.
- **Regulatory Compliance:** Align the business continuity plan with industry-specific cloud policies and regulations. This involves understanding and adhering to data protection laws, compliance frameworks, and security standards relevant to the organization's sector.
- **Risk Assessment:** Conduct a thorough risk assessment to identify potential vulnerabilities and prioritize critical business functions. This step ensures that resources are allocated efficiently to safeguard the most essential aspects of the organization.
- **Cloud Provider Collaboration:** Collaborate with cloud service providers to integrate their disaster recovery and business continuity features into the overall plan. Leverage cloud provider tools and services to enhance the effectiveness of the business continuity strategy.

- **Regular Testing and Updates:** Implement a testing schedule to regularly evaluate the effectiveness of the business continuity plan. This includes simulated drills, scenario-based exercises, and updates based on lessons learned from testing.
- **Employee Training:** Provide comprehensive training to employees on their roles and responsibilities during a data loss incident. Ensure that employees are well-versed in the business continuity plan and can execute their designated tasks effectively.
- **Communication Strategies:** Develop clear and concise communication strategies to keep stakeholders informed during an incident. This includes communication channels, escalation procedures, and transparency in updating both internal and external parties.
- **Documentation and Documentation Access:** Ensure thorough documentation of the business continuity plan and make it easily accessible to relevant personnel. This documentation should include step-by-step procedures, contact lists, and any necessary authorization processes.

Industry Cloud Policies, Rules, and Frameworks

- **Identify Applicable Regulations:** Determine the specific industry cloud policies, rules, and frameworks that apply to the organization. This may include data protection laws, industry-specific compliance standards, and security regulations.
- **Adherence and Integration:** Ensure that the business continuity plan aligns with and adheres to the identified industry cloud policies. Integrate compliance requirements seamlessly into the overall strategy to mitigate legal and regulatory risks.
- **Continuous Monitoring:** Establish mechanisms for continuous monitoring of changes in industry cloud policies. Regularly update the business continuity plan to reflect any modifications in regulations or compliance frameworks.

4.4.2 Case Studies Showcasing Successful Business Continuity Practices

1. Healthcare Industry: Navigating Data Loss with Resilience

In a recent data loss incident within the healthcare industry, a prominent healthcare organization showcased resilience by implementing a business continuity plan meticulously crafted to comply with stringent healthcare data protection regulations. The incident involved the accidental deletion of critical patient records due to a system glitch [20].

Scenario

Data Loss Incident: A technical glitch led to the unintentional deletion of a substantial portion of patient records, jeopardizing access to crucial medical histories, treatment plans, and diagnostic information.

Response and Recovery:

- **Quick Activation of Business Continuity Plan:** The healthcare organization swiftly activated its business continuity plan, a well-documented strategy aligned with healthcare data protection regulations, ensuring compliance with laws such as the Health Insurance Portability and Accountability Act.
- **Data Recovery Protocols:** The business continuity plan incorporated robust data recovery protocols. Utilizing regular backups, incremental backups, and versioning systems, the organization efficiently restored the deleted patient records to their latest consistent state.

Impact on Patient Care:

- **Minimal Disruption to Patient Care:** The swift recovery of patient records played a pivotal role in maintaining uninterrupted patient care. Healthcare providers regained access to critical information, allowing them to make informed decisions promptly.
- **Positive Patient Outcomes:** The organization's adherence to healthcare data protection regulations not only ensured legal compliance but also positively impacted patient outcomes. Quick data recovery prevented potential medical errors and delays in treatment.

2. Financial Services Sector: Safeguarding Critical Transactions

In the financial services sector, a disruptive event threatened the integrity of critical financial transaction data. The incident required a robust business continuity plan to swiftly recover data and mitigate the impact on business operations and customer trust [21].

Scenario

Disruptive Event: A sudden system failure occurred during peak trading hours, leading to the potential loss of critical financial transaction data, including stock trades, fund transfers, and customer account balances.

Response and Recovery:

- Business Continuity Plan Activation: The financial institution activated its well-defined business continuity plan, emphasizing quick response and recovery in line with industry regulations and financial data protection standards.
- Snapshot-Based Recovery: Leveraging the use of regular snapshots of transactional databases, the organization rapidly restored the financial transaction data to its latest consistent state. Automated snapshot creation and synchronization ensured real-time representation.

Impact on Business Operations and Customer Trust:

- **Operational Continuity:** The business continuity plan's efficiency in recovering critical financial data ensured minimal disruption to trading activities, preserving the operational continuity of the financial institution.

- **Customer Trust Preservation:** By swiftly restoring accurate account balances and transaction records, the financial institution retained customer trust. Transparent communication during the incident reassured customers, showcasing the institution's commitment to data integrity.

3. E-commerce Platform: Effective Communication and Contingency Planning

In the dynamic realm of e-commerce, an e-commerce platform faced a data loss incident that necessitated effective communication strategies and contingency planning. The organization's business continuity plan proved instrumental in ensuring minimal disruption to customer services and order fulfillment [22].

Scenario:

Data Loss Incident: A cybersecurity breach resulted in the unauthorized deletion of customer order records, creating challenges in order processing, shipping, and inventory management.

Response and Recovery:

- **Business Continuity Plan Implementation:** The e-commerce platform activated its business continuity plan, focusing on effective communication and contingency planning to address the multifaceted challenges posed by the data loss incident.
- **Communication Protocols:** Clear communication protocols were established, ensuring transparent communication with customers regarding the incident, potential delays, and remediation efforts. Social media, email, and the platform's website served as key communication channels.
- **Contingency Measures:** The business continuity plan incorporated contingency measures, such as leveraging redundant order databases, to continue processing orders despite the loss of some data. Inventory management systems were recalibrated to account for potential discrepancies.

Impact on Customer Services and Order Fulfillment:

- **Minimal Disruption to Customer Services:** The proactive communication strategies ensured that customers were informed promptly, mitigating frustration and dissatisfaction. The organization provided reassurance and outlined steps taken to address the situation.
- **Order Fulfillment Efficiency:** Despite the data loss, the business continuity plan's contingency measures enabled the platform to efficiently fulfill orders. Redundant systems and recalibrated processes minimized disruptions in shipping and inventory management.

Best Practices:

1. Proactive Preparedness: Navigating the Future with Strategic Readiness

In the ever-evolving landscape of business continuity, proactive preparedness stands as a cornerstone for resilience. This imperative is especially pronounced when aligning business continuity practices with industry cloud policies, rules, and frameworks. Proactivity involves anticipating potential risks, understanding regulatory landscapes, and establishing a solid foundation for response mechanisms. Key Components of Proactive Preparedness are [23]:

i. **Risk Identification and Assessment:**
   - **Anticipating Challenges:** Proactive preparedness begins with a comprehensive identification of potential risks. This involves a meticulous assessment of both internal and external factors that could pose threats to data integrity and operational continuity.

ii. **Regulatory Alignment:**
   - **Compliance Mapping:** Successful business continuity practices necessitate aligning with industry cloud policies and regulations. This entails mapping out the specific compliance requirements laid out by regulatory frameworks and ensuring that the business continuity plan adheres to these standards.

iii. **Preemptive Strategy Development:**
   - **Scenario Planning:** Proactive preparedness involves scenario planning, where organizations simulate potential disruptions and design preemptive strategies. This prepares the organization to respond swiftly and effectively in the face of unexpected challenges.

iv. **Education and Training:**
   - **Building Competencies:** Ensuring that the workforce is well-educated and trained in the intricacies of the business continuity plan is paramount. Proactive measures include ongoing training programs to enhance the team's readiness for various scenarios.

Benefits of Proactive Preparedness:

- **Reduced Downtime:** Anticipating and addressing potential risks proactively minimizes downtime during disruptions, ensuring that operations can swiftly resume.
- **Enhanced Compliance:** Aligning with industry cloud policies ensures that the organization remains compliant with legal and regulatory frameworks, reducing the risk of penalties and legal ramifications.
- **Stakeholder Confidence:** Proactive preparedness builds stakeholder confidence by demonstrating a commitment to data security, regulatory compliance, and the overall resilience of the organization.

2. Continuous Improvement in BCP

Emphasizing the importance of continuous improvement in BCP is paramount for organizations navigating the dynamic landscape of cloud computing and data management. This involves a proactive approach through regular testing, updates, and adherence to evolving industry cloud regulations [24].

- **Regular Testing and Simulation:** Conducting regular testing is the linchpin of continuous improvement. Organizations should simulate various scenarios, including data loss incidents, cyberattacks, and system failures, to evaluate the efficacy of their business continuity plan.
- **Scenario-Based Exercises:** Designing scenario-based exercises helps teams respond to hypothetical but plausible situations. This proactive testing not only identifies weaknesses in the plan but also fosters a culture of preparedness among stakeholders.
- **Lessons Learned Analysis:** After each testing phase, conduct a comprehensive analysis of lessons learned. This involves scrutinizing the outcomes of simulations, identifying areas of improvement, and refining the business continuity plan based on real-world insights.
- **Technology Updates:** Given the rapid evolution of technology, updating systems and tools integral to the business continuity plan is crucial. Continuous improvement involves integrating the latest technologies that enhance data recovery, communication, and overall resilience.
- **Feedback Mechanisms:** Establishing feedback mechanisms from stakeholders involved in testing and plan execution is essential. This feedback loop helps organizations gain insights into the practical aspects of the plan's implementation and provides valuable perspectives for refinement.
- **Adherence to Cloud Regulations:** Staying abreast of evolving industry cloud regulations is fundamental. Continuous improvement in BCP involves regular reviews to ensure compliance with data protection laws, privacy regulations, and other industry-specific cloud standards.
- **Agile Response to Changes:** Agility is a cornerstone of continuous improvement. Organizations should adopt an agile mindset that allows for swift adjustments to the business continuity plan in response to technological advancements, regulatory changes, or shifts in industry best practices.

3. Adaptability to Industry Specifics in BCP

Stressing the need for adaptability in BCP underscores the importance of tailoring strategies to the specifics of each industry. This involves considering compliance requirements, unique operational challenges, and the intricacies of data management within the industry's context [25].

- **Customization for Compliance:** Industries operate under distinct regulatory frameworks. Business continuity plans must be customized to align seamlessly with these compliance requirements, ensuring that the organization not only meets legal obligations but also builds a robust defense against potential breaches.
- **Understanding Operational Nuances:** Each industry has its own set of operational nuances and critical functions. An adaptable business continuity plan takes into account these specifics, identifying key operational areas that require special attention during data loss incidents.

- **Risk Assessment for Industry Challenges:** Conducting a thorough risk assessment that considers industry-specific challenges is vital. This involves analyzing potential threats unique to the sector and devising strategies that address these challenges effectively.
- **Integration with Industry Standards:** Adaptable business continuity plans integrate seamlessly with industry standards. Whether it is data encryption practices, secure communication protocols, or specific data recovery methodologies, the plan should align with the established standards of the industry.
- **Collaboration with Industry Peers:** Foster collaboration and knowledge exchange with industry peers. Understanding how other organizations within the same sector approach BCP provides valuable insights for adapting and enhancing one's own strategy.
- **Training Tailored to Industry Dynamics:** Employee training programs should be tailored to industry dynamics. This includes educating staff on industry-specific threats, compliance nuances, and the role they play in maintaining continuity during data loss incidents.
- **Scalability to Industry Growth:** An adaptable business continuity plan anticipates and accommodates the industry's growth. Scalability is crucial, ensuring that the plan remains effective as the organization expands, introduces new technologies, or adapts to changing market demands.

4.5 CONCLUSION

In conclusion, this chapter has provided a comprehensive exploration of the critical dimensions involved in safeguarding data integrity within the dynamic landscape of cloud environments. The journey began by unraveling the complexities of potential data loss incidents in cloud settings, shedding light on the intricate challenges that organizations may face. Real-world examples and case studies illustrated the diversity of scenarios, emphasizing the multifaceted nature of threats to data integrity. Moving forward, the chapter delved into the architectural principles of building resilient data storage systems within the cloud. The deep dive into construction methodologies, including redundant storage, distributed databases, and fault-tolerant design, illuminated the path toward fortifying data against loss. The exploration of cutting-edge technologies showcased the ongoing evolution of strategies to enhance data resilience, providing a glimpse into the future of robust storage architectures. The discussion then shifted to the critical realm of backup and recovery strategies. A comprehensive examination of these strategies, encompassing regular backups, incremental backups, and snapshots, underscored their pivotal role in fortifying against data loss. Practical insights into their implementation within cloud environments bridged the gap between theory and real-world applicability. Finally, the chapter emphasized the shield of continuity through BCP. Strategic insights into crafting and executing these plans in the face of data loss incidents provided a roadmap for organizations to navigate challenges effectively. The inclusion of case studies showcased instances where effective business continuity practices not only mitigated the impact of data loss but also inspired thoughtful planning for future resilience.

4.6 FUTURE SCOPE

Looking ahead, the future scope for research in this domain is vast and promising. One avenue for exploration is the integration of Artificial Intelligence and Machine Learning to enhance predictive capabilities and preemptively address potential data threats. Investigating how quantum computing might impact data storage and security in the cloud is another compelling direction, considering the evolving landscape of quantum technologies.

Blockchain, with its promise of immutability, offers a rich field for future study. Evaluating the feasibility and effectiveness of blockchain in ensuring data integrity within cloud environments could pave the way for innovative solutions. Furthermore, understanding the challenges and opportunities associated with global regulatory compliance is crucial as organizations navigate diverse regulatory frameworks worldwide.

The future of disaster recovery strategies in the cloud is also a focal point for exploration. Advancements in technologies and methodologies that contribute to rapid and efficient recovery from catastrophic data loss incidents will be pivotal. As the world becomes more interconnected, businesses must seek innovative ways to navigate compliance requirements and ensure data resilience across diverse regions.

In embracing these future directions, researchers and practitioners alike can contribute to the ongoing evolution of best practices, strategies, and technologies. This chapter serves as a foundational guide, and the exploration and discovery in the realm of data resilience within cloud environments are poised to continue. The journey ahead holds the promise of further innovation and insights that will shape the future landscape of secure and resilient data management in the cloud.

REFERENCES

1. Mehraj, S., & Banday, M. T. (2020, January). Establishing a zero trust strategy in cloud computing environment. In *2020 International Conference on Computer Communication and Informatics (ICCCI)* (pp. 1–6). IEEE.
2. Kunduru, A. R. (2023). The perils and defenses of enterprise cloud computing: a comprehensive review. *Central Asian Journal of Mathematical Theory and Computer Sciences*, **4**(9), 29–41.
3. Shahid, M. A., Islam, N., Alam, M. M., Mazliham, M. S., & Musa, S. (2021). Towards resilient method: an exhaustive survey of fault tolerance methods in the cloud computing environment. *Computer Science Review*, **40**, 100398.
4. Welsh, T., & Benkhelifa, E. (2020). On resilience in cloud computing: A survey of techniques across the cloud domain. *ACM Computing Surveys (CSUR)*, **53**(3), 1–36.
5. Wazid, M., Das, A. K., Hussain, R., Succi, G., & Rodrigues, J. J. (2019). Authentication in cloud-driven IoT-based big data environment: Survey and outlook. *Journal of Systems Architecture*, **97**, 185–196.
6. Adhikari, M., Amgoth, T., & Srirama, S. N. (2019). A survey on scheduling strategies for workflows in cloud environment and emerging trends. *ACM Computing Surveys (CSUR)*, **52**(4), 1–36.
7. Tabrizchi, H., & Kuchaki Rafsanjani, M. (2020). A survey on security challenges in cloud computing: issues, threats, and solutions. *The Journal of Supercomputing*, **76**(12), 9493–9532.

8. Alouffi, B., Hasnain, M., Alharbi, A., Alosaimi, W., Alyami, H., & Ayaz, M. (2021). A systematic literature review on cloud computing security: threats and mitigation strategies. *IEEE Access*, **9**, 57792–57807.
9. Helali, L., & Omri, M. N. (2021). A survey of data center consolidation in cloud computing systems. *Computer Science Review*, **39**, 100366.
10. Gupta, I., Singh, A. K., Lee, C. N., & Buyya, R. (2022). Secure data storage and sharing techniques for data protection in cloud environments: A systematic review, analysis, and future directions. *IEEE Access*, 10.
11. Cortez, E. K., & Dekker, M. (2022). A corporate governance approach to cybersecurity risk disclosure. *European Journal of Risk Regulation*, **13**(3), 443–463.
12. Mishra, S., Anderson, K., Miller, B., Boyer, K., & Warren, A. (2020). Microgrid resilience: A holistic approach for assessing threats, identifying vulnerabilities, and designing corresponding mitigation strategies. *Applied Energy*, **264**, 114726.
13. Dantas, V. (2021). *Architecting Google Cloud Solutions: Learn to Design Robust and Future-Proof Solutions with Google Cloud Technologies*. Packt Publishing Ltd.
14. Mulder, J. (2020). *Multi-Cloud Architecture and Governance: Leverage Azure, AWS, GCP, and VMware vSphere to Build Effective Multi-Cloud Solutions*. Packt Publishing Ltd.
15. Kishor, K., Saxena, N., & Pandey, D. (Eds.). (2023). *Cloud-Based Intelligent Informative Engineering for Society 5.0*. CRC Press.
16. Naidu, R., Guruprasad, N., & Gowda, V. D. (2020). Design and implementation of cryptcloud system for securing files in cloud. *Advances in Mathematics: Scientific Journal*, **9**(7), 4485–4493.
17. Diogenes, Y., & Ozkaya, E. (2019). *Cybersecurity–Attack and Defense Strategies: Counter Modern Threats and Employ State-of-the-Art Tools and Techniques to Protect your Organization Against Cybercriminals*. Packt Publishing Ltd.
18. Oladoyinbo, T. O., Adebiyi, O. O., Ugonnia, J. C., Olaniyi, O. O., & Okunleye, O. J. (2023). Evaluating and establishing baseline security requirements in cloud computing: an enterprise risk management approach. *Asian Journal of Economics, Business and Accounting*, **23**(21), 222–231.
19. Dittakavi, R. S. S. (2022). Evaluating the efficiency and limitations of configuration strategies in hybrid cloud environments. *International Journal of Intelligent Automation and Computing*, **5**(2), 29–45.
20. Lin, W., Xu, M., He, J., & Zhang, W. (2023). Privacy, security and resilience in mobile healthcare applications. *Enterprise Information Systems*, **17**(3), 1939896.
21. Scott, H. S., Gulliver, J., & Nadler, H. (2019). Cloud computing in the financial sector: A global perspective. *Program on International Financial Systems*.
22. Zhang, R., Fang, L., He, X., & Wei, C. (2023). *The Whole Process of E-commerce Security Management System: Design and Implementation*. Springer Nature.
23. Makura, S. M., Venter, H. S., Ikuesan, R. A., Kebande, V. R., & Karie, N. M. (2020, February). Proactive forensics: Keystroke logging from the cloud as potential digital evidence for forensic readiness purposes. In *2020 IEEE International Conference on Informatics, IoT, and Enabling Technologies (ICIoT)* (pp. 200–205). IEEE.
24. Yenugula, M., Sahoo, S., & Goswami, S. (2024). Cloud computing for sustainable development: An analysis of environmental, economic and social benefits. *Journal of Future Sustainability*, **4**(1), 59–66.
25. Niemimaa, M., Järveläinen, J., Heikkilä, M., & Heikkilä, J. (2019). Business continuity of business models: Evaluating the resilience of business models for contingencies. *International Journal of Information Management*, **49**, 208–216.

5 Cryptographic Bastions

Mastering Cloud Security through Advanced Access Control and Encryption Strategies

Het Joshi and Neeraj Phadke

5.1 INTRODUCTION TO CLOUD PROVIDERS

A Cloud Provider is a company or an organization that delivers Cloud Computing services and resources. The services offered may include the following: Computing Power—Storage and Databases—Networking—Analytics—Software Applications. These organizations or companies operate large-scale data centers and provide the users with their computation resources on a pay-as-you-go subscription basis [1,2]. Users leverage these resources to host and run applications, store data, and perform various other computations tasks without having to maintain their own physical hardware setup. Examples of popular Cloud Providers are Google Cloud Platform (GCP), Amazon Web Services (AWS), Microsoft Azure, and others. Widely embraced for its prowess in supporting Business-Critical architectures, Artificial Intelligence, and machine learning applications, GCP stands at the forefront of empowering data-intensive applications [3,4].

Beyond its robust computing capabilities, GCP distinguishes itself with additional features, including the Open Cloud and Multicloud approaches. These strategic frameworks imbue GCP with a spectrum of functionalities, such as unparalleled Interoperability, unwavering commitment to Vendor Neutrality, active Community Involvement, and the capacity to seamlessly facilitate Hybrid and Multicloud Architectures [5].

In essence, GCP's multifaceted offerings position it as a versatile and dynamic Cloud Computing solution, capable of meeting the intricate demands of modern businesses and fostering collaboration within the broader technological landscape [6].

5.1.1 Overview of GCP, AWS, and Other Key Players

Key Services of the GCP

1. **Compute Engine:**
   - *Description:* It is a secure and customizable service that lets us create and run Virtual Machines on Google's Cloud infrastructure. They have

DOI: 10.1201/9781003455448-5

a good library of predefined machine types to choose from and also provide an option for creating our own custom machine types to better fit our requirements.
   - *Use Cases:* Scalable and customizable computing resources for a variety of workloads.
2. **App Engine:**
   - *Description:* Cloud computing platform as a service for developing and hosting web applications in Google-managed data centers. Applications are containerized and run across multiple servers which drastically increases the scalability of our app. It also helps manage the scalability for the app—If the number of requests increases for an application, the app engine automatically allocates more resources for the web application to handle additional demand.
   - *Use Cases:* Ideal for web applications and services requiring automatic scaling.
3. **Google Kubernetes Engine:**
   - *Description:* Managed Kubernetes service for orchestrating containerized applications.
   - *Use Cases:* Efficient deployment, management, and scaling of containerized applications.
4. **Cloud Storage:**
   - *Description:* Object storage service for storing and retrieving any amount of data.
   - *Use Cases:* Data storage, backup, and serving static content for websites.

Amazon Web Services

Amazon web services is one of the most comprehensive and widely used Cloud Service. It offers over 200 fully featured services from data centers situated all across the globe. It also provides more features within those services from infrastructure technologies like—compute, storage and database management to emerging technologies such as—machine learning and Artificial Intelligence, data lakes and analytics, and Internet of Things. This provides much more functionality to the user [7–10].

AWS services are provided to users through a global network of AWS server farms distributed across various regions. Charges are determined by a "Pay-as-you-go" model, encompassing factors such as usage, selected hardware, operating system, software, and chosen networking features. Subscribers have the flexibility to pay for individual components, whether it is a single virtual AWS computer, a dedicated physical machine, or clusters of either. This pricing structure takes into account considerations like availability, redundancy, security, and service options chosen by the subscriber.

Key services of AWS

1. **Amazon EC2 (Elastic Compute Cloud):**
   - *Description:* Users have the capability to access a virtual cluster of computers through AWS, ensuring exceptionally high availability.

Interaction with this virtual cluster can be achieved over the Internet using REST APIs, a Command Line Interface (CLI), or the AWS console. These virtual computers, provided by AWS, closely mimic the features of physical computers, encompassing attributes such as hardware components like central processing units (CPUs) and graphics processing units (GPUs), local/RAM memory, hard-disk/SSD storage, a selection of operating systems, networking capabilities, and pre-loaded application software like web servers, databases, and customer relationship management (CRM) tools.
   - *Use Cases:* Running applications, hosting websites, and handling various computing workloads.
2. **Amazon S3 (Simple Storage Service):**
   - *Description:* Object storage service for scalable and secure data storage.
   - *Use Cases:* Storing and retrieving any amount of data, hosting static websites.
3. **AWS Lambda:**
   - *Description:* Serverless computing service for executing code in response to events.
   - *Use Cases:* Running code without provisioning or managing servers.
4. **Amazon Relational Database Service:**
   - *Description:* Managed relational database service for MySQL, PostgreSQL, Oracle, SQL Server, and MariaDB.
   - *Use Cases:* Hosting and managing relational databases in the Cloud.
5. **Amazon Virtual Private Cloud:**
   - *Description:* Networking service for creating isolated virtual networks within the AWS Cloud.
   - *Use Cases:* Building secure and scalable network architectures.

Microsoft Azure

Microsoft Azure is a comprehensive Cloud Computing platform that offers a wide range of services, including computing, analytics, storage, and networking. It provides a global network of data centers and is known for its integration with Microsoft products such as Windows Server, Active Directory, and SQL Server. Azure supports hybrid Cloud Environments, enabling seamless integration between on-premises data centers and the Cloud. With a focus on enterprise solutions, Azure is suitable for businesses of all sizes [11–13].

Key Features of Microsoft Azure:

1. **Hybrid Cloud Capabilities:**
   - *Feature:* Azure excels in supporting hybrid Cloud scenarios, allowing seamless integration between on-premises data centers and the Cloud. This is beneficial for businesses with existing infrastructure investments.

2. **Integrated with Microsoft Ecosystem:**
   - *Feature:* Azure integrates smoothly with Microsoft's suite of products and services, such as Windows Server, Active Directory, and SQL Server. This integration facilitates a cohesive environment for organizations already utilizing Microsoft technologies.
3. **Comprehensive Artificial Intelligence and Analytics Services:**
   - *Feature:* Azure offers a rich set of AI and analytics services, including Azure machine learning and Azure Synapse Analytics. This enables businesses to derive insights from data and implement machine learning solutions.
4. **Global Network of Data Centers:**
   - *Feature:* Azure boasts a vast global network of data centers, ensuring low-latency access to services from various regions. This global presence is valuable for businesses with a geographically distributed user base.

IBM Cloud

The IBM Cloud encompasses a whole suite of Cloud Services which include infrastructure, platform and Software as a service. The IBM Cloud is widely used for its efficiency in AI and Blockchain. It also offers a robust set of tools and solutions specially crafted for enterprise needs. It provides industry-specific solutions, ensuring compliance and security for various sectors. IBM Cloud has a global network of data centers and is recognized for its hybrid Cloud capabilities, allowing businesses to integrate their existing infrastructure with Cloud Services seamlessly [14,15].

Key Features of IBM Cloud:

1. **AI and Blockchain Expertise:**
   - *Feature:* IBM Cloud is known for its expertise in AI and Blockchain technologies. It provides specialized services for implementing AI solutions and leveraging blockchain for enhanced security and transparency.
2. **Industry-Specific Solutions:**
   - *Feature:* IBM Cloud offers industry-specific solutions tailored to sectors such as healthcare, finance, and manufacturing. These solutions address unique regulatory and compliance requirements of different industries.
3. **Hybrid Cloud Integration:**
   - *Feature:* IBM Cloud emphasizes hybrid Cloud Capabilities, allowing businesses to seamlessly integrate on-premises infrastructure with Cloud Services. This flexibility supports a gradual transition to the Cloud.
4. **Global Network and Security Focus:**
   - *Feature:* IBM Cloud provides a global network of data centers and places a strong emphasis on security. This includes robust identity and access management, encryption, and compliance features.

Table 5.1 presents a comparative overview of various features offered by different Cloud Service Providers (CSPs), including Microsoft Azure, IBM Cloud, GCP, and AWS. Microsoft Azure is recognized for its excellent support for hybrid Cloud Scenarios and smooth integration with the Microsoft ecosystem. IBM Cloud stands out with its emphasis on hybrid Cloud capabilities, specialized AI and analytics

TABLE 5.1
Overview of Features of Different Cloud Service Providers

Feature	Microsoft Azure	IBM Cloud	Google Cloud Platform (GCP)	Amazon Web Services (AWS)
Hybrid Cloud Capabilities	Excellent support for hybrid Cloud Scenarios.	Emphasizes hybrid Cloud Capabilities.	Offers hybrid Cloud Solutions.	AWS outposts provides on-premises Cloud Services.
Integrated with Microsoft ecosystem	Smooth integration with Microsoft products.	Integrates with Microsoft technologies.	N/A	N/A
AI and analytics services	Comprehensive AI and analytics services.	Specialized AI and analytics expertise.	Robust AI and machine learning services.	Offers a wide range of AI and analytics services.
Global network of data centers	Vast global network ensuring low-latency access.	Global presence with a network of data centers.	Global infrastructure with data centers worldwide.	Extensive global network of data centers.
Industry-specific solutions	N/A	Offers industry-specific solutions.	N/A	N/A
Blockchain expertise	N/A	Strong expertise in blockchain technologies.	N/A	N/A
Hybrid Cloud integration	Supports seamless integration with on-premises.	Emphasizes hybrid Cloud Capabilities.	Facilitates hybrid Cloud Integration.	AWS provides hybrid Cloud Solutions.
Networking expertise	N/A	Extensive networking expertise.	Networking solutions prioritizing connectivity.	Networking solutions with a focus on reliability.
Collaboration tools	N/A	Provides collaboration tools.	N/A	N/A
Security solutions	N/A	Strong emphasis on security.	Robust security solutions.	Comprehensive security features and services.
Internet of Things (IoT) integration	N/A	Supports IoT solutions.	Comprehensive IoT solutions.	Offers IoT services and solutions.
Simplicity and ease of use	N/A	N/A	N/A	Known for simplicity and ease of use.
Developer-friendly tools	N/A	N/A	N/A	Offers a wide range of developer tools and services.
Cost-effective solutions	N/A	N/A	N/A	Known for providing cost-effective Cloud Solutions.
Scalability and performance	N/A	N/A	Designed for scalability and predictable performance.	Scalable architecture for high-performance computing.

Note: "N/A" indicates that the specific feature may not be a prominent focus or publicly disclosed by the respective Cloud Service provider.

expertise, industry-specific solutions, strong blockchain technologies, extensive networking expertise, and robust security solutions. Google Cloud Platform offers robust AI and machine learning services, a global network of data centers, and comprehensive Internet of Things (IoT) solutions, with a focus on simplicity and ease of use.

5.1.2 Unique Security Considerations for Each Provider

Amazon Web Services is known for its on-premises Cloud Services through AWS Outposts, a wide array of AI and analytics services, an extensive global network, comprehensive security features, IoT services, developer-friendly tools, cost-effective solutions, and scalable architecture designed for high-performance computing. Each provider showcases unique strengths such as Hybrid Cloud Integration, global data center presence, and sector-specific offerings, catering to different needs in the Cloud Computing landscape [16].

5.2 ACCESS MANAGEMENT IN THE CLOUD

Access Management is crucial for regulating the user access via various methods and practices. It ensures the securing of resources and data integrity. Access management is required because sometimes we might not want everyone to have the same level of exposure to data within an organization.

Example: A programmer might not need access to the data and work of the Marketing and Sales department. The other way also holds true. To add a layer of partition as well, Access Control methods are necessary to implement.

Among the various strategies that can be employed, a few of them are as listed below:

- **Role-Based Access Control**—assigns roles to users based on their responsibilities.
- **Multifactor Authentication (MFA)**—requires users to provide multiple forms of identification such as passwords, biometrics, or one-time codes.
- **Principle of Least Privilege (PoLP)**—principle of granting users the minimum required access for their tasks.

Continuous Monitoring and **incident response** strategies help detect and respond effectively toward unauthorized activities in real time. Along with this, **regular compliance checks** and regular **audits** ensure that access management aligns with the established policies.

5.2.1 Role-Based Access Control

Function-Based Role-based security, another name for access control, is a technique whereby we grant end users permissions according to their roles within the company. Fine-grained control can be achieved with RBAC, which is also a simpler, more manageable method of implementing access control that is less prone to error than individually granted permissions.

RBAC is popular in large organizations that require granting access to hundreds or thousands of their employees based on their roles and responsibilities. As of late, it is also gaining traction outside these large organizations due to its ease of implementation and effectiveness. In this system, the User-Access Provisioning is done based on the needs of the group, roles and their respective responsibilities. Each role is given a set of permissions and individuals can be assigned multiple roles concurrently [17,18].

Example:

Role-Based Access Control (RBAC) functions like an organizational maestro, distributing access rights with precision. The Chief Architect, akin to a Software Director, oversees the entire composition. Project Managers assume the role of coordinators, orchestrating development tasks efficiently. Developers are assigned specific roles—Back-end, Front-end, Database—with access rights tailored to their responsibilities. The Security team plays the crucial role of guardians, implementing robust access control measures to fortify the digital infrastructure. Admins, like meticulous custodians, regulate access to sensitive systems. This structured approach ensures that each team member operates within the bounds of their responsibilities, fostering a secure and well-organized tech environment.

A brief outline on how to about Implementing RBAC is as follows:

- **Role Definition:** Clearly defining roles and their associated responsibilities within the Cloud Environment.
- **Permission Assignment:** Assigning specific permissions to roles rather than individual users, simplifying access control.
- **Dynamic Role Assignment:** Implementing dynamic assignment to adapt to changes in organizational structure or responsibilities.
- **Regular Audits:** Conducting regular audits to review and update roles and permissions based on evolving business needs.

5.2.2 Multifactor Authentication

Traditionally, authentication (proving to the service you are who you say you are) has been carried out using a Username and a Password. This method has been proved to be insecure and inefficient. Usernames were easy to guess and discover leading to a weak layer of security. Further, many people use simple passwords and retain the same across different connected accounts worsening the security [19,20].

To combat this issue, almost all social networking websites and other big industry players have switched to Multifactor Authentication (MFA) or as some us would have heard—"Two-Factor Authentication." This method along with using regular username and password also requires you to provide a "factor" to prove who you are. This factor can be of three kinds commonly:

- **Something you know:** Password, PIN, Security Questions
- **Something you have:** One-Time key, Physical USB
- **Something you are:** Fingerprint, Facial recognition

Below are a few widely used ways to implement Multifactored Authentication:

- **Biometric Authentication:** Integrating fingerprint scans, facial recognition, or other bio metric factors for enhanced user verification.
- **Time-Based One-Time Passwords (TOTP):** Utilizing time-sensitive codes generated by authenticator apps to prevent unauthorized access.
- **Device Authentication:** Verifying user identity based on the device they are using, adding an additional authentication factor.
- **Adaptive Authentication:** Employing adaptive methods that adjust authentication requirements based on user behavior and risk levels.

5.2.3 Best Practices for Access Policies

Maintaining well-defined and effective access policies is crucial for maintaining and ensuring a well-organized computing environment [21–28]. Below are some of the best practices for access policies:

1. **Principle of Least Privilege**

   One of the fundamental ideas of computer security and access control, it supports the idea of granting users the bare minimum of privileges on systems according to their individual job requirements. To put it another way, users under PoLP are granted the minimal access levels or permissions necessary to carry out their duties.

   The idea is applied in a variety of situations, such as creating staff profiles in an internal database or writing programs that provide resources only to the processes that require them to carry out a given task. Reducing the possibility of harm in the event that a system is compromised is the aim of every situation.

   Key aspects of this are listed below: Clear understanding of user roles—Minimize risk of data misuse—Track and manage privileges—Regulatory Framework Compliance.
2. **Regular Review and Revoking of Privileges:**

   Regular security review must be conducted in order to understand user roles and their responsibilities. The privileges for each user must be updated and redundant or roles that are no longer required to be assigned to the user must be revoked. This practice helps better control the roles and access management system. If the roles are not revoked it may cause un-desirable outcomes or data leaks.
3. **Security Audits:**

   One crucial aspect of access control is conducting routine audits and reporting. This entails a methodical and documented assessment of the degree to which the organization's access controls conform to accepted security norms and policies.

   - **Defining the Audit Scope**: The first step in conducting an audit is defining its scope. This determines which systems, locations, and procedures are evaluated. This may include specific departments, physical locations, or specific information systems.

- **Data Collection**: Once the scope is defined, data collection begins. This includes examining access logs, interviewing system users, and reviewing system configurations and access control lists. The goal is to collect accurate information about who has access to resources, how access is managed, and whether unauthorized access has occurred.
- **Evaluation of Results**: The collected data is analyzed to evaluate the effectiveness of the access controls. This includes verifying that access rights match job roles, verifying that unnecessary access rights are revoked, and identifying instances of unauthorized access or other security events.
- **Reports**: Audit results are compiled into reports that verify effectiveness. Flag non-compliance with access control policies and identify areas for improvement. The report should provide a clear and concise summary of the audit findings, including recommendations to address identified issues.

4. **Granting Temporary Access:**

   As needed, provide temporary authorizations. An access control mechanism called temporary permissions enables organizations to give users more access rights when needed, but only for a set amount of time. When users must complete tasks that are outside the scope of their normal roles but are urgent at the moment, this method is especially helpful. Certain circumstances may call for the issuance of temporary permits. For instance, a developer might require temporary access to a production database in order to complete a task, or a system administrator might require extra permissions in order to troubleshoot a problem. Since it only gives users the access they require to complete their tasks and only for that duration, this method complies with the principle of least privilege (PoLP).

5.3 FINE-GRAINED ACCESS CONTROL POLICIES

In the complex landscape of access management, Fine-Grained Access Control Policies emerge as a sophisticated and detailed approach to controlling user privileges. This section describes important principles and best practices for implementing fine-grained access controls and provides organizations with the tools to tailor access rights to their specific needs.

5.3.1 Granular Permission Assignments

Granular permission assignments refer to the practice of allocating user permissions at a highly detailed level within an information system. Instead of providing broad, sweeping access rights, granular permissions allow system administrators to specify exact access rights for each user or user group, down to individual files, data fields, or actions.

Example: In a healthcare system, a nurse might be granted permission to view patient records but not to alter them, whereas a doctor can both view and update these records. An IT administrator, on the other hand, might have permissions to access system logs but not patient data. This level of detailed permission assignment minimizes the risk of unauthorized access or data breaches.

5.3.2 Attribute-Based Access Control Implementation

ABAC is a flexible access control method that assigns user permissions based on attributes. These attributes can be related to the user (such as role, department, or clearance level), the resource (like file type or sensitivity level), the action (read, write, edit), or the context (such as time of day or location).

Example: A financial company implements ABAC in its systems. An employee in the finance department can access financial reports but only during working hours and from the office network. The same employee attempting to access these documents from a home network or after hours would be denied, as the context attributes (time and location) do not match the defined access policy.

5.3.3 Case Studies Demonstrating the Need for Fine-Grained Control

Healthcare Sector

Scenario: A large hospital faced a data breach where sensitive patient information was leaked.

Problem: The investigation revealed that the breach occurred due to overly broad access permissions for staff.

Solution: Implementing granular permission assignments and ABAC. Nurses received access only to the patient data necessary for their duties, and access logs were monitored for unusual activity.

Outcome: This change significantly reduced the risk of unauthorized access, protecting patient confidentiality.

Financial Services Industry

Scenario: A bank experienced insider trading allegations.

Problem: Employees in non-trading roles accessed sensitive market information.

Solution: The bank implemented granular permissions, restricting market-sensitive data only to authorized trading personnel. ABAC was used to control data access based on role, location, and time.

Outcome: This prevented unauthorized access to sensitive information, mitigating the risk of illegal trading activities.

Educational Institution

Scenario: A university's research data were accidentally modified, leading to a loss of critical academic work.

Problem: Students had the same access rights as faculty members, allowing them to modify or delete research data.

Solution: The University instituted granular permissions, differentiating access rights between students and faculty. ABAC was used to further refine access based on the nature of the project and individual roles.

Outcome: This protected academic research from unauthorized alterations, preserving the integrity of scholarly work.

5.4 ENCRYPTION FUNDAMENTALS IN CLOUD ENVIRONMENTS

Cloud encryption is a crucial process where data, before being transferred to Cloud Storage, undergoes encoding or modification. This process involves the use of mathematical algorithms and keys to convert the original data, known as plaintext—which can include text, data, numbers, or images—into a unique, encrypted format called ciphertext. This transformation effectively obscures the data, making it inaccessible and unintelligible to unauthorized or suspicious parties. This method of encryption serves as a primary defense mechanism, ensuring that sensitive information is protected from unauthorized access and potential cybercriminals. In this framework, the Cloud Service provider encrypts the data and then shares the encryption key with the client. These keys are essential as they allow the client to decrypt and access the original message or data when needed. Thus, Cloud Encryption is a vital component in safeguarding data privacy and security in the Cloud Computing environment.

5.4.1 Understanding Encryption Algorithms

1. **Data at Rest:**
   - **Definition:** Data at rest refers to stored data that is not actively being used or transmitted. It is in a static state and resides in storage systems, databases, or other data repositories.
   - **Characteristics:**
     - **Location:** Data are stored on disk drives, databases, or other persistent storage media.
     - **Access:** Not actively in use or being processed.
     - **Security Concerns:** Focus on encrypting stored data to protect against unauthorized access.
   - **Use Cases:**
     - Storing files in Cloud Storage.
     - Database contents when not actively queried.
     - Archived data.
2. **Data in Transit:**
   - **Definition:** Data in transit refers to data actively moving from one location to another, typically over a network. This state involves data being transmitted between systems or devices.
   - Characteristics:
     - **Location:** Data are in motion, traveling over networks.
     - **Access:** Actively being transferred between systems.
     - **Security Concerns:** Focus on securing the transmission using encryption to prevent interception or tampering.
   - Use Cases:
     - Uploading or downloading files to/from Cloud Storage.
     - Data being transmitted between Cloud Services.
     - User accessing a Cloud-based application.

3. **Data in Use:**
   - **Definition:** Data in use refers to data that are actively being processed, analyzed, or utilized by an application, service, or computation.
   - **Characteristics:**
     - **Location:** Actively being processed in the memory or CPU of a system.
     - **Access:** Actively being utilized by applications or services.
     - **Security Concerns:** Focus on protecting data during active processing, including access controls and encryption.
   - **Use Cases:**
     - Running computations on Cloud-based virtual machines.
     - Processing and analyzing data in Cloud-based applications.
     - Real-time interactions with data through Cloud services.

5.4.2 Importance of Data Encryption in the Cloud

Types of Encryption:

There are mainly two types of encryption techniques used which are (i) Symmetric Encryption and (ii) Asymmetric Encryption. We will dive deep into each of them in detail to know more about each of the two types.

Symmetric-Key Encryption:

Symmetric Encryption is a cryptographic method where the same key is used for both the encryption and decryption of the data. The key produced must be kept anonymous and both ends of the users should keep it that way. Symmetric Encryption is generally faster than asymmetric encryption, making it suitable for encrypting large amounts of data.

Practical Symmetric Encryption Examples:

1. Popular messaging apps (e.g., WhatsApp, telegram)
2. BitLocker
3. Data Storage Encryption
4. Virtual Machine Disk Encryption

Types of Symmetric Encryption Algorithms:

1. Advanced Encryption Standard Encryption:

Advanced Encryption Standard (AES) is a widely used Symmetric Encryption algorithm designed to secure sensitive data. It is a high level encryption type. It was established as a standard by the U.S. National Institute of Standards and Technology (NIST) in 2001, replacing the Data Encryption Standard (DES). AES is known for its security, efficiency, and versatility, and it has become a fundamental building block in various security protocols and systems.

Key Features of AES:

1. **Symmetric Encryption:**
   - In both the enciphering and deciphering same key is used.
2. **Key Lengths:**
   - 128, 192, and 256 bits are the three key lengths supported. More long a key is better and more secure the data are but then it requires more efforts and computational.
3. **Block Cipher:**
   - AES operates as a block cipher, processing fixed-size blocks of data. For AES, the block size is 128 bits (16 bytes).
4. **Substitution-Permutation Network:**
   - AES employs a substitution-permutation network (SPN) structure, which involves multiple rounds of substitution and permutation operations. These rounds are dependent upon how long the key is in following ways: 10 rounds for 128-bit keys, 12 rounds for 192-bit keys, and 14 rounds for 256-bit keys.

Real-Life Applications:

- Data Encryption
- Wireless Security (Wi-Fi)
- Secure Sockets Layer (SSL)/TLS Protocols
- Disk Encryption Tools
- VPN (Virtual Private Network) Encryption

2. Blowfish

Blowfish is a symmetric-key block cipher designed by Bruce Schneier in 1993. It is known for its simplicity, speed, and flexibility. While Blowfish is not as widely used as some other symmetric-key algorithms like AES, it is still considered a strong encryption algorithm and has applications in various scenarios, including Cloud Computing.

Use Cases in Cloud Computing:

1. Secure Communication
2. File Encryption
3. Password Protection
4. Legacy Systems ### 3. 3DES:

Triple Data Encryption Standard, also known as Triple DES or TDEA, is a symmetric-key block cipher that applies the DES algorithm three times to each data block. It was designed to provide an additional layer of security by using multiple iterations of the DES algorithm, compensating for the relatively small block size of DES.

Key Features of 3DES:

1. **Key Length:**
   - The effective key length of 3DES is determined by the keying option used:
     - **2-Key 3DES:** The key length is 112 bits.
     - **3-Key 3DES:** The key length is 168 bits.
2. **Block Cipher:**
   - 3DES operates as a block cipher, processing data in fixed-size blocks. The block size is 64 bits.
3. **Triple Application of DES:**
   - 3DES applies the DES algorithm thrice for every block of data:
     - **Encryption:** Data are encrypted with the first key.
     - **Decryption:** The result is decrypted with the second key.
     - **Encryption:** The final result is encrypted with the third key.
4. **Keying Options:**
   - 3DES supports different keying options:
     - **2-Key 3DES:** Uses two independent keys for the three stages of encryption.
     - **3-Key 3DES:** Uses three independent keys, providing a higher level of security.

Asymmetric Encryption Algorithms

Asymmetric Encryption, also known as public key cryptography. This utilizes two keys namely private and public key. These keys are mathematically related but have different functions. In this type of encryption method private key as the name suggests is kept secret and restricted while the private key is openly shared. Once the data are encrypted by a specific public key it can only be decrypted by its corresponding or co-related private key and not some random key.

Two Practical Asymmetric Encryption Examples:

1. Secure email communications (e.g., PGP, S/MIME)
2. Digital signatures for document originality and integrity (e.g., Adobe Sign, DocuSign)
3. Access control
4. Digital wallets and cryptocurrencies ## common asymmetric encryption algorithms

RSA Algorithm

SA (Rivest–Shamir–Adleman) is one of the most widely used asymmetric encryption algorithms. It is named after its inventors Ron Rivest, Adi Shamir, and Leonard Adleman, who introduced it in 1977. RSA is widely employed in various security applications, including secure communication, digital signatures, and key exchange, making it a fundamental component of the security infrastructure in Cloud Computing.

RSA's security relies on the difficulty of factoring large composite numbers into their prime components. As computing power increases, key lengths must be adjusted to maintain security. RSA continues to be a foundational algorithm in securing various aspects of Cloud Computing and information exchange on the Internet.

Key Features of RSA:

1. **Mathematical Basis:**
   - RSA relies on the mathematical properties of large prime numbers, specifically the difficulty of factoring the product of two large primes.
2. **Key Generation:**
   - The security of RSA is based on the challenge of factoring the product of two large prime numbers. The public and private keys are generated using mathematical operations involving these primes.
3. **Public Key Distribution:**
   - The public key can be openly distributed, allowing anyone to encrypt data intended for the owner of the corresponding private key.
4. **Private Key Secrecy:**
   - The private key must be kept secret and utilized during decryption of the data that has been encrypted with the corresponding public key.
5. **Digital Signatures:**
   - RSA is usually used in creating digital signatures, providing a way to verify the authenticity and integrity of data.

Elliptic Bend Cryptography

This is an asymmetric key algorithm that utilizes the mathematical properties of elliptic curves over finite fields to provide a high level of security with shorter key lengths compared to traditional asymmetric algorithms like RSA. Elliptic Curve Cryptography (ECC) is gaining popularity in Cloud Computing and other security applications due to its efficiency and strong cryptographic properties.

ECC's efficiency and strong security make it a compelling choice for various security applications, particularly in environments where resource constraints, such as limited bandwidth or computational power, are significant considerations, as is often the case in Cloud Computing.

5.4.3 Balancing Performance and Security

Table 5.2 contrasts symmetric and asymmetric encryption, highlighting their distinct characteristics. Symmetric Encryption, utilizing a single shared secret key for both encrypting and decrypting data, is known for its computational efficiency, making it suitable for encrypting large volumes of data. However, it requires a secure method for distributing the shared key between parties. On the other hand, asymmetric encryption employs a pair of keys—a public key for encryption and a private key for decryption. While public keys can be openly distributed, private keys must be kept confidential. Asymmetric Encryption is computationally more demanding, making it slower and less scalable for bulk data encryption compared to Symmetric Encryption. The security of Symmetric Encryption hinges on the shared key's strength and secrecy, whereas Asymmetric Encryption's security is based on the complexity of mathematical problems, such as factorizing large numbers. Symmetric Encryption is widely used in scenarios like data and file encryption, as seen in AES and DES. Asymmetric Encryption, exemplified by RSA (Rivest–Shamir–Adleman) and ECC, is optimal for key exchanges, digital signatures, and securing communication channels, offering a different set of advantages and applications compared to Symmetric Encryption.

TABLE 5.2
Symmetric Encryption vs Asymmetric Encryption

Feature	Symmetric Encryption	Asymmetric Encryption
Key type	Uses a single shared secret key for both encryption and decryption.	Utilizes a pair of public and private keys for encryption and decryption.
Key distribution	Requires secure distribution of the shared key between communicating parties.	Public keys can be freely distributed, while private keys must remain confidential.
Computational complexity	Generally faster and computationally less intensive.	Slower due to complex mathematical operations involved.
Scalability	Efficient for bulk data encryption and large-scale operations.	Less efficient for large-scale operations due to higher computational overhead.
Security strength	Dependent on the strength and secrecy of the shared key.	Relies on the mathematical difficulty of certain problems (e.g., factorizing large numbers).
Use cases	Commonly used for data encryption, file encryption, and secure communication.	Ideal for key exchange, digital signatures, and securing communication channels.
Examples	AES (Advanced Encryption Standard), DES (Data Encryption Standard).	RSA (Rivest–Shamir–Adleman), ECC (Elliptic Curve Cryptography).

5.5 KEY MANAGEMENT IN CLOUD SECURITY

5.5.1 What is Cloud Key Management?

The management of cryptographic keys in a cryptosystem is known as key management. To accomplish security in a framework, cryptographic algorithms are utilized to create keys which are subsequently encrypted and decrypted to give the requested data in a secure manner. Cloud key management refers to a service that is hosted on the Cloud, where symmetric and asymmetric cryptographic keys can be managed as on-premises.

This forms the basis of all data privacy and security. Encryption keys are utilized to encrypt and decryption purpose, if these are compromised or lost then all the privacy and protection strategies applied to it will not be of much use. Keys also guarantee the protected transmission of information across an Internet connection. A standard way to refer to key management is "KMS" which is a short form of Key Management System. Further in the chapter KMS will be used in place of mentioning its full form every time.

5.5.2 Centralized vs. Decentralized Key Management

Centralized Key Management

Definition and Functionality: Centralized key management involves the consolidation of cryptographic key generation, distribution, and storage within a single, dedicated entity or service. This central authority is responsible for overseeing all key-related operations.

Security Advantages:

1. **Enhanced Control:** Centralized systems provide a unified control point, allowing administrators to implement and enforce security policies consistently.
2. **Streamlined Auditing:** Monitoring and auditing key-related activities becomes more straightforward, contributing to improved compliance and accountability.
3. **Rapid Updates:** Centralized systems facilitate swift updates and changes to key management policies across the entire infrastructure.

Drawbacks:

1. **Single Point of Failure:** The centralization of keys creates a potential vulnerability, as a breach or compromise of the central system could lead to a catastrophic compromise of all encrypted data.
2. **Scalability Challenges:** As Cloud Environments scale, managing a centralized key system may become logistically challenging and resource-intensive.

Decentralized Key Management

Definition and Functionality: Decentralized key management distributes cryptographic key generation, distribution, and storage across multiple entities or services. This approach aims to eliminate a single point of failure and enhance security through a distributed model.

Security Advantages:

1. **Resilience against Breaches:** Decentralization mitigates the impact of a single point of failure, as compromising one key does not jeopardize the security of the entire system.
2. **Improved Redundancy:** The distributed nature of decentralized systems enhances redundancy and fault tolerance, minimizing the risk of data loss due to a localized issue.

Drawbacks:

1. **Complexity:** Decentralized systems can be more complex to implement and manage, potentially requiring sophisticated coordination among distributed entities.
2. **Potential for Inconsistency:** Ensuring consistent security policies and practices across a decentralized infrastructure may pose challenges, leading to potential vulnerabilities.

The choice between centralized and decentralized key management in the Cloud is not a one-size-fits-all decision. Organizations must carefully assess their specific needs, considering factors such as the sensitivity of data, scalability requirements, and the overall security posture. Striking a balance between centralized control and decentralized resilience may be the key to achieving a robust and adaptive key management strategy in the dynamic landscape of Cloud Computing.

5.5.3 Automated Key Rotation Strategies

Why is Key Rotation Important for Data Security?

Key rotation is a security practice that involves regularly updating cryptographic keys used in encryption algorithms to enhance the overall security of a system. This process helps mitigate the risk associated with compromised or weakened keys over time. Key rotation is applied to both symmetric and asymmetric encryption keys, and it is a common practice in various security protocols and systems.

Importance of Key Rotation:

1. **Mitigating Risks:**
   - Regularly changing cryptographic keys reduces the window of opportunity for attackers to compromise and exploit keys. It limits the impact of compromised keys on the security of the system.
2. **Adapting to Evolving Threats:**
   - As security threats evolve and new vulnerabilities are discovered, key rotation allows organizations to adapt and respond to emerging risks, ensuring that their encryption mechanisms remain robust.
3. **Regulatory Compliance:**
   - Many regulatory standards and compliance frameworks mandate the periodic rotation of cryptographic keys. Adhering to these requirements is crucial for organizations operating in regulated industries.
4. **Long-Term Security:**
   - Over time, cryptographic algorithms and technologies may become vulnerable due to advancements in computational power. Key rotation allows for the adoption of stronger encryption algorithms and technologies as needed.
5. **Data Resilience:**
   - Key rotation contributes to data resilience by minimizing the impact of key compromise or accidental loss. Even if a key is compromised, the exposure is limited to the duration between key rotations.

Key Rotation Strategies:

1. **Time-Based Rotation:** Keys are rotated at predefined time intervals, regardless the fact that these are compromised or not.
   - **Advantages:**
     - Predictable and easy to implement.
     - Ensures regular updates to cryptographic keys.
   - **Considerations:**
     - Might cause unnecessary key changes if there is no proof of compromise.
     - Timing should be balanced to ensure security without causing disruptions.
2. **Event-Based Rotation:** Keys are rotated in response to specific events, such as a security incident or suspicion of key compromise.

- **Advantages:**
  - Adaptable and responsive to security incidents.
  - Reduces unnecessary key changes during periods of stability.
- **Considerations:**
  - Requires effective monitoring and detection mechanisms.
  - The timing of rotations may vary depending on the occurrence of events.

3. **Usage-Based Rotation:** Keys are rotated based on the number of encryption or decryption operations performed.
   - **Advantages:**
     - Adapts to the actual usage patterns of keys.
     - Provides a balance between security and operational efficiency.
   - **Considerations:**
     - Requires monitoring and logging of key usage.
     - May be challenging to implement in systems with dynamic usage patterns.

Choosing the appropriate key rotation strategy depends on the specific security requirements, operational considerations, and the nature of the data and systems involved. Implementing key rotation as part of a comprehensive key management strategy contributes significantly to the overall security posture of an organization.

5.5.4 Ensuring Key Confidentiality

Auditing and monitoring key rotation is a crucial aspect of maintaining secure, compliant, and consistent information encryption practices. These processes involve tracking key-related activities, identifying potential security incidents, and ensuring adherence to organizational policies and industry regulations.

The majority of CSPs and Key Management Systems (KMS) come equipped with built-in logging capabilities that record key rotation events. These logs serve to retain information for a predefined period, aligning with organizational policies and regulatory requirements, ensuring traceability, and facilitating incident response.

Key logs typically encompass details such as:

- Key creation, modification, and deletion
- Key usage, including encryption and decryption operations
- Changes in access control, such as granting or revoking permissions
- Updates to key metadata, including descriptions and aliases

While logging is considered a fundamental component for reviewing key activities, monitoring is another pivotal aspect that enables the timely detection of potential security incidents or policy violations. Monitoring key rotation can be achieved through the use of built-in tools provided by KMS or CSPs or by integrating with third-party Security Information and Event Management (SIEM) solutions.

Effective monitoring of key rotation involves identifying unusual key access or usage patterns, detecting potential key compromise or unauthorized attempts to rotate keys, and making things such that key rotation occurs at specified interval as per the rules and guidelines of the company or organization. This ensures a proactive approach to security, helping organizations respond swiftly to emerging threats and maintaining the integrity of their cryptographic key management practices.

5.6 SERVER-SIDE ENCRYPTION

Server-side encryption (SSE) is a security feature implemented by CSPs to protect data at rest in their storage systems. With SSE, the Cloud Provider automatically encrypts the data before it is stored and decrypts it when it is retrieved. This ensures that stored data remain confidential and secure, adding an extra layer of protection beyond the physical security measures employed by the data center.

Here is an overview of server-side encryption and some standard encryption algorithms used in SSE:

1. **SSE with Amazon 'Simple Storage Service':**

   Amazon S3 (Simple Storage Service) provides a feature called SSE, which helps protect data stored in S3 buckets by encrypting it at the server level. SSE offers different methods for managing encryption keys, and one of these methods is SSE-S3, where Amazon S3 manages the encryption keys on behalf of the user.

   Server-Side Encryption with Amazon S3 Managed Keys (SSE-S3) is a straightforward and secure method to encrypt data at rest in Amazon S3 buckets. It simplifies the encryption process by automating key management, allowing users to focus on managing their data and applications while AWS ensures the security of the stored information.
2. **SSE with Azure Storage:**

   SSE with Azure Storage is a security feature that enhances the protection of data stored in Azure Storage services, such as Azure Blob Storage. SSE ensures that data at rest is encrypted, adding an extra layer of security to safeguard sensitive information. SSE in Azure Storage integrates with Azure's robust identity and access management features, allowing users to control access to their encrypted data through Azure Active Directory and Azure Role-Based Access Control. This SSE functionality aligns with best practices for securing data in Cloud Storage, meeting compliance requirements and providing a secure foundation for various Cloud-based applications and services.
3. **SSE with Google Cloud Storage:**

   SSE with Google Cloud Storage is a security feature designed to protect data at rest by automatically encrypting it before storing it in Google Cloud Storage. Google Cloud Storage offers multiple SSE options, including Google-managed encryption keys (GMEK), Customer-supplied encryption keys (CSEK), and Customer-managed encryption keys (CMEK).

Encryption options in Google Cloud Storage include:

- **Google-Managed Encryption Keys:** This pre-fixed mode ensures transparency to the client, requiring only GCP IAM (Identity and Access Management) permissions to access the bucket and its objects.
- **Customer-Supplied Encryption Keys:** In this option, customers generate encryption keys using their own methods. These keys are then sent to Google servers to encrypt data before standard Google Storage Encryption is applied. It is important to note that Google holds the key in memory only for the duration of the operation. If the client loses the key, the data are not possible to decrypt.
- **Customer-Managed Encryption Keys:** With CMEK, customers create encryption keys using Google Key Management Service (KMS). These keys are employed by Google servers to encrypt data before applying standard Google Storage Encryption. This option provides customers with enhanced control over key management while benefiting from the security of Google Cloud Storage.

5.6.1 Encrypting Data at Rest: Methods and Considerations

Data at rest refers to information stored persistently on storage devices. Encrypting data at rest are a crucial practice to prevent unauthorized access in the event of a breach. Various methods exist for encrypting data at rest:

- **Full Disk Encryption:** This method involves encrypting the entire storage device, ensuring that all data, including the operating system and application files, is protected. Full Disk Encryption (FDE) provides a comprehensive and transparent way to secure data at rest.
- **File-Level Encryption:** Unlike FDE, file-level encryption selectively encrypts individual files or directories. This approach offers more granular control over encryption but may require more management overhead.
- **Database Encryption:** For organizations relying on databases, encrypting data at the database level adds an additional layer of protection. This method secures sensitive information within the database, safeguarding against unauthorized access.

Considerations for encrypting data at rest include key management, performance impact, and compliance requirements. Robust key management is essential to ensure secure storage and retrieval of encryption keys, while organizations must assess the potential impact on system performance to strike a balance between security and functionality.

5.6.2 Secure Data Transfer with Encryption in Transit

Encryption in transit focuses on securing data while it is being transmitted between systems. This prevents eavesdropping and man-in-the-middle attacks, ensuring the confidentiality and integrity of the transmitted information. Common protocols for encryption in transit include:

- **Transport Layer Security (TLS):** TLS, the successor to SSL, is a widely adopted protocol for securing communication over a network. It encrypts data during transit, providing a secure channel between the client and server.
- **Secure File Transfer Protocols:** Protocols like Secure File Transfer Protocol (SFTP) and Secure Copy Protocol (SCP) ensure encrypted file transfers. These protocols are essential for safeguarding sensitive data during transmission.

Implementing encryption in transit requires configuring servers and applications to use secure protocols, obtaining and managing digital certificates, and staying informed about potential vulnerabilities in encryption protocols.

5.6.3 Implementing SSE in Cloud Storage

Cloud storage services offer SSE as a built-in feature to enhance the security of stored data. The implementation typically involves the following components:

- **Key Management:** CSPs manage encryption keys, either allowing users to bring their own keys (BYOK) or handling key management on behalf of the users. BYOK provides customers with more control over their encryption keys.
- **Encryption Algorithms:** Cloud providers use robust encryption algorithms to secure data at rest. Commonly used algorithms include AES with varying key lengths.
- **Access Controls:** Implementing SSE is complemented by robust access controls. This ensures that only authorized users and services can access and decrypt the stored data.

Organizations considering SSE in Cloud Storage must understand the encryption options provided by their chosen Cloud Provider, assess key management capabilities, and align their encryption strategy with regulatory and compliance requirements.

5.7 CONCLUSION

As we reach the conclusion of this chapter on Cloud Security, we have traversed a detailed and intricate landscape that is vital for safeguarding data in Cloud Environments. Our comprehensive journey began with an enlightening introduction to key Cloud Providers, including the GCP and AWS, offering a foundational understanding of the industry's major players. Progressing into the realm of "Access Management in the Cloud," we explored the implementation of RBAC and MFA strategies, underscoring the importance of robust access policies in maintaining Cloud Security. This was followed by an in-depth analysis in "Fine-Grained Access Control Policies," where we investigated precise permission assignments and the application of Attribute-Based Access Control (ABAC). Real-world case studies were examined to demonstrate the critical nature of exacting control measures.

A crucial aspect of Cloud Security, "Encryption Fundamentals in Cloud Environments," was then addressed. Here, we delved into the complexities of encryption algorithms, balancing the need for strong security with performance considerations. This section highlighted the indispensable role of data encryption in safeguarding Cloud-based information. Our exploration continued with "Key Management in Cloud Security," where we differentiated between centralized and decentralized key management approaches. The segment detailed automated key rotation strategies and emphasized the paramount importance of maintaining key confidentiality to ensure overall data security.

Lastly, "SSE Techniques" provided an overview of various methods for encrypting data at rest, securing data transfers with encryption in transit, and the practical aspects of implementing SSE in Cloud Storage systems. Throughout this chapter, we have combined theoretical insights with practical methodologies, enhanced by illustrative case studies, to forge a holistic understanding of Cloud Security. This intricate examination is not just an academic exercise; it is an essential guide for researchers, practitioners, and Cloud Computing enthusiasts. It empowers them with the necessary knowledge and tools to effectively navigate the complex and ever-evolving domain of securing data in Cloud Environments. In conclusion, as Cloud Computing continues to advance and integrate into the fabric of modern technology, the importance of Cloud Security cannot be overstated. The insights and methodologies discussed in this chapter are crucial for anyone involved in the field of Cloud Computing, offering guidance and knowledge that are imperative in today's digitally driven world. This chapter serves as a comprehensive resource, illuminating the path toward a more secure and resilient Cloud Computing future.

REFERENCES

1. Sharma, A., Singh, S. K., Chhabra, A., Kumar, S., Arya, V., & Moslehpour, M. (2023). "A novel deep federated learning-based model to enhance privacy in critical infrastructure systems," *International Journal of Software Science and Computational Intelligence*, 15(1), 1–23. doi: 10.4018/ijssci.334711.
2. Murthy, J. S., Shekar, A. C., Bhattacharya, D., Namratha, R., & Sripriya, D. (2021). A novel framework for multimodal twitter sentiment analysis using feature learning. In *Advances in Computing and Data Sciences: 5th International Conference, ICACDS 2021, Nashik, India, April 23–24, 2021, Revised Selected Papers, Part II 5* (pp. 252–261). Springer International Publishing.
3. Liu, J., Fan, Y., Sun, R., Liu, L., Wu, C., & Mumtaz, S. (2023). "Blockchain-aided privacy-preserving medical data sharing scheme for e-healthcare system," *IEEE Internet of Things Journal*, 10(24), 21377–21388. doi: 10.1109/jiot.2023.3287636.
4. Wang, N., Han, Q., Fu, J., & Liu, J. (2023). "Multi-user personalized Ciphertext retrieval scheme based on deep learning," *IEEE Internet of Things Journal*, 10(24), 22791–22805. doi: 10.1109/jiot.2023.3305359.

5. Murthy, J. S., & Siddesh, G. M. (2024). A smart video analytical framework for sarcasm detection using novel adaptive fusion network and SarcasNet-99 model. *The Visual Computer*, 1–13, Springer.
6. Murthy, J. S., Matt, S. G., Venkatesh, S. K. H., & Gubbi, K. R. (2022). A real-time quantum-conscious multimodal option mining framework using deep learning. *IAES International Journal of Artificial Intelligence*, **11**(3), 1019.
7. Yu, Z., Gao, H., Cong, X., Wu, N., & Song, H. (2023). "A survey on cyber-physical systems security," *IEEE Internet of Things Journal*, 10(24), 21670–21686. doi: 10.1109/jiot.2023.3289625.
8. Tabrizchi, H., & Kuchaki Rafsanjani, M. (2020). "A survey on security challenges in cloud computing: Issues threats and solutions," *Journal of Supercomputing*, **76**(12), 9493–9532.
9. Butt, U. A., Mehmood, M., Shah, S. B. H., Amin, R., Shaukat, M. W., Raza, S. M., et al. (2020). "A review of machine learning algorithms for cloud computing security," *Electronics*, **9**(9), 1379.
10. Murthy, J. S., Siddesh, G. M., & Srinivasa, K. G. (2019). A real-time twitter trend analysis and visualization framework. *International Journal on Semantic Web and Information Systems (IJSWIS)*, **15**(2), 1–21.
11. Ali, M., Jung, L. T., Laghari, A. A., Sodhro, A. A., Belhaouari, S. B., Gillani, Z., et al. (2023). "A Confidentiality-based data Classification-as-a-Service (C2aaS) for cloud security," *Alexandria Engineering Journal*, **64**, 749–760.
12. Omer, M. A., Yazdeen, A. A., Malallah, H. S., & Abdulrahman, L. M. (2022). "A *survey on cloud security: concepts, types, limitations, and chall*enges," *Journal of Applied Science and Technology Trends*, **3**(02), 47–57.
13. Murthy, J. S., & Chitlapalli, S. S. (2022). Conceptual Analysis and Applications of Bigdata in Smart Society. In *Society 5.0: Smart Future Towards Enhancing the Quality of Society* (pp. 57–67). Singapore: Springer Nature Singapore.
14. Chauhan, M., & Shiaeles, S. (2023). "An analysis of cloud security frameworks, problems and proposed solutions," *Network*, **3**, 422–450.
15. Murthy, J. S., Siddesh, G. M., & Srinivasa, K. G. (2018). A Distributed Framework for Real-Time Twitter Sentiment Analysis and Visualization. In *Recent Findings in Intelligent Computing Techniques: Proceedings of the 5th ICACNI 2017*, Volume 3 (pp. 55–61). Springer Singapore.
16. Surianarayanan, C., & Chelliah, P. R. (2023). "Integration of the internet of things and cloud: Security challenges and solutions-a review," *International Journal of Cloud Applications and Computing (IJCAC)*, **13**(1), 1–30.
17. Ahamad, D., Hameed, S. A., & Akhtar, M. (2022). "A multi-objective privacy preservation model for cloud security using hybrid Jaya-based shark smell optimization," *Journal of King Saud University-Computer and Information Sciences*, **34**(6), 2343–2358.
18. Murthy, J. S., Siddesh, G. M., Lai, W. C., Parameshachari, B. D., Patil, S. N., & Hemalatha, K. L. (2022). ObjectDetect: A Real-Time Object Detection Framework for Advanced Driver Assistant Systems Using YOLOv5. *Wireless Communications and Mobile Computing*, 2022(1), 9444360.
19. Bajaj, P., Arora, R., Khurana, M., & Mahajan, S. (2022). "Cloud security: the future of data storage," in *Cyber Security and Digital Forensics*: *Proceedings of ICCSDF 2021* (pp. 87–98). Springer Singapore.
20. Murthy, J. S., Chitlapalli, S. S., Anirudha, U. N., & Subramanya, V. (2022, April). A Real-Time Driver Assistance System Using Object Detection and Tracking. In *International Conference on Advances in Computing and Data Sciences* (pp. 150–159). Cham: Springer International Publishing.

21. Anas, M., Imam, R., & Anwer, F. (2022, January). "Elliptic curve cryptography in cloud security: a survey," in *2022 12th International Conference on Cloud Computing, Data Science & Engineering (Confluence)* (pp. 112–117). IEEE.
22. Murthy, J. S., Siddesh, G. M., & Srinivasa, K. G. (2019). TwitSenti: a real-time Twitter sentiment analysis and visualization framework. *Journal of Information & Knowledge Management*, **18**(02), 1950013.
23. Murthy, J. S. (2019). Edgecloud: A distributed management system for resource continuity in edge to cloud computing environment. In *The Rise of Fog Computing in the Digital Era* (pp. 108–128). IGI Global.
24. Varun, P., & Ashokkumar, K. (2022). "Intrusion detection system in cloud security using deep convolutional network," *Applied Mathematics & Information Sciences*, **16**, 581–588.
25. Mallisetty, S. B., Tripuramallu, G. A., Kamada, K., Devineni, P., Kavitha, S., & Krishna, A. V. P. (2023, January). "A review on cloud security and its challenges," in *2023 International Conference on Intelligent Data Communication Technologies and Internet of Things (IDCIoT)* (pp. 798–804). IEEE.
26. Murthy, J. S., & Siddesh, G. M. (2023, October). AI Based Criminal Detection and Recognition System for Public Safety and Security using novel CriminalNet-228. In *International Conference on Frontiers in Computing and Systems* (pp. 3–20). Singapore: Springer Nature Singapore.
27. Murthy, J. S., & Siddesh, G. M. (2023, October). A Real-Time Framework for Automatic Sarcasm Detection Using Proposed Tensor-DNN-50 Algorithm. In *International Conference on Frontiers in Computing and Systems* (pp. 109–124). Singapore: Springer Nature Singapore.
28. Murthy, J.S., Dhanashekar, K., Siddesh, G.M. (2024). A Real-Time Video Surveillance-Based Framework for Early Plant Disease Detection Using Jetson TX1 and Novel LeafNet-104 Algorithm. In: Kole, D.K., Roy Chowdhury, S., Basu, S., Plewczynski, D., Bhattacharjee, D. (eds) Proceedings of 4th International Conference on Frontiers in Computing and Systems. COMSYS 2023. Lecture Notes in Networks and Systems, vol 975. Springer, Singapore. https://doi.org/10.1007/978-981-97-2614-1_23

6 Harnessing Data Provenance and Security Attribution for Resilient Cloud Systems

L. Suresh and Sangay Chedup

6.1 OVERVIEW OF DATA PROVENANCE IN CLOUD COMPUTING

6.1.1 Definition and Significance of Data Provenance in Cloud Computing

Data provenance in cloud computing is a concept that revolves around systematically documenting and monitoring the entire lifecycle of data within a cloud-based system as shown in Figure 6.1. It involves keeping track of the origin of data, its movement or flow between different processes or services, and any transformations applied to it throughout its journey within the cloud infrastructure. In essence, data provenance serves as a comprehensive record-keeping system, capturing crucial details about how data is created, altered, and accessed within the cloud environment. This documentation extends from the initial data creation to its eventual storage, retrieval, and potential deletion [1].

In the exploration of securing data provenance within IoT networks, Siddiqui et al. [2] proposed a robust framework. Their work focuses on the outsourcing of attribute-based signatures and the strategic application of bloom filters. The study underscores the importance of fortifying provenance data in the intricate context of the Internet of Things. Through the integration of attribute-based signatures, the authors contribute to an access-controlled and resilient framework for managing provenance in IoT environments.

Jaigirdar, Rudolph, and Bain [3] contribute to the evolving landscape of IoT provenance models with their creation, Prov-IoT. The model stands out for its heightened security awareness, catering to the imperative need for enhanced security in IoT data tracking. The paper meticulously details the design and implementation of Prov-IoT, shedding light on its security features. The research by Jaigirdar et al. adds valuable insights into the evolving field of IoT provenance, addressing security considerations essential for maintaining the integrity of provenance data.

Gao et al. [4] present a significant contribution with their big data provenance model designed explicitly for data security supervision. Their research takes advantage of the PROV-DM model to offer a structured and comprehensive solution. By leveraging the PROV-DM model, the authors provide a strategic approach for the supervision

DOI: 10.1201/9781003455448-6

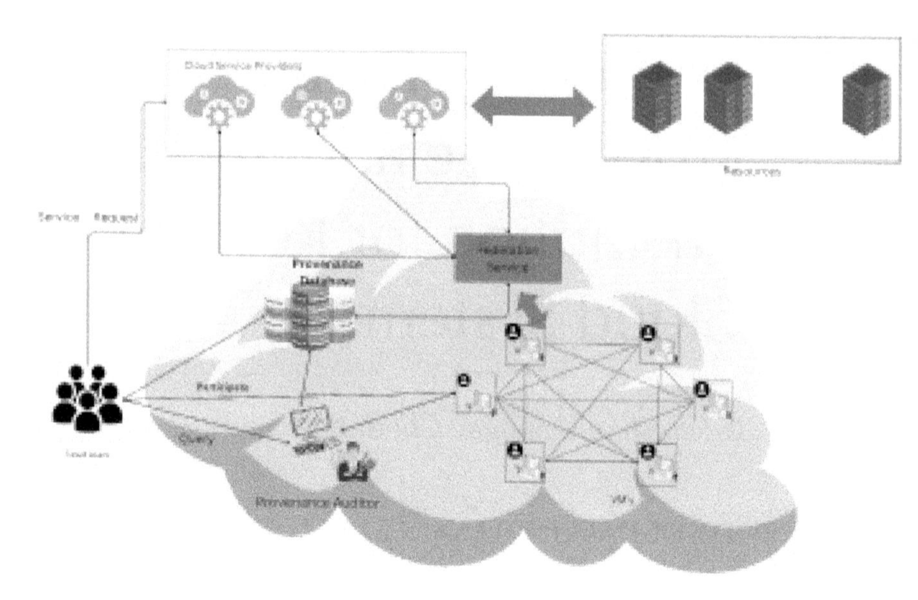

FIGURE 6.1 Architecture of data provenance in Cloud.

and security assurance of large-scale data. The work by Gao et al. stands as a pivotal resource in the realm of securing and overseeing provenance in big data scenarios.

Honar Pajooh et al. [5] introduced an innovative IoT big data provenance scheme that uniquely integrates blockchain within the Hadoop ecosystem. Their work explores the synergies between blockchain, IoT, and big data provenance. The authors' contribution lies in offering a novel approach to secure data tracking, ensuring a decentralized and tamper-proof provenance ledger. The strategic integration of blockchain within the Hadoop ecosystem adds a layer of security and transparency to the provenance of IoT big data.

Abiodun and collaborators [6] provide a comprehensive survey focusing on data provenance for cloud forensic investigations. Their work encapsulates a thorough examination of the security aspects, challenges, solutions, and future perspectives of data provenance in cloud environments. The authors, through this survey, offer valuable insights into the multifaceted role of data provenance in the intricate landscape of cloud forensic investigations. Their work serves as a crucial resource for understanding and addressing the challenges associated with ensuring data provenance in cloud environments.

6.1.1.1 The Tracking Elements in Data Provenance Encompass a Range of Factors

- **Data Creation:** The point at which data is generated or introduced into the cloud system.
- **Modifications:** Any changes or transformations made to the data, including preprocessing, aggregations, or any other alterations.
- **Access Records:** Details about who accessed the data, when, and for what purpose. This includes both human users and automated processes.

6.1.1.2 The Primary Objectives of Maintaining Data Provenance are

- **Transparency:** Data provenance ensures transparency by providing a clear and detailed account of how data evolves within the cloud. This transparency is crucial for understanding the data's history and context.
- **Traceability:** The ability to trace the lineage of data from its origin to its current state allows for a comprehensive understanding of data dependencies and relationships.
- **Accountability:** By recording the actions performed on the data and who performed them, data provenance establishes accountability. This is vital for identifying responsible parties in case of errors, security breaches, or compliance issues.

6.1.1.3 The Significance of Data Provenance in Cloud Computing is Multifaceted

- **Enhancing Data Governance:** Data provenance contributes to effective data governance by providing the necessary insights for managing, controlling, and optimizing data-related processes. This is critical for maintaining data quality and reliability.
- **Ensuring Compliance:** Many industries and regulatory frameworks mandate strict adherence to data handling and storage regulations. Data provenance aids in demonstrating compliance by offering a detailed account of how data is managed and secured.
- **Augmenting Security:** Security in cloud environments relies on understanding and controlling data access and modifications. Data provenance plays a pivotal role in security by enabling the tracking of every action performed on the data, facilitating the identification of potential security threats or unauthorized activities.

6.1.2 Use Cases: Financial Analytics and Provenance Tracking in Cloud Environments

Example: Utilizing TensorFlow on Google Cloud Platform (GCP) for Provenance Tracking in Financial Analytics Models

Financial analytics, particularly in the context of risk assessment and portfolio management, can benefit significantly from data provenance. Let us explore how TensorFlow on GCP can be employed for provenance tracking in the development and deployment of financial analytics models.

1. **Selecting TensorFlow for Financial Analytics:** Choose TensorFlow as the machine learning framework for financial analytics due to its flexibility and extensive capabilities in handling complex models often required in risk assessment and portfolio optimization.
2. **Setting Up GCP Environment:** Establish the necessary infrastructure on GCP, configuring virtual machines, storage solutions, and networking to support the financial analytics workload. Ensure compliance with industry standards and security protocols.

3. **Data Ingestion and Preprocessing:** Ingest financial datasets, including historical market data, economic indicators, and relevant financial reports, into the GCP environment. Apply TensorFlow for data preprocessing to clean, normalize, and transform the data into a suitable format for analysis.
4. **Building Risk Assessment Models:** Utilize TensorFlow to construct machine learning models for risk assessment. This involves designing models that can predict potential financial risks based on historical data, market trends, and other relevant factors. The provenance tracking in TensorFlow captures details about the model architecture, training data, and hyperparameters.
5. **Provenance Tracking During Model Training:** TensorFlow's provenance tracking mechanisms record essential information throughout the model training phase. This includes details about the financial datasets used, any feature engineering or transformations applied, and the specific configurations employed during the training process.
6. **Deployment for Portfolio Optimization:** Deploy the trained risk assessment models to assess and optimize investment portfolios. During deployment, the provenance tracking continues to document the version of the model in use, deployment configurations, and any adjustments made to the model for real-world application.
7. **Real-Time Monitoring and Updating:** Implement real-time monitoring to track the performance of the risk assessment models. If market conditions change or if the model's accuracy diminishes, update the model accordingly. Provenance tracking ensures that every update is documented, providing a historical record of model evolution.
8. **Comprehensive Provenance View for Auditing:** The use of TensorFlow on GCP for provenance tracking in financial analytics results in a comprehensive view of the entire lifecycle of risk assessment models. This includes insights into the origin of financial data, preprocessing steps, model training specifics, deployment configurations, and any subsequent updates. Such a detailed provenance trail is invaluable for auditing purposes, regulatory compliance, and ensuring transparency in financial decision-making processes.

6.1.3 Importance of Security Attribution in Cloud Environments

Security attribution plays a pivotal role in the landscape of data provenance, particularly within cloud environments characterized by shared resources and diverse interactions among users and services. This fundamental aspect involves the assignment of responsibility for security events, thereby establishing a clear understanding of who has accessed, modified, or attempted unauthorized actions on the data. The significance of security attribution lies in its ability to identify security breaches, enforce policies, and ensure regulatory compliance within the complex and dynamic realm of cloud computing [7,8].

6.1.3.1 Understanding the Landscape

- **Shared Resources in Cloud Environments:** Cloud environments inherently operate on shared resources, where multiple users and services coexist. This shared nature introduces complexity and challenges in tracking and controlling access to sensitive data.

- **Diverse Interactions:** Cloud services facilitate diverse interactions, ranging from data storage and processing to the deployment of applications. With various entities interacting within the cloud ecosystem, the potential for security incidents increases, necessitating a mechanism to attribute actions to specific actors.

6.1.3.2 The Role of Security Attribution

- **Clear Assignment of Responsibility:** Security attribution ensures that every action on data is attributed to a specific entity, whether it be a user or an automated process. This clear assignment of responsibility is crucial for accountability and forms the foundation for understanding the chain of events during a security incident.
- **Identification of Security Breaches:** By attributing security events to specific actors, security attribution aids in the rapid identification of security breaches. Whether it is unauthorized access, data modifications, or other malicious activities, knowing who is responsible enables swift response and containment of the security incident.
- **Policy Enforcement:** Effective security attribution supports the enforcement of security policies within a cloud environment. Policies can include access control rules, data encryption requirements, and other security measures. Attribution allows organizations to ensure that policies are followed and take corrective action when deviations occur.
- **Ensuring Regulatory Compliance:** Many industries and jurisdictions have stringent regulatory requirements regarding data security and privacy. Security attribution provides the necessary documentation to demonstrate compliance with these regulations. It serves as a tool for audits, proving that security measures are in place and that any security incidents are thoroughly investigated.

Example

Consider a scenario in a cloud-based financial application where a user attempts to access sensitive customer data without proper authorization. Security attribution would identify the user attempting this unauthorized access, providing a detailed record of the event. This information is invaluable for investigating the incident, taking appropriate action, and, if necessary, reporting the breach to regulatory authorities.

6.1.4 Role of Security Attribution in Protecting Machine Learning Systems

Example: Amazon Web Services (AWS) CloudTrail for Tracing Security Events in Machine Learning Pipelines

The protection of machine learning (ML) systems in cloud environments demands a robust approach to security, and security attribution emerges as a pivotal element in this context. AWS CloudTrail, a service provided by AWS, exemplifies the critical role of security attribution in safeguarding ML systems. This service is designed to capture and log API calls, offering organizations the capability to trace user activity and changes to resources. In the realm of machine learning pipelines, CloudTrail becomes a powerful tool for tracking security events, providing valuable insights into potential threats and unauthorized access to ML models and datasets.

6.1.4.1 Understanding the Role of Security Attribution

- **Capturing API Calls:** AWS CloudTrail serves as a watchful guardian by capturing and logging every API call made within the AWS ecosystem. API calls are fundamental to the interaction between users, services, and resources, making them a critical source of information for security analysis.
- **Tracing User Activity:** Security attribution involves tracing user activity to specific individuals or entities. CloudTrail, through its comprehensive logging, enables organizations to attribute API calls to specific users. This ensures accountability and transparency, crucial for understanding who is interacting with ML resources.
- **Logging Changes to Resources:** ML systems rely on various resources, including datasets, models, and computing instances. CloudTrail logs changes made to these resources, such as modifications to ML model configurations or alterations to training datasets. This logging capability is central to identifying and mitigating security risks.

6.1.4.2 Example of AWS CloudTrail in ML Pipelines

Consider a scenario where an unauthorized user attempts to access a critical ML model hosted on AWS. CloudTrail, through its logging mechanisms, captures this attempt and attributes it to the specific user account involved. The security team can then investigate the incident, determine the potential threat, and take appropriate action to prevent unauthorized access.

6.1.4.3 Key Contributions to Protecting ML Systems

- **Threat Detection:** CloudTrail's role in security attribution contributes significantly to threat detection in ML systems. Unusual or unauthorized activities, such as unauthorized model access or changes to training data, can be promptly identified through the detailed logs provided by CloudTrail.
- **Incident Response:** In the event of a security incident, CloudTrail facilitates an efficient incident response. Security teams can quickly access the logs, determine the scope and impact of the incident, and take corrective measures to mitigate potential risks.
- **Compliance Assurance:** Security attribution is vital for compliance with industry regulations and security best practices. CloudTrail's logging capabilities provide the documentation needed to demonstrate adherence to security policies and regulatory requirements governing ML systems.

6.1.5 Case Study: Azure Sentinel for Cross-Cloud Security Attribution in a Multicloud Architecture

Microsoft's Azure Sentinel, a cloud-native Security Information and Event Management (SIEM) solution, serves as a powerful case study illustrating the significance of security attribution in a multicloud architecture. The steps involved in this case study showcase how Azure Sentinel, by aggregating data from various cloud platforms, enables organizations to correlate security events across different environments, emphasizing the importance of a unified approach to security attribution.

1. **Understanding Azure Sentinel:** Azure Sentinel is a cloud-native SIEM solution designed by Microsoft to provide advanced security analytics and threat intelligence across an organization's entire infrastructure. It is tailored to operate seamlessly in cloud environments, making it suitable for multicloud architectures.
2. **Deployment in a Multicloud Environment:** Organizations deploy Azure Sentinel within their multicloud architecture, ensuring compatibility with various cloud platforms, such as AWS, GCP, and Azure itself. The deployment involves integrating Sentinel with each cloud provider to gather security-related data.
3. **Aggregating Data from Multiple Cloud Platforms:** Azure Sentinel acts as a central hub, collecting and aggregating security-related data from different cloud platforms. This includes logs, events, and other security telemetry, providing a comprehensive view of activities across the entire multicloud ecosystem.
4. **Correlating Security Events:** One of the key features of Azure Sentinel is its ability to correlate security events. By analyzing data from multiple cloud platforms simultaneously, Sentinel can identify patterns and relationships that may indicate security threats or incidents. This correlation is essential for a holistic understanding of the security landscape.
5. **Attributing Security Events Across Cloud Environments:** Security attribution in Azure Sentinel involves associating specific security events with the responsible entities across different cloud environments. This attribution is achieved by analyzing user identities, access logs, and other contextual information to determine who initiated or was affected by a particular security event.
6. **Unified Approach to Security Attribution:** Azure Sentinel promotes a unified approach to security attribution, emphasizing the importance of treating security events consistently across diverse cloud environments. This consistency ensures that security policies and investigative processes are applied uniformly, regardless of the underlying cloud infrastructure.
7. **Advanced Analytics and Threat Intelligence:** Leveraging advanced analytics and threat intelligence, Azure Sentinel goes beyond mere event correlation. It identifies anomalies, detects potential threats, and provides actionable insights to security teams, enabling them to proactively respond to emerging security challenges in a multicloud environment.
8. **Response and Remediation:** Azure Sentinel facilitates a coordinated response to security incidents. Once security events are attributed and analyzed, the platform allows organizations to implement response and remediation actions. This may include isolating affected resources, updating access controls, or initiating incident response protocols.
9. **Continuous Monitoring and Adaptation:** The case study emphasizes the importance of continuous monitoring and adaptation. Azure Sentinel's capabilities allow organizations to evolve their security strategies based on the evolving threat landscape, ensuring ongoing protection in the dynamic multicloud environment.

6.2 DATA PROVENANCE IN ML

6.2.1 Tracing Data Lineage in Distributed ML Workflows

Example: Apache Atlas for Data Governance in Hadoop Ecosystem on Azure

In distributed ML workflows, tracing data lineage is crucial for understanding how data moves and transforms throughout the process. An exemplary tool for this is Apache Atlas, often used for data governance in the Hadoop ecosystem, which can be extended to Azure.

Steps

- **Integration with Hadoop Ecosystem on Azure:** Deploy Apache Atlas in the Azure environment, integrating it seamlessly with the Hadoop ecosystem components. This integration ensures that data lineage is captured across the distributed processing framework.
- **Metadata Capture:** Apache Atlas captures metadata related to data entities, processes, and relationships within the Hadoop ecosystem. This metadata includes information about data sources, transformations, and storage locations.
- **Data Lineage Visualization:** Utilize Apache Atlas to visualize data lineage, providing a clear and comprehensive view of how data moves through various stages of the distributed ML workflow. This visualization aids in understanding dependencies and identifying potential bottlenecks.
- **Policy Enforcement:** Leverage Apache Atlas to enforce data governance policies by defining rules and constraints on data movement and transformations. This ensures that the distributed ML workflow adheres to organizational and regulatory standards.

6.2.2 Current Research Trends in Data Provenance

In the rapidly evolving landscape of data provenance, current research trends focus on addressing emerging challenges and leveraging innovative technologies. Some key trends include [9–15]:

- **Blockchain for Immutable Provenance Records:** Exploring the integration of blockchain technology to create immutable and tamper-proof provenance records, ensuring the integrity of the data lineage.
- **AI-Driven Provenance Analysis:** Investigating the application of artificial intelligence techniques for automated analysis of provenance data, facilitating insights, anomaly detection, and proactive decision-making.
- **Standardization and Interoperability:** Emphasizing efforts to standardize data provenance formats and establish interoperability between different provenance systems, enabling seamless collaboration in heterogeneous cloud environments.

6.2.3 Provenance-Aware ML Algorithms

Example: Google Cloud AI Platform's Integration with Kubeflow for Provenance-aware ML Models

Provenancc-aware ML algorithms ensure transparency and accountability in model development and deployment. An illustrative example is the integration of Google Cloud AI Platform with Kubeflow.

6.2.3.1 Integration Steps

- **Kubeflow Integration:** Integrate Google Cloud AI Platform with Kubeflow, a popular open-source ML platform designed for Kubernetes. This integration enables end-to-end ML workflow orchestration.
- **Provenance Tracking during Training:** During the training phase, the integrated solution captures provenance information, such as model configurations, hyperparameters, and the lineage of training data. This information is stored and can be queried for auditing and reproducibility.
- **Model Deployment with Provenance Metadata:** When deploying ML models using Google Cloud AI Platform, include provenance metadata in the deployment. This metadata includes details about the model version, training data sources, and the training process, providing a comprehensive view of the model's lineage.

6.2.4 Real-Time Provenance Tracking in Cloud-Native Environments

Real-time provenance tracking is essential for immediate insights into data activities within cloud-native environments. Key considerations for achieving real-time provenance tracking include:

- **Streaming Data Processing:** Implementing mechanisms for streaming data processing to capture and analyze data events in real time, ensuring that provenance information is up-to-date and responsive to dynamic changes.
- **Event-Driven Architecture:** Adopting an event-driven architecture that triggers provenance tracking activities in response to data events, ensuring timely recording of data lineage.
- **Integration with Cloud-Native Services:** Integrating real-time provenance tracking capabilities with cloud-native services and architectures, leveraging serverless computing, microservices, and event-driven infrastructure for agility and scalability.

6.3 SECURITY ATTRIBUTION IN CLOUD ENVIRONMENTS

6.3.1 Understanding Security Attribution

6.3.1.1 Definition

Security attribution in cloud environments is the process of systematically assigning responsibility for security events, allowing organizations to identify and trace the actions of users, services, or entities interacting with shared resources. It involves associating specific security incidents with the responsible parties, providing transparency and accountability in the dynamic and multi-user landscape of cloud computing [16,17].

6.3.1.2 Purpose

The primary purpose of security attribution is to enhance the security posture of cloud environments by facilitating the identification of security breaches, adherence to security policies, and ensuring regulatory compliance. Understanding who accessed, modified, or attempted unauthorized actions on data or resources is critical for effective incident response and mitigation.

6.3.2 Application of Security Attribution in Federated Learning

Example: AWS Security Hub for Tracking Security Incidents in Federated Learning Systems

In the context of federated learning, where ML models are trained across decentralized devices or servers, security attribution is essential for maintaining the integrity of the learning process. AWS Security Hub serves as an example of a tool that aids in tracking security incidents in federated learning systems.

6.3.2.1 Application Steps

- **Integration with Federated Learning Infrastructure:** Integrate AWS Security Hub with the federated learning infrastructure, ensuring that it can capture and analyze security-related data from the decentralized components.
- **Monitoring User Activities:** Utilize Security Hub to monitor and attribute user activities within the federated learning system. This includes tracking model updates, data exchanges, and any anomalies that may indicate security threats.
- **Incident Detection and Attribution:** AWS Security Hub employs advanced analytics to detect security incidents. When an incident is identified, the tool attributes the incident to specific users or entities involved, enabling swift and targeted response.
- **Centralized Incident Dashboard:** Security Hub provides a centralized incident dashboard, offering a unified view of security events across the federated learning environment. This allows security teams to correlate incidents and identify patterns indicative of potential threats.

6.3.3 Challenges and Solutions in Security Attribution Across Clouds

6.3.3.1 Challenges

- **Heterogeneity of Cloud Environments:** The diverse and heterogeneous nature of cloud environments, especially in multicloud scenarios, poses challenges in standardizing security attribution processes.
- **Cross-Cloud User Identity Management:** Managing user identities consistently across different cloud providers can be challenging, leading to difficulties in accurately attributing security events.

6.3.3.2 Solutions

- **Standardization Efforts:** Industry-wide efforts to standardize security event formats and user identity management protocols can help address the heterogeneity challenge.

- **Unified Identity and Access Management:** Implementing a unified identity and access management system that spans across multiple clouds facilitates more accurate security attribution by ensuring consistent user identification.

6.3.4 Federated Security Models for Cross-Cloud Attribution

Federated security models represent a strategic approach to address the complexities associated with securing data and resources across multiple cloud environments. The primary objective is to establish a cohesive and interoperable framework that harmonizes security practices, policies, and attribution mechanisms, ensuring a consistent and reliable security posture irrespective of the underlying cloud infrastructure [18–20].

- **Standardized Security Policies:** In federated security models, organizations define and implement standardized security policies that can be uniformly applied across diverse cloud environments. These policies encompass access controls, encryption standards, authentication protocols, and other security measures.
- **Common Event Formats:** To achieve interoperability and seamless collaboration, federated security models advocate for the adoption of common event formats. This involves standardizing the way security events are recorded and reported across different cloud platforms, allowing for consistent interpretation and analysis.
- **Attribution Mechanisms:** Federated security models emphasize the establishment of standardized attribution mechanisms. These mechanisms ensure that security events are accurately attributed to the responsible entities, enabling a uniform understanding of the chain of events leading to a security incident.

6.3.4.1 Benefits

1. **Consistency:**
   - **Definition:** Federated security models prioritize the establishment of consistent security practices.
   - **Implementation:** Regardless of the diverse cloud infrastructures in use, federated security models ensure that security policies are consistently applied. This consistency is crucial for avoiding discrepancies in security implementations that could arise from the heterogeneity of cloud providers.
   - **Impact:** Organizations benefit from a unified and reliable security approach, simplifying management and reducing the risk of security vulnerabilities caused by inconsistencies in policy enforcement.
2. **Interoperability:**
   - **Definition:** Federated security models promote interoperability by facilitating seamless collaboration between different cloud environments.
   - **Collaboration:** Organizations operating in a multicloud or hybrid cloud setup often face challenges related to disparate security infrastructures.

Federated security models address this by promoting the adoption of standardized practices that enable efficient collaboration and information sharing between clouds.

- **Efficiency:** Interoperability reduces friction in security operations, allowing security teams to work more efficiently. This is particularly important for incident response, where the ability to share and correlate security events across cloud platforms is crucial.

6.3.5 Emerging Technologies for Security Attribution

6.3.5.1 Trends

The landscape of security attribution in cloud environments is continually evolving, with emerging technologies playing a pivotal role in enhancing the efficiency, accuracy, and responsiveness of security processes [21,22]. Two notable trends in this domain are:

1. **AI-Driven Attribution:**
    - **Integration of Artificial Intelligence:** The integration of AI into security attribution processes signifies a paradigm shift toward automation and advanced analysis.
    - **Automated Analysis:** AI-driven attribution involves the automation of the analysis of security events. ML algorithms can process vast amounts of data, identify patterns, and discern meaningful insights without human intervention.
    - **Identification of Patterns:** AI-driven systems excel in identifying complex patterns and correlations within security data. This capability is particularly valuable for recognizing subtle indicators of security threats that might go unnoticed through traditional methods.
    - **Enhanced Efficiency and Accuracy:** By automating the attribution process, AI-driven systems significantly enhance efficiency and accuracy. Rapid analysis and identification of potential security incidents enable organizations to respond proactively, minimizing the impact of security breaches.
2. **Behavioral Analytics:**
    - **Understanding User Behavior:** Behavioral analytics focuses on understanding normal patterns of user behavior within a system. It establishes baselines by analyzing historical data, allowing it to identify deviations or anomalies from established norms.
    - **Anomaly Detection:** The primary goal of behavioral analytics is to detect anomalies that may indicate unauthorized or suspicious actions. This includes deviations from regular login times, atypical access patterns, or unexpected data transfers.
    - **Continuous Monitoring:** Behavioral analytics involves continuous monitoring of user activities, creating a dynamic understanding of evolving patterns. This real-time analysis ensures that anomalies are detected promptly, reducing the time window for potential security threats.

- **Risk Assessment:** By assessing user behavior, behavioral analytics contributes to risk assessment. It helps in assigning risk scores to users or entities based on their actions, allowing organizations to prioritize and respond to potential threats more effectively.

6.3.5.2 Significance of Emerging Technologies

- **Adaptive and Proactive Security:** AI-driven attribution and behavioral analytics contribute to the evolution of security from a reactive to a proactive stance. The ability to adapt to changing threat landscapes and proactively identify potential risks is crucial for staying ahead of sophisticated cyber adversaries.
- **Efficient Resource Utilization:** Automation through AI-driven processes reduces the burden on human resources, enabling security teams to focus on strategic tasks that require human intuition and decision-making. This efficient resource utilization is especially beneficial in the face of the increasing volume and complexity of security data.
- **Enhanced Threat Detection:** The combination of AI-driven attribution and behavioral analytics enhances threat detection capabilities. By identifying patterns that may not be apparent through traditional methods, these technologies contribute to a more comprehensive and nuanced understanding of potential security incidents.
- **Real-Time Response:** Real-time analysis provided by behavioral analytics ensures that security teams can respond promptly to emerging threats. Timely identification of anomalies allows for immediate action, reducing the dwell time of adversaries within a system.

6.3.6 Blockchain-based Security Attribution in Cloud Environments

6.3.6.1 Concept

The exploration of blockchain technology for enhancing security attribution in cloud environments marks a significant advancement in ensuring the integrity, transparency, and trustworthiness of security processes. The core concept involves leveraging blockchain to create an immutable and tamper-proof ledger of security events, revolutionizing the way attribution is handled in complex cloud infrastructures [23–25].

6.3.6.1.1 Immutable Ledger

- **Decentralized Integrity:** Blockchain's immutability stems from its decentralized architecture. Once a security event is recorded on the blockchain, it becomes a part of a chain of blocks, and altering any information within a block would require changing subsequent blocks across the entire network, which is computationally infeasible.
- **Trustworthy Audit Trail:** The immutability of blockchain ensures the creation of a trustworthy audit trail. Security events, once entered into the blockchain, remain unaltered, providing a reliable and indisputable record of all activities within the cloud environment.

6.3.6.2 Benefits

1. The decentralized and tamper-proof nature of blockchain ensures the integrity of security event data. Once recorded, the information remains unchanged, providing a high level of confidence in the accuracy and authenticity of the recorded events.
2. Blockchain-based security attribution creates indisputable records. This is particularly crucial for compliance, audits, and investigations, as the blockchain provides a verifiable and permanent record of all security-related activities.

6.3.6.2.1 Distributed Trust

- **Elimination of Central Authority:** Blockchain's distributed architecture eliminates the need for a central authority in managing and verifying security events. Instead of relying on a single entity, trust is distributed across the entire network of participants, enhancing the resilience of the attribution process.
- **Fostering Trust in Attribution:** The decentralized nature of blockchain fosters trust in the attribution process. Participants in the network can independently verify the authenticity of security events, reducing the reliance on a single point of control and minimizing the risk of manipulation or tampering.

6.3.6.3 Benefits

1. **Reduced Dependency on Central Authorities:** Blockchain reduces dependency on central authorities for managing security events. The distributed trust model ensures that the attribution process is not vulnerable to a single point of failure or compromise, enhancing the overall resilience of the security framework.
2. The distributed nature of trust in blockchain enhances transparency. Participants can independently verify the integrity of the security attribution process, fostering a more open and accountable security environment.

6.3.6.4 Challenges and Considerations

- **Scalability:** While blockchain offers strong immutability and distributed trust, scalability remains a challenge. Ensuring the efficient processing of a large number of security events within a cloud environment requires addressing scalability concerns.
- **Integration Complexity:** Integrating blockchain-based security attribution into existing cloud environments may introduce complexities. Organizations need to carefully plan and execute the integration process to minimize disruptions.

6.4 INTERPLAY BETWEEN DATA PROVENANCE AND SECURITY ATTRIBUTION

6.4.1 Synergies and Interdependencies

6.4.1.1 Synergies

The interplay between data provenance and security attribution represents a symbiotic relationship aimed at fortifying the overall security posture of cloud environments. The synergies lie in the shared goal of providing transparency, traceability, and accountability, crucial elements for maintaining the integrity of data and security operations.

6.4.1.2 Enhancing Security Posture Through Provenance-Aware Security Systems

6.4.1.2.1 Unified Data Governance and Security

Example: Azure Purview

Azure Purview is an exemplary tool that illustrates the integration of data provenance and security attribution. It serves as a unified platform for data governance, enabling organizations to not only track the lineage of data (provenance) but also enhance security through advanced attribution mechanisms.

6.4.1.3 Key Components

- **Data Discovery:** Provenance-aware security systems, like Azure Purview, facilitate data discovery by providing insights into the origin, transformations, and usage of data. This is essential for understanding the context in which security events occur.
- **Unified Policies:** The integration of provenance and security allows organizations to establish unified policies that govern both data governance and security practices. This ensures a holistic approach to managing and protecting data throughout its lifecycle.
- **Real-Time Monitoring:** Provenance-aware security systems enable real-time monitoring of data activities. This includes tracking changes, access patterns, and modifications, contributing to proactive security measures.

6.4.1.4 Benefits

- **Comprehensive Insights:** The combined approach provides comprehensive insights into both the data's journey (provenance) and the security events associated with it. This holistic view enhances the organization's ability to respond effectively to incidents.
- **Streamlined Compliance:** Unified data governance and security policies streamline compliance efforts by addressing both provenance and attribution requirements. This is particularly beneficial in industries with stringent regulatory frameworks.

6.4.2 Leveraging Provenance Data for Improved Security Attribution

6.4.2.1 ML Models for Predictive Security Attribution

6.4.2.1.1 Integration of Provenance Data

- **Proactive Security Measures:** Provenance data, detailing the history and transformations of data, can be leveraged to enhance security attribution. By integrating this information into security systems, organizations can develop a proactive understanding of the normal patterns of data usage and user behavior.
- **Predictive Analytics:** ML models applied to provenance data enable predictive analytics for security attribution. These models can learn normal behavior and detect anomalies, aiding in the identification of potential security threats before they escalate.

6.4.2.1.2 Benefits

- **Early Threat Detection:** Predictive security attribution allows for early detection of abnormal activities. ML models can identify deviations from established norms, signaling potential security incidents before they manifest into significant threats.
- **Adaptive Security Strategies:** The integration of provenance data into ML models supports the development of adaptive security strategies. As the models learn from evolving data patterns, security measures can be adjusted dynamically to respond to emerging threats.
- **Reduced False Positives:** Predictive security attribution contributes to reducing false positives by distinguishing between regular and anomalous behavior based on learned patterns. This improves the accuracy of security alerts and minimizes unnecessary interventions.

6.5 REAL-WORLD CASE STUDIES

6.5.1 Case Study 1: Provenance-based Security in a Multicloud Environment

Example: AWS CloudWatch and X-Ray Integration for Provenance-based Security in a Hybrid AWS-Azure Environment

6.5.1.1 Scenario

Multicloud Environment: The organization operates in a multicloud environment, utilizing both AWS and Azure services for its infrastructure.

6.5.1.2 Implementation

- **AWS CloudWatch and X-Ray Integration:** The organization integrates AWS CloudWatch and X-Ray services to establish a provenance-based security system. CloudWatch monitors and logs AWS resources, while X-Ray provides insights into the performance and traces of applications.
- **Cross-Cloud Compatibility:** The integration is designed to be cross-cloud compatible, allowing the organization to capture and correlate provenance data across both AWS and Azure services.

6.5.1.3 Benefits

- **Unified Security Posture:** The integration of AWS CloudWatch and X-Ray creates a unified security posture by providing visibility into the provenance of data and activities across the multicloud environment.
- **Holistic Incident Response:** Provenance-based security enhances incident response capabilities, allowing security teams to trace security events, identify the root causes, and respond promptly, irrespective of the cloud provider.

6.5.2 Case Study 2: Incident Response and Attribution in Cloud-based Systems

Example: Google Cloud Security Command Center for Incident Response in Google Cloud Environment

6.5.2.1 Scenario

Google Cloud Environment: The organization relies on Google Cloud services for its cloud infrastructure.

6.5.2.2 Implementation

Google Cloud Security Command Center: The organization implements the Google Cloud Security Command Center to centralize and streamline incident response activities.

Attribution and Forensics: The Security Command Center facilitates attribution by providing a centralized view of security events, enabling security teams to conduct forensic analysis and attribute incidents to specific entities.

6.5.2.3 Benefits

Centralized Incident Dashboard: The Security Command Center offers a centralized incident dashboard, allowing security teams to correlate events, attribute incidents, and respond efficiently.

Automated Incident Detection: Leveraging ML and real-time analysis, the Security Command Center automates incident detection, enhancing the speed and accuracy of attribution in cloud-based systems.

6.5.3 Case Study 3

Successful Implementation of Data Provenance in a Cloud-native Infrastructure

Example: Azure Data Factory for End-to-End Provenance Tracking in Azure Cloud-native Data Workflows

6.5.3.1 Scenario

Azure Cloud-native Infrastructure: The organization utilizes Azure services for its cloud-native data workflows.

6.5.3.2 Implementation

- **Azure Data Factory:** The organization implements Azure Data Factory to orchestrate end-to-end data workflows, encompassing data ingestion, processing, and storage.
- **Provenance Tracking:** Azure Data Factory is configured to capture detailed provenance information at each stage of the data workflow. This includes the source of data, transformations applied, and the destination.

6.5.3.3 Benefits

- **Comprehensive Data Lineage:** The implementation of Azure Data Factory enables the organization to establish comprehensive data lineage, enhancing transparency and traceability throughout the data lifecycle.
- **Auditing and Compliance:** Provenance tracking in Azure Data Factory supports auditing and compliance efforts by providing a detailed record of data movements and transformations, contributing to regulatory adherence.

6.6 FUTURE DIRECTIONS AND TRENDS

6.6.1 Evolving Landscape of Data Provenance and Security Attribution

6.6.1.1 Integration of AI and ML in Advanced Provenance Systems

Example: AWS SageMaker for Building AI-enhanced Provenance Models

Evolving Landscape:

Dynamic Nature of Cloud Security: The landscape of data provenance and security attribution is expected to evolve in response to the dynamic nature of cloud environments, emerging cyber threats, and the increasing complexity of data workflows.

Integration of AI and ML:

AI-enhanced Provenance Systems: Future directions involve the integration of AI and ML techniques into advanced provenance systems. AWS SageMaker stands as an example, allowing organizations to build AI-enhanced models for more sophisticated and context-aware provenance tracking [26].

Predictive Provenance: AI algorithms can predict and identify patterns in data provenance, enabling proactive security measures. Predictive analytics in provenance systems can anticipate potential security threats and deviations from normal data flow patterns [27,28].

6.6.2 Potential Research Avenues

6.6.2.1 Addressing Privacy Concerns in Provenance Data Collection in Cloud-based ML Systems

6.6.2.1.1 Privacy Concerns

- **Inherent Challenges in ML Systems:** As machine learning systems in the cloud become more prevalent, addressing privacy concerns in provenance data collection is a crucial research avenue. The inherent challenges of collecting and managing provenance data while preserving user privacy need innovative solutions.
- **Anonymization Techniques:** Research may focus on developing effective anonymization techniques that balance the need for detailed provenance information with the imperative to protect sensitive user data.

6.6.3 Anticipated Technological Advancements

6.6.3.1 Blockchain and Decentralized Technologies

- **Enhancing Trust and Security:** Anticipated technological advancements include further exploration of blockchain and decentralized technologies to enhance the trust and security of provenance data. The immutable nature of blockchain could be leveraged for creating secure and transparent provenance ledgers.
- **Interoperable Provenance Platforms:** Technological advancements may lead to the development of interoperable provenance platforms that can seamlessly operate across different cloud providers and environments, promoting consistency in security practices.

6.6.4 Next-Generation Provenance Tools and Platforms

6.6.4.1 Unified Provenance and Attribution Platforms

- **Holistic Security Solutions:** Future trends involve the emergence of next-generation provenance tools and platforms that provide unified solutions for both data provenance and security attribution. These platforms are expected to offer comprehensive insights into the entire lifecycle of data, enabling a more holistic approach to cloud security.
- **User-Friendly Interfaces:** User-friendly interfaces and intuitive dashboards are anticipated to become integral components of next-generation provenance platforms, making it easier for security professionals to navigate and interpret complex provenance and attribution data.

6.7 CHALLENGES AND CONSIDERATIONS

6.7.1 Ethical and Legal Implications

6.7.1.1 Privacy-Preserving Techniques in Data Provenance

6.7.1.1.1 Balancing Transparency and Privacy

- **Ethical Considerations:** The collection of detailed provenance data raises ethical considerations, especially in the context of user privacy. Striking a balance between transparency and privacy is a challenge that requires careful consideration.
- **Privacy-Preserving Techniques:** Future research and development should focus on privacy-preserving techniques in data provenance. Encryption, differential privacy, and other privacy-enhancing technologies can help safeguard sensitive information while still providing valuable provenance insights.

6.7.1.2 Scalability and Performance Challenges

6.7.1.3 Optimizing Provenance Tracking for Large-Scale ML Deployments

6.7.1.3.1 Increasing Volume and Complexity

- **Growing Challenges:** As the volume and complexity of data workflows, especially in ML deployments, continue to increase, scalability and performance challenges emerge. Optimizing provenance tracking for large-scale deployments becomes crucial.
- **Distributed Provenance Systems:** Future efforts should focus on developing distributed provenance systems that can efficiently handle the scale and distributed nature of modern cloud environments, ensuring minimal impact on system performance.

6.7.2 User Acceptance and Adoption Challenges

6.7.2.1 Training and Education Initiatives for Provenance-Aware Security Practices

6.7.2.1.1 Awareness and Education

- **Understanding the Importance:** User acceptance and adoption of provenance-aware security practices can be challenging due to a lack of awareness regarding the importance and benefits of provenance.
- **Training Initiatives:** Recommendations include investing in training and education initiatives to raise awareness among security professionals and end-users about the significance of provenance data in bolstering security postures.

6.8 RECOMMENDATIONS FOR PRACTITIONERS

6.8.1 Best Practices for Implementing Data Provenance and Security Attribution

6.8.1.1 Utilizing Cloud-Specific Tools for Provenance and Attribution

Example: Azure Monitor and AWS CloudTrail Integration for Comprehensive Cloud Security

6.8.1.1.1 Cloud-Specific Tools

- **Leveraging Native Capabilities:** Practitioners are recommended to utilize cloud-specific tools for provenance and attribution. Integrating native capabilities such as Azure Monitor and AWS CloudTrail provides comprehensive visibility and control over security events in cloud environments.
- **Holistic Cloud Security:** Integration of cloud-specific tools allows for a holistic approach to cloud security, combining provenance data with attribution insights to create a unified and robust security posture.

6.9 CONCLUSION

In conclusion, this book chapter has undertaken a comprehensive exploration of data provenance and security attribution in the context of cloud computing. We started by defining the significance of data provenance and delving into real-world applications, showcasing its crucial role in ML environments. Security attribution emerged as a linchpin in protecting ML systems, demonstrated through examples like AWS CloudTrail and Azure Sentinel. The interplay between data provenance and security attribution highlighted synergies that enhance overall security postures, illustrated by tools such as Azure Purview. The chapter progressed to dissecting data provenance in ML, presenting current research trends, and exemplifying real-time tracking in cloud-native environments. Security attribution, especially in federated learning, and emerging technologies like blockchain-based attribution, were explored, offering insights into the evolving landscape.

6.10 FUTURE SCOPE

The future of data provenance and security attribution holds exciting prospects. The integration of AI and ML into advanced provenance systems, showcased by AWS SageMaker, anticipates more intelligent and context-aware tracking. Addressing privacy concerns in cloud-based ML systems stands as a vital research avenue, ensuring that provenance data collection respects user privacy. Technological advancements, such as blockchain-based security attribution, promise a more transparent and secure future. Next-generation tools and platforms are expected to provide unified solutions, simplifying the complexity of provenance and attribution in cloud environments. Challenges like ethical considerations, scalability, and user acceptance call for continued research and innovative solutions. Practitioners are recommended to embrace cloud-specific tools, illustrated by examples like Azure Monitor and AWS CloudTrail, for a comprehensive approach to data provenance and security attribution. In essence, this chapter provides a foundation for navigating the intricate intersection of data provenance and security attribution, setting the stage for ongoing advancements and practical implementations in the dynamic realm of cloud computing.

REFERENCES

1. Pan, B., Stakhanova, N., & Ray, S. (2023). Data provenance in security and privacy. *ACM Computing Surveys*, *55*(14s), 1–35.
2. Siddiqui, M. S., Rahman, A., Nadeem, A., & Alzahrani, A. M. (2019). Secure data provenance in internet of things based networks by outsourcing attribute based signatures and using bloom filters. *International Journal of Advanced Computer Science and Applications*, *10*(5). http://dx.doi.org/10.14569/IJACSA.2019.0100529
3. Murthy, J. S., Matt, S. G., Venkatesh, S. K. H., & Gubbi, K. R. (2022). A real-time quantum-conscious multimodal option mining framework using deep learning. *IAES International Journal of Artificial Intelligence*, *11*(3), 1019.
4. Gao, Y., Chen, X., & Du, X. (2020). A big data provenance model for data security supervision based on PROV-DM model. *IEEE Access*, *8*, 38742–38752.

5. Honar Pajooh, H., Rashid, M. A., Alam, F., & Demidenko, S. (2021). IoT Big Data provenance scheme using blockchain on Hadoop ecosystem. *Journal of Big Data*, *8*, 1–26.
6. Murthy, J. S., Siddesh, G. M., & Srinivasa, K. G. (2018). A Distributed Framework for Real-Time Twitter Sentiment Analysis and Visualization. In *Recent Findings in Intelligent Computing Techniques: Proceedings of the 5th ICACNI 2017*, Volume 3 (pp. 55–61). Springer Singapore.
7. Tabrizchi, H., & Kuchaki Rafsanjani, M. (2020). A survey on security challenges in cloud computing: issues, threats, and solutions. *The Journal of Supercomputing*, *76*(12), 9493–9532.
8. Gupta, I., Singh, A. K., Lee, C. N., & Buyya, R. (2022). Secure data storage and sharing techniques for data protection in cloud environments: A systematic review, analysis, and future directions. *IEEE Access*, *10*, 71247–71277.
9. Noor, U., Anwar, Z., Amjad, T., & Choo, K. K. R. (2019). A machine learning-based FinTech cyber threat attribution framework using high-level indicators of compromise. *Future Generation Computer Systems*, *96*, 227–242.
10. Murthy, J. S., Siddesh, G. M., & Srinivasa, K. G. (2019). A real-time twitter trend analysis and visualization framework. *International Journal on Semantic Web and Information Systems (IJSWIS)*, 15(2), 1–21.
11. Barre, M., Gehani, A., & Yegneswaran, V. (2019). Mining data provenance to detect advanced persistent threats. In 11th *International Workshop on Theory and Practice of Provenance* (*TaPP 2019*).
12. Murthy, J. S., & Chitlapalli, S. S. (2022). Conceptual Analysis and Applications of Bigdata in Smart Society. In *Society 5.0: Smart Future Towards Enhancing the Quality of Society* (pp. 57–67). Singapore: Springer Nature Singapore.
13. Werder, K., Ramesh, B., & Zhang, R. (2022). Establishing data provenance for responsible artificial intelligence systems. *ACM Transactions on Management Information Systems* (*TMIS*), *13*(2), 1–23.
14. Murthy, J. S., Shekar, A. C., Bhattacharya, D., Namratha, R., & Sripriya, D. (2021). A novel framework for multimodal twitter sentiment analysis using feature learning. In *Advances in Computing and Data Sciences: 5th International Conference, ICACDS 2021, Nashik, India, April 23–24, 2021, Revised Selected Papers*, Part II 5 (pp. 252–261). Springer International Publishing.
15. Zipperle, M., Gottwalt, F., Chang, E., & Dillon, T. (2022). Provenance-based intrusion detection systems: A survey. *ACM Computing Surveys*, *55*(7), 1–36.
16. Murthy, J. S., Siddesh, G. M., Lai, W. C., Parameshachari, B. D., Patil, S. N., & Hemalatha, K. L. (2022). ObjectDetect: A Real-Time Object Detection Framework for Advanced Driver Assistant Systems Using YOLOv5. *Wireless Communications and Mobile Computing*, 2022(1), 9444360.
17. Jaigirdar, F. T., Tan, B., Rudolph, C., & Bain, C. (2023). Security-aware provenance for transparency in IoT data propagation. *IEEE Access*, *11*, 55677–55691. http://dx.doi.org/10.1109/ACCESS.2023.3280928
18. Yang, X., Zhao, Y., Chen, Q., Yu, Y., Du, X., & Guizani, M. (2022). Accountable and verifiable secure aggregation for federated learning in IoT networks. *IEEE Network*, *36*(5), 173–179.
19. Murthy, J. S., Chitlapalli, S. S., Anirudha, U. N., & Subramanya, V. (2022, April). A Real-Time Driver Assistance System Using Object Detection and Tracking. In *International Conference on Advances in Computing and Data Sciences* (pp. 150–159). Cham: Springer International Publishing.
20. Yuan, H., Ma, C., Zhao, Z., Xu, X., & Wang, Z. (2022, July). A privacy-preserving oriented service recommendation approach based on personal data cloud and federated learning. In 2022 *IEEE International Conference on Web Services* (*ICWS*) (pp. 322–330). IEEE.

21. Murthy, J. S., & Siddesh, G. M. (2024). A smart video analytical framework for sarcasm detection using novel adaptive fusion network and SarcasNet-99 model. *The Visual Computer*, 1–13, Springer.
22. Murthy, J. S., Siddesh, G. M., & Srinivasa, K. G. (2019). TwitSenti: a real-time Twitter sentiment analysis and visualization framework. *Journal of Information & Knowledge Management*, 18(02), 1950013.
23. A. Al-Sulami, Z., Ali, N., & Ramli, R. (2023). Blockchain adoption in Healthcare: Models, Challenges, and Future Work. *Journal of Basrah Researches (Sciences)*, *49*(2), 79–93. https://doi.org/10.56714/bjrs.49.2.8.
24. Habib, G., Sharma, S., Ibrahim, S., Ahmad, I., Qureshi, S., & Ishfaq, M. (2022). Blockchain technology: benefits, challenges, applications, and integration of blockchain technology with cloud computing. *Future Internet*, *14*(11), 341.
25. Murthy, J. S. (2019). Edgecloud: A distributed management system for resource continuity in edge to cloud computing environment. In *The Rise of Fog Computing in the Digital Era* (pp. 108–128). IGI Global.
26. Murthy, J. S., & Siddesh, G. M. (2023, October). AI Based Criminal Detection and Recognition System for Public Safety and Security using novel CriminalNet-228. In *International Conference on Frontiers in Computing and Systems* (pp. 3–20). Singapore: Springer Nature Singapore.
27. Murthy, J. S., & Siddesh, G. M. (2023, October). A Real-Time Framework for Automatic Sarcasm Detection Using Proposed Tensor-DNN-50 Algorithm. In *International Conference on Frontiers in Computing and Systems* (pp. 109–124). Singapore: Springer Nature Singapore.
28. Murthy, J.S., Dhanashekar, K., Siddesh, G.M. (2024). A Real-Time Video Surveillance-Based Framework for Early Plant Disease Detection Using Jetson TX1 and Novel LeafNet-104 Algorithm. In: Kole, D.K., Roy Chowdhury, S., Basu, S., Plewczynski, D., Bhattacharjee, D. (eds) Proceedings of 4th International Conference on Frontiers in Computing and Systems. COMSYS 2023. Lecture Notes in Networks and Systems, vol 975. Springer, Singapore. https://doi.org/10.1007/978-981-97-2614-1_23

7 Identity Threads in the Cloud Tapestry

A Comprehensive Study of Federated Identity Management and Its Role in Ensuring Cloud Security

K. Dhanashekar

7.1 FEDERATED CLOUD ENVIRONMENTS AND IDENTITY MANAGEMENT

In the dynamic landscape of modern cloud computing, the synergy between federated cloud environments and robust identity management is instrumental. Their roles are particularly critical in fostering secure and efficient collaboration, especially within the expansive domain of machine learning that spans multiple cloud environments. Federated cloud environments denote a distributed computing architecture where multiple cloud platforms seamlessly interoperate. This collaboration enables organizations to harness the strengths of different cloud service providers, fostering flexibility, scalability, and resource optimization. Federated setups are crucial in accommodating the diverse requirements of complex applications, such as machine learning models that demand significant computational resources [1,2].

7.1.1 Why Cloud Federation?

Cloud Federation is a strategy in cloud computing that involves integrating and coordinating services from multiple cloud providers. This approach offers several advantages as shown in Figure 7.1:

- **Access to a Range of Services:** By federating, organizations can utilize specific services from various providers, taking advantage of each provider's unique strengths.
- **Improved Reliability:** Distributing applications and data across multiple clouds enhances overall system reliability. If one provider experiences issues, others can maintain service continuity.

DOI: 10.1201/9781003455448-7

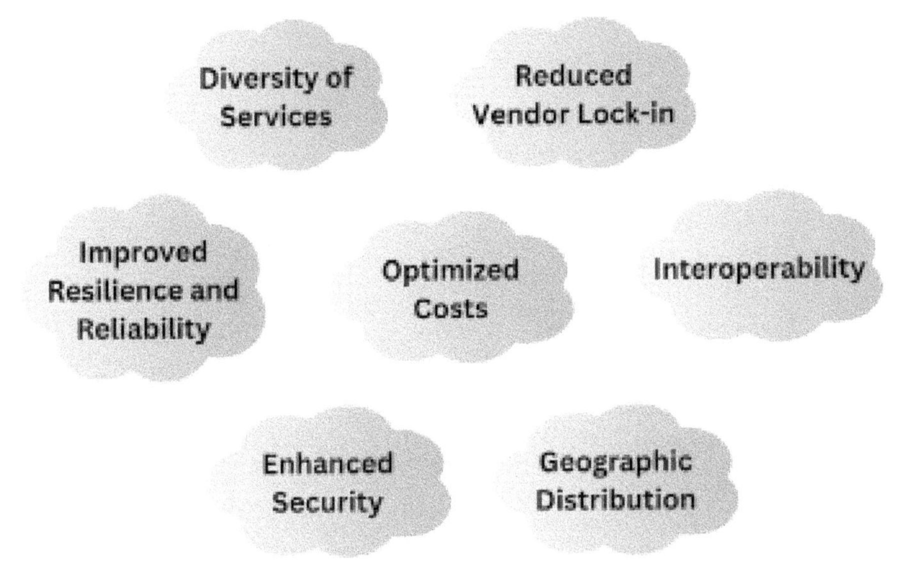

FIGURE 7.1 Advantages of cloud federation.

- **Cost Management:** Cloud Federation enables businesses to choose the most economical services for different tasks, optimizing overall cloud spending.
- **Compliance and Data Sovereignty:** It helps in complying with regional data laws by using local cloud providers where necessary, addressing data residency requirements.
- **Scalability and Enhanced Performance:** Organizations can scale resources more effectively by selecting providers that offer the best performance for particular tasks or applications.
- **Risk Reduction:** By using multiple providers, businesses can reduce risks such as vendor lock-in and service outages, ensuring a more robust cloud environment.
- **Greater Flexibility:** Federation allows for agility in choosing or switching providers, based on changing needs or service offerings.
- **Innovation Benefits:** Leveraging various technologies and innovations from different providers can keep businesses at the forefront of technological advancements.

In essence, Cloud Federation presents a flexible and efficient model for utilizing cloud services, balancing cost, performance, and risk while ensuring compliance and capitalizing on the latest technological developments.

7.1.2 Cloud Federation Architecture

Cloud Federation Architecture refers to a framework that enables the integration and cooperation of various cloud service providers to create a comprehensive and versatile cloud environment as shown in Figure 7.2. This architecture is designed

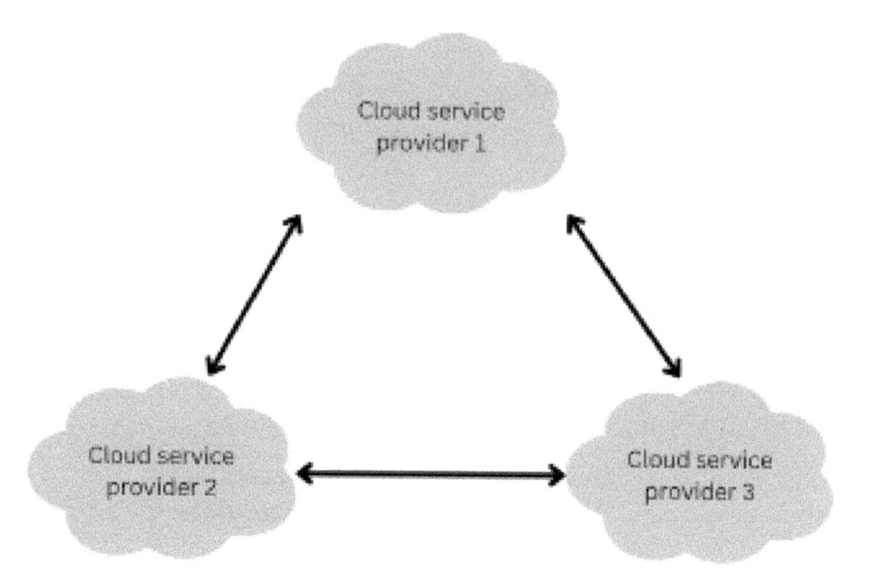

FIGURE 7.2 Overview of cloud federation.

to seamlessly manage and utilize services from different cloud providers, each potentially offering distinct capabilities such as Infrastructure-as-a-Service (IaaS), Platform-as-a-Service (PaaS), or Software-as-a-Service (SaaS). Here is an explanation of how Cloud Federation Architecture functions with respect to different cloud service providers as shown in Figure 7.3:

1. **Interoperability:** A core aspect of Cloud Federation Architecture is interoperability among different cloud services. This involves establishing standardized protocols and APIs that enable different cloud systems to communicate and share data and resources effectively. For example, a federated cloud might allow a user to deploy a service on Amazon Web Services (AWS) while leveraging AI tools from Google Cloud, all managed under a single umbrella.
2. **Unified Management Interface:** Cloud Federation Architecture typically includes a centralized management interface or gateway that allows users to manage resources across various clouds. This could involve a dashboard or a set of tools that provide visibility and control over resources located in different cloud environments, simplifying management tasks.
3. **Identity and Access Management:** In a federated cloud environment, managing access and identity across various providers is crucial. Federation architectures often incorporate unified Identity and Access Management (IAM) systems that allow users to authenticate once and gain access to resources across different clouds, adhering to the set permissions and policies.
4. **Automated Orchestration and Optimization:** This architecture usually incorporates automated tools for resource orchestration and optimization.

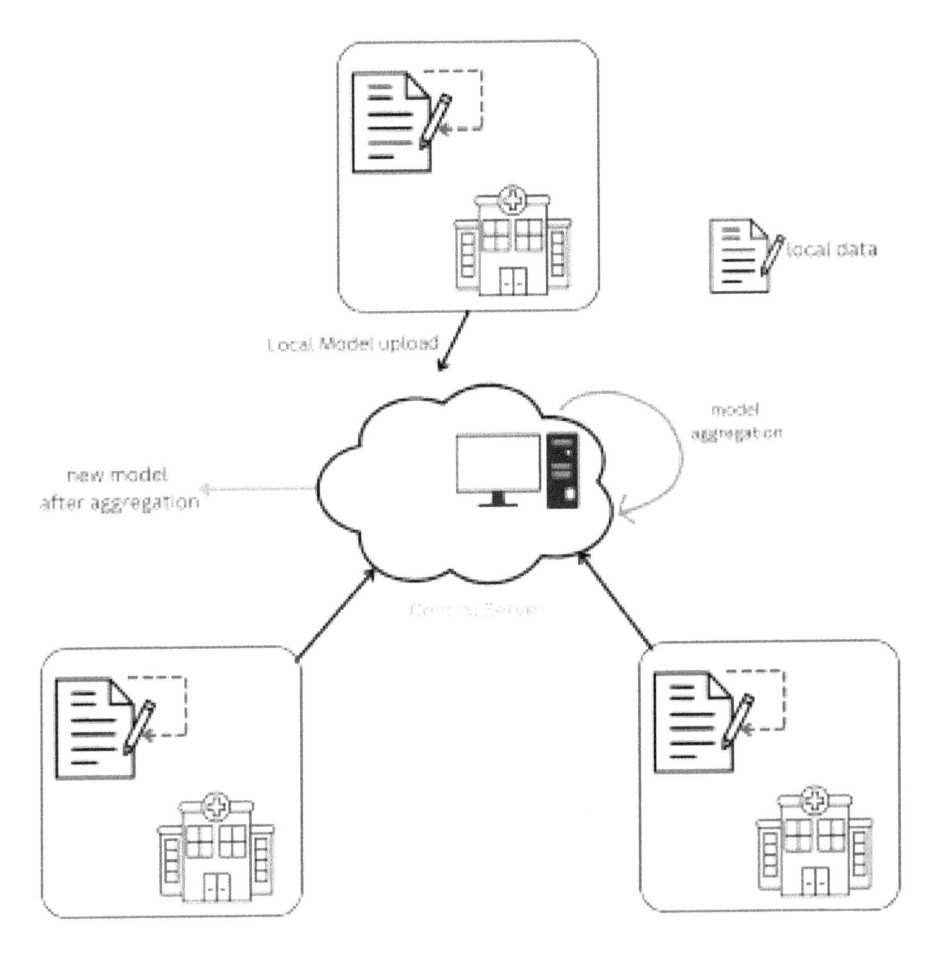

FIGURE 7.3 Cloud federation architecture.

These tools can dynamically allocate resources from different clouds based on performance requirements, cost-efficiency, or compliance needs, ensuring the best use of the federated cloud resources.

5. **Data Integration and Portability:** Data integration is essential in a federated cloud, where data might be stored across multiple cloud environments. The architecture ensures that data can move seamlessly between different clouds, maintaining consistency and integrity. This aspect is crucial for tasks like analytics, where data from various sources might be aggregated.
6. **Compliance and Security:** Federated Cloud Architecture must address security and compliance challenges across different jurisdictions and providers. This includes consistent application of security policies and adherence to various regulatory requirements, which can be complex in a multi-cloud environment.
7. **Network Connectivity and Performance Optimization:** Ensuring high-performance connectivity between different cloud services is a key aspect

of the architecture. This may involve using dedicated network links or optimizing network configurations to reduce latency and improve data transfer speeds between different cloud environments.

Identity management forms the linchpin of secure cloud collaboration. It encompasses processes and technologies that ensure the appropriate authentication, authorization, and management of user identities and their access to resources within cloud ecosystems. Effective identity management is indispensable for maintaining data confidentiality, integrity, and accessibility, especially in scenarios where collaboration spans across diverse cloud environments. Within the realm of machine learning, Federated Cloud Environments and Identity Management jointly play a pivotal role. Machine learning models often demand extensive computational power, and federated cloud setups provide the infrastructure needed for such resource-intensive tasks. Meanwhile, identity management ensures that access to these resources is controlled, authenticated, and authorized, mitigating security risks associated with collaborative endeavors [3,4].

The integration of federated cloud environments and robust identity management is paramount for ensuring secure collaboration in the cloud. As organizations increasingly rely on collaborative machine learning initiatives that transcend the boundaries of individual cloud providers, the seamless orchestration of federated environments and effective identity management becomes a linchpin for success [5,6].

7.1.3 Role of Identity Management in Machine Learning Collaborations Across Clouds

Identity management holds a crucial position in orchestrating machine learning collaborations that traverse diverse cloud environments. It involves the seamless integration of identity across multiple platforms to enable secure and efficient collaboration. In this context, federated identity becomes instrumental, allowing users to access resources and collaborate seamlessly across different cloud providers [7,8].

Example: AWS Cognito for Federated Identity in Cross-Cloud Machine Learning Models

Practically implementing federated identity in cross-cloud machine learning models involves utilizing AWS Cognito, a comprehensive identity management service provided by AWS. Below are detailed steps that illustrate the utilization of AWS Cognito for federated identity in the context of cross-cloud machine learning collaborations:

1. **AWS Cognito Setup:**
    - Access the AWS Management Console and navigate to the AWS Cognito service.
    - Create a new user pool within AWS Cognito, defining user attributes and policies based on the collaboration requirements.
    - Configure identity providers, including social identity providers or external identity providers, to establish federated identity capabilities.

2. **Cross-Cloud Integration:**
    - Identify the various cloud environments involved in the machine learning collaboration. This could include AWS, Azure, Google Cloud Platform (GCP), or other providers.
    - Establish trust relationships between AWS Cognito and the identity management services of other cloud providers to enable seamless cross-cloud authentication.
3. **User Registration and Authentication:**
    - Implement user registration mechanisms within the AWS Cognito user pool, allowing users from different clouds to register and authenticate.
    - Leverage federated identity protocols like OAuth or OpenID Connect to ensure secure and standardized authentication across diverse cloud platforms.
4. **Machine Learning Model Access Control:**
    - Define access control policies within AWS Cognito, specifying which users or groups have permissions to access machine learning resources.
    - Integrate AWS IAM for fine-grained access control, aligning with the principle of least privilege.
5. **Real-Time Collaboration:**
    - Implement real-time collaboration features within the machine learning models, ensuring that users authenticated through AWS Cognito can seamlessly collaborate across different cloud environments.
6. **Monitoring and Security Audits:**
    - Set up monitoring and logging mechanisms within AWS Cognito to track user activities and security events.
    - Regularly audit security logs to identify any anomalies or potential security threats, ensuring the ongoing integrity of the federated identity system.
7. **Scalability and Optimization:**
    - Ensure that the federated identity solution scales effectively as the machine learning collaboration grows.
    - Optimize the configuration and performance of AWS Cognito to handle increased user loads and evolving collaboration requirements.

7.1.4 Significance of Identity Management in Ensuring Cloud Security

In the intricate landscape of federated cloud environments, robust identity management emerges as a linchpin for safeguarding the security of cloud ecosystems. Beyond its conventional role in user authentication, identity management plays a pivotal role in orchestrating access, privileges, and interactions within the federated cloud environment. This section delves into the profound significance of identity management in ensuring cloud security, emphasizing its role as a comprehensive framework for maintaining a secure and well-regulated cloud ecosystem [9,10].

Example: Azure Active Directory for Secure Identity Management in Azure Cloud Environments

Illustrating the practical implementation of robust identity management, the example focuses on the utilization of Azure Active Directory within the Azure Cloud Environment. Azure Active Directory stands out as a comprehensive solution that extends beyond basic user authentication, providing a robust infrastructure for managing and securing identities in a federated cloud setup. Below are detailed steps outlining the significance of Azure Active Directory and its implementation for secure identity management in Azure:

1. **Azure Active Directory Configuration:** Navigate to the Azure Portal and access the Azure Active Directory service. Configure user attributes, policies, and security settings within Azure Active Directory to align with the security requirements of the federated cloud environment.
2. **Identity Federation across Clouds:** Establish trust relationships between Azure Active Directory and the identity management services of other cloud providers involved in the federated environment. Enable seamless and secure identity federation, ensuring that users from different clouds can access resources within the Azure Cloud Environment.
3. **Access Control Policies:** Define granular access control policies within Azure Active Directory, specifying which users or groups have permission to access various resources. Integrate Azure IAM for precise control over resource access, enhancing the overall security posture.
4. **Security Monitoring and Auditing:** Implement monitoring and auditing features within Azure Active Directory to track user activities and security events. Regularly review security logs to identify potential threats, ensuring proactive security measures and compliance with federated cloud security standards.
5. **Integration with Azure Security Center:** Ensure seamless integration with Azure Security Center to leverage advanced threat protection features. Monitor and respond to security alerts, enhancing the ability to detect and mitigate potential security risks in real time.

7.2 IDENTITY MANAGEMENT IN FEDERATED CLOUDS

In the complex domain of federated cloud environments, identity management assumes a paramount role in orchestrating secure and seamless interactions across diverse cloud platforms. This section navigates through the nuances of federated identity models, authentication and authorization mechanisms, and emerging research trends, exemplifying practical implementations for a comprehensive understanding [11–13].

7.2.1 Federated Identity Models

In the context of federated cloud environments, federated identity models, specifically Security Assertion Markup Language (SAML) and OAuth, play a crucial role in facilitating Cross-Cloud Identity Federation.

7.2.1.1 Security Assertion Markup Language

- **Definition:** SAML is an XML-based open standard for exchanging authentication and authorization data between parties, in particular, between an identity provider (IdP) and a service provider (SP).
- **Functionality:** SAML enables the secure sharing of authentication and authorization information, allowing users to access services and resources across different cloud platforms without the need for separate credentials for each.
- **Cross-Cloud Integration:** SAML is instrumental in the Cross-Cloud Identity Federation, as it establishes a standardized method for communication between IdPs and service providers, ensuring interoperability.

7.2.1.2 OAuth (Open Authorization)

- **Definition:** OAuth is an open standard for access delegation, commonly used for granting access to resources between applications without sharing credentials.
- **Functionality:** OAuth allows users to grant limited access to their resources (e.g., profile information) to another entity without exposing their credentials. It is widely used in scenarios where one application needs to access resources on behalf of a user.
- **Cross-Cloud Integration:** OAuth facilitates Cross-Cloud Identity Federation by providing a secure and standardized framework for authorization. It allows entities to obtain access tokens to access resources on different cloud platforms without compromising user credentials.

7.2.1.2.1 Significance of SAML and OAuth in Cross-Cloud Identity Federation:

- **Interoperability:** SAML and OAuth serve as common protocols, promoting interoperability between different cloud platforms. This interoperability is crucial for establishing a seamless and secure identity federation process.
- **Single Sign-On:** Both SAML and OAuth contribute to the implementation of Single Sign-On, enabling users to authenticate once and access services across multiple clouds, enhancing user experience and security.

Example: GCP Identity Platform for Seamless Integration with SAML and OAuth

- **Integration with GCP Identity Platform:** Access the GCP Console and navigate to the Identity Platform service. Configure SAML and OAuth settings to establish seamless integration with federated identity models. Define trust relationships with identity providers from other clouds, ensuring a cohesive federated identity ecosystem.
- **Cross-Cloud Authentication:** Enable SAML-based authentication to allow users from different cloud environments to access GCP resources securely. Implement OAuth for delegated authorization, granting controlled access to federated users based on defined policies.
- **Single Sign-On across Clouds:** Implement Single Sign-On (SSO) functionality, allowing users to log in once and access resources across multiple cloud platforms without the need for repeated authentications. Ensure a streamlined and user-friendly experience, enhancing collaboration in federated environments.

7.2.2 Authentication and Authorization Mechanisms

In the realm of federated cloud environments, the authentication and authorization mechanisms, with a specific focus on IAM services, are pivotal in controlling access effectively. Using AWS as an illustrative example, the implementation steps for configuring IAM services for access control in federated cloud environments are detailed below:

1. **IAM User Configuration:**
   - **Access the AWS Management Console:** Log in to the AWS Management Console using administrator credentials.
   - **Navigate to IAM Service:** From the console, navigate to the IAM service.
2. **Configuration Steps:**
   - **Define IAM Users:** Create IAM users within the IAM service to represent federated identities. This involves specifying user details and creating user accounts.
   - **Assign Permissions:** Based on the principle of least privilege, assign relevant permissions to IAM users. This step ensures that federated identities have the minimum required access to AWS resources.
3. **Federated Identity Integration:**
   - **Integrate with IdPs:** Enable integration between AWS IAM and identity providers by configuring federation standards such as SAML.
   - **Configure Trust Relationships:** Establish trust relationships between AWS IAM and the identity provider. This configuration enables federated users to assume roles securely and access AWS resources.
4. **Access Policies and Permissions:**
   - **Define Access Policies:** Within AWS IAM, define access policies that dictate what actions federated users are allowed to perform on AWS resources.
   - **Fine-Grained Permissions:** Implement fine-grained permissions to exercise precise control over resource access in the federated environment. This involves specifying detailed permissions for specific actions, resources, and conditions.

7.2.2.1 Using AWS as an Example, the Following Steps Outline the Implementation:

- **IAM User Configuration:** Access the AWS Management Console and navigate to the IAM service. Define IAM users representing federated identities and assign relevant permissions based on the principle of least privilege.
- **Federated Identity Integration:** Integrate AWS IAM with identity providers using federation standards like SAML. Configure trust relationships to enable federated users to assume roles and access AWS resources securely.
- **Access Policies and Permissions:** Define access policies within IAM, specifying which actions federated users can perform on AWS resources.
- Implement fine-grained permissions to ensure precise control over resource access in the federated environment.

7.2.3 Research Trends in Federated Identity Management

The field of federated identity management is evolving, incorporating innovative research trends to address emerging challenges and enhance security. Here are ten research trends in federated identity management, each accompanied by a scenario and example [14–20]:

1. **Machine Learning-Based Adaptive Authentication:**
   Scenario: In a dynamic cloud collaboration environment, the need for adaptive authentication arises to counter evolving security threats.
   Research explores the integration of machine learning algorithms that analyze user behavior patterns for real-time risk assessment. For instance, detecting anomalies in login behavior triggers additional authentication steps.
2. **Blockchain for Identity Verification:**
   Scenario: Ensuring trust and integrity in identity verification processes is crucial in federated environments.
   Example: Researchers investigate the use of blockchain technology to create decentralized and tamper-resistant identity verification systems. This enhances the reliability of identity assertions across federated clouds.
3. **Biometric Authentication in Federated Systems:**
   Scenario: Traditional authentication methods may fall short of providing robust security. Biometric authentication adds an extra layer of identity verification.
   Example: Research focuses on integrating biometric data, such as fingerprints or facial recognition, into federated identity management systems for secure and user-friendly access.
4. **Zero-Trust Security Models:**
   Scenario: With the increasing sophistication of cyber threats, adopting a zero-trust security model becomes imperative.
   Example: Researchers explore the implementation of zero-trust architectures in federated identity management, requiring continuous verification of user identity and device health regardless of their location.
5. **Context-Aware Access Control:**
   Scenario: Users accessing federated resources may have different levels of trust based on their context.
   Example: Research investigates context-aware access control mechanisms, considering factors like location, device type, and network conditions to dynamically adjust access permissions.
6. **Privacy-Preserving Identity Management:**
   Scenario: Protecting user privacy is a critical concern in federated systems.
   Example: Researchers explore cryptographic techniques, such as homomorphic encryption, to enable identity verification without revealing sensitive user information.

7. **Multi-Cloud Identity Federation:**
   Scenario: Organizations increasingly leverage multiple cloud providers for diverse services.
   Example: Research addresses the challenges of identity federation across multiple cloud platforms, ensuring seamless and secure collaboration between users in a multi-cloud environment.
8. **Quantum-Safe Identity Protocols:**
   Scenario: The advent of quantum computing poses a threat to traditional cryptographic methods.
   Example: Research explores quantum-safe identity protocols that remain secure even in the era of quantum computing, safeguarding federated identities from potential threats.
9. **Self-Sovereign Identity:**
   Scenario: Users desire more control over their identity information.
   Example: Research focuses on self-sovereign identity models, empowering users to manage and share their identity attributes without relying on central authorities.
10. **Decentralized Identity Ecosystems:**
    Scenario: Centralized identity systems may present single points of failure.
    Example: Research explores decentralized identity ecosystems using technologies like decentralized identifiers (DIDs) and verifiable credentials, promoting a more resilient and user-centric federated identity landscape.

7.3 REAL-WORLD CASE STUDIES

In this section, we delve into real-world case studies that exemplify the successful implementation of federated identity management in diverse cloud scenarios. These cases illustrate the practical applications of identity federation solutions and their impact on security, collaboration, and compliance [21,22].

7.3.1 Case Study 1: Seamless Identity Federation Across Multiple Cloud Providers

Example: Azure AD B2B for Secure Collaboration and Identity Federation with External Partners

- **Overview:** In this case study, we explore how Azure Active Directory Business-to-Business (Azure AD B2B) facilitates seamless identity federation across various cloud providers, ensuring secure collaboration with external partners. The scenario involves organizations working jointly on projects that span multiple cloud environments.
- **Implementation:** Azure AD B2B enables organizations to extend their identities to external users, granting them secure access to resources. This is achieved through features like guest user invitations, allowing partners to

use their existing credentials. The federation is seamless, providing a unified identity experience across different clouds.
- **Impact:** The implementation of Azure AD B2B enhances collaboration efficiency and security by simplifying the onboarding of external partners. It ensures a consistent and secure identity management approach, fostering a collaborative ecosystem that transcends individual cloud boundaries.

7.3.2 Case Study 2: Challenges and Solutions in Identity Management for Hybrid Clouds

Example: AWS SSO for Simplified Identity Management in Hybrid AWS-Azure Environments

- **Overview:** This case study delves into the complexities of identity management in hybrid cloud environments, where organizations operate across both AWS and Azure. The challenges include maintaining consistent user identities and access controls.
- **Implementation:** AWS SSO offers a solution by providing centralized access to multiple AWS accounts and applications. It streamlines user access across hybrid environments, enforcing uniform identity policies. Integration with Azure AD ensures synchronization of user attributes, simplifying identity management challenges.
- **Impact:** The implementation of AWS SSO streamlines identity management in hybrid cloud setups. It reduces the administrative burden, enhances user experience with SSO capabilities, and ensures that identity policies are uniformly enforced across AWS and Azure environments.

7.3.3 Case Study 3: Achieving Compliance through Federated Identity Systems

Example: Google Cloud Identity Aware Proxy for Ensuring Compliance in Cross-Cloud Environments

- **Overview:** This case study explores how federated identity systems contribute to achieving compliance requirements in scenarios where data and applications span multiple cloud environments.
- **Implementation:** Google Cloud Identity Aware Proxy (IAP) is employed to enforce access controls and security policies across cross-cloud environments. By integrating IAM with IAP, organizations ensure that only authorized users, devices, and applications can access sensitive data, meeting compliance standards.
- **Impact:** The implementation of Google Cloud IAP enhances security and compliance by providing fine-grained access controls. It ensures that data integrity and privacy regulations are adhered to in cross-cloud environments, contributing to a secure and compliant federated identity ecosystem.

7.4 SECURITY IMPLICATIONS AND CONSIDERATIONS

In this section, we delve into the security implications of federated identity management, addressing associated risks and providing strategies for risk mitigation. The focus is on safeguarding machine learning models and employing key security measures offered by cloud platforms [23,24].

7.4.1 Risks Associated with Federated Identity Management

7.4.1.1 Addressing Security Challenges in Machine Learning Models with Federated Identity

Federated identity management introduces unique security challenges, particularly in the context of machine learning models that span multiple cloud environments. This subsection identifies and addresses risks associated with securing machine learning models in federated identity ecosystems.

Example: Azure Key Vault for Secure Storage of Machine Learning Model Keys

Azure Key Vault is exemplified as a solution for secure storage of machine learning model keys. Storing sensitive information like model encryption keys in Azure Key Vault enhances security by providing centralized and highly secure key management. This ensures that only authorized applications and services can access and use the machine learning models.

Utilizing Azure Key Vault mitigates the risk of unauthorized access to machine learning model keys. It enhances the confidentiality and integrity of machine learning models, preventing potential security breaches and unauthorized use of sensitive information.

7.4.2 Strategies for Mitigating Security Risks

7.4.2.1 Role of Azure Security Center and AWS IAM in Risk Mitigation

To mitigate security risks associated with federated identity management, this subsection explores the strategic role of Azure Security Center and AWS IAM. These cloud services contribute to overall security by implementing access controls, monitoring, and threat detection.

Azure Security Center provides advanced threat protection across hybrid cloud workloads. It employs machine learning to detect and respond to threats, ensuring a proactive security approach. AWS IAM, on the other hand, enables granular control over access to AWS resources, defining roles, permissions, and policies.

The strategic implementation of Azure Security Center and AWS IAM enhances the security posture of federated identity environments. It provides real-time threat detection, automated responses, and fine-grained access controls, reducing the risk of unauthorized access and potential security incidents.

7.5 INTEROPERABILITY AND STANDARDS

In this section, we delve into the significance of interoperability in federated cloud environments, emphasizing the importance of adhering to established standards for identity management. The focus is on OpenID Connect and OAuth 2.0, with practical examples using AWS Cognito to illustrate compliance with these standards.

7.5.1 Importance of Interoperable Identity Management Systems

7.5.1.1 Compliance with OpenID Connect Standards in Federated Cloud Environments

In the ever-evolving landscape of cloud computing, achieving interoperability is paramount for facilitating seamless collaboration across diverse cloud platforms. This section underscores the critical importance of adopting interoperable identity management systems and specifically delves into the significance of complying with OpenID Connect (OIDC) standards.

7.5.1.1.1 Implementation Steps

1. **Understanding OpenID Connect (OIDC):** OpenID Connect is an authentication layer built on top of the OAuth 2.0 framework, extending it to include an identity layer for user authentication.

   Key aspects of OIDC that enhance user authentication in federated cloud environments include:

   - **User Authentication:** OIDC enables clients to verify the identity of end-users using authentication performed by an authorization server. Authentication is based on the exchange of identity tokens between the client, IdP, and authorization server.
   - **Standardized Identity Tokens:** OIDC defines a set of standardized identity tokens, such as ID tokens, which contain user profile information and authentication claims. These tokens are used to convey information about the authenticated user.
   - **Single Sign-On:** OIDC supports SSO, allowing users to authenticate once and access multiple services without needing to re-enter credentials. This is particularly beneficial in federated cloud environments where users interact with diverse services.
   - **Scope and Consent:** OIDC introduces scopes that define the access levels granted to clients. Users provide consent for sharing specific information, ensuring privacy and control over their data.
   - **JSON Web Tokens (JWT):** OIDC relies on JWTs for token representation, providing a compact and self-contained way to transmit information between parties. JWTs enhance security and efficiency in identity management.

   Understanding these aspects of the OIDC standard empowers organizations to implement secure and standardized user authentication mechanisms within federated cloud environments. It establishes a foundation for consistent and interoperable identity management, facilitating seamless collaboration across diverse cloud platforms.

2. **Integration with AWS Cognito**

   Integration with AWS Cognito is a pivotal step in establishing a robust identity management system within federated cloud environments. AWS Cognito, a comprehensive identity management service offered by AWS, facilitates the implementation of OpenID Connect (OIDC) standards, ensuring secure and standardized user authentication. The following steps outline the process of integrating AWS Cognito as an OpenID Connect Provider:

- **Access the AWS Management Console:** Log in to the AWS Management Console using appropriate credentials. Navigate to the AWS Cognito service to initiate the integration process.
- **Create an OIDC IdP within AWS Cognito:** Within the AWS Cognito console, create an OIDC IdP. Configure the IdP settings to align with OIDC standards, ensuring compatibility with the framework.
- **Configure AWS Cognito for OIDC Standards:** Define the necessary parameters within AWS Cognito to adhere to OIDC standards. Specify details such as client ID, client secret, authorization endpoint, token endpoint, and other relevant settings.
- **Integrate AWS Cognito as an OpenID Connect Provider:** Establish the integration between AWS Cognito and the OIDC framework. Verify that the integration ensures secure authentication practices and supports the exchange of standardized identity tokens.

This integration process with AWS Cognito as an OpenID Connect Provider is crucial for organizations aiming to enhance the interoperability and security of their federated identity management systems. By configuring AWS Cognito to comply with OIDC standards, users can benefit from consistent and reliable authentication practices across diverse cloud platforms. This integration not only streamlines user access but also contributes to the overall success of federated cloud environments by providing a secure and standardized identity management solution.

7.5.2 Current Standards and Protocols in Federated Identity Management

7.5.2.1 Leveraging OAuth 2.0 for Secure Authorization in Cross-Cloud Systems

In the dynamic landscape of federated identity management, this subsection delves into the pivotal role of OAuth 2.0, emphasizing its significance in ensuring secure authorization across diverse cloud systems. OAuth 2.0 stands as a cornerstone for standardized and secure access control mechanisms within federated environments.

7.5.2.2 Implementation Steps

7.5.2.2.1 Understanding OAuth 2.0

OAuth 2.0 is a sophisticated and widely adopted protocol designed to streamline secure authorization workflows in a variety of applications and systems. To gain a comprehensive understanding, delve into the intricate framework of OAuth 2.0. Explore its key components, including authorization servers, resource servers, and the diverse grant types that form the foundation of its operation.

- **Authorization Servers:** These servers play a central role in the OAuth 2.0 flow by verifying the identity of users and providing access tokens upon successful authentication. Understanding their function is crucial for grasping the overall authentication process.
- **Resource Servers:** Responsible for hosting and providing access to protected resources, resource servers interact with authorization servers to ensure that access is granted only to authenticated and authorized users.
- **Grant Types:** OAuth 2.0 supports various grant types, each tailored for specific use cases. Familiarize yourself with grant types such as authorization code, implicit, client credentials, and refresh token to comprehend the versatility of the OAuth 2.0 protocol.

7.5.2.3 Implementation in Cross-Cloud Systems

Practical implementation of OAuth 2.0 across diverse cloud platforms is essential for establishing secure authorization mechanisms in federated environments. Follow these steps to ensure a consistent and standardized implementation:

- **Apply OAuth 2.0 Protocols:** Implement OAuth 2.0 protocols in the architecture of federated cloud environments. This involves integrating OAuth 2.0 within the IAM systems of each participating cloud platform.
- **Ensure Consistent Implementation:** Guarantee uniformity by implementing OAuth 2.0 consistently across different cloud platforms. This ensures that the authorization process remains standardized, irrespective of the cloud SP.
- **Configure Authorization Servers and Resource Servers:** Set up and configure authorization servers and resource servers to seamlessly interact. This interaction is crucial for the secure exchange of access tokens, facilitating standardized authorization practices.

Leveraging OAuth 2.0 signifies a substantial enhancement in the security and standardization of authorization mechanisms within federated identity management. By adopting OAuth 2.0, organizations ensure that access controls are uniformly implemented across diverse cloud systems, fostering a secure, interoperable, and collaborative environment.

7.6 FUTURE DEVELOPMENTS AND TRENDS

In anticipating the future landscape of identity management within federated cloud environments, several developments and trends are expected to shape the way organizations approach security and access control. This section explores the evolving aspects and future trajectories [25].

7.6.1 Evolving Landscape of Identity Management in Federated Clouds

7.6.1.1 Integration of Machine Learning in Dynamic Identity Policies

As federated cloud environments become more complex and dynamic, the integration of machine learning (ML) emerges as a pivotal trend in shaping dynamic identity policies. ML algorithms can adapt and learn from user behavior, contextual data, and system interactions to dynamically refine identity policies in real time.

Example: Azure ML for Adaptive Identity Management Policies

7.6.1.1.1 Implementation Steps

- **Data Collection and Analysis:** Utilize Azure ML to collect and analyze vast datasets related to user behavior, access patterns, and system activities.
- **Model Training:** Train ML models using historical data to recognize patterns, anomalies, and contextual information relevant to identity management.
- **Dynamic Policy Generation:** Implement dynamic policy generation mechanisms that leverage ML insights. These policies continuously adapt based on evolving user needs, potential threats, and contextual changes within the federated environment.
- **Real-Time Policy Enforcement:** Integrate the trained models into the identity management infrastructure to enforce policies in real time. This ensures that access controls remain adaptive and responsive to changing circumstances.

7.6.1.1.2 Significance

The integration of ML in dynamic identity policies enhances the ability of organizations to respond to evolving security challenges. By leveraging Azure ML, organizations can create adaptive identity policies that proactively address potential risks and ensure a more secure and responsive federated cloud environment.

7.7 FUTURE OUTLOOK

As technology continues to advance, the integration of ML in identity management is poised to become a standard practice. This proactive approach not only enhances security but also streamlines user experiences by tailoring access controls based on individual user behaviors and contextual factors within federated cloud environments. Organizations adopting these adaptive policies are better equipped to navigate the complexities of identity management in an ever-evolving cloud landscape.

7.8 CONCLUSION

In conclusion, this comprehensive exploration of federated identity management within the ever-evolving realm of cloud computing illuminates the pivotal role of identity in ensuring security and collaboration. The study seamlessly traverses through the intricacies of identity management, emphasizing its relevance in ML collaborations, federated identity models, authentication mechanisms, and ongoing research trends. Real-world case studies provide tangible examples, offering insights into seamless identity federation, addressing challenges in hybrid cloud scenarios, and strategically implementing federated identity systems for compliance. Security considerations take center stage, with the study addressing associated risks and presenting effective mitigation strategies. The significance of interoperability is underscored, emphasizing adherence to standards like OpenID Connect and the use of OAuth 2.0 for secure authorization in cross-cloud systems. Looking ahead, the study anticipates a dynamic future for federated identity management, envisioning an evolving landscape with the integration of ML into dynamic identity policies, exemplified by tools such as Azure ML. In summary, this study serves as a guiding compass for organizations navigating the complexities of securing identity within the expansive cloud landscape. By weaving together theoretical insights, practical examples, and future trends, it contributes valuable knowledge to the ongoing discourse on fortifying cloud environments through robust identity management practices. As organizations continue to adapt to the changing cloud landscape, the understanding gained from this study empowers them to navigate the intricate intersections of security, collaboration, and identity within federated cloud environments.

REFERENCES

1. Stergiou, C. L., Psannis, K. E., & Gupta, B. B. (2021). InFeMo: Flexible big data management through a federated cloud system. *ACM Transactions on Internet Technology (TOIT)*, **22**(2), 1–22.
2. Rosa, M. J., Ralha, C. G., Holanda, M., & Araujo, A. P. (2021). Computational resource and cost prediction service for scientific workflows in federated clouds. *Future Generation Computer Systems*, **125**, 844–858.
3. Murthy, J. S., Chitlapalli, S. S., Anirudha, U. N., & Subramanya, V. (2022, April). A Real-Time Driver Assistance System Using Object Detection and Tracking. In *International Conference on Advances in Computing and Data Sciences* (pp. 150–159). Cham: Springer International Publishing.
4. Liu, T., Di, B., An, P., & Song, L. (2021). Privacy-preserving incentive mechanism design for federated cloud-edge learning. *IEEE Transactions on Network Science and Engineering*, **8**(3), 2588–2600.
5. Keshavarzi, A., Haghighat, A. T., & Bohlouli, M. (2021). Clustering of large scale QoS time series data in federated clouds using improved variable Chromosome Length Genetic Algorithm (CQGA). *Expert Systems with Applications*, 164, 113840.
6. Murthy, J. S., Siddesh, G. M., & Srinivasa, K. G. (2018). A Distributed Framework for Real-Time Twitter Sentiment Analysis and Visualization. In *Recent Findings in Intelligent Computing Techniques: Proceedings of the 5th ICACNI 2017*, Volume 3 (pp. 55–61). Springer Singapore.
7. Singh, A. K., & Saxena, D. (2022). A cryptography and machine learning based authentication for secure data-sharing in federated cloud services environment. *Journal of Applied Security Research*, **17**(3), 385–412.
8. Murthy, J. S., Shekar, A. C., Bhattacharya, D., Namratha, R., & Sripriya, D. (2021). A novel framework for multimodal twitter sentiment analysis using feature learning. In *Advances in Computing and Data Sciences: 5th International Conference, ICACDS 2021, Nashik, India, April 23–24, 2021, Revised Selected Papers, Part II 5* (pp. 252–261). Springer International Publishing.
9. Chikhaoui, A., Lemarchand, L., Boukhalfa, K., & Boukhobza, J. (2021). Multi-objective optimization of data placement in a storage-as-a-service federated cloud. *ACM Transactions on Storage (TOS)*, **17**(3), 1–32.

10. Kar, B., Yahya, W., Lin, Y. D., & Ali, A. (2023). Offloading using traditional optimization and machine learning in federated cloud–edge–fog systems: A survey. *IEEE Communications Surveys & Tutorials*, **25**(2), 1199–1226.
11. Murthy, J. S., Siddesh, G. M., Lai, W. C., Parameshachari, B. D., Patil, S. N., & Hemalatha, K. L. (2022). ObjectDetect: A Real-Time Object Detection Framework for Advanced Driver Assistant Systems Using YOLOv5. *Wireless Communications and Mobile Computing*, 2022(1), 9444360.
12. Fogli, M., Kudla, T., Musters, B., Pingen, G., Van den Broek, C., Bastiaansen, H., ... & Webb, S. (2021, May). Performance evaluation of kubernetes distributions (k8s, k3s, kubeedge) in an adaptive and federated cloud infrastructure for disadvantaged tactical networks. In *2021 International Conference on Military Communication and Information Systems (ICMCIS)* (pp. 1–7). IEEE.
13. Murthy, J. S., Matt, S. G., Venkatesh, S. K. H., & Gubbi, K. R. (2022). A real-time quantum-conscious multimodal option mining framework using deep learning. *IAES International Journal of Artificial Intelligence*, 11(3), 1019.
14. Ebadifard, F., & Babamir, S. M. (2021). Federated geo-distributed clouds: Optimizing resource allocation based on request type using autonomous and multi-objective resource sharing model. *Big Data Research*, 24, 100188.
15. Murthy, J. S., Siddesh, G. M., & Srinivasa, K. G. (2019). A real-time twitter trend analysis and visualization framework. *International Journal on Semantic Web and Information Systems (IJSWIS)*, 15(2), 1–21.
16. Verma, A., Bhattacharya, P., Bodkhe, U., Saraswat, D., Tanwar, S., & Dev, K. (2023). FedRec: Trusted rank-based recommender scheme for service provisioning in federated cloud environment. *Digital Communications and Networks*, **9**(1), 33–46.
17. Karthikeyan, R., Sundaravadivazhagan, B., Cyriac, R., Balachandran, P. K., & Shitharth, S. (2023). Preserving resource handiness and exigency-based migration algorithm (PRH-EM) for energy efficient federated cloud management systems. *Mobile Information Systems*, 2023, 1–11.
18. Murthy, J. S., & Siddesh, G. M. (2024). A smart video analytical framework for sarcasm detection using novel adaptive fusion network and SarcasNet-99 model. *The Visual Computer*, 1–13, Springer.
19. Zhao, Y., Zhang, J., & Cao, Y. (2023). Manipulating vulnerability: Poisoning attacks and countermeasures in federated cloud-edge-client learning for image classification. *Knowledge-Based Systems*, 259, 110072.
20. Ramezani, F., Abrishami, S., & Feizi, M. (2023). A market-based framework for resource management in cloud federation. *Journal of Grid Computing*, **21**(1), 3.
21. Murthy, J. S. (2019). Edgecloud: A distributed management system for resource continuity in edge to cloud computing environment. In *The Rise of Fog Computing in the Digital Era* (pp. 108–128). IGI Global.
22. Subashchandrabose, U., John, R., Anbazhagu, U. V., Venkatesan, V. K., & Thyluru Ramakrishna, M. (2023). Ensemble federated learning approach for diagnostics of multi-order lung cancer. *Diagnostics*, **13**(19), 3053.
23. Murthy, J. S., & Chitlapalli, S. S. (2022). Conceptual Analysis and Applications of Bigdata in Smart Society. In *Society 5.0: Smart Future Towards Enhancing the Quality of Society* (pp. 57–67). Singapore: Springer Nature Singapore.
24. Kar, B., Lin, Y. D., & Lai, Y. C. (2023). Cost optimization of omnidirectional offloading in two-tier cloud-edge federated systems. *Journal of Network and Computer Applications*, 215, 103630.
25. Murthy, J. S., Siddesh, G. M., & Srinivasa, K. G. (2019). TwitSenti: a real-time Twitter sentiment analysis and visualization framework. *Journal of Information & Knowledge Management*, 18(02), 1950013.

8 Anticipating the Evolution of Data Accountability through Technological Advancements and Regulatory Landscape Changes

Yash Gawankar and Srinivas Naik

8.1 INTRODUCTION TO DATA ACCOUNTABILITY IN CLOUD

8.1.1 Definition and Scope: A Multifaceted Responsibility

Data accountability in the cloud transcends a simple definition. It intricately weaves responsibilities and duties for managing, handling, and safeguarding the diverse data types entrusted to cloud services. This shared endeavor necessitates collaboration between Cloud Service Providers (CSPs) and their customers to ensure data integrity, confidentiality, and accessibility.

A Spectrum of Data, Demanding Different Protections: Cloud data is not a singular entity. It spans a vast spectrum, encompassing sensitive personal identifiable information (PII), confidential financial data, valuable intellectual property, vital operational data, and even seemingly insignificant digital traces [1]. Each data type demands distinct considerations and protective measures. For example, stringent encryption and access controls are paramount for PII, while robust backup and disaster recovery solutions might be crucial for operational data.

Shared Responsibility: A Collaborative Imperative: Data protection in the cloud is not a solo act. Both CSPs and users share the responsibility. CSPs bear the onus of maintaining and securing the underlying cloud infrastructure, employing robust security measures like intrusion detection and vulnerability management [2]. Conversely, users remain accountable for the data they store, access, or process within these environments. This includes implementing data governance policies, user access controls, and proper data encryption practices.

Moving Beyond a Binary: While the CSP-user dichotomy forms the core of shared responsibility, the accountability landscape extends further. Recent research

DOI: 10.1201/9781003455448-8

recognizes the roles of data brokers, third-party applications, and government regulators in this intricate web [3]. Each entity plays a role in ensuring responsible data handling and mitigating potential risks.

Beyond Technical Safeguards: Expanding Accountability: The focus on data accountability is evolving beyond mere technical security controls. Growing concerns around ethical implications, potential biases, and discriminatory outcomes associated with data processing in the cloud demand a broader perspective [4]. Addressing these concerns requires transparency, explainability in AI/machine learning (ML) models, and mechanisms to mitigate algorithmic bias.

Data Accountability: A Continuously Evolving Landscape: As cloud technologies and data landscapes evolve, so too must our understanding of accountability. By leveraging advancements such as verifiable computing, provenance tracking, and blockchain-based solutions, we can enhance transparency and auditability. Embracing the dynamic nature of data, with solutions like real-time data flow monitoring and adaptive risk assessment, further strengthens the accountability framework.

Data accountability in the cloud is a complex and ever-evolving endeavor. Through collaborative efforts, shared responsibility, and a comprehensive understanding of the multifaceted ecosystem, we can navigate this landscape and ensure the responsible and ethical stewardship of data entrusted to the cloud.

8.1.2 Navigating the Research Landscape: A Charting of Uncharted Waters

Data accountability in the cloud resembles a captivating, yet uncharted territory. Its dynamic nature unfolds like an epic saga, constantly evolving and encompassing intriguing areas of research. Let's delve into some of these key domains:

1. **Legal Frontiers: Navigating the Regulatory Labyrinth:** The legal landscape plays a pivotal role in shaping data accountability. Researchers diligently analyze the implications of evolving regulations like General Data Protection Regulation (GDPR) and California Consumer Privacy Act (CCPA) on cloud environments. They provide vital guidance to CSPs and users, illuminating compliance strategies and best practices [4]. Recent efforts focus on emerging regulations like Schrems II and the CLOUD Act, exploring their impact on cross-border data transfers and government access to cloud data.
2. **Technical Fortifications: Bolstering Cloud Defenses:** The research frontier does not solely reside in legal realms. Technical advancements play a crucial role in fortifying data security within clouds. Researchers tirelessly explore sophisticated encryption methods, robust access control protocols, and cutting-edge intrusion detection systems. Continuous efforts focus on homomorphic encryption for secure in cloud data processing and homomorphic ML for privacy-preserving analysis.

3. **Empowering the Cloud Citizens: Granting Users the Reins:** User empowerment takes center stage in the data accountability narrative. Researchers strive to equip users with the tools and knowledge to take control of their cloud-stored data. Transparency initiatives shed light on previously opaque cloud practices, demystifying data handling processes and ensuring informed consent [1]. Recent research explores empowering users to audit their own data usage within cloud services and demand accountability from CSPs.
4. **Governance and Compliance: Laying the Ground Rules:** Robust governance frameworks are vital for navigating the complexities of data accountability in the cloud. Researchers meticulously develop models that delineate roles, responsibilities, and accountability mechanisms for various stakeholders within cloud environments [2]. Recent efforts focus on integrating ethical considerations into governance frameworks and adapting existing models to cater to the dynamic nature of cloud technologies and data landscapes.
5. **Unveiling the Shadows: Auditing and Reporting in the Cloud:** Even the most fortified systems may encounter vulnerabilities. Researchers delve into effective auditing mechanisms and incident reporting protocols within cloud services. These efforts ensure clear visibility into data handling practices, enabling swift responses to security breaches and obscured data practices [3]. Recent research explores leveraging blockchain technology for tamper-proof audit trails and developing user-friendly dashboards for real-time data governance insights.

By illuminating these research frontiers, we gain a deeper understanding of the multifaceted nature of data accountability in the cloud. This ongoing exploration paves the way for a more secure, transparent, and ethical future for cloud computing, where data is treated with the respect it deserves.

8.2 REGULATORY COMPLIANCE IN CLOUD ENVIRONMENTS: TAMING THE DIGITAL WILD WEST

8.2.1 GDPR, CCPA, and the Regulatory Mosaic: A Kaleidoscope of Data Protection Regimes

The cloud, with its immense storage and computational power, has revolutionized data utilization, creating a dynamic digital landscape brimming with opportunities and challenges. While offering unparalleled accessibility and agility, the cloud simultaneously generates vast amounts of data, intertwining intricate privacy concerns and ethical dilemmas. To ensure responsible stewardship of this digital wealth, a new wave of legal regulations has emerged, aiming to confine the "data wild west" within the boundaries of accountability and compliance.

GDPR and CCPA: These regulatory acronyms represent formidable benchmarks in data protection.

- **GDPR**: Standing as a comprehensive framework within the European Union, GDPR grants individuals extensive control over their data and imposes strict demands on transparency, user rights, security measures, and breach notifications by data controllers and processors, including CSPs [7].
- **CCPA** in California: While less expansive than GDPR, the CCPA empowers Californians with significant rights to access, rectify, delete, and restrict the sale of their personal information. It places clear expectations for businesses operating within California regarding communication, transparency, and robust security practices.

8.2.2 Comparative Analysis: Decoding the Regulatory Rosetta Stone

Compliance with this diverse set of regulations necessitates a detailed understanding of their nuanced requirements. A comparative analysis serves as the "Rosetta Stone," deciphering the intricacies of these regulations and their interplay.

- **Transparency and User Rights:** Both GDPR and CCPA emphasize user transparency and access rights. However, GDPR goes further by granting individuals rights like data portability and restriction of processing, while CCPA focuses on opting out of data sales and sharing [8].
- **Data Security:** Both demand robust security measures, but GDPR adds complexity with its emphasis on risk-based assessments and encryption, compared to CCPA's focus on reasonable security practices.
- **Data Breach Notification:** Prompt reporting of breaches is common, but GDPR enforces stricter timeframes and broader notification requirements compared to CCPA [8].

8.2.3 Cloud Providers in the Crosshairs: Compliance as a Competitive Differentiator

CSPs face the regulatory storm directly, being responsible not only for ensuring their platforms comply with regulations but also for aiding customers in meeting their data protection obligations.

- **Developing Robust Compliance Frameworks:** CSPs must establish internal policies aligned with relevant regulations for data management, security, and breach response [7].
- **Regular Audits and Assessments:** Conducting frequent assessments helps identify and rectify compliance vulnerabilities [5,7].
- **Transparency and Reporting:** Clear communication about data privacy practices and prompt reporting of breaches to regulators and affected individuals is imperative [5,8].
- **Collaboration with Customers:** CSPs play a vital role in educating and equipping customers to fulfill their own data protection obligations [5,6].

8.3 ACCOUNTABILITY MODELS IN CLOUD COMPUTING: NAVIGATING THE SHARED RESPONSIBILITY MAZE

The shared responsibility model has long formed the cornerstone of accountability in cloud computing. However, the dynamic nature of technology and increasingly complex regulatory landscapes necessitate revisiting this model and exploring advanced frameworks for data accountability within the cloud ecosystem. This section delves into the evolving landscape of cloud accountability, examining the shared responsibility model, emerging frameworks, and the integration of accountability into service level agreements (SLAs).

8.3.1 Shared Responsibility Model Revisited

The shared responsibility model defines distinct zones of control and responsibility between cloud providers and customers. Providers manage the infrastructure layer, ensuring its security and availability. Customers are responsible for the data layer, including its security, privacy, and compliance with relevant regulations. This model, while seemingly clear, suffers from several limitations:

- Ambiguity in Responsibility Boundaries: Demarcating precise boundaries between cloud and customer control can be challenging, leading to disputes and finger-pointing in case of data breaches or regulatory non-compliance [9].
- Shifting Security Threats: The evolving landscape of cyber threats and vulnerabilities calls for a more nuanced approach to responsibility. Static definitions of control zones may not adequately address novel threats requiring collaborative efforts [10].
- Limited Customer Visibility: Lack of transparent access to cloud security practices and audit logs can hinder customers' ability to effectively fulfill their security obligations and exercise proper due diligence [11].

These limitations highlight the need for a more dynamic and collaborative approach to accountability in cloud computing.

8.3.2 Popular Shared Responsibility Models: AWS and Azure

Amazon AWS: The AWS model states in Figure 8.1 that AWS is responsible for the security of the underlying infrastructure, while customers are responsible for the security of their data and applications. This division of responsibility can vary depending on the AWS service being used, but it is important for customers to understand the model in order to make informed decisions about how to secure their data and applications in the cloud.

Microsoft Azure: In the context of Azure as shown in Figure 8.2, the shared responsibility model defines the division of security responsibilities between Microsoft and the customer. When you move your workload to the cloud, some security responsibilities are transferred to Microsoft, while others remain your

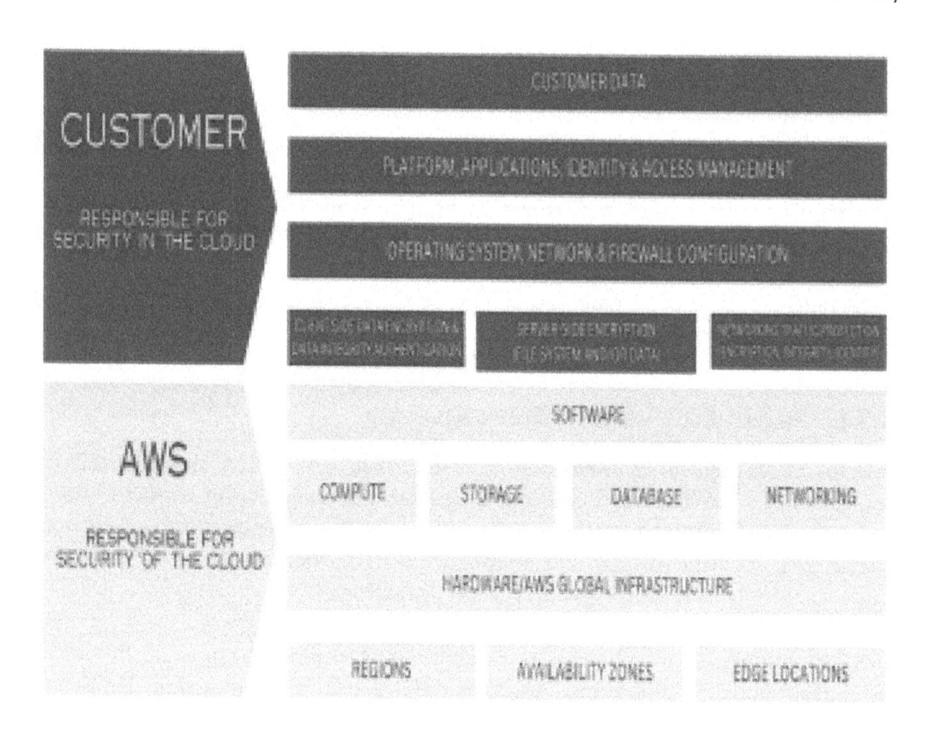

FIGURE 8.1 AWS: shared responsibility model for cloud security.

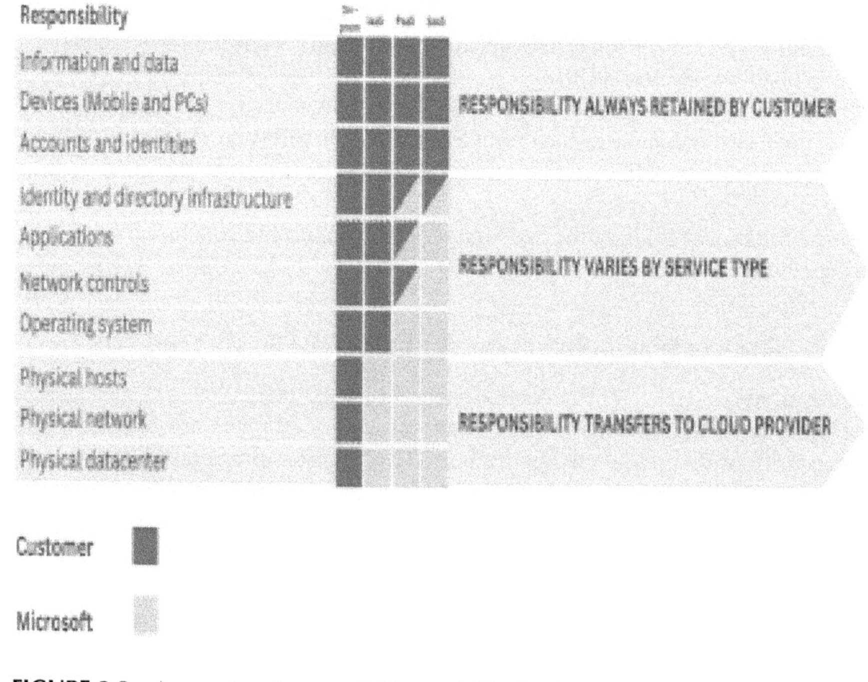

FIGURE 8.2 Azure: shared responsibility model in the cloud.

responsibility. The specific responsibilities that are transferred depend on the type of deployment you choose (SaaS, PaaS, IaaS, or on-premises). Regardless of the deployment type, you are always responsible for protecting your data and identities, on-premises resources, and the cloud components you control. Microsoft is responsible for securing the underlying infrastructure.

8.3.3 Advanced Accountability Frameworks

Several frameworks emerging in recent years aim to address the limitations of the shared responsibility model and enhance cloud accountability. These frameworks emphasize:

- Shared Accountability: Moving beyond rigid boundaries, acknowledging the intertwined nature of cloud provider and customer responsibilities in ensuring data security and compliance.
- Continuous Monitoring and Auditing: Employing automated tools and continuous monitoring techniques to proactively identify and address potential security risks and compliance issues [9].
- Transparency and Collaboration: Fostering open communication and collaboration between cloud providers and customers, enabling joint incident response, threat intelligence sharing, and proactive risk mitigation strategies.
- Compliance-oriented Design: Integrating compliance considerations into the development and deployment of cloud services, ensuring alignment with relevant regulations from the outset.

These frameworks are still evolving, but they offer promising avenues for building a more robust and collaborative model of accountability in the cloud.

8.3.4 Integrating Accountability into Cloud SLAs

SLAs play a crucial role in defining cloud service expectations and outlining remedies for non-compliance. Integrating accountability provisions into SLAs can further strengthen data protection and transparency within the cloud ecosystem:

- Explicit Definitions of Security and Compliance Obligations: Clearly articulating both provider and customer responsibilities regarding data security, privacy, and compliance with specific regulations.
- Transparent Reporting and Auditing Mechanisms: Establishing clear protocols for incident reporting, security audits, and access to security logs, empowering customers to actively monitor and verify compliance.
- Financial Incentives and Penalties: Including provisions for financial rewards for exceeding security and compliance benchmarks and penalties for non-compliance, incentivizing both parties to prioritize data protection.
- Dispute Resolution Mechanisms: Defining transparent and efficient mechanisms for resolving disputes arising from potential breaches of security or compliance obligations within the SLA framework.

By incorporating these elements, SLAs can transform from mere service guarantees to powerful tools for driving accountability and fostering a culture of shared responsibility within the cloud.

8.4 ADVANCED AUDITING AND MONITORING MECHANISMS: SHINING A LIGHT ON DATA ACCOUNTABILITY IN THE CLOUD

8.4.1 Real-time Auditing Tools in Cloud Platforms: Guardians of the Ephemeral

The dynamic nature of cloud computing renders traditional, periodic audits insufficient. Real-time auditing tools emerge as vigilant sentinels, continuously monitoring digital activities and providing granular insights into user actions, data access, and system configurations. These tools offer multifaceted benefits:

- Proactive Threat Detection: By continuously analyzing user activities and system events, real-time auditing tools can swiftly identify anomalous behaviors or suspicious actions, potentially preventing data breaches before they occur [14,16].
- Enhanced Compliance Measures: They furnish comprehensive audit logs and reports that attest to compliance with data protection regulations. This simplifies compliance audits, mitigates risks, and ensures adherence to industry standards [12,15].
- Operational Efficiency: Real-time monitoring allows for swift identification and resolution of performance issues, thereby significantly enhancing the operational efficiency of cloud services [13,17].

Prominent cloud platforms like AWS CloudTrail and Google Cloud Audit Logs, along with third-party tools such as Splunk and Sumo Logic, offer robust real-time auditing capabilities. These tools enable comprehensive tracking, analysis, and real-time visibility into cloud activities.

8.4.2 Log Analysis Techniques for Accountability: Decoding the Digital Rosetta Stone

The logs generated by real-time auditing tools can often appear cryptic and overwhelming. Employing advanced log analysis techniques becomes imperative to unlock their inherent value. These techniques utilize sophisticated algorithms to:

- Detect Anomalous Activity: Leveraging ML algorithms enables the identification of unusual patterns in user behavior, system configurations, or data access attempts. These anomalies may signify potential security threats or compliance violations. [21]

- Correlate Events Across Logs: By interconnecting events sourced from various logs and data sources, analysts can construct a holistic depiction of user activities and data flows. This facilitates forensic investigations and incident response, enabling a comprehensive understanding of cloud-related incidents. [23]
- Transform Logs into Actionable Insights: Generating reports and visualizations from raw logs empowers stakeholders to comprehend data access trends, identify areas of concern, and make informed decisions regarding data security and compliance measures. [22]

EFK vs PLG Architecture

Choosing between EFK and PLG architectures for log management boils down to a balance between power and efficiency. EFK, with its Elasticsearch engine, thrives on complex searches and intricate filtering, but at the cost of resource-intensiveness and intricate configuration. PLG, built around Loki, focuses on lightweight scalability and easy integration with monitoring systems, offering simpler queries and label-based filtering. If in-depth log analysis is crucial, EFK's robust search is unmatched. But for streamlined log aggregation and basic filtering, PLG's streamlined architecture shines. Ultimately, the choice depends on your specific needs and priorities: deep log exploration or efficient ingestion and basic analysis.

8.4.3 Google Cloud and AWS Monitoring Toolkits: A Guided Tour of the Digital Citadel

Google Cloud and AWS offer robust and comprehensive monitoring toolkits that empower organizations with profound insights into the health, performance, and security of their cloud resources. These toolkits encompass:

- Cloud Monitoring: Offering real-time and historical data on resource utilization, performance metrics, and custom-defined metrics, providing a holistic view of the cloud environment [18,13].
- Cloud Security Command Center: A centralized platform designed for monitoring security events, investigating potential threats, and managing the overall security posture across the cloud infrastructure [12,15].
- Identity and Access Management (IAM): Providing fine-grained control over user permissions and access privileges to cloud resources, thereby ensuring accountability and data access control [19,16].

Leveraging these tools alongside real-time auditing and log analysis techniques enables organizations to establish a robust monitoring ecosystem. This ecosystem ensures continuous visibility into the cloud environment, fostering data accountability and enabling proactive measures for risk mitigation and compliance adherence.

8.5 CASE STUDIES ON IMPLEMENTING DATA ACCOUNTABILITY: NAVIGATING THE LABYRINTH OF RESPONSIBILITY

8.5.1 SUCCESS STORIES IN ACHIEVING DATA ACCOUNTABILITY: BEACONS OF RESPONSIBLE PRACTICE

Several organizations have demonstrated exemplary practices in ensuring data accountability within the cloud, showcasing how technology and responsible stewardship can go hand in hand. Here are some noteworthy examples:

- **Garanti, a Brazilian insurance company**: Leveraged Google Cloud's IAM and Cloud Audit Logs to establish robust access controls and comprehensive audit trails. This implementation not only ensured compliance with local data protection regulations (e.g., LGPD) but also enhanced customer trust and reinforced a culture of data accountability within the organization.
- **The City of Munich**: Migrated its IT infrastructure to AWS, utilizing services like Key Management Service (KMS) and CloudTrail. These tools enabled the encryption of sensitive data at rest and in transit, as well as meticulous tracking of user access. This resulted in heightened data security, enhanced accountability, and facilitated streamlined compliance audits, particularly relevant for government entities.
- **Blackboard, an educational technology company**: Implemented a robust data governance program centered on ISO 27001, integrating it seamlessly with their cloud environment. This initiative aimed to define clear roles, responsibilities, and accountability mechanisms for efficient data management across the organization. This approach showcases a commitment to data accountability not only through technology but also through established governance frameworks.

Additional Considerations:

- **Beyond Technology**: While cloud technologies like IAM, CloudTrail, and KMS offer valuable tools, true data accountability requires a holistic approach. Organizations should consider implementing data governance frameworks that go beyond technology, encompassing policies, procedures, and training programs to foster a culture of data responsibility.
- **Continuous Improvement**: Data accountability is an ongoing journey, not a destination. Organizations should adopt a continuous improvement mindset, regularly reviewing their data governance practices and adapting them to evolving regulations and technological advancements.

These success stories underscore the effectiveness of integrating advanced cloud technologies with robust data governance practices. They exemplify how strategic implementation can significantly contribute to achieving and maintaining data accountability in the cloud, fostering trust and building a foundation for responsible data stewardship.

8.5.2 Challenges Encountered and Mitigation Strategies: Charting a Course Through Turbulent Waters

Navigating the Labyrinth: Challenges and Solutions for Data Accountability in the Cloud

While success stories illuminate the path, implementing data accountability in the cloud requires careful consideration of several challenges:

1. **Ambiguous Roles and Responsibilities:**
   1. The shared responsibility model of cloud computing, where both the organization and the CSP share security obligations, can lead to confusion regarding ultimate accountability for data security. This ambiguity can create gaps in data protection and leave organizations vulnerable.[12,15]
   2. **Solutions:**
   - Clearly define roles and responsibilities: Establish precise contracts with the CSP outlining each party's data security obligations. Internally, designate data ownership and access control within the organization. [19,16]
   - Implement shared responsibility model best practices: Leverage frameworks like the Cloud Security Alliance (CSA) Shared Responsibility Matrix and NIST SP 800-161 to clarify respective roles and guide implementation.
2. **Data Sprawl and Shadow IT:**
   3. The rapid creation and storage of data across diverse cloud services, often fueled by unauthorized "shadow IT", can create a chaotic landscape. This disorganization makes it difficult to track, audit, and control access, increasing the risk of data breaches and compliance violations. [14,13]
   4. **Solutions:**
   - Implement data discovery and classification tools: Utilize automated tools to locate and categorize data across all cloud environments, facilitating data governance and access control. [21,23]
   - Enforce data governance policies: Establish clear policies for data lifecycle management, including storage, access, and deletion, and ensure consistent enforcement across all departments and cloud services. [20]
3. **Lack of Security Awareness and Training:**
   5. Inadequate employee awareness and training regarding data security best practices in the cloud can lead to human errors and accidental data leaks. This risk is further amplified by the dynamic nature of cloud environments and evolving compliance regulations.
   6. **Solutions:**
   - Regularly conduct data security awareness training: Educate employees on cloud-specific security threats, proper data handling practices, and reporting procedures for suspicious activities. [18,22]
   - Implement robust security protocols: Enforce multi-factor authentication, strong password policies, and access controls to minimize the impact of human error and malicious activities. [15]

Proactive addressing of these challenges through effective communication, rigorous data governance frameworks, and continuous training initiatives can help organizations navigate the complexities of data accountability in the cloud. By fostering a culture of data responsibility and leveraging available tools and best practices, organizations can ensure secure and compliant data management in the cloud environment.

8.5.3 Comparative Analysis of Accountability Practices in Google Cloud and AWS: Choosing the Right Vessel for Your Journey

Choosing your Cloud Ally: Comparing Google Cloud and AWS for Data Accountability

While both Google Cloud and AWS offer comprehensive tools and services to support data accountability in the cloud, their approaches differ in key aspects, influencing your selection process:

Data Protection Regulations:

- **Google Cloud:** Often boasts stronger built-in compliance features for specific regulations like GDPR and HIPAA, easing adherence with pre-configured settings. [14,15]
- **AWS:** Provides a broader range of customizable tools that can be tailored to diverse regulatory requirements, offering greater flexibility but requiring more configuration. [12,19]

Transparency and Reporting:

- **Google Cloud:** Typically delivers detailed audit logs and reports, offering granular insights into data access and activity, readily facilitating traceability and accountability. [22,16]
- **AWS:** Offers similar capabilities but may require additional configuration and integration with third-party tools to achieve comparable levels of transparency and granular reporting. [23]

Open-Source and Community:

- **Google Cloud:** Embraces an open-source philosophy with robust community support, fostering wider collaboration and access to a wealth of community-developed tools and resources for data accountability. [21,13]
- **AWS:** Adopts a more proprietary approach, potentially limiting access to certain functionalities and relying primarily on vendor-specific resources for accountability measures. [17,20]

Choosing the Right Cloud for Data Accountability:

The optimal platform depends on your specific needs, priorities, and existing infrastructure. Carefully evaluate:

- Regulatory compliance requirements: If adherence to specific regulations is paramount, Google Cloud's pre-configured compliance features might be advantageous.

- Desired level of transparency: If granular data access insights are crucial, Google Cloud's detailed audit logs might be preferable.
- Existing infrastructure and skills: Consider compatibility with your current IT environment and existing skill sets within your team when choosing between open-source and proprietary approaches.

Navigating the Evolving Landscape:

Data accountability demands constant adaptation. Organizations must:

- Stay agile: Remain informed about technological advancements and evolving regulatory landscapes to adjust their data governance strategies accordingly.
- Draw from success stories: Leverage insights from successful case studies to implement best practices and overcome similar challenges.
- Utilize valuable resources: Seek guidance from organizations like the CSA, International Organization for Standardization (ISO), and NIST Cybersecurity Framework to solidify your journey toward responsible data stewardship.

By carefully considering these factors and actively shaping your data accountability approach, you can confidently choose the best cloud platform to ensure secure and compliant data management in the ever-evolving cloud environment.

8.6 FUTURE TRENDS IN DATA ACCOUNTABILITY

Future Trends in Data Accountability: Navigating the Uncharted Waters

As data continues its relentless surge through the cloud, the quest for accountability in this dynamic landscape takes center stage. While established principles and practices form the bedrock, the future of data accountability promises a fascinating convergence of technological advancements and evolving regulatory frameworks. Let's delve into three key trends that are poised to reshape the landscape:

8.6.1 ML for Anomaly Detection: Unveiling the Shadows of Misconduct

The sheer volume and velocity of data in the cloud pose a formidable challenge for traditional data security and accountability measures. Enter ML for anomaly detection, a powerful tool poised to revolutionize the game. ML algorithms, trained on vast datasets of past activities and user behavior, can identify subtle anomalies in data access, usage patterns, and system configurations, potentially revealing malicious intent or data breaches before they wreak havoc [24–26].

ML-powered anomaly detection holds immense promise for enhancing data accountability in several ways:

- Proactive Threat Identification: By continuously monitoring data flows and user activities, ML can flag suspicious behavior in real-time, enabling timely intervention and mitigation of potential data breaches.

- Improved Regulatory Compliance: ML algorithms can help organizations comply with data protection regulations by detecting and reporting potential violations, reducing the risk of hefty fines and reputational damage.
- Enhanced Transparency and Trust: By providing granular insights into data access and usage patterns, ML can foster transparency and trust between organizations and their stakeholders, solidifying data accountability practices.

However, ethical considerations and potential biases within ML algorithms must be addressed to ensure responsible and fair use in data accountability.

8.6.2 Blockchain and Distributed Ledger Technologies: Democratizing Data Governance

Blockchain technology, with its immutable and decentralized nature, offers a fascinating potential for transforming data accountability. By creating a distributed ledger where every data transaction is recorded and verified transparently, blockchain empowers individuals to take control of their data and fosters a more collaborative data governance ecosystem.

Blockchain-enabled data accountability could bring about a paradigm shift in several ways:

- Empowering Individuals: Individuals can gain greater control over their data, deciding who can access it and for what purposes, leading to a more empowered and responsible data ecosystem.
- Enhanced Auditability and Transparency: The transparent and immutable nature of blockchain records makes it easier to track data usage and identify potential breaches or misuse, increasing accountability for data controllers.
- Reduced Reliance on Third-Party Intermediaries: Decentralized data governance eliminates the need for centralized data repositories, reducing the risk of data breaches and fostering trust between data subjects and controllers.

However, scalability challenges, complex technical infrastructure, and regulatory hurdles remain obstacles that need to be overcome for the widespread adoption of blockchain for data accountability.

8.6.3 Anticipated Evolution in Regulatory Frameworks: Keeping Pace with the Digital Tornado

The ever-evolving landscape of data usage and technology necessitates a dynamic regulatory framework to ensure effective data accountability. We can anticipate several key trends:

- Focus on Data Governance and Compliance: Regulations are likely to shift from a purely technical focus to emphasize data governance practices and compliance mechanisms, placing responsibility on organizations to implement robust data management systems.
- Sector-Specific Regulations: The increasing diversity of data usage across industries will likely lead to the development of sector-specific regulations tailored to the unique challenges and risks of each domain.
- International Collaboration and Harmonization: Recognizing the global nature of data flows, international collaboration and harmonization of data protection regulations will become increasingly important to ensure consistency and effectiveness.

Conclusion

The cloud has revolutionized data storage and processing, but it has also introduced new challenges for data accountability. This chapter has explored the multifaceted landscape of data accountability in cloud environments, examining the interplay between technological advancements, regulatory compliance, and evolving accountability models. While significant progress has been made, achieving robust and transparent data accountability in the cloud remains an ongoing endeavor. The fragmented nature of the regulatory landscape, with GDPR, CCPA, and other regulations setting different standards, presents a significant challenge for CSPs and data owners alike. Moving forward, greater harmonization and international cooperation are crucial to ensure consistent and effective data protection. The shared responsibility model, while a cornerstone of cloud accountability, necessitates collaborative efforts between cloud providers and data owners. Advanced accountability frameworks, coupled with real-time auditing tools and log analysis techniques, can offer a more comprehensive approach to data stewardship. Integrating accountability into SLAs can further strengthen the commitment to data protection. The emergence of cutting-edge technologies like ML and blockchain holds immense promise for the future of data accountability. ML can facilitate anomaly detection and automate data governance processes, while blockchain can enable secure and tamper-proof data provenance tracking.

Future Scope

The evolution of data accountability in the cloud is far from over. Several key areas require further exploration and development:

- ML for Enhanced Accountability: Research into applying ML algorithms for anomaly detection, predictive analysis of data usage patterns, and automated enforcement of data protection policies can significantly improve the effectiveness of accountability measures.
- Blockchain for Secure Data Provenance: Integrating blockchain technology into cloud platforms can provide a tamper-proof record of data access and usage, enhancing transparency and trust.

- Evolving Regulatory Frameworks: Anticipating the development of new regulations and adapting existing frameworks to address emerging technologies like AI and IoT is crucial to ensure comprehensive data protection in the cloud.
- Standardization and Harmonization: International collaboration and efforts to harmonize data protection regulations across jurisdictions are essential for fostering a level playing field and facilitating seamless data transfer in the global cloud ecosystem.
- User Education and Empowerment: Educating users about their data rights and responsibilities is critical for promoting active participation in data governance and fostering a culture of data accountability.

By embracing these advancements and fostering a collaborative approach, we can move toward a future where data accountability in the cloud is not just a compliance obligation, but a cornerstone of trust and responsible data stewardship.

REFERENCES

1. Kache, H., et al. (2020). Contextual data sensitivity: A framework for assessing data privacy risks in the cloud. In *Proceedings of the 2020 ACM Web* Conference (pp. 3295–3301).
2. Khan, M. U., et al. (2020). Shared responsibility model for cloud security: A systematic review. *Future Generation Computer Systems*, 110, 800–815.
3. Thatcher, J., et al. (2021). Towards collective data accountability in the cloud: A socio-technical framework. *MIS Quarterly*, 45(4), 1423–1451.
4. Murthy, J. S., & Siddesh, G. M. (2024). A smart video analytical framework for sarcasm detection using novel adaptive fusion network and SarcasNet-99 model. *The Visual Computer*, 1–13, Springer.
5. Acquisti, A., Taylor, C., & Wagman, J. (2023). Data protection in the age of artificial intelligence: Rethinking the regulatory framework. *Washington Law Review*, 98(3), 1139–1214.
6. Murthy, J. S., Siddesh, G. M., & Srinivasa, K. G. (2018). A Distributed Framework for Real-Time Twitter Sentiment Analysis and Visualization. In *Recent Findings in Intelligent Computing Techniques: Proceedings of the 5th ICACNI 2017,* Volume 3 (pp. 55–61). Springer Singapore.
7. Baba, M. H. (2023). Cloud computing and data privacy: A comparative study of GDPR, CCPA, and PDPA. *International Journal of Information Security and Privacy*, 17(1), 23–42.
8. Citron, D. K., & de Laat, M. (2020). The GDPR and the CCPA: A comparative analysis. *European Journal of Law and Technology*, 13(1), 1–26.
9. Murthy, J. S. (2019). Edgecloud: A distributed management system for resource continuity in edge to cloud computing environment. In *The Rise of Fog Computing in the Digital Era* (pp. 108–128). IGI Global.
10. Gantz, J., Granato, P., & Antonelli, C. (2022). *Emerging Cloud Threat Landscapes* (Tech. Rep.). Gartner.
11. Kuo, P.-H., Huang, Y.-J., & Huang, Y.-M. (2020). Cloud Security Accountability and Transparency Model. *Security and Communication Networks*, 13(7): 1801–1819.

12. Murthy, J. S., Chitlapalli, S. S., Anirudha, U. N., & Subramanya, V. (2022, April). A Real-Time Driver Assistance System Using Object Detection and Tracking. In *International Conference on Advances in Computing and Data Sciences* (pp. 150–159). Cham: Springer International Publishing.
13. Murthy, J. S., Shekar, A. C., Bhattacharya, D., Namratha, R., & Sripriya, D. (2021). A novel framework for multimodal twitter sentiment analysis using feature learning. In *Advances in Computing and Data Sciences: 5th International Conference, ICACDS 2021, Nashik, India, April 23–24, 2021, Revised Selected Papers, Part II 5* (pp. 252–261). Springer International Publishing.
14. Monnappa, K. V., & Latif, S. (2020). A survey on cloud security auditing tools and techniques. *Journal of King Saud University-Computer and Information Sciences*, 32(6), 2055–2065.
15. Rong, Y., Li, Y., & Zhang, Y. (2022). A survey of cloud security compliance auditing: Challenges and solutions. *IEEE Transactions on Cloud Computing*, 10(2), 463–476.
16. Shukla, A., Singh, G., & Sharma, Y. D. (2023). Cloud security auditing: A comprehensive review of recent advancements and challenges. *Computer Science Review*, 46, 100453.
17. Murthy, J. S., & Chitlapalli, S. S. (2022). Conceptual Analysis and Applications of Bigdata in Smart Society. In *Society 5.0: Smart Future Towards Enhancing the Quality of Society* (pp. 57–67). Singapore: Springer Nature Singapore.
18. Ahmed, M. A., & Hassan, M. A. (2020). Cloud performance anomaly detection: A comprehensive survey. *IEEE Transactions on Network and Service Management*, 17(4), 1451–1472.
19. Murthy, J. S., Matt, S. G., Venkatesh, S. K. H., & Gubbi, K. R. (2022). A real-time quantum-conscious multimodal option mining framework using deep learning. *IAES International Journal of Artificial Intelligence*, 11(3), 1019.
20. Al-Ani, A., Al-Riabi, A., & Alsari, A. (2021). Towards a real-time log analysis framework for cloud security auditing. *International Journal of Computer Network and Information Security*, 13(1), 31–42.
21. Murthy, J. S., Siddesh, G. M., & Srinivasa, K. G. (2019). A real-time twitter trend analysis and visualization framework. *International Journal on Semantic Web and Information Systems (IJSWIS)*, 15(2), 1–21.
22. Hwang, I., Koo, J., & Park, J. (2020). A cloud log analysis and visualization system for security management. *International Journal of Network Security*, 23(5), 504–512.
23. Murthy, J. S., Siddesh, G. M., & Srinivasa, K. G. (2019). TwitSenti: a real-time Twitter sentiment analysis and visualization framework. *Journal of Information & Knowledge Management,* 18(02), 1950013.
24. Murthy, J. S., & Siddesh, G. M. (2023, October). AI Based Criminal Detection and Recognition System for Public Safety and Security using novel CriminalNet-228. In *International Conference on Frontiers in Computing and Systems* (pp. 3–20). Singapore: Springer Nature Singapore.
25. Murthy, J. S., & Siddesh, G. M. (2023, October). A Real-Time Framework for Automatic Sarcasm Detection Using Proposed Tensor-DNN-50 Algorithm. In *International Conference on Frontiers in Computing and Systems* (pp. 109–124). Singapore: Springer Nature Singapore.
26. Murthy, J.S., Dhanashekar, K., Siddesh, G.M. (2024). A Real-Time Video Surveillance-Based Framework for Early Plant Disease Detection Using Jetson TX1 and Novel LeafNet-104 Algorithm. In: Kole, D.K., Roy Chowdhury, S., Basu, S., Plewczynski, D., Bhattacharjee, D. (eds) Proceedings of 4th International Conference on Frontiers in Computing and Systems. COMSYS 2023. Lecture Notes in Networks and Systems, vol 975. Springer, Singapore. https://doi.org/10.1007/978-981-97-2614-1_23

9 Secure Multiparty Computation

Protocols, Collaborative Data Processing, and Real-World Applications in Industry

Sahana D. Gowda

9.1 INTRODUCTION TO PRIVACY-PRESERVING COMPUTATION

Privacy-preserving computation stands at the forefront of data security, offering innovative solutions to protect sensitive information in collaborative computing environments. As organizations increasingly rely on shared data processing and analysis, preserving the confidentiality of individual data becomes paramount. This section delves into the foundations of privacy-preserving computation, examining its evolution, principles, and the growing need for robust techniques.

9.1.1 The Crucial Intersection of Security and Privacy

In the landscape of cloud computing, the convergence of security and privacy within privacy-preserving computation is a pivotal consideration. This subsection delves into the intricate relationship between safeguarding sensitive information and the delicate balance required to ensure both data security and user privacy as shown [1].

Cloud environments serve as hubs for collaborative data processing and analysis, amplifying the importance of this intersection. Encryption, while fundamental, is only one facet of the broader challenge of maintaining the integrity of data while respecting user privacy. The delicate equilibrium between these two concerns is essential to foster trust in cloud-based collaborations [2].

9.1.1.1 Security

Security in the context of computing and information technology refers to the measures and protocols implemented to protect computer systems, networks, and data from unauthorized access, attacks, damage, or theft [3]. It encompasses a broad spectrum of practices aimed at ensuring the confidentiality, integrity, and availability of information. Key aspects of security include:

DOI: 10.1201/9781003455448-9

- **Confidentiality:** Ensuring that sensitive information is accessible only to authorized individuals or systems.
- **Integrity:** Maintaining the accuracy and reliability of data and information, safeguarding against unauthorized modifications.
- **Availability:** Ensuring that systems and data are accessible and usable when needed, minimizing downtime and disruptions.
- **Authentication:** Verifying the identity of users or systems, typically through passwords, biometrics, or multifactor authentication.
- **Authorization:** Granting appropriate permissions to authenticated users, specifying what actions or resources they are allowed to access.
- **Network Security:** Implementing measures to protect networks from unauthorized access, data interception, and malicious activities.
- **Data Encryption:** Utilizing cryptographic techniques to encode data, rendering it unreadable without the correct decryption key.
- **Intrusion Detection and Prevention:** Employing tools and technologies to detect and respond to unauthorized or malicious activities within a system or network.

9.1.1.1.1 Secure Multiparty Sharing

Secure Multiparty Sharing (SMPS) is a concept in the field of cryptography and data security. It refers to the ability for multiple parties, each holding their own private data, to jointly compute a function over their data inputs while keeping those inputs private. This ensures that no participating party learns anything more about the other parties' private data than what can be inferred from the output of the computation itself as shown in Figure 9.1. Here is an overview of SMPS:

- **Objective:** The main goal of SMPS is to enable collaborative computation or data analysis without compromising the confidentiality of each party's data. It is particularly useful in situations where sharing raw data is not possible due to privacy concerns, regulatory restrictions, or commercial confidentiality.

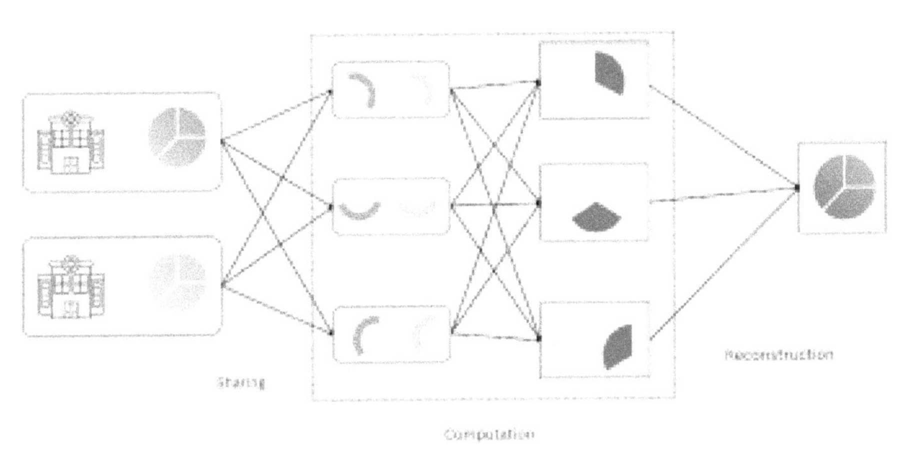

FIGURE 9.1 Secure multiparty sharing.

- **How it Works:** In SMPS, a desired computation is broken down into parts that can be processed separately by each participant. The participants then perform computations on their own data and share only specific, non-revealing pieces of information. Advanced cryptographic techniques are used to ensure that these shared pieces do not expose the private data.
- **Cryptography Techniques:** SMPS often involves techniques like homomorphic encryption (which allows computations on encrypted data), secret sharing (where a secret is divided into parts), and zero-knowledge proofs (which prove a statement is true without revealing the statement itself).
- **Applications:** This approach is used in various fields such as collaborative data analysis, privacy-preserving data mining, secure voting systems, and more. For instance, in the healthcare sector, SMPS can enable researchers to collectively analyze patient data from multiple hospitals without any hospital revealing its individual patient records.
- **Challenges:** SMPS is complex and can be computationally intensive. Ensuring the efficiency and scalability of these cryptographic protocols, especially for large-scale applications, is an ongoing area of research.
- **Privacy and Trust:** SMPS helps in building trust among parties that need to collaborate but are either competitive or have strict privacy requirements. By guaranteeing data privacy, it enables cooperation that would otherwise be risky or impossible.

9.1.1.2 Privacy

Privacy, in the context of computing and information technology, revolves around the protection of individuals' personal information and the right to control the collection, use, and dissemination of their data [4]. It involves practices and policies that safeguard sensitive information from unauthorized access or misuse. Key components of privacy include:

- **Data Protection:** Implementing measures to secure personal and sensitive information, preventing unauthorized access or disclosure.
- **Consent and Transparency:** Ensuring individuals are informed about how their data will be used and obtaining their consent for such usage.
- **Anonymity:** Protecting individuals' identities by removing or encrypting personally identifiable information when possible.
- **Compliance with Regulations:** Adhering to legal requirements and industry standards related to data privacy, such as GDPR, HIPAA, or CCPA.
- **User Control:** Providing individuals with mechanisms to control and manage their personal information, including the ability to opt out of certain data processing activities.
- **Ethical Data Practices:** Upholding ethical standards in the collection, processing, and storage of data to ensure fairness, transparency, and respect for individuals' rights.

Both security and privacy are integral components of responsible and ethical information management in the digital age, aiming to create a trustworthy and resilient computing environment.

9.1.1.2.1 Secure Multiparty Computation

Secure Multiparty Computation (SMC) is an advanced concept in the field of cryptography and computer science. It allows multiple parties, each holding their own private data, to jointly perform a computation on their combined data without revealing their individual inputs to each other as shown in Figure 9.2. This technique enables trustless collaboration in sensitive computations, ensuring data privacy and security. Here is a deeper look into SMC:

- **Primary Goal:** SMC aims to enable parties to jointly compute a function over their inputs while keeping those inputs confidential. The outcome of the computation is made available to participants, but the individual data points are not revealed.
- **Use Cases:** This approach is valuable in scenarios where sharing raw data is impractical or forbidden due to privacy concerns, legal constraints, or proprietary interests. It is used in various sectors including finance, healthcare, and governmental organizations for purposes such as collaborative research, joint financial transactions, and private voting systems.
- **Cryptography Techniques:** To achieve secure computation, SMC utilizes cryptographic methods like homomorphic encryption (which allows operations on encrypted data), secret sharing (dividing a secret into parts), and zero-knowledge proofs (verifying the truth of a statement without revealing the statement itself).
- **How It Works:** In a typical SMC scenario, each participant encrypts their input and then shares it with the group. Computations are performed on the

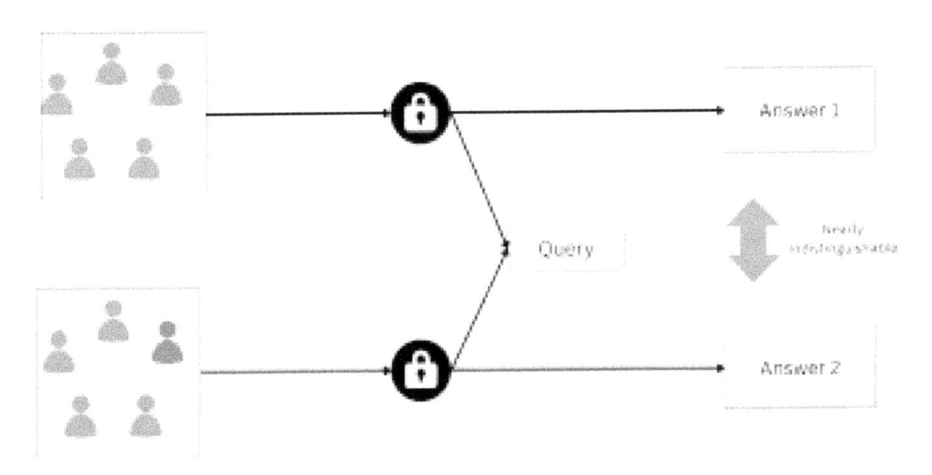

FIGURE 9.2 Secure multiparty computation.

encrypted data, and the process is structured so that the final result can be decrypted to reveal only the intended outcome, not the individual inputs.

- **Security and Privacy:** SMC is designed to protect against various threats, including attempts by participants to learn about others' data or external attacks. It ensures data privacy even if some of the participants are not trustworthy.
- **Challenges:** Implementing SMC is complex and can be resource-intensive. It often requires significant computational power and can be slower than non-secure computations. Researchers are continually working on optimizing these protocols for better efficiency and scalability.
- **Building Trust:** SMC is particularly valuable in building trust among entities that need to collaborate but do not fully trust each other. It facilitates secure cooperation while mitigating risks associated with data breaches or unauthorized data access.

Example: Balancing Security and Privacy in Healthcare Collaborative Research

In the healthcare sector, collaborative research often involves sharing patient data to derive valuable insights. The challenge lies in finding the right balance between facilitating research and upholding the confidentiality and privacy rights of patients. Here is a detailed explanation with steps and potential cloud implementation:

1. **Data Classification and Encryption:** Classify patient data based on sensitivity (e.g., personally identifiable information, medical records). Encrypt sensitive data using strong encryption algorithms. Utilize cloud-based encryption services to protect data both in transit and at rest.
2. **Access Control and Authentication:** Implement strict access controls, allowing only authorized personnel to access patient data. Utilize multifactor authentication to ensure the identity of users. Leverage cloud-based identity and access management (IAM) services for fine-grained access control.
3. **Secure Data Transmission:** Use secure communication protocols (e.g., HTTPS) for transmitting patient data. Employ Virtual Private Clouds (VPCs) to create isolated network environments with secure communication channels.
4. **Audit Trails and Monitoring:** Implement audit trails to log access and modifications to patient data. Set up continuous monitoring for unusual activities. Leverage cloud-native monitoring and logging services to track user activities and system changes.
5. **Data Minimization and De-Identification:** Minimize the amount of patient data shared to only what is necessary for research. De-identify data by removing or encrypting personally identifiable information. Use cloud services that support data anonymization and de-identification.
6. **Compliance with Healthcare Regulations:** Ensure compliance with healthcare regulations (e.g., HIPAA) governing patient data. Regularly update security measures to align with evolving regulations. Choose cloud providers with compliance certifications and implement healthcare-specific cloud services.

7. **Secure Collaboration Platforms:** Utilize secure collaboration platforms that offer end-to-end encryption. Train researchers on secure data handling practices. Explore cloud-based collaboration tools with built-in security features.
8. **Data Lifecycle Management:** Establish clear data lifecycle management policies, including data retention and disposal. Regularly review and update data management practices. Leverage cloud storage services with lifecycle management capabilities.

The crucial intersection of security and privacy is imperative in the realm of information technology and computing due to several critical needs:

1. **Safeguarding Sensitive Information:** Organizations deal with vast amounts of sensitive data, such as personal, financial, and healthcare information. Ensuring the security and privacy of this data is paramount to prevent unauthorized access, breaches, and misuse.
2. **Protecting User Confidentiality:** Users entrust organizations with their personal information. The intersection ensures that user confidentiality is maintained, fostering trust and confidence in the use of digital services.
3. **Legal and Ethical Compliance:** There are legal and ethical obligations to protect individuals' privacy rights. Compliance with data protection laws and regulations necessitates a careful balance between security measures and privacy considerations.
4. **Preventing Identity Theft and Fraud:** Security and privacy measures help in preventing identity theft and fraudulent activities. Unauthorized access to personal information can lead to financial losses, reputational damage, and legal consequences.
5. **Facilitating Secure Collaboration:** In collaborative environments, especially across industries or research domains, striking the right balance ensures that data can be shared securely. This is crucial for advancements in research, innovation, and industry collaborations.
6. **Mitigating Risks of Data Breaches:** Data breaches are a significant risk, and the intersection ensures robust security measures to prevent unauthorized access. Addressing vulnerabilities in the intersection helps mitigate the risks associated with data breaches.
7. **Preserving Individual Rights:** Individuals have the right to privacy, and the intersection safeguards these rights. It ensures that individuals have control over their personal information and how it is used.
8. **Building Trust in Technology:** Trust is foundational in the adoption of technology. The intersection of security and privacy builds and maintains trust between users, organizations, and technology providers, encouraging widespread adoption of digital services.
9. **Supporting Ethical Data Practices:** Ethical considerations play a vital role in handling data responsibly. The intersection ensures that data practices align with ethical standards, promoting fair, transparent, and responsible use of information.

10. **Adapting to Evolving Threats:** The landscape of cyber threats is dynamic. The intersection addresses the need to adapt security and privacy measures to evolving threats, including new technologies, sophisticated cyber-attacks, and emerging risks.

9.1.2 Research Challenges and Opportunities

As privacy-preserving computation advances, it encounters both challenges and opportunities. This subsection critically examines the existing research landscape, identifying obstacles that range from scalability issues to the trade-off between privacy and utility. Simultaneously, it highlights the opportunities for innovation and the potential societal impact of developing effective privacy-preserving technologies [5–10].

9.1.2.1 Challenges

1. **Scalability Challenges:** Deploying privacy-preserving technologies at scale, such as implementing homomorphic encryption for large datasets in a cloud environment, may pose computational and performance challenges.
2. **Trade-Off Between Privacy and Utility:** Striking a balance between privacy and utility can be challenging in scenarios like collaborative machine learning, where adding privacy measures may impact the accuracy of the model.
3. **Ensuring Data Accuracy:** Techniques like differential privacy can introduce noise, affecting the accuracy of analytics results, especially in precision-dependent applications like healthcare diagnostics.
4. **Legal and Regulatory Compliance:** Adhering to diverse data protection regulations, like GDPR or HIPAA, can be challenging when implementing privacy-preserving computation across international boundaries.
5. **User Acceptance and Adoption:** Users may resist adopting privacy-preserving technologies in social media platforms due to concerns about changes in user experience and the perceived inconvenience of added privacy measures.
6. **Interoperability Issues:** Ensuring interoperability between different privacy-preserving systems, especially in heterogeneous environments, poses challenges when sharing data across platforms and services.
7. **Complexity of Encryption Algorithms:** Implementing complex homomorphic encryption algorithms in resource-constrained devices, like Internet of Things (IoT) sensors, can be challenging due to computational limitations.
8. **Potential for Adversarial Attacks:** Adversarial attacks exploiting vulnerabilities in privacy-preserving protocols, such as membership inference attacks on federated learning models, pose security challenges.
9. **Ethical Considerations:** Ethical challenges arise in scenarios where privacy-preserving technologies unintentionally perpetuate biases or discriminate against certain groups, raising concerns about fairness and justice.
10. **Resource Intensiveness:** Resource-intensive privacy-preserving computations, like SMPC for large datasets, may strain computing resources and lead to increased operational costs.

9.1.2.2 Opportunities

1. **Development of Efficient Encryption Algorithms:** Innovations in developing more efficient and lightweight encryption algorithms can pave the way for secure and scalable privacy-preserving computation in resource-constrained environments.
2. **Advancements in Homomorphic Encryption:** Continuous advancements in homomorphic encryption can enable more practical applications, such as secure data processing in cloud environments without compromising computational efficiency.
3. **Integration of Privacy by Design:** Embedding privacy features directly into the design phase of applications can provide opportunities for seamless integration of privacy-preserving measures, ensuring a more robust privacy architecture.
4. **Global Standards and Frameworks:** The establishment of global standards and frameworks for privacy-preserving computation can streamline compliance efforts and facilitate more consistent implementation across industries and regions.
5. **User-Friendly Privacy Solutions:** The development of user-friendly privacy-preserving solutions, such as intuitive privacy controls in social media, can enhance user acceptance and adoption, making privacy measures more accessible.
6. **Research in Hybrid Privacy Models:** Ongoing research in hybrid privacy models that combine differential privacy with other techniques can provide opportunities for achieving a better balance between privacy and utility.
7. **Open-Source Collaboration:** Open-source collaboration in privacy-preserving technologies can foster innovation, allowing researchers and developers worldwide to contribute, share knowledge, and collectively address challenges.
8. **Blockchain for Privacy Assurance:** Leveraging blockchain technology for privacy-preserving computation can offer opportunities for secure and transparent data transactions while ensuring data integrity and user control.
9. **Ethical AI Development:** Focusing on ethical considerations in AI development can lead to opportunities for creating privacy-preserving solutions that prioritize fairness, transparency, and accountability in algorithmic decision-making.
10. **Public Awareness and Education:** Opportunities exist in raising public awareness and education about privacy-preserving technologies, fostering a better understanding of the importance of privacy and encouraging informed decision-making by users.

9.2 HOMOMORPHIC ENCRYPTION: THEORY AND APPLICATIONS

Homomorphic encryption stands as a pivotal concept in privacy-preserving computation, allowing computations to be performed on encrypted data without the need for decryption. This section delves into the theory and practical applications of homomorphic encryption, exploring algorithms, cloud implementations, and the support provided by major cloud service providers [11,12].

9.2.1 What is Homomorphic Encryption?

Homomorphic encryption is a cryptographic technique that enables computations to be performed on encrypted data without decrypting it. The primary goal is to maintain data privacy during processing. Let us delve into a high-level overview of homomorphic encryption and its mathematical underpinnings using a simplified example.

Homomorphic encryption involves three main operations: encryption, computation, and decryption. There are different levels of homomorphic encryption, such as partially homomorphic and fully homomorphic encryption. For simplicity, we'll focus on a simplified example using a partially homomorphic encryption scheme.

9.2.1.1 Mathematical Derivation

9.2.1.1.1 Key Generation

- Alice generates a pair of keys: a public key (pk) and a private key (sk).
- The public key is shared openly, and the private key is kept secret.

9.2.1.1.2 Encryption

- Alice wants to send a message m to Bob.
- She encrypts the message using the public key: $c = E(pk,m)$, Here, c is the ciphertext.

9.2.1.1.3 Computation

- Bob, who possesses the private key, performs a computation on the ciphertext without decrypting it.
- Let us consider a simple example: $c' = c2$
- This operation represents a mathematical computation (in this case, squaring) applied to the encrypted message.

9.2.1.1.4 Decryption

- When Bob sends back c' to Alice, she decrypts it using her private key: $m' = D(sk,c')$.
- The result m' is the squared value of the original message m.

Example: Suppose Alice wants to keep the number 3 confidential but still wants Bob to compute its square. Using homomorphic encryption:

9.2.1.1.5 Key Generation

- pk (public key) and sk (private key) are generated.

9.2.1.1.6 Encryption

- Alice encrypts 3: $c = E(pk,3)$.

9.2.1.1.7 Computation

- Bob computes the square without decrypting: $c' = c2$

9.2.1.1.8 Decryption

- Alice decrypts the result:
- $m' = D(sk,c')$

The decrypted result m' is the square of the original number, i.e., 9

9.2.2 Homomorphic Encryption Algorithms

Homomorphic encryption algorithms form the foundation of secure data processing while maintaining privacy. Notable algorithms like Paillier, RSA, and fully homomorphic encryption schemes are discussed, elucidating their mathematical underpinnings and the specific use cases they cater to. Understanding these algorithms is paramount for implementing effective privacy-preserving solutions.

1. **Paillier Encryption Algorithm:** The Paillier Encryption Algorithm is a cryptographic system with partially homomorphic properties, particularly recognized for its additive homomorphism. This characteristic allows for homomorphic addition of plaintexts, making it a valuable tool for secure computations while preserving the privacy of sensitive data.

   1. The key generation process involves selecting two large prime numbers, p and q, computing the public modulus n, and determining the least common multiple λ. A random integer g is chosen to satisfy specific conditions, forming the public key (n,g). The private key (λ,μ) is then calculated, where μ depends on g and λ. The pseudocode of the same is given in Algorithm 1 below.

Algorithm 1: Key_Generation_Paillier

Input: Security parameter λ

Output: Public key (n, g) and Private key (λ, μ)

1. Select two large prime numbers p and q.
2. Compute $n = pq$ and $\lambda = 1\text{cm}(p - 1, q - 1)$.
3. Select a random integer g such that $g\hat{\ }n \bmod n\hat{\ }2 = 1$.
4. Compute $\mu = L(g\hat{\ }\lambda \bmod n\hat{\ }2)\hat{\ }(-1) \bmod n$, where $L(x) = (x - 1)/n$.
5. Output (n, g) as the public key and (λ, μ) as the private key.

   2. For encryption, a random integer r is chosen, and the ciphertext c is computed using the plaintext message m, the public key (n,g), and the random factor r. The pseudocode of the same is given in Algorithm 2 below.

Algorithm 2: Encryption_Paillier

Input: Public key (n, g), Plaintext message m

Output: Ciphertext c

1. Select a random integer r such that $1 \le r < n$.
2. Compute $c = g\hat{\ }m * r\hat{\ }n \bmod n\hat{\ }2$.

3. Output c as the ciphertext.

3. Decryption, on the other hand, utilizes the private key (λ,μ) to reverse the encryption process. It involves computing a function of the ciphertext, yielding the original plaintext message. The pseudocode of the same is given in Algorithm 3 below.

Algorithm 3: Decryption_Paillier

Input: Input: Private key (λ, μ), Ciphertext c

Output: Plaintext message m

1. Compute $L(c^\wedge\lambda \bmod n^\wedge 2)$.
2. Compute $m = \mu * L(c^\wedge\lambda \bmod n^\wedge 2) \bmod n$.
3. Output m as the plaintext message.

4. In practical terms, the Paillier Encryption Algorithm finds applications in scenarios where secure computation with additive homomorphism is crucial. The key generation ensures a secure foundation, encryption transforms the plaintext, and decryption allows the recovery of the original message, contributing to the delicate balance between security and privacy.

2. **RSA Encryption Algorithm:** The RSA Encryption Algorithm, primarily renowned for public key encryption, exhibits homomorphic properties under specific circumstances. Here, we delve into the key generation, encryption, and decryption processes, outlining each step without delving into mathematical equations.

5. For key generation, two large prime numbers, p and q, are selected, and their product n is computed. The totient function $\varphi(n)$ is determined based on p and q. An integer e is then chosen such that it is coprime with $\varphi(n)$, and its modular multiplicative inverse d is computed. The resulting public key is (n,e), and the private key is d. The pseudocode of the same is given in Algorithm 4 below.

Algorithm 4: Key_Generation_RSA

Input: Security parameter λ

Output: Public key (n, e) and Private key (d)

1. Select two large prime numbers p and q.
2. Compute $n = pq$ and $\varphi(n) = (p - 1)(q - 1)$.
3. Select an integer e such that $1 < e < \varphi(n)$ and $gcd(e, \varphi(n)) = 1$.
4. Compute d as the modular multiplicative inverse of e modulo $\varphi(n)$.
5. Output (n, e) as the public key and d as the private key.
6. The encryption process involves taking the plaintext message m and raising it to the power of e, followed by a modulus operation with n. This yields the ciphertext c, which is the output of the encryption algorithm. The pseudocode of the same is given in Algorithm 5 below.

Algorithm 5: Encryption_RSA

Input: Public key (n, e), Plaintext message m

Output: Ciphertex

1. Compute $c = m$^e mod n.
2. Output c as the ciphertext.

6. Decryption utilizes the private key d, and the ciphertext c is raised to the power of d with a modulus operation using n. The result is the retrieval of the original plaintext message m, concluding the decryption algorithm. The pseudocode of the same is given in Algorithm 6 below.

Algorithm 6: Decryption_RSA

Input: Private key (d), Ciphertext c

Output: Plaintext message m

1. Compute $m = c$^d mod n.
2. Output m as the plaintext message.

7. In practical applications, RSA's homomorphic nature, especially in scenarios involving secure computations, makes it a versatile choice for privacy-preserving operations. The key generation ensures a secure foundation, encryption transforms the plaintext, and decryption allows the recovery of the original message, contributing to the delicate balance between security and privacy.

3. **Fully Homomorphic Encryption (FHE)** represents a breakthrough in cryptographic techniques, allowing for advanced homomorphic capabilities by enabling both addition and multiplication operations on encrypted data. This section explores the intricacies of FHE, shedding light on its fundamental principles and real-world applications.

8. At its core, FHE is designed to operate on data in its encrypted form, offering a unique level of privacy and security. Traditional encryption methods, while securing data during storage and transmission, typically require decryption for any meaningful computation. FHE, however, empowers computations to be performed directly on encrypted data, preserving its confidentiality throughout the process.

9. The primary distinction of FHE lies in its support for both addition and multiplication operations. This dual functionality significantly expands the scope of computations that can be carried out on encrypted data. Addition and multiplication are fundamental operations in mathematical computations, and FHE's ability to handle both unlocks a wide range of applications, from secure data processing in the cloud to privacy-preserving machine learning.

9.2.2.1 Key Characteristics of Fully Homomorphic Encryption

- **Addition and Multiplication Support:** FHE allows computations involving addition and multiplication on encrypted data, providing a versatile set of operations.
- **Preserving Data Confidentiality:** The encryption remains intact throughout the computation process, ensuring that sensitive information is never exposed.
- **Versatility in Applications:** FHE finds applications in scenarios where privacy is paramount, such as SMPC, privacy-preserving machine learning, and collaborative data processing.

9.2.2.2 Real-World Implications and Applications

- **Secure Cloud Computing:** FHE enables secure computations on data stored in the cloud without the need for decryption, ensuring that sensitive information is never revealed to the cloud service provider.
- **Privacy-Preserving Machine Learning:** In machine learning applications, FHE allows for training and inference on encrypted data, maintaining the privacy of individual data points while deriving valuable insights.
- **Collaborative Data Processing:** FHE facilitates secure collaboration on data across different entities, allowing computations on encrypted data without compromising confidentiality.

9.2.3 Implementing Homomorphic Encryption in Cloud Scenarios

The adoption of homomorphic encryption in cloud scenarios presents a paradigm shift in securing sensitive data while allowing meaningful computations. This subsection delves into the intricacies of implementing homomorphic encryption in the cloud, offering practical insights through real-world scenarios.

1. **Secure Data Sharing in Healthcare**
   - **Scenario:** Healthcare providers need to collaboratively analyze patient data without compromising individual privacy.
   - **Implementation:** Homomorphic encryption enables secure sharing of encrypted patient records, allowing computations on the encrypted data without exposing sensitive details.
2. **Privacy-Preserving Analytics in Financial Computations**
   - **Scenario:** Financial institutions aim to perform collaborative analytics on transaction data without revealing customer-specific details.
   - **Implementation:** Homomorphic encryption is integrated into cloud-based financial systems, enabling secure computations on encrypted transaction records while preserving customer privacy.
3. **Confidential Data Processing in Government Clouds:**
   - **Scenario:** Government agencies require secure processing of confidential data stored in the cloud for policy analysis.

- **Implementation:** Homomorphic encryption ensures that sensitive governmental data remains encrypted during computations, maintaining the confidentiality of policy-related information.

4. **Secure Data Collaboration in Research Environments**
   - **Scenario:** Research institutions need to collaborate on sensitive research data without exposing individual contributions.
   - **Implementation:** Homomorphic encryption is employed to enable encrypted data collaboration, allowing researchers to jointly analyze information while protecting the privacy of individual datasets.
5. **Privacy-Enhanced Cloud-Based Machine Learning**
   - **Scenario:** Organizations want to leverage cloud-based machine learning services without disclosing proprietary training datasets.
   - **Implementation:** Homomorphic encryption is applied to machine learning models in the cloud, enabling secure model training and inference without the need to decrypt sensitive training data.

9.2.4 Google Cloud and AWS Support for Homomorphic Encryption

Major cloud service providers, including Google Cloud and AWS, play a crucial role in advancing the adoption of homomorphic encryption. This part explores the support and tools offered by Google Cloud and AWS for implementing homomorphic encryption in cloud environments. Examining specific services, such as Google's Confidential VMs or AWS's Key Management Service, showcases the commitment of these platforms to enhancing data security and privacy through homomorphic encryption.

9.2.4.1 Google Cloud's Contribution

9.2.4.1.1 Confidential VMs

- **Overview:** Google Cloud offers Confidential VMs, a specialized computing environment designed to keep workloads confidential and isolated.
- **Homomorphic Integration:** Confidential VMs provide a secure infrastructure for implementing homomorphic encryption, ensuring that computational processes on sensitive data remain confidential throughout.

9.2.4.2 AWS's Commitment

9.2.4.2.1 AWS Key Management Service (KMS)

- **Overview:** AWS KMS is a fully managed service for creating and controlling cryptographic keys used to encrypt data.
- **Homomorphic Integration:** AWS KMS plays a pivotal role in homomorphic encryption scenarios by providing a secure key management infrastructure, allowing users to generate and manage encryption keys securely.

9.2.4.3 Comparative Analysis

9.2.4.3.1 Google Cloud vs. AWS

- **Overview:** A comparative analysis sheds light on the unique offerings of Google Cloud and AWS in supporting homomorphic encryption.

- **Tools Evaluation:** Specific tools provided by each platform, such as Google's Confidential VMs and AWS's KMS, are evaluated in terms of their homomorphic encryption capabilities and ease of integration.

9.2.4.4 Real-World Implementation

In the realm of homomorphic encryption, real-world implementation through diverse use cases stands as a testament to the efficacy of this advanced cryptographic technique. Google Cloud and AWS, with their specialized tools like Confidential VMs and KMS, have played pivotal roles in bringing these success stories to fruition.

1. **Healthcare Data Collaboration**
   - **Overview:** Homomorphic encryption finds significant application in healthcare scenarios where collaboration among institutions is vital for research.
   - **Tools in Action:** Confidential VMs on Google Cloud and KMS on AWS enable secure and confidential data sharing among healthcare organizations, ensuring compliance with privacy regulations.
2. **Financial Computations in the Cloud**
   - **Overview:** Financial institutions often grapple with the challenge of performing complex computations on sensitive data securely.
   - **Tools in Action:** The deployment of homomorphic encryption tools provided by both Google Cloud and AWS facilitates secure financial computations, preserving the confidentiality of critical financial information.
3. **Privacy-Preserving Analytics**
   - **Overview:** Organizations handling large datasets for analytics face the challenge of balancing insights with data privacy.
   - **Tools in Action:** Leveraging tools like Confidential VMs and KMS, companies can perform analytics on encrypted data, ensuring privacy is maintained throughout the analytical process.
4. **Secure Cloud-based Machine Learning**
   - **Overview:** Machine learning models often require collaborative efforts involving multiple stakeholders, raising concerns about data privacy.
   - **Tools in Action:** Confidential VMs on Google Cloud and KMS on AWS contribute to the secure execution of machine learning algorithms on encrypted data, fostering collaborative model development.
5. **Encrypted Data Processing in Government Initiatives**
   - **Overview:** Government agencies dealing with sensitive information necessitate secure data processing mechanisms.
   - **Tools in Action:** The implementation of homomorphic encryption tools provided by major cloud platforms ensures that confidential government data is processed securely and remains shielded from unauthorized access.

9.3 DIFFERENTIAL PRIVACY IN CLOUD ENVIRONMENTS

The bedrock of differential privacy, a groundbreaking concept in safeguarding individual privacy while extracting valuable insights, is explored in this section. Moreover, a deep dive into the practical implementation of differential privacy within cloud analytics is undertaken. The narrative extends further by presenting a comparative analysis of the tools offered by two major cloud service providers, Google Cloud and AWS [13–16].

1. **Foundations of Differential Privacy**
   - **Overview:** At the heart of this exploration lies the fundamental concept of differential privacy, which ensures that the inclusion or exclusion of a single data point does not significantly impact the outcome of a computation.
   - **Implementation:** Cloud environments present a unique set of challenges for implementing differential privacy due to distributed data and diverse data processing scenarios.
2. **Differential Privacy in Cloud Analytics:**
   - **Overview:** The integration of differential privacy into cloud analytics reflects a commitment to balancing data utility with individual privacy rights.
   - **Implementation:** Cloud analytics platforms, such as Google Cloud and AWS, deploy differential privacy mechanisms to process data securely while adhering to stringent privacy standards.
3. **Comparative Analysis of Tools:**
   - **Overview:** Google Cloud and AWS, as leading cloud service providers, offer differential privacy tools to empower organizations in their data analytics endeavors.
   - **Strengths and Limitations:** A meticulous comparative analysis delves into the strengths and limitations of the differential privacy tools provided by both platforms. This analysis considers factors such as ease of integration, scalability, and the level of privacy preservation achieved.

9.3.1 Case Scenarios

- **Scenario 1 –** Secure Data Aggregation: Differential privacy tools in Google Cloud and AWS enable secure aggregation of data from multiple sources without compromising individual privacy, ensuring accurate analytics without divulging sensitive details.
- **Scenario 2 –** Privacy-Preserving Machine Learning:* Organizations leverage the differential privacy mechanisms on both cloud platforms to enable collaborative machine learning, fostering innovation while maintaining data privacy.
- **Scenario 3 –** Comparative Analysis Benchmark:* A benchmarking exercise compares the performance of differential privacy tools in various scenarios, offering insights into their efficacy and applicability.

9.4 SMPC IN INDUSTRY

In the realm of industrial data processing, the spotlight is on Secure Multiparty Computation (SMPC), a transformative paradigm that underpins collaborative efforts while ensuring data security. This section takes a comprehensive dive into the protocols and practical applications of SMPC, shedding light on its vital role in facilitating secure collaborations within various industry sectors.

1. **Understanding SMPC Protocols**
   - **Overview:** Secure Multiparty Computation involves multiple parties jointly analyzing their data without revealing individual inputs, thereby preserving confidentiality.
   - **Protocols:** This section elucidates key SMPC protocols, such as Yao's Garbled Circuits, Oblivious Transfer, and Secret Sharing, providing a foundation for secure collaborative computation.
2. **Practical Applications of SMPC**
   - **Overview:** The practical applications of SMPC span a spectrum of industries, from finance to healthcare, where collaborative data processing is paramount.
   - **Industry Use Cases:** Real-world scenarios are explored to illustrate how SMPC is employed in industries like finance for secure collaborative financial modeling and in healthcare for collaborative research without exposing sensitive patient data.
3. **Collaborative Data Processing in Real-World Scenarios**

   10. **Overview:** The section extends beyond theory to showcase how SMPC is leveraged in authentic industry settings for collaborative data processing.

9.4.1 Real-World Examples

- **Financial Sector Collaboration:** In financial institutions, SMPC ensures secure collaborative financial modeling, enabling organizations to collectively analyze market trends without revealing proprietary information.
- **Healthcare Research:** SMPC facilitates collaborative research in healthcare by allowing multiple entities to analyze patient data collectively, fostering medical advancements while preserving patient privacy.
- **Supply Chain Security:** Industries with intricate supply chains utilize SMPC for secure collaborative planning, enabling efficient coordination without exposing sensitive supply chain data.

9.5 PRIVACY-PRESERVING MACHINE LEARNING IN CLOUD

In the evolving landscape of machine learning, privacy preservation has emerged as a critical consideration. This chapter delves into the intricate domain of privacy-preserving machine learning within cloud environments, unraveling the nuances of federated learning use cases, addressing practical challenges, and exploring cutting-edge solutions. The spotlight is also on the strategic utilization of leading cloud platforms, namely Google Cloud AI Platform and AWS SageMaker, to foster privacy-preserving practices in machine learning [17–20].

1. **Federated Learning Use Cases**
   11. The chapter begins by elucidating the concept of federated learning, an innovative approach where models are trained across decentralized devices, preserving data privacy. Real-world use cases, ranging from mobile applications to edge computing, exemplify the versatility and applicability of federated learning.
2. **Practical Challenges and Solutions**
   - **Navigating the Privacy Dilemma:** The discourse extends to the practical challenges encountered in privacy-preserving machine learning, including concerns about data security, model robustness, and communication overhead.
   - **Innovative Solutions:** The chapter presents innovative solutions, such as cryptographic techniques, secure aggregation protocols, and privacy-enhancing technologies, designed to overcome the challenges posed by privacy-preserving machine learning in cloud environments.
3. **Leveraging Cloud Giants for Privacy-Preserving ML**
   - **Google Cloud AI Platform:** The narrative explores how the Google Cloud AI Platform serves as a catalyst for implementing privacy-preserving machine learning. From model training to deployment, Google Cloud offers a secure environment for organizations aiming to safeguard sensitive information.
   - **AWS SageMaker:** The discussion extends to AWS SageMaker, showcasing how Amazon's robust machine learning service integrates privacy-preserving mechanisms. By leveraging SageMaker, organizations can embark on privacy-centric machine learning journeys without compromising the scalability and efficiency of their models.

9.6 CASE STUDIES ON PRIVACY-PRESERVING COMPUTATION

9.6.1 Case Study 1: Healthcare Data Sharing

- **Scenario:** In the healthcare sector, a case study focuses on enabling collaborative research by securely sharing patient data. The challenge lies in balancing the need for researchers to access valuable insights for medical advancements while ensuring the confidentiality and privacy rights of patients.
- **Implementation:** Privacy-preserving computation techniques, including homomorphic encryption, are employed to enable secure data sharing. The encryption allows computations to be performed on the encrypted data

directly, preserving patient privacy. The case study evaluates the effectiveness of this approach in facilitating collaborative healthcare research without compromising data security.

- **Success Metrics:** The success of the implementation is measured by the number of research collaborations facilitated, advancements in medical knowledge, and, critically, the maintenance of patient confidentiality. Metrics include the number of participating healthcare institutions, the speed of data processing, and feedback from researchers on the usability of the privacy-preserving framework.

9.6.2 Case Study 2: Financial Computations in the Cloud

- **Scenario:** A financial institution aims to conduct complex computations involving sensitive financial data in a cloud environment. The challenge is to ensure the confidentiality of financial transactions while allowing secure collaborative data processing.
- **Implementation:** SMPC protocols are implemented to enable secure collaboration on financial computations. This involves distributed computation where multiple parties jointly compute a function over their inputs while keeping those inputs private. The case study assesses the feasibility and efficiency of SMPC in financial scenarios.
- **Success Metrics:** The success of this case study is measured by the accuracy of financial computations, the time taken for collaborative processing, and the level of security achieved. Metrics include the speed of transaction processing, the accuracy of computed results, and feedback from financial analysts on the usability of the privacy-preserving protocols.

9.6.3 Case Study 3: Privacy-Preserving Machine Learning

- **Scenario:** Organizations aim to leverage machine learning models for data analysis without compromising the privacy of individual user data. This case study explores the implementation of federated learning use cases in the cloud environment.
- **Implementation:** Federated Learning, supported by tools like Google Cloud AI Platform and AWS SageMaker, is implemented to enable collaborative machine learning across distributed datasets. The case study evaluates the accuracy of machine learning models, the efficiency of training, and the level of privacy preservation achieved through federated learning.
- **Success Metrics:** Success is gauged by the accuracy of machine learning predictions, the model's performance on diverse datasets, and the level of privacy maintained. Metrics include model accuracy, training time, and user feedback on the perceived privacy protection achieved by the federated learning approach.

9.7 FUTURE DIRECTIONS IN PRIVACY-PRESERVING TECHNOLOGIES

The concluding section outlines next-generation privacy-preserving tools and anticipates the impact of AI advancements on privacy preservation in the future [21–25].

9.7.1 Next-Generation Privacy-Preserving Tools

The assessment of privacy-preserving tools involves a comprehensive examination of emerging technologies in the field. An emphasis on the need for advanced cryptographic techniques, secure computation protocols, and innovative approaches to fortify privacy in an ever-changing digital landscape.

9.7.1.1 Focus Areas

- **Post-Quantum Cryptography:** The discussion centers around post-quantum cryptographic techniques, exploring encryption methods resilient to quantum threats. Tools like NTRUEncrypt or Falcon are considered as successors to current cryptographic algorithms.
- **Advanced Homomorphic Encryption Schemes:** Delving into sophisticated homomorphic encryption approaches, the exploration includes advancements beyond current schemes, envisioning tools that can perform complex computations on encrypted data. Potential tools may include improvements upon existing schemes like BFV (Brakerski-Vaikuntanathan-Fan) or CKKS (Cheon-Kim-Kim-Song).
- **Improved Differential Privacy Mechanisms:** The section envisions tools that enhance differential privacy, ensuring stronger protection of individual data in aggregate analyses. Innovations may include refined noise injection methods or mechanisms that balance privacy and utility more effectively.

9.7.2 Anticipating AI Advancements on Privacy Preservation

As AI technologies progress, the section anticipates their impact on privacy preservation. Recognition of the need for privacy-aware AI algorithms and models to align technological progress with ethical considerations [26–28].

9.7.2.1 Focus Areas

1. **Federated Learning Enhancements:** Envisaging improvements in federated learning, the section explores tools that enhance collaborative model training across decentralized devices while preserving individual data privacy. Potential enhancements may include optimized federated learning frameworks like TensorFlow Federated.
2. **Privacy-Respecting AI Models:** The exploration extends to the development of AI models designed with inherent respect for privacy constraints. This involves researching and implementing algorithms that minimize data exposure while maintaining model accuracy.

3. **Integration into Mainstream AI Frameworks:** Anticipating the integration of privacy-preserving techniques into mainstream AI frameworks, the focus is on ensuring that privacy considerations become integral to the development and deployment of AI applications. This might involve extensions to popular frameworks like PyTorch or TensorFlow to seamlessly incorporate privacy-preserving functionalities.

9.8 CONCLUSION

In conclusion, this chapter has provided a comprehensive exploration of privacy-preserving computation, addressing key aspects such as homomorphic encryption, differential privacy, SMPC, and privacy-preserving machine learning in cloud environments. By navigating through theoretical foundations, practical implementations, and real-world case studies, we have underscored the critical importance of securing sensitive data while enabling collaborative data processing and machine learning. The comparative analysis of tools offered by major cloud providers, Google Cloud and AWS, has offered valuable insights into the diverse landscape of privacy-preserving technologies. The field of privacy-preserving computation is rapidly evolving, presenting exciting avenues for future research and development. The next generation of privacy-preserving tools is anticipated to integrate advanced cryptographic techniques, machine learning, and decentralized computing. Exploring novel protocols and mechanisms for SMPC, advancing the capabilities of homomorphic encryption, and addressing challenges in implementing differential privacy will be pivotal. Additionally, as AI continues to advance, the impact on privacy preservation warrants continuous attention. The integration of privacy-preserving technologies into emerging domains, such as edge computing and the IoT, holds promise for enhancing data security and confidentiality. Moreover, collaborations between academia and industry are crucial to bridge the gap between theoretical advancements and practical applications. Standardization efforts and the establishment of best practices will contribute to a more cohesive and interoperable landscape for privacy-preserving computation. As industries increasingly recognize the value of protecting user privacy, continued research and innovation in this domain will play a pivotal role in shaping the future of secure and collaborative data processing.

REFERENCES

1. Alghamdi, W., Salama, R., Sirija, M., Abbas, A. R., & Dilnoza, K. (2023). Secure multi-party computation for collaborative data analysis. In E3S *Web of Conferences* (Vol. 399, p. 04034). EDP Sciences.
2. Murthy, J. S., Siddesh, G. M., & Srinivasa, K. G. (2019). TwitSenti: a real-time Twitter sentiment analysis and visualization framework. *Journal of Information & Knowledge Management*, 18(02), 1950013.
3. Zhao, Y., Pan, S., Zhao, Y., Liao, H., Ye, L., & Zheng, Y. (2024). Ultra-short-term wind power forecasting based on personalized robust federated learning with spatial collaboration. *Energy*, *288*, 129847.

4. Murthy, J. S., & Siddesh, G. M. (2024). A smart video analytical framework for sarcasm detection using novel adaptive fusion network and SarcasNet-99 model. *The Visual Computer*, 1–13, Springer.
5. Tiwari, K., Sarkar, N., & George, J. P. (2023). Confidential training and inference using secure multi-party computation on vertically partitioned dataset. *Scalable Computing: Practice and Experience*, *24*(4), 1065–1076.
6. Sanon, S. P., Reddy, R., Lipps, C., & Schotten, H. D. (2023, January). Secure federated learning: an evaluation of homomorphic encrypted network traffic prediction. In 2023 *IEEE 20th Consumer Communications & Networking Conference* (*CCNC*) (pp. 1–6). IEEE.
7. Murthy, J. S., Siddesh, G. M., & Srinivasa, K. G. (2018). A Distributed Framework for Real-Time Twitter Sentiment Analysis and Visualization. In *Recent Findings in Intelligent Computing Techniques: Proceedings of the 5th ICACNI 2017*, Volume 3 (pp. 55–61). Springer Singapore.
8. Sotthiwat, E., Zhen, L., Li, Z., & Zhang, C. (2021, May). Partially encrypted multi-party computation for federated learning. In *2021 IEEE/ACM 21st International Symposium on Cluster, Cloud and Internet Computing* (*CCGrid*) (pp. 828–835). IEEE.
9. Gong, Y., Chen, C., & Liu, Z. (2023, April). Privacy computing technology in the context of energy Internet. In 2023 *5th International Conference on Communications, Information System and Computer Engineering* (*CISCE*) (pp. 372–376). IEEE.
10. Murthy, J. S., Matt, S. G., Venkatesh, S. K. H., & Gubbi, K. R. (2022). A real-time quantum-conscious multimodal option mining framework using deep learning. *IAES International Journal of Artificial Intelligence*, 11(3), 1019.
11. Nalagandla, R., & Pattanaik, O. (2023). *Cloud Data Security: Advanced Cryptography Algorithms* (No. 10784). EasyChair.
12. Murthy, J. S., Shekar, A. C., Bhattacharya, D., Namratha, R., & Sripriya, D. (2021). A novel framework for multimodal twitter sentiment analysis using feature learning. In *Advances in Computing and Data Sciences: 5th International Conference, ICACDS 2021, Nashik, India, April 23–24, 2021, Revised Selected Papers, Part II 5* (pp. 252–261). Springer International Publishing.
13. Farahani, B., & Monsefi, A. K. (2023). Smart and collaborative industrial IoT: A federated learning and data space approach. *Digital Communications and Networks*, *9*(2), 436–447.
14. Farahani, B., & Monsefi, A. K. (2023). Smart and collaborative industrial IoT: A federated learning and data space approach. *Digital Communications and Networks*, *9*(2), 436–447.
15. Murthy, J. S., Siddesh, G. M., & Srinivasa, K. G. (2019). A real-time twitter trend analysis and visualization framework. *International Journal on Semantic Web and Information Systems (IJSWIS)*, 15(2), 1–21.
16. Wolfe, P. F. W. (2021). *Enabling secure multi-party computation with FPGAs in the datacenter* (Doctoral dissertation, Boston University).
17. Zhang, C., Luo, X., Fan, Q., Wu, T., & Zhu, L. (2023). Enabling privacy-preserving multi-server collaborative search in smart healthcare. *Future Generation Computer Systems*, *143*, 265–276.
18. Murthy, J. S., Chitlapalli, S. S., Anirudha, U. N., & Subramanya, V. (2022, April). A Real-Time Driver Assistance System Using Object Detection and Tracking. In *International Conference on Advances in Computing and Data Sciences* (pp. 150–159). Cham: Springer International Publishing.
19. Huang, A., Liu, Y., Chen, T., Zhou, Y., Sun, Q., Chai, H., & Yang, Q. (2021). Starfl: Hybrid federated learning architecture for smart urban computing. *ACM Transactions on Intelligent Systems and Technology* (*TIST*), *12*(4), 1–23.

20. Murthy, J. S., Siddesh, G. M., Lai, W. C., Parameshachari, B. D., Patil, S. N., & Hemalatha, K. L. (2022). ObjectDetect: A Real-Time Object Detection Framework for Advanced Driver Assistant Systems Using YOLOv5. *Wireless Communications and Mobile Computing,* 2022(1), 9444360.
21. Liu, Y., Fan, T., Chen, T., Xu, Q., & Yang, Q. (2021). Fate: An industrial grade platform for collaborative learning with data protection. *The Journal of Machine Learning Research*, *22*(1), 10320–10325.
22. Murthy, J. S. (2019). Edgecloud: A distributed management system for resource continuity in edge to cloud computing environment. In *The Rise of Fog Computing in the Digital Era* (pp. 108-128). IGI Global.
23. Ntizikira, E., Lei, W., Alblehai, F., Saleem, K., & Lodhi, M. A. (2023). Secure and privacy-preserving intrusion detection and prevention in the internet of unmanned aerial vehicles. *Sensors*, *23*(19), 8077.
24. Stephanie, V., Khalil, I., Atiquzzaman, M., & Yi, X. (2022). Trustworthy privacy-preserving hierarchical ensemble and federated learning in healthcare 4.0 with blockchain. *IEEE Transactions on Industrial Informatics*, *19*(7), 7936–7945. doi: 10.1109/TII.2022.3214998.
25. Murthy, J. S., & Chitlapalli, S. S. (2022). Conceptual Analysis and Applications of Bigdata in Smart Society. In *Society 5.0: Smart Future Towards Enhancing the Quality of Society* (pp. 57-67). Singapore: Springer Nature Singapore.
26. Murthy, J. S., & Siddesh, G. M. (2023, October). AI Based Criminal Detection and Recognition System for Public Safety and Security using novel CriminalNet-228. In *International Conference on Frontiers in Computing and Systems* (pp. 3–20). Singapore: Springer Nature Singapore.
27. Murthy, J. S., & Siddesh, G. M. (2023, October). A Real-Time Framework for Automatic Sarcasm Detection Using Proposed Tensor-DNN-50 Algorithm. In *International Conference on Frontiers in Computing and Systems* (pp. 109–124). Singapore: Springer Nature Singapore.
28. Murthy, J.S., Dhanashekar, K., Siddesh, G.M. (2024). A Real-Time Video Surveillance-Based Framework for Early Plant Disease Detection Using Jetson TX1 and Novel LeafNet-104 Algorithm. In: Kole, D.K., Roy Chowdhury, S., Basu, S., Plewczynski, D., Bhattacharjee, D. (eds) Proceedings of 4th International Conference on Frontiers in Computing and Systems. COMSYS 2023. Lecture Notes in Networks and Systems, vol 975. Springer, Singapore. https://doi.org/10.1007/978-981-97-2614-1_23

10 Role-Based Virtuosity in Virtual Environments

A Technical Exploration of Access Control and Authentication Mechanisms

U. N. Anirudh and S. L. Shiva Darshan

10.1 INTRODUCTION TO SECURE VIRTUAL ENVIRONMENTS

In the rapidly evolving landscape of technology, the integration of virtualized cloud environments has become ubiquitous, providing flexibility, scalability, and efficiency in resource utilization. As organizations increasingly rely on virtualization to streamline operations, the imperative to ensure the security of these virtualized environments becomes paramount. This section delves into the foundational aspects of secure virtual environments, exploring the definition of security in the context of virtualized cloud environments and examining the latest advancements in research related to virtualization security [1,2].

10.1.1 Defining Security in Virtualized Cloud Environments

Security in virtualized cloud environments encompasses a multifaceted approach aimed at safeguarding the integrity, confidentiality, and availability of data and resources. The dynamic nature of virtualization introduces unique challenges, demanding a comprehensive understanding of potential threats and vulnerabilities. Key elements of security in this context include network security, data encryption, access controls, and the isolation of virtualized instances. Ensuring the resilience of virtual environments against cyber threats is crucial to maintaining the trust of users and stakeholders [3,4].

As organizations migrate their operations to cloud-based platforms, the need for robust security measures intensifies. The definition of security in virtualized cloud environments extends beyond traditional paradigms, considering factors such as hypervisor security, virtual machine isolation, and secure migration protocols. A holistic security strategy must address the evolving nature of virtualized infrastructures, aligning with industry best practices and compliance standards to mitigate risks effectively [5,6].

DOI: 10.1201/9781003455448-10

10.1.2 State-of-the-Art Research in Virtualization Security

The landscape of virtualization security is continually evolving, with researchers exploring innovative approaches to address emerging threats and vulnerabilities. State-of-the-art research in virtualization security encompasses a wide range of topics, including but not limited to [7–10]:

- **Hypervisor Security:** Investigating techniques to fortify the security of hypervisors, the foundational layer of virtualization, is a crucial area of research. This involves identifying and mitigating vulnerabilities that could be exploited to compromise the entire virtualized environment.
- **Container Security:** As containerization gains prominence, researchers focus on enhancing the security of containerized applications. This includes secure orchestration, image integrity verification, and isolation mechanisms to prevent unauthorized access.
- **Machine Learning in Threat Detection:** Leveraging machine learning algorithms for real-time threat detection and anomaly detection within virtualized environments is an emerging trend. This approach enables proactive responses to potential security incidents, enhancing overall system resilience.
- **Secure Migration Protocols:** Research efforts also address secure migration strategies for virtual machines and workloads, ensuring that data transfers between different virtualized instances are protected from interception or manipulation.

10.2 VIRTUALIZATION TECHNOLOGIES: A TECHNICAL DEEP DIVE

Virtualization technologies have revolutionized the way IT infrastructures are designed and managed, offering unparalleled flexibility and efficiency. This section offers a technical deep dive into the core components of virtualization technologies, with a focus on hypervisors and containers as shown in Figure 10.1, a comparative analysis of virtual machine security, and an exploration of the utilization of Google Kubernetes Engine (GKE) and AWS Elastic Container Service (ECS) in contemporary IT environments [11–13].

10.2.1 Hypervisors and Containers in Detail

Hypervisors are a central element in virtualization technology. They function as a layer of software directly above the physical hardware, enabling the creation and management of virtual machines (VMs). There are two main types of hypervisors:

- **Type 1 Hypervisors:** Also known as bare-metal hypervisors, these are installed directly on the host's hardware to control the hardware and to manage guest operating systems. Examples include VMware ESXi and Microsoft Hyper-V.
- **Type 2 Hypervisors:** These run on a conventional operating system just like other computer programs. Examples include VMware Workstation and Oracle VirtualBox.

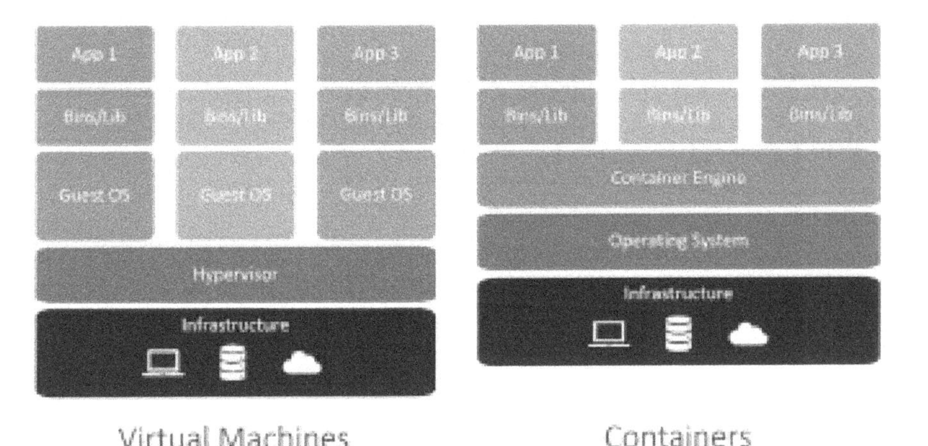

FIGURE 10.1 Virtual machines vs containers.

Containers, on the other hand, are a lighter-weight form of virtualization. Unlike VMs, which virtualize entire operating systems, containers share the host system's kernel and isolate the application processes from the rest of the system. Docker is a widely used platform for developing and running containers, providing an efficient, standardized way to package applications and their dependencies into a single object.

10.2.2 Comparative Analysis of Virtual Machine Security

Security in VMs is a critical consideration. VMs, depending on their configuration and usage, present various security challenges and advantages. Some key aspects of VM security include [14,15]:

- **Isolation:** VMs are typically well-isolated from each other, which can prevent a security breach in one VM from spreading to others.
- **Snapshot and Reversion Capabilities:** The ability to take snapshots and revert to previous states can be a powerful tool in recovering from security incidents.
- **Patch Management:** VMs require diligent patch management, just like physical servers, to protect against vulnerabilities.

However, VMs also face specific security challenges, such as hypervisor vulnerabilities, which could potentially compromise all hosted VMs. Additionally, the complexity of VM environments can create challenges in maintaining consistent security policies.

10.2.3 Leveraging GKE and AWS ECS

GKE and AWS ECS are modern platforms designed to manage containerized applications. GKE is a managed environment for deploying, managing, and scaling containerized applications using Google infrastructure. It offers automated scaling, monitoring, and management of containerized applications.

AWS ECS is a highly scalable, high-performance container orchestration service that supports Docker containers and allows users to easily run applications on a managed cluster of Amazon EC2 instances. ECS simplifies container management, allowing automated scaling and integration with AWS services.

Both GKE and ECS provide robust, scalable environments for container orchestration but differ in their integration with respective cloud environments and specific features. GKE integrates deeply with other Google Cloud services and is known for its robustness in Kubernetes operations, while ECS is known for its seamless integration with AWS services and features such as AWS Fargate, which allows running containers without having to manage servers or clusters.

10.3 NETWORK SECURITY IN VIRTUAL ENVIRONMENTS

Network security within virtual environments is a critical aspect of modern IT infrastructure. As virtualization becomes more prevalent, the strategies to secure these networks have evolved. This section delves into isolation strategies and network segmentation, explores advanced virtual network configurations, and examines the network security features available in Google Cloud and AWS, supplemented by practical examples [16–18].

10.3.1 Isolation Strategies and Network Segmentation

Isolation and segmentation are key strategies for enhancing security in virtual networks. These tactics involve dividing a network into smaller parts to limit access and reduce the potential impact of security breaches.

- **VLANs (Virtual Local Area Networks):** VLANs are a common method of network segmentation. For example, a company might have separate VLANs for its HR department, sales team, and IT infrastructure, each isolated from the others to prevent unauthorized access and mitigate risks.
- **Firewall Rules and Access Control Lists (ACLs):** These are used to control traffic between network segments. For instance, an organization may implement ACLs on their routers or firewalls to restrict traffic between the production network and the administrative network.

10.3.2 Advanced Virtual Network Configurations

Advanced virtual network configurations enable more granular control over traffic and enhanced security features.

- **Software-Defined Networking (SDN):** SDN allows network administrators to manage network services through the abstraction of lower-level functionality. For instance, using SDN, an organization can dynamically adjust network routes and policies based on current network conditions and threats.

- **Virtual Network Function (VNF):** VNFs are used to deploy network services like firewalls, load balancers, and intrusion detection systems as virtualized services. For example, a company might deploy a virtual firewall as a VNF to protect its virtualized server environment.

10.3.3 Network Security Features in Google Cloud and AWS

Both Google Cloud and AWS offer a range of network security features designed for virtual environments.

10.3.3.1 Google Cloud

- **Virtual Private Cloud (VPC):** Google Cloud's VPC allows organizations to create a private network within the Google Cloud infrastructure. For instance, a business might use VPC to create a segregated network environment for a sensitive project.
- **Cloud Armor:** This provides DDoS and web attack protection. A retail company might utilize Cloud Armor to protect its e-commerce site from DDoS attacks during high-traffic events like Black Friday.

10.3.3.2 AWS

- **Amazon VPC:** Similar to Google's VPC, Amazon VPC lets users provision a logically isolated section of the AWS Cloud. A company could use it to host a secure and scalable backend for a mobile app.
- **Security Groups and Network ACLs:** These features offer stateful and stateless traffic control, respectively. An enterprise might configure Security Groups for its EC2 instances to ensure only traffic from specific IP addresses can access the instances.

10.4 ENSURING DATA INTEGRITY AND CONFIDENTIALITY IN VIRTUALIZED ENVIRONMENTS

In the realm of virtualized environments, maintaining data integrity and confidentiality is paramount. This section explores the encryption protocols for VMs and containers, secure data transmission protocols, and real-world implementation scenarios in Google Cloud and AWS. It includes examples and industry case studies to illustrate these concepts [19,20].

10.4.1 Encryption Protocols for VMs and Containers

Encryption is crucial in safeguarding data in VMs and containers. It ensures that data remains confidential and unaltered during storage and transit.

- **VM Encryption:** VMware, for instance, offers VM encryption. This solution encrypts VM files, ensuring that data is unreadable to unauthorized users. In a healthcare scenario, a hospital might use VM encryption to protect patient records, complying with regulations like HIPAA.

- **Container Image Encryption:** Projects like Docker Content Trust provide mechanisms to verify the integrity and publisher of all the data in a container image. In a software development company, this means ensuring that the container images used in production are secure and tamper-proof.

10.4.2 Secure Data Transmission Protocols

Secure data transmission is critical for preventing data breaches during transit.

- **TLS/SSL:** Transport Layer Security (TLS) and its predecessor, Secure Sockets Layer (SSL), are widely used protocols for secure data transmission. An e-commerce site, for example, employs TLS to secure customer transactions and protect sensitive data like credit card information.
- **SSH (Secure Shell):** SSH is used for secure data communication, particularly in administrative contexts. A cloud service provider might use SSH for secure administrative access to servers.

10.4.3 Real-World Implementation Scenarios in Google Cloud and AWS

Various industries have leveraged Google Cloud and AWS to ensure data integrity and confidentiality in their virtualized environments [21,22].

10.4.3.1 Google Cloud Case Study

- **Confidential VMs:** Google Cloud offers Confidential VMs, which are designed to encrypt data in use. A financial services firm could use Confidential VMs to protect sensitive client data while performing computations, ensuring data confidentiality even from cloud administrators.

10.4.3.2 AWS Case Study

- **Amazon RDS Encryption:** AWS provides encryption at rest for databases using Amazon RDS. For instance, a retail company could utilize Amazon RDS encryption to protect customer data, ensuring that this information is encrypted when stored in the database.
- **AWS KMS (Key Management Service):** This service is used to create and manage encryption keys. A software company might use AWS KMS to manage keys that encrypt its application data, ensuring both security and compliance with industry standards.

10.5 IDENTITY AND ACCESS MANAGEMENT IN VIRTUALIZED CLOUD

Identity and Access Management (IAM) is a cornerstone of security in virtualized cloud environments, ensuring that only authorized individuals have access to specific resources. This section examines Role-Based Access Control (RBAC) in virtual environments, advanced authentication mechanisms, and the integration of IAM best practices with Google Cloud Identity and Access Management and AWS Identity and Access Management, supported by examples and industry case studies.

10.5.1 RBAC in Virtual Environments

RBAC is a method of restricting network access based on individual user roles within an enterprise. In virtual environments, RBAC is crucial for maintaining fine-grained control over resources [23].

Example: In a hospital's virtualized data environment, RBAC could be used to ensure that only doctors can access patient medical records, while administrative staff have access only to non-sensitive patient information.

Case Study: A global bank implemented RBAC across its virtualized cloud infrastructure. By defining roles such as 'administrator', 'user', and 'auditor', the bank could assign specific permissions and access levels, ensuring that employees accessed only the data necessary for their roles, significantly reducing the risk of data breaches.

10.5.2 Advanced Authentication Mechanisms

Advanced authentication mechanisms are essential in reinforcing security, especially in cloud-based virtual environments.

- **Multi-Factor Authentication (MFA):** MFA requires users to provide multiple proofs of identity. For instance, a tech company might require employees to use a password and a biometric scan to access its virtualized cloud environment.
- **Single Sign-On (SSO):** SSO allows users to log in once and gain access to multiple related but independent software systems. A multinational corporation could implement SSO to simplify access to various services across its global offices while maintaining security.

10.5.3 Integrating IAM Best Practices with Google Cloud Identity and Access Management and AWS Identity and Access Management

Integrating IAM best practices with platforms like Google Cloud IAM and AWS IAM is vital for cloud security.

- **Google Cloud IAM Case Study:** A media streaming service used Google Cloud IAM to manage user access to its cloud resources. By defining custom roles and permissions, the company could easily control who had the ability to modify the streaming infrastructure and access sensitive data, thus enhancing overall security.
- **AWS IAM Case Study:** An e-commerce platform utilized AWS IAM for securely managing access to its AWS services. By implementing fine-grained access controls, the platform ensured that developers could only access resources necessary for their job functions, minimizing the potential for accidental or malicious changes to critical resources.
- **Best Practices Implementation:** Both case studies illustrate best practices like least privilege access, regular audits of IAM permissions, and the use of automated tools to manage user permissions at scale.

10.6 MONITORING AND INCIDENT RESPONSE IN VIRTUALIZED ENVIRONMENTS

Effective monitoring and incident response are vital for maintaining the security and integrity of virtualized environments. This involves using real-time monitoring tools, developing robust incident response strategies, and utilizing the toolkits provided by cloud services like Google Cloud and AWS [24,25].

10.6.1 Real-Time Monitoring Tools for Virtualized Infrastructures

Real-time monitoring tools provide insights into the performance and security of virtualized infrastructures, allowing for prompt detection and resolution of issues.

- **Example:** VMware vRealize Operations: This tool offers comprehensive monitoring capabilities across virtualized environments. It provides operational insights and analytics, helping organizations to optimize performance and predict resource needs. For instance, a financial institution might use vRealize Operations to monitor their VMs' performance and ensure they are running optimally for high-frequency trading platforms.
- **Example:** SolarWinds Virtualization Manager: SolarWinds offers a solution for managing VMware and Hyper-V environments. It helps in identifying and fixing inefficiencies in virtual environments. A large e-commerce company could leverage this tool to monitor their virtual servers and ensure that customer-facing applications have the necessary resources, especially during peak shopping periods.

10.6.2 Incident Response Strategies in Virtualized Environments

Having a well-defined incident response strategy is crucial for minimizing the impact of security incidents in virtual environments.

- **Regular Drills and Scenario Planning:** Regularly conducting incident response drills can prepare an organization for various scenarios. For instance, a cloud service provider might simulate a data breach or DDoS attack to train their team in rapid and effective response.
- **Forensic Analysis and Segregation:** In the event of an incident, conducting a forensic analysis to understand the cause and segregating affected systems to contain the breach are essential steps. A healthcare organization, for example, might isolate affected VMs immediately upon detecting a ransomware infection, preventing its spread to other parts of the network.

10.6.3 Google Cloud and AWS Toolkits for Monitoring and Incident Response

Both Google Cloud and AWS provide comprehensive toolkits for monitoring and incident response.

- **Google Cloud Monitoring and Logging:** Google Cloud offers integrated monitoring and logging services that allow for real-time tracking of cloud resources and applications. An online gaming company could use these tools to monitor their gaming servers hosted on Google Cloud, ensuring high availability and performance.
- **AWS CloudWatch and AWS CloudTrail:** AWS CloudWatch provides monitoring for AWS cloud resources, while CloudTrail tracks user activity and API usage. A fintech startup could use CloudWatch to monitor their application's health and CloudTrail to audit changes in their AWS environment, ensuring compliance with financial regulations.
- **Incident Response Tools:** Both Google Cloud and AWS offer tools and guidelines for incident response. AWS, for example, provides the AWS Incident Response Whitepaper to guide organizations in developing and implementing effective incident response strategies.

10.7 CASE STUDIES ON SECURE VIRTUAL ENVIRONMENTS

In this section, we delve into industry use cases with an emphasis on Google Cloud and AWS deployments, analyzing the security challenges faced and the resolutions achieved. Each case study will be explored with detailed implementation steps.

10.7.1 Case Study 1: E-Commerce Company Migrating to AWS

Challenge: An e-commerce company faced challenges in scaling its operations and ensuring data security during high-traffic events like Black Friday sales.

Resolution: The company decided to migrate to AWS for its scalability and robust security features.

10.7.1.1 Implementation Steps

1. **Infrastructure Assessment and Planning:**
   - Conducted a comprehensive assessment of the existing e-commerce infrastructure.
   - Developed a migration plan focusing on minimal downtime and security.
2. **AWS Environment Setup:**
   - Configured AWS VPC for isolated network environment.
   - Established AWS IAM roles and policies for secure access control.
3. **Data Migration and Encryption:**
   - Migrated data to AWS S3, implementing server-side encryption for data at rest.
   - Utilized AWS Database Migration Service for secure database transfer.
4. **Application Deployment and Auto-Scaling:**
   - Deployed e-commerce applications on AWS Elastic Beanstalk for automated scaling and management.
   - Implemented AWS Auto-Scaling to handle traffic surges during peak times.

5. **Security Measures and Monitoring:**
   - Integrated AWS WAF (Web Application Firewall) to protect against web exploits.
   - Set up AWS CloudTrail and AWS Config for continuous monitoring and auditing.
6. **Regular Security Audits and Compliance Checks:**
   - Conducted regular security audits using AWS Trusted Advisor.
   - Ensured compliance with PCI DSS standards for payment processing.

10.7.2 Case Study 2: Financial Services Firm Adopting Google Cloud

Challenge: A financial services firm needed to enhance its data analytics capabilities while ensuring compliance with financial regulations and data security.

Resolution: The firm chose Google Cloud for its advanced data analytics tools and compliance features.

10.7.2.1 Implementation Steps

1. **Compliance and Security Planning:**
   - Evaluated regulatory requirements specific to the financial industry.
   - Drafted a security and compliance roadmap aligning with GDPR and other financial regulations.
2. **Google Cloud Setup and Data Encryption:**
   - Configured Google Cloud resources, ensuring all data is encrypted at rest and in transit.
   - Used Google Cloud Key Management Service for managing encryption keys.
3. **Big Data Analytics and Private Connectivity:**
   - Deployed BigQuery for large-scale data analytics.
   - Set up Cloud Interconnect for secure, private connections between Google Cloud and on-premises environments.
4. **Identity and Access Management:**
   - Implemented RBAC using Google Cloud IAM.
   - Integrated multi-factor authentication for enhanced security.
5. **Monitoring and Incident Response:**
   - Utilized Google Cloud's operations suite for real-time monitoring and logging.
   - Developed an incident response strategy using Google Cloud's security command center.
6. **Regular Compliance Audits:**
   - Conducted periodic audits using Google Cloud's compliance and security tools.
   - Regularly reviewed access logs and security settings to maintain a high-security posture.

10.8 FUTURE TRENDS IN VIRTUALIZATION SECURITY

The landscape of virtualization security is continuously evolving, with new trends, security measures, and emerging technologies shaping its future. This section explores these dimensions, particularly in the context of Google Cloud and AWS.

10.8.1 Evolving Security Measures in Virtual Environments

1. **Zero Trust Architecture (ZTA):** A security concept where trust is never assumed and verification is required from everyone trying to access resources in the network. This approach is becoming integral in virtual environments for preventing data breaches.
2. **AI-Driven Threat Detection:** Leveraging artificial intelligence to predict and identify potential threats in real time, enhancing the ability to respond to security incidents quickly and effectively.
3. **Quantum-Resistant Cryptography:** As quantum computing evolves, developing cryptography that can withstand quantum attacks is becoming crucial for protecting sensitive data in virtual environments.
4. **Microsegmentation:** This involves breaking down security perimeters into small zones to maintain separate access for separate parts of the network. It is becoming more prevalent in cloud environments to enhance security and limit the spread of attacks.
5. **Blockchain for Data Integrity:** Utilizing blockchain technology to ensure data integrity and prevent unauthorized data manipulation in distributed virtual environments.
6. **Enhanced Endpoint Security:** With the rise of IoT and mobile devices, securing every endpoint that accesses the virtual environment is critical for preventing security breaches.
7. **Automated Security Compliance:** Implementing automated tools for continuous monitoring and ensuring compliance with ever-evolving regulations and standards.
8. **Extended Detection and Response (XDR):** An emerging approach that provides a more comprehensive threat detection and response by combining multiple security products into a cohesive security operation.
9. **Federated Identity Management:** As cloud services proliferate, managing identities across multiple platforms and environments is essential for security and compliance.
10. **Serverless Security Architectures:** With the rise of serverless computing, ensuring the security of these environments, where traditional perimeter defenses are not applicable, is becoming increasingly important.

10.8.2 Integrating Emerging Technologies for Enhanced Virtualization Security in Google Cloud and AWS

1. **Machine Learning for Anomaly Detection:** Both AWS and Google Cloud are integrating machine learning algorithms to detect anomalies in network traffic and user behavior, thereby identifying potential threats early [26–28].
2. **IoT Security Management:** As IoT devices increasingly interact with cloud environments, AWS and Google Cloud are focusing on enhanced security measures specific to IoT.
3. **Implementation of Confidential Computing:** This involves encrypting data in use, which is particularly important in multi-tenant cloud environments. Google Cloud's Confidential VMs and AWS Nitro Enclaves are examples.
4. **Cloud Access Security Brokers:** These are security policy enforcement points placed between cloud service users and cloud applications to monitor activity and enforce security policies.
5. **Secure Access Service Edge:** This emerging framework combines network security functions with wide-area networking capabilities to support the dynamic, secure access needs of organizations.
6. **Integration of DevSecOps:** Emphasizing security in the DevOps process, Google Cloud and AWS offer tools and best practices for integrating security into the software development lifecycle.
7. **Edge Computing Security:** As edge computing grows, ensuring the security of these distributed computing environments becomes vital. Both AWS and Google Cloud are developing solutions to secure edge deployments.
8. **Automated Patch Management:** Automated tools for patch management are becoming integral in Google Cloud and AWS to ensure that all systems are up-to-date with the latest security patches.
9. **Enhanced Data Loss Prevention (DLP):** DLP technologies are evolving to offer more sophisticated monitoring and protection of sensitive data across virtual environments.
10. **Adoption of Security as a Service:** This model allows businesses to outsource their security needs to cloud providers, which is being increasingly adopted in AWS and Google Cloud ecosystems for streamlined and enhanced security management.

REFERENCES

1. Almutairy, N. M., Al-Shqeerat, K. H., & Al Hamad, H. A. (2019). A taxonomy of virtualization security issues in cloud computing environments. *Indian Journal of Science and Technology*, **12**(3), 1–19.
2. Murthy, J. S., Shekar, A. C., Bhattacharya, D., Namratha, R., & Sripriya, D. (2021). A novel framework for multimodal twitter sentiment analysis using feature learning. In *Advances in Computing and Data Sciences: 5th International Conference, ICACDS 2021, Nashik, India, April 23–24, 2021, Revised Selected Papers, Part II 5* (pp. 252–261). Springer International Publishing.

3. Lewis, N., & Rhee, K. H. (2014). Towards secure virtual machine migration in vehicular cloud environment. *Advanced Science and Technology Letters*, **66**, 85–89.
4. Abu-Alhaija, M., Turab, N. M., & Hamza, A. (2022). Extensive study of cloud computing technologies, threats and solutions prospective. *Computer Systems Science & Engineering*, **41**(1), 225–240.
5. Murthy, J. S., Siddesh, G. M., Lai, W. C., Parameshachari, B. D., Patil, S. N., & Hemalatha, K. L. (2022). ObjectDetect: A Real-Time Object Detection Framework for Advanced Driver Assistant Systems Using YOLOv5. *Wireless Communications and Mobile Computing*, 2022(1), 9444360.
6. Benkhelifa, E., Hani, A. B., Welsh, T., Mthunzi, S., & Guegan, C. G. (2019). Virtual environments testing as a cloud service: a methodology for protecting and securing virtual infrastructures. *IEEE Access*, **7**, 108660–108676.
7. Valencia-Arias, A., Gutiérrez, C. A. E., Agudelo, L. C. A., & Gutiérrez, M. S. E. (2024). Tendencias investigativas en el uso de Cloud Computing en contenerización entre 2015 y 2023. *Revista Virtual Universidad Católica del Norte*, **72**, 306–344.
8. Murthy, J. S., Siddesh, G. M., & Srinivasa, K. G. (2019). TwitSenti: a real-time Twitter sentiment analysis and visualization framework. *Journal of Information & Knowledge Management*, 18(02), 1950013.
9. Tamane, S. (2015). A review on virtualization: A cloud technology. *International Journal on Recent and Innovation Trends in Computing and Communication*, **3**(7), 4582–4585.
10. Murthy, J. S., Siddesh, G. M., & Srinivasa, K. G. (2018). A Distributed Framework for Real-Time Twitter Sentiment Analysis and Visualization. In *Recent Findings in Intelligent Computing Techniques: Proceedings of the 5th ICACNI 2017,* Volume 3 (pp. 55–61). Springer Singapore.
11. Wahid, K. F., Kuntze, N., & Rudolph, C. (2013, September). Trusted virtual machine management for virtualization in critical environments. In *1st International Symposium for ICS & SCADA Cyber Security Research 2013* (*ICS-CSR 2013*) *1* (pp. 48–55).
12. Chen, L., Xian, M., Liu, J., & Wang, H. (2020, April). Research on virtualization security in cloud computing. In *IOP Conference Series*: *Materials Science and Engineering* (Vol. 806, No. 1, p. 012027). IOP Publishing.
13. Murthy, J. S., Matt, S. G., Venkatesh, S. K. H., & Gubbi, K. R. (2022). A real-time quantum-conscious multimodal option mining framework using deep learning. *IAES International Journal of Artificial Intelligence,* 11(3), 1019.
14. Chadha, K., & Bajpai, A. (2012). Security aspects of cloud computing. *International Journal of Computer Applications*, **40**(8), 43–47.
15. Murthy, J. S., Chitlapalli, S. S., Anirudha, U. N., & Subramanya, V. (2022, April). A Real-Time Driver Assistance System Using Object Detection and Tracking. In *International Conference on Advances in Computing and Data Sciences* (pp. 150-159). Cham: Springer International Publishing.
16. Abu-Alhaija, M., Turab, N. M., & Hamza, A. (2022). Extensive study of cloud computing technologies, threats and solutions prospective. *Computer Systems Science & Engineering*, **41**(1), 225–240. https://doi.org/10.32604/csse.2022.019547.
17. Murthy, J. S., & Chitlapalli, S. S. (2022). Conceptual Analysis and Applications of Bigdata in Smart Society. In *Society 5.0: Smart Future Towards Enhancing the Quality of Society* (pp. 57-67). Singapore: Springer Nature Singapore.
18. Sierra-Arriaga, F., Branco, R., & Lee, B. (2020). Security issues and challenges for virtualization technologies. *ACM Computing Surveys (CSUR)*, **53**(2), 1–37.
19. Tank, D., Aggarwal, A., & Chaubey, N. (2019). Virtualization vulnerabilities, security issues, and solutions: a critical study and comparison. *International Journal of Information Technology*, **14**, 847–862.

20. Murthy, J. S. (2019). Edgecloud: A distributed management system for resource continuity in edge to cloud computing environment. In *The Rise of Fog Computing in the Digital Era* (pp. 108–128). IGI Global.
21. Rashid, A., & Chaturvedi, A. (2019). Virtualization and its role in cloud computing environment. *International Journal of Computer Sciences and Engineering*, **7**(4), 1131–1136.
22. Murthy, J. S., Siddesh, G. M., & Srinivasa, K. G. (2019). A real-time twitter trend analysis and visualization framework. *International Journal on Semantic Web and Information Systems (IJSWIS)*, 15(2), 1–21.
23. Kumar, R., & Goyal, R. (2019). On cloud security requirements, threats, vulnerabilities and countermeasures: A survey. *Computer Science Review*, **33**, 1–48.
24. Caprolu, M., Di Pietro, R., Lombardi, F., & Raponi, S. (2019, July). Edge computing perspectives: Architectures, technologies, and open security issues. In *2019 IEEE International Conference on Edge Computing* (*EDGE*) (pp. 116–123). IEEE.
25. Murthy, J. S., & Siddesh, G. M. (2024). A smart video analytical framework for sarcasm detection using novel adaptive fusion network and SarcasNet-99 model. *The Visual Computer*, 1–13, Springer.
26. Murthy, J. S., & Siddesh, G. M. (2023, October). AI Based Criminal Detection and Recognition System for Public Safety and Security using novel CriminalNet-228. In *International Conference on Frontiers in Computing and Systems* (pp. 3–20). Singapore: Springer Nature Singapore.
27. Murthy, J. S., & Siddesh, G. M. (2023, October). A Real-Time Framework for Automatic Sarcasm Detection Using Proposed Tensor-DNN-50 Algorithm. In *International Conference on Frontiers in Computing and Systems* (pp. 109–124). Singapore: Springer Nature Singapore.
28. Murthy, J.S., Dhanashekar, K., Siddesh, G.M. (2024). A Real-Time Video Surveillance-Based Framework for Early Plant Disease Detection Using Jetson TX1 and Novel LeafNet-104 Algorithm. In: Kole, D.K., Roy Chowdhury, S., Basu, S., Plewczynski, D., Bhattacharjee, D. (eds) Proceedings of 4th International Conference on Frontiers in Computing and Systems. COMSYS 2023. Lecture Notes in Networks and Systems, vol 975. Springer, Singapore. https://doi.org/10.1007/978-981-97-2614-1_23

11 Fortifying Cyber Resilience in the Ever-Changing Sky of Cloud Security

Jamuna S. Murthy, Wen-Cheng Lai, and K. Dhanashekar

11.1 INTRODUCTION TO CLOUD RISK MANAGEMENT AND GOVERNANCE

In this section, we delve into the critical aspects of Cloud Risk Management and governance, understanding the evolution of risk management in cloud environments, exploring the landscape of cloud data governance, and examining the impact of data privacy legislation on cloud operations [1,2].

11.1.1 Defining Risk in Cloud Environments

Defining Risk: Risk in cloud environments refers to the potential for adverse events or outcomes that can impact the confidentiality, integrity, and availability of data and services hosted in the cloud. It encompasses a wide range of factors, including security threats, data breaches, compliance issues, and operational disruptions [3,4].

Examples:

- **Security Vulnerabilities:** Weaknesses in cloud infrastructure or misconfigurations that can be exploited by malicious actors.
- **Data Breaches:** Unauthorized access to sensitive data stored in the cloud, leading to potential exposure or theft.
- **Compliance Risks:** Failure to adhere to regulatory requirements, leading to legal consequences and reputational damage.
- **Service Outages:** Disruptions in cloud services that can impact business operations and availability.

11.1.2 The Evolution of Cloud Risk Management

Cloud risk management has evolved in response to the dynamic nature of cloud computing. Initially, concerns were centered around traditional IT risk factors. However,

DOI: 10.1201/9781003455448-11

as cloud adoption grew, unique challenges emerged, requiring a shift in risk management strategies to address the intricacies of cloud environments as shown in Figure 11.1 [5,6].

Examples:

- **Traditional IT Risks:** Initially, organizations focused on risks such as hardware failures, software vulnerabilities, and network breaches.
- **Cloud-Specific Risks:** With the move to the cloud, new risks like shared infrastructure vulnerabilities, data privacy concerns, and vendor lock-in became prominent.
- **Shift to Shared Responsibility Model:** The adoption of a shared responsibility model clarified the division of security responsibilities between cloud service providers and customers.

11.1.3 Cloud Data Governance Landscape

Cloud data governance involves establishing policies, procedures, and controls to ensure the proper management, accessibility, and security of data in cloud environments. It encompasses data classification, access controls, and data lifecycle management [7,8].

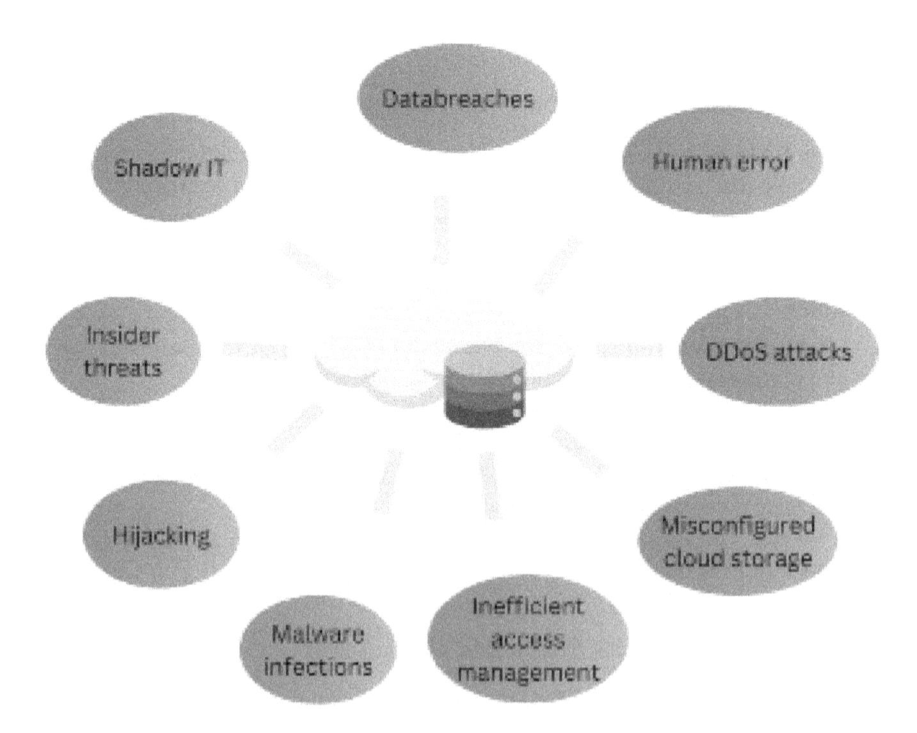

FIGURE 11.1 Overview of Cloud Risk Management.

Examples:

- **Data Classification:** Categorizing data based on sensitivity to apply appropriate security measures. For instance, confidential financial data may require stricter controls than non-sensitive information.
- **Access Controls:** Implementing granular access controls to ensure that only authorized individuals can access specific datasets in the cloud.
- **Data Lifecycle Management:** Defining processes for data creation, storage, archival, and deletion to optimize resource usage and comply with data protection regulations.

11.1.4 Overview of Data Privacy Legislation and Its Impact on Cloud Operations

Data privacy legislation, such as GDPR (General Data Protection Regulation) and CCPA (California Consumer Privacy Act), imposes strict requirements on the collection, processing, and storage of personal data. Cloud operations must align with these regulations to avoid legal consequences and maintain customer trust [9,10].

Examples:

- **GDPR Compliance:** Ensuring that cloud operations adhere to GDPR requirements, including obtaining user consent for data processing and implementing measures to protect personal data.
- **CCPA Requirements:** Complying with CCPA mandates, such as providing consumers with the right to know what personal information is collected and the right to request its deletion.
- **Global Impact:** Many organizations, even those outside the European Union (EU) or California, must adhere to these regulations if they process data of EU or California residents.

11.2 CURRENT TRENDS IN CLOUD RISK MANAGEMENT

11.2.1 Dynamic Threat Landscape in Cloud Computing

The threat landscape in cloud computing is characterized by its dynamic and evolving nature. As cloud technologies advance, threat actors continually adapt and exploit vulnerabilities. Threats include data breaches, unauthorized access, denial-of-service attacks, and increasingly sophisticated tactics [11,12].

Examples:

- **Data Breaches:** Cybercriminals exploit vulnerabilities to gain unauthorized access to sensitive data stored in the cloud, leading to potential exposure or misuse.
- **Misconfigurations:** Improperly configured cloud resources can be exploited by attackers to access sensitive information or disrupt services.
- **Phishing Attacks:** Social engineering attacks targeting cloud users through deceptive emails or messages to gain unauthorized access credentials.

11.2.2 Emerging Risks and Challenges in Cloud Environments

New challenges and risks continually arise in cloud environments due to technological advancements, increased adoption, and evolving cyber threats. These challenges include complexities in managing multi-cloud environments, addressing insider threats, and ensuring the security of serverless architectures [13].

Examples:

- **Multi-Cloud Complexity:** Organizations using multiple cloud service providers face challenges in maintaining consistent security policies, access controls, and visibility across diverse cloud environments.
- **Insider Threats:** Malicious or unintentional actions by employees or authorized users pose risks to data integrity and confidentiality.
- **Serverless Security:** The adoption of serverless computing introduces security challenges related to code vulnerabilities, event injection attacks, and inadequate monitoring.

11.2.3 Trends in Risk Assessment and Mitigation Strategies

Organizations are adopting advanced risk assessment and mitigation strategies to proactively identify and address potential threats. This includes leveraging automation, threat intelligence, and real-time monitoring for swift response to security incidents [14].

Examples:

- **Automated Risk Assessment:** Using automated tools to continuously assess the security posture of cloud environments, identifying vulnerabilities, and prioritizing remediation efforts.
- **Threat Intelligence Integration:** Incorporating threat intelligence feeds to stay informed about the latest threats and tactics used by cyber adversaries.
- **Real-Time Monitoring and Response:** Implementing solutions, such as Amazon Web Services (AWS) Security Hub, that enable real-time monitoring for immediate threat detection and automated response.

Example: Utilizing AWS Security Hub for Real-Time Threat Detection in USA-based Cloud Deployments

AWS Security Hub

AWS Security Hub is a cloud security service that provides a comprehensive view of high-priority security alerts and compliance status across AWS accounts. It aggregates, correlates, and prioritizes security findings from various AWS services.

Example Implementation

A USA-based organization deploys AWS Security Hub to enhance its Cloud Risk Management strategy. The organization configures Security Hub to centralize security findings from multiple AWS accounts. The service continuously monitors for security threats, such as unauthorized access attempts or misconfigurations, and provides real-time alerts.

Key Benefits:

- **Centralized Visibility**: AWS Security Hub provides a unified dashboard, offering centralized visibility into security findings across AWS environments.
- **Automated Threat Detection:** Security Hub uses automated threat detection mechanisms to identify and prioritize potential risks.
- **Integration with AWS Services:** It integrates with various AWS services, allowing organizations to streamline security operations and response efforts.

11.3 CLOUD DATA GOVERNANCE FRAMEWORKS

11.3.1 Frameworks for Effective Cloud Data Governance

Cloud data governance frameworks are essential for establishing policies, procedures, and controls to ensure the proper management, security, and compliance of data in cloud environments. Effective frameworks offer guidance on data handling, access controls, and compliance measures [15,16].

Example: Google Cloud Platform's (GCP) Cloud Data Governance Best Practices

GCP provides a comprehensive set of best practices for cloud data governance. This framework encompasses guidelines for data classification, access controls, auditing, and compliance. It offers organizations a structured approach to implement robust data governance practices in their cloud deployments.

11.3.1.1 Key Components of GCP's Cloud Data Governance Best Practices

- **Data Classification:** Categorizing data based on sensitivity to apply appropriate security measures.
- **Access Controls:** Implementing granular access controls to ensure authorized access to data.
- **Audit Logging:** Enabling comprehensive audit logging to track data access and modifications.
- **Compliance Management:** Incorporating measures to align with regulatory and compliance requirements.
- **Data Lifecycle Management:** Defining processes for data creation, storage, archival, and deletion.

11.3.2 Data Classification and Labeling in Cloud Environments

11.3.2.1 Data Classification and Labeling

Data classification involves categorizing data based on its sensitivity and importance. Labeling data allows organizations to apply consistent security controls and access policies, ensuring that appropriate protections are in place for different types of data.

Examples:

- **Sensitive Data Types:** Classifying data into categories such as public, internal, confidential, or regulated based on its sensitivity.
- **Labeling Mechanisms:** Assigning labels or tags to data sets, indicating their classification level.
- **Automated Classification Tools:** Implementing automated tools that analyze content and assign appropriate classifications based on predefined policies.

11.3.3 Role of Cloud Service Providers in Data Governance

Cloud Service Providers (CSPs) play a crucial role in facilitating and enhancing data governance in the cloud. They provide tools, services, and features that enable organizations to implement effective data governance practices seamlessly [17].

Case Study: AWS Lake Formation for Streamlined Data Governance in a UK-based Cloud Project

AWS offers a case study on the implementation of AWS Lake Formation for streamlined data governance in a UK-based cloud project. AWS Lake Formation is a service that simplifies and accelerates the process of building, securing, and managing data lakes.

Key Aspects of the Case Study:

- **Unified Data Lake:** AWS Lake Formation enables the creation of a unified data lake, consolidating diverse data sources for streamlined governance.
- **Fine-Grained Access Controls:** The service provides fine-grained access controls, allowing organizations to manage and enforce access policies based on user roles and data classifications.
- **Automated Data Lake Construction:** AWS Lake Formation automates the process of building and configuring data lakes, reducing the complexity and time required for setup.

11.4 INTEGRATION OF TECHNOLOGIES IN CLOUD RISK MANAGEMENT

11.4.1 Artificial Intelligence and Machine Learning in Risk Prediction

Definition: Artificial Intelligence (AI) and Machine Learning (ML) refer to the utilization of algorithms and statistical models that enable systems to learn and make predictions or decisions without explicit programming [18,19].

Scenario: Consider a European cloud infrastructure using Cisco's SecureX Platform. This platform employs AI and ML to continuously analyze vast amounts of data, including network traffic, user behavior, and threat intelligence feeds.

Key Aspects:

- **Behavioral Analysis:** AI and ML algorithms learn the normal behavior of users and systems, enabling the detection of anomalous activities.
- **Threat Detection:** The system can predict potential security threats by analyzing patterns and identifying deviations from the norm.
- **Automated Response:** In the event of a detected threat, AI-driven automation can trigger predefined response actions, such as isolating affected systems or alerting security teams.

Example: Cisco's SecureX Platform for AI-driven Threat Detection in European Cloud Infrastructures

Cisco's SecureX Platform illustrates the integration of AI and ML in risk management. The platform leverages these technologies to enhance threat detection, providing proactive security measures for European cloud infrastructures.

Scenario: A user in a European organization accesses cloud resources. The SecureX Platform continuously monitors user behavior, network traffic, and system interactions. Using AI and ML, it identifies a deviation from the user's normal behavior, indicating a potential security threat.

Automated Response:

SecureX, with AI-driven automation, immediately isolates the affected user account, preventing further unauthorized access. Simultaneously, it generates an alert for the security team to investigate the incident.

11.4.2 Automation and Orchestration for Rapid Incident Response

Definition: Automation involves the use of technology to perform tasks without human intervention, while orchestration refers to coordinating and managing multiple automated processes to achieve a specific outcome.

Scenario: In Cloud Risk Management, automation and orchestration streamline incident response by automating routine tasks and coordinating various security processes.

Key Aspects:

- **Automated Incident Triage:** Automation can quickly triage security incidents, prioritizing them based on severity and potential impact.
- **Workflow Orchestration:** Orchestration coordinates different security tools and processes, ensuring a cohesive response to incidents.
- **Efficient Resource Allocation:** Automation reduces the time spent on manual tasks, allowing security teams to focus on more complex aspects of incident investigation.

11.4.3 Blockchain Technology in Ensuring Data Integrity and Security

Definition:

Blockchain is a decentralized and distributed ledger technology that records transactions across multiple computers in a secure, transparent, and tamper-resistant manner.

Scenario:

Blockchain technology is applied to enhance data integrity and security in cloud environments.

Key Aspects:

- **Immutable Recordkeeping:** Transactions recorded on a blockchain are immutable, meaning they cannot be altered or deleted once added to the ledger.
- **Decentralization:** Blockchain operates on a decentralized network, reducing the risk of a single point of failure or manipulation.
- **Smart Contracts:** Self-executing smart contracts can automate and enforce predefined security protocols based on specific conditions.

Case Study: Leveraging Azure Blockchain for Enhanced Data Privacy Compliance in a Multinational Cloud Project

Scenario

In a multinational cloud project, Azure Blockchain is employed to ensure enhanced data privacy compliance.

Implementation

- **Data Provenance:** Blockchain records the origin and changes made to sensitive data, providing a transparent and auditable trail.
- **Consent Management:** Smart contracts enforce data access and usage policies, ensuring compliance with privacy regulations across multiple jurisdictions.
- **Immutable Audit Trail:** Any attempts to tamper with or access data without proper authorization trigger alerts, and the immutable nature of the blockchain ensures a trustworthy audit trail.

11.5 DATA PRIVACY LEGISLATION AND COMPLIANCE

11.5.1 Overview of Data Privacy Laws in the USA, UK, and Europe

Data privacy laws govern the collection, processing, and protection of personal information. This section provides an overview of data privacy laws in the USA, UK, and Europe, emphasizing the legal frameworks that organizations must adhere to when handling personal data.

Key Aspects:

- **USA:** The USA follows a sectoral approach with various federal and state laws such as HIPAA, GLBA, and the CCPA.
- **UK:** The UK's Data Protection Act (DPA) 2018 aligns with the GDPR and regulates the processing of personal data.
- **Europe:** The GDPR is a comprehensive regulation applicable across EU member states, setting high standards for data protection.

11.5.2 Impact of GDPR on Cloud Data Governance

The GDPR significantly influences how organizations manage and protect personal data, introducing stringent requirements for data processing, consent, and data subject rights. Cloud data governance must align with GDPR principles to ensure compliance.

Key Impacts:

- **Data Subject Rights**: GDPR grants individuals rights over their personal data, including the right to access, rectify, and erase their information.
- **Data Protection Impact Assessments (DPIA):** Organizations must conduct DPIAs for high-risk processing activities, ensuring they evaluate and mitigate privacy risks.
- **Cross-Border Data Transfers:** GDPR places restrictions on transferring personal data outside the EU, necessitating compliance mechanisms like Standard Contractual Clauses.

11.5.3 Navigating Cloud Operations under CCPA and Other Regional Legislations

Various regions have introduced their own data privacy regulations, such as the CCPA in California. Organizations operating in these regions must understand and comply with regional legislations, often facing complex requirements for data handling and consumer rights.

Key Considerations:

- **CCPA Compliance:** The CCPA grants California residents rights over their personal information, including the right to know, delete, and opt out of the sale of their data.
- **Global Variations:** Other regions, like Brazil with the LGPD, and India with the Personal Data Protection Bill, introduce variations in data privacy requirements, adding complexity for multinational organizations.
- **Harmonizing Compliance:** Organizations with a global presence must navigate and harmonize compliance efforts to meet the diverse requirements of regional legislations.

Example: AWS Key Management Service (KMS) for Ensuring GDPR Compliance in European Cloud Deployments

AWS KMS is a fully managed service that simplifies the creation and control of encryption keys. It is an example of a tool that aids organizations in achieving GDPR compliance in their European cloud deployments.

Implementation:

- **Data Encryption:** AWS KMS enables organizations to encrypt sensitive data, a key requirement for GDPR compliance.
- **Key Management Controls:** KMS provides robust key management controls, allowing organizations to manage access to keys and meet GDPR's security and confidentiality requirements.

- **Auditability:** KMS logs and audit trails support GDPR compliance efforts by providing evidence of key usage and access, aiding in accountability and transparency.

11.6 REAL-WORLD INDUSTRY EXAMPLES AND CASE STUDIES

11.6.1 Industry Best Practices in Cloud Risk Management

The best practices adopted by industries in managing risks associated with cloud environments are:

- **Comprehensive Risk Assessment:** Industries conduct thorough risk assessments to identify and prioritize potential risks specific to their cloud deployments.
- **Continuous Monitoring:** Regular and continuous monitoring of cloud environments is crucial for identifying and responding to emerging threats promptly.
- **User Education and Training:** Industries prioritize educating and training users on security best practices to enhance overall security awareness.
- **Integration of Advanced Technologies:** Leveraging advanced technologies such as AI and ML for predictive threat analysis and response.

Case Study: GCP's Confidential VMs in Securing Sensitive Data in USA-based Financial Cloud Projects

GCP Confidential VMs feature in a case study showcasing how industries secure sensitive data in USA-based financial cloud projects.

Implementation:

- **Confidential Computing:** GCP's Confidential VMs use confidential computing technology to keep data encrypted even during processing.
- **Protection against Memory Attacks:** The case study demonstrates how Confidential VMs protect against memory attacks, enhancing security for financial data.
- **Industry Collaboration:** The implementation involves collaboration between the cloud provider and financial industries to ensure regulatory compliance and security standards.

11.6.2 Cloud Data Governance Success Stories

The success stories in implementing effective cloud data governance practices within industries are:

- **Clear Data Classification Policies:** Industries define and implement clear data classification policies to appropriately handle diverse types of data.
- **Automated Governance Tools:** Success stories often involve the use of automated governance tools for consistent and efficient management of data.

- **Stakeholder Collaboration:** Effective cloud data governance requires collaboration among stakeholders, including IT teams, data owners, and compliance officers.

Case Study: AWS Control Tower Implementation for Effective Governance in UK Government Cloud Projects

This case study focuses on the successful implementation of AWS Control Tower for effective governance in UK government cloud projects.

Implementation:

- **Account Vending:** AWS Control Tower automates the creation of new accounts, ensuring standardized and compliant account setups.
- **Centralized Governance:** The case study illustrates how AWS Control Tower provides centralized governance by enforcing predefined policies across multiple AWS accounts.
- **Continuous Compliance Monitoring:** Industries benefit from continuous compliance monitoring, ensuring adherence to regulatory requirements and security standards.

11.6.3 Compliance Challenges and Solutions in Multinational Cloud Deployments

The challenges industries face in achieving compliance in multinational cloud deployments and solutions to overcome them are [20]:

Key Challenges:

Diverse Regulatory Landscapes: Multinational cloud deployments often involve navigating diverse regulatory landscapes with varying data protection requirements.

Cross-Border Data Transfer Concerns: Challenges arise concerning the secure transfer of data across borders while adhering to different jurisdictional laws.

Consistent Policy Enforcement: Ensuring consistent policy enforcement across multiple regions poses a significant challenge.

Example: Utilizing Azure Policy for Cross-Border Data Compliance in a European Enterprise Cloud Initiative

This example highlights the utilization of Azure Policy for addressing cross-border data compliance challenges in a European enterprise cloud initiative.

Implementation:

- **Policy Enforcement:** Azure Policy is implemented to enforce consistent data compliance policies across the enterprise's European cloud deployments.
- **Automated Compliance Checks:** The solution involves automated compliance checks, ensuring adherence to specific regulations governing cross-border data transfers.
- **Documentation and Reporting:** Azure Policy facilitates documentation and reporting, helping industries demonstrate compliance to relevant authorities.

11.7 COLLABORATIVE APPROACHES IN CLOUD SECURITY

11.7.1 Collaborative Security Models with CSPs

The collaborative security models established between organizations and CSPs to enhance overall cloud security are:

- **Shared Responsibility Model:** Emphasizes the shared responsibility for security between the organization and the CSP, clarifying the respective roles and obligations.
- **Continuous Communication:** Collaboration involves continuous communication and cooperation to address emerging security challenges and updates.
- **Security Best Practices:** Organizations work collaboratively with CSPs to implement and adhere to security best practices specific to the cloud environment.

11.7.2 Partnering with Cybersecurity Companies for Enhanced Cloud Protection

The strategic partnerships formed between organizations and cybersecurity companies to bolster cloud protection through specialized expertise and technologies are [21,22]:

- **Specialized Threat Intelligence:** Cybersecurity companies contribute specialized threat intelligence to enhance detection and response capabilities in the cloud.
- **Advanced Security Solutions:** Partnerships involve the integration of advanced security solutions to fortify defenses against evolving cyber threats.
- **Tailored Security Strategies:** Collaborations allow for the development of tailored security strategies based on the organization's unique cloud architecture and requirements.

Example: Integrating Cisco Umbrella for Cloud-based Threat Intelligence and Protection

This example illustrates the integration of Cisco Umbrella as part of a collaborative approach to leveraging cloud-based threat intelligence and protection.

Implementation:

Threat Intelligence Integration: Cisco Umbrella is integrated to provide real-time threat intelligence, enhancing the organization's ability to identify and respond to potential threats.

Secure Web Gateway Functionality: The solution includes the deployment of Cisco Umbrella's secure web gateway functionality, safeguarding against malicious web activities.

Cloud-Native Security: The integration ensures that security measures align with the dynamic and scalable nature of cloud environments.

11.8 FUTURE DIRECTIONS AND INNOVATIONS

11.8.1 Evolving Trends in Cloud Risk Management and Governance

The future of Cloud Risk Management and governance is shaped by dynamic trends that address emerging challenges and opportunities [23].

Key Trends:

- **Zero Trust Architecture:** The evolution toward implementing Zero Trust Architecture involves continuous verification and strict access controls, transforming traditional security paradigms.
- **Automated Threat Detection and Response:** Increasing reliance on AI and ML for automated threat detection and response, enhancing the speed and efficiency of security operations.
- **Regulatory Evolution:** Evolving regulatory landscapes necessitate a proactive approach to compliance, with organizations integrating automated tools to ensure adherence to changing requirements.
- **Edge Security:** The growing adoption of edge computing requires innovative approaches to extend security measures to the edge, protecting data closer to its source.

11.8.2 Integration of Quantum Computing for Advanced Cloud Security

The emergence of quantum computing introduces both challenges and opportunities in reshaping the landscape of cloud security [24].

Key Considerations:

- **Quantum-Resistant Encryption:** As quantum computers pose a threat to current encryption methods, the integration of quantum-resistant encryption becomes paramount to ensure data security.
- **Quantum Key Distribution:** Quantum Key Distribution emerges as a potential solution for secure key exchange, leveraging quantum principles to establish unhackable cryptographic keys.
- **Post-Quantum Cryptography:** The development and implementation of post-quantum cryptographic algorithms become essential to prepare for the era of quantum computing.

11.8.3 Anticipated Changes in Data Privacy Legislation and Their Impacts

As the digital landscape evolves, data privacy legislation is expected to undergo changes, influencing how organizations manage and protect sensitive information.

- **Global Harmonization:** Efforts toward global harmonization of data privacy laws may increase, aiming to create consistent standards for organizations operating across borders.
- **Enhanced Individual Rights:** Anticipated changes may include the strengthening of individual rights over personal data, requiring organizations to provide greater transparency and control to data subjects.
- **Stricter Enforcement Measures:** Regulators may implement stricter enforcement measures, imposing significant penalties for non-compliance to encourage robust data protection practices.
- **Focus on Emerging Technologies:** Changes in legislation may specifically address the impact of emerging technologies, such as AI and IoT, on data privacy.

11.9 CHALLENGES AND CONSIDERATIONS IN CLOUD RISK MANAGEMENT

11.9.1 Balancing Security and Innovation in Cloud Projects

The intersection of security and innovation in cloud projects poses a significant challenge, requiring organizations to strike a delicate balance to foster creativity while ensuring robust security measures [25].

Key Considerations:

- **Dynamic Nature of Innovation:** Rapid technological advancements demand constant innovation, but this dynamism can introduce new security vulnerabilities.
- **Risk-Aware Innovation:** Organizations need to adopt a risk-aware approach to innovation, assessing potential security implications throughout the development lifecycle.
- **Collaborative Culture:** Establishing a collaborative culture that encourages communication between security teams and innovators is crucial for proactive risk management.
- **Agile Security Practices:** Incorporating agile security practices allows organizations to adapt security measures in real time without impeding innovation.

11.9.2 Addressing Cross-Border Data Governance Challenges

As organizations operate globally, cross-border data governance challenges arise, necessitating thoughtful strategies to navigate diverse regulatory landscapes.

Key Challenges:

- **Diverse Regulatory Requirements:** Different regions have varying data protection regulations, requiring organizations to navigate a complex web of compliance requirements.

- **Data Transfer Limitations:** Transferring data across borders may face restrictions, compelling organizations to implement secure and compliant cross-border data transfer mechanisms.
- **Jurisdictional Complexity:** Determining the jurisdiction under which data falls and understanding the associated legal obligations pose considerable challenges.
- **Data Residency Concerns:** Some regions may mandate data residency requirements, influencing where data can be stored and processed.

11.9.3 Ethical Considerations in Cloud Risk Management and Data Privacy

Ethical Considerations in Cloud Risk Management and Data Privacy:

The ethical dimension of Cloud Risk Management and data privacy requires organizations to consider the broader societal impact of their actions and decisions.

Key Ethical Considerations:

- **Transparency and Consent:** Ensuring transparency in data practices and obtaining informed consent from individuals are ethical imperatives, building trust and respecting privacy.
- **Fair Data Usage:** Ethical Cloud Risk Management involves using data fairly, avoiding discriminatory practices, and ensuring equitable treatment of individuals.
- **Accountability and Responsibility:** Organizations must be accountable for the impact of their technologies on society, taking responsibility for mitigating negative consequences.
- **Bias Mitigation:** Ethical considerations extend to addressing biases in algorithms and decision-making processes to prevent discriminatory outcomes.

11.10 RECOMMENDATIONS FOR ORGANIZATIONS AND PRACTITIONERS

11.10.1 Best Practices for Cloud Risk Management

Organizations and practitioners can enhance their Cloud Risk Management by adopting proven best practices that prioritize security and resilience.

Key Recommendations:

- **Comprehensive Risk Assessment:** Conduct regular and comprehensive risk assessments to identify, evaluate, and prioritize potential risks in the cloud environment.
- **Implement Zero Trust Architecture:** Embrace the Zero Trust Architecture model, ensuring continuous verification and strict access controls to mitigate the risk of unauthorized access.

- **Regular Security Audits:** Conduct regular security audits to assess the effectiveness of security measures, identify vulnerabilities, and address emerging threats.
- **Employee Training and Awareness:** Invest in employee training programs to enhance security awareness, emphasizing the role of individuals in maintaining a secure cloud environment.
- **Collaborative Incident Response Planning:** Develop and regularly update incident response plans, fostering collaboration between security teams, IT personnel, and other stakeholders for swift and effective responses.

11.10.2 Strategies for Effective Cloud Data Governance

Ensuring effective cloud data governance requires strategic approaches to manage and protect data throughout its lifecycle.

Key Recommendations:

- **Clear Data Classification Policies:** Establish clear data classification policies to categorize and handle data based on sensitivity, ensuring appropriate protection measures are applied.
- **Automated Governance Tools:** Leverage automated governance tools to enforce consistent data management policies, streamline compliance, and enhance overall governance efficiency.
- **Role-based Access Control:** Implement role-based access control mechanisms to restrict data access based on job roles, minimizing the risk of unauthorized data exposure.
- **Data Lifecycle Management:** Define and implement data lifecycle management practices, covering data creation, usage, storage, archiving, and eventual disposal in a secure and compliant manner.
- **Regular Data Audits:** Conduct regular data audits to ensure adherence to governance policies, identify potential compliance gaps, and maintain data integrity.

11.10.3 Continuous Compliance in the Ever-Changing Landscape of Data Privacy Legislation

Continuous Compliance in Data Privacy Legislation

Amidst the dynamic nature of data privacy legislation, organizations must adopt strategies to achieve and maintain compliance.

Key Recommendations:

- **Proactive Regulatory Monitoring:** Stay informed about changes in data privacy legislation by proactively monitoring regulatory updates, ensuring timely adjustments to compliance strategies.
- **Automation for Compliance Checks:** Implement automated tools for continuous compliance checks, enabling organizations to assess adherence to evolving regulations in real time.

- **Cross-Functional Compliance Teams:** Form cross-functional compliance teams involving legal, IT, and data protection experts to collectively address the challenges posed by varied and dynamic regulatory landscapes.
- **Documentation and Reporting:** Maintain detailed documentation of compliance efforts, including policies, audits, and corrective actions, to demonstrate adherence to regulatory requirements during inspections or audits.
- **Invest in Legal Consultation:** Engage legal professionals specializing in data privacy to provide insights, interpret regulatory changes, and guide compliance efforts effectively.

11.11 CONCLUSION AND FUTURE SCOPE

In conclusion, this chapter provides a holistic view of fortifying cyber resilience in the dynamic realm of cloud security. It navigates through the foundations of risk management, governance frameworks, and compliance challenges, showcasing practical applications in real-world scenarios. The integration of cutting-edge technologies and collaborative security models emphasizes the industry's proactive approach to addressing evolving threats. As we delve into the future, the chapter highlights the importance of staying abreast of trends, leveraging quantum computing for enhanced security, and preparing for shifts in data privacy legislation. The ethical considerations underscore the responsibility of organizations in fostering a secure and ethically sound cloud ecosystem.

The future scope of this work lies in the continuous exploration and adaptation to emerging technologies, evolving threats, and regulatory changes. As the cloud landscape evolves, future research can delve deeper into the practical implementation of quantum computing in securing cloud environments. The ethical considerations raised here open avenues for further research on responsible AI deployment and the societal impact of cloud technologies. Additionally, ongoing developments in data privacy legislation warrant continuous examination, providing opportunities for researchers and practitioners to contribute to the evolving discourse on compliance and privacy in the cloud. This chapter lays the groundwork for ongoing discussions and proactive measures in the dynamic field of cloud security.

REFERENCES

1. Taherdoost, H. (2023). An overview of trends in information systems: emerging technologies that transform the information technology industry. *Cloud Computing and Data Science*, **4**(1), 1–16.
2. Weyns, D., Andersson, J., Caporuscio, M., Flammini, F., Kerren, A., & Löwe, W. (2021). A research agenda for smarter cyber-physical systems. *Journal of Integrated Design and Process Science*, **25**(2), 27–47.
3. Kumar, R., Kumar, P., & Singhal, V. (2019, March). A survey: Review of cloud IoT security techniques, issues and challenges. In *Proceedings of 2nd International Conference on Advanced Computing and Software Engineering (ICACSE)*.
4. Castaldo, C. (2021). *Start-Up Secure: Baking Cybersecurity into Your Company from Founding to Exit*. John Wiley & Sons.

5. Wang, Z., Shi, D., Zhao, J., Chu, Z., Guo, D., Eze, C., ... & Burke, A. F. (2023). Battery health diagnostics: Bridging the gap between academia and industry. *eTransportation*, **19**(3), 100309.
6. Pandey, B., & Ahmad, S. (2022). *Introduction to the Cyber Ranges*. CRC Press.
7. Aslan, Ömer, Semih Serkant Aktuğ, Merve Ozkan-Okay, Abdullah Asim Yilmaz, and Erdal Akin. (2023). A comprehensive review of cyber security vulnerabilities, threats, attacks, and solutions. *Electronics*, **12**(6), 1333..
8. Hossain, N. U. I., Rahman, S., & Liza, S. A. (2023). Cyber-susiliency index: A comprehensive resiliency-sustainability-cybersecurity index for healthcare supply chain networks. *Decision Analytics Journal*, **9**, 100319.
9. Alyahya, S., Khan, W. U., Ahmed, S., Marwat, S. N. K., & Habib, S. (2022). Cyber secure framework for smart agriculture: Robust and tamper-resistant authentication scheme for IoT devices. *Electronics*, **11**(6), 963.
10. Keys, D. P., Wright, V. L., Chanoski, S. D., Freeman, S. G., Mitchell, J. R., & Samford, M. (2022). *Prioritizing ICS Beachhead Systems for Cyber Vulnerability Testing* (No. INL/RPT-22-66453-Rev000). Idaho National Lab. (INL), Idaho Falls, ID (United States).
11. Carlo, A., Mantı, N. P., WAM, B. A. S., Casamassima, F., Boschetti, N., Breda, P., & Rahloff, T. (2023). The importance of cybersecurity frameworks to regulate emergent AI technologies for space applications. *Journal of Space Safety Engineering*, **10**(4), 474–482.
12. Mershad, K., Dahrouj, H., Sarieddeen, H., Shihada, B., Al-Naffouri, T., & Alouini, M. S. (2021). Cloud-enabled high-altitude platform systems: Challenges and opportunities. *Frontiers in Communications and Networks*, **2**, 716265.
13. Driouch, O., Bah, S., & Guennoun, Z. (2023). A holistic approach to build a defensible cybersecurity architecture for new space missions. *New Space*, **11**(4), 203–218.
14. Monge, M. A. S., & Vidal, J. M. (2021). Conceptualization and cases of study on cyber operations against the sustainability of the tactical edge. *Future Generation Computer Systems*, **125**, 869–890.
15. Arefifar, S. A., Alam, M. S., & Hamadi, A. (2023). A review on self-healing in modern power distribution systems. *Journal of Modern Power Systems and Clean Energy*, **11**(6), 1719–1733.
16. Malek, A. F., Mokhlis, H., Mansor, N. N., Jamian, J. J., Wang, L., & Muhammad, M. A. (2023). Power distribution system outage management using improved resilience metrics for smart grid applications. *Energies*, **16**(9), 3953.
17. Robinson, A. R., Schmidt, H., Haley, P. J., Lalis, S., Tian, R., Leslie, W. G., & Cho, W. (2023). Toward Dynamic Data-Driven Systems for Rapid Adaptive Interdisciplinary Ocean Forecasting In N.M. Patrikalakis, P.F.J. Lermusiaux, C. Evangelinos, J.J. McCarthy (Eds.), *Handbook of Dynamic Data Driven Applications Systems: Volume 2*, 377. Springer.
18. Stevens, T. (2023). *What Is Cybersecurity For?*. Policy Press.
19. Grzegorzewski, M. (2023). Russia's 2022 Cyber-enabled warfare against Ukraine: Why Russia failed to perform to expectations. In *The Great Power Competition Volume 5: The Russian Invasion of Ukraine and Implications for the Central Region* (pp. 47–73). Cham: Springer Nature Switzerland.
20. Sood, K., Grima, S., Sharma, G., & Balusamy, B. (Eds.). (2024). *The Application of Emerging Technology and Blockchain in the Insurance Industry*. CRC Press.
21. Ince, S., Espes, D., Lallet, J., Gogniat, G., & Santoro, R. (2023). Authentication and Confidentiality in FPGA-Based Clouds. In *Security of FPGA-Accelerated Cloud Computing Environments* (pp. 1–27). Cham: Springer International Publishing.

22. Salman, Z., Alomary, A., & Hammad, M. (2024). A secure cloud framework for big data analytics using a distributed model. *International Journal of Computing and Digital Systems*, **15**(1), 1–10.
23. Baseer, K. K., Pasha, M. J., Subhashini, R., Srinivasan, S., Patra, J. P., & Reddy, V. J. (2024). Joint data integrity and loss recovery mechanism for secure storage in cloud computing. *International Journal of Intelligent Systems and Applications in Engineering*, **12**(2), 800–809.
24. Shukla, A. K., & Sharma, A. (2024). Cloud data security by hybrid machine learning and cryptosystem approach. *International Journal of Intelligent Systems and Applications in Engineering*, **12**(2s), 01–14.
25. Shukla, A. K., & Sharma, A. (2024). Cloud data security by hybrid machine learning and cryptosystem approach. *International Journal of Intelligent Systems and Applications in Engineering*, **12**(2s), 01–14.

12 SCiphered Clouds and Quantum Secrets

Navigating Secure Information Flow with Emerging Encryption Technologies

Jamuna S. Murthy and K. G. Srinivasa

12.1 INTRODUCTION TO SECURE INFORMATION FLOW IN CLOUD ENVIRONMENTS

In the dynamic landscape of cloud computing, securing the flow of information is paramount. This chapter delves into the fundamentals of information flow security within cloud environments, exploring its definition, the importance of secure data transmission, and an overview of emerging encryption technologies dedicated to enhancing cloud security [1,2].

12.1.1 Defining Information Flow Security in Cloud Computing

Information flow security is a critical aspect of ensuring the confidentiality, integrity, and availability of data in cloud computing environments. As technology continues to advance, organizations are increasingly relying on cloud services to store, process, and manage their data. However, this shift toward cloud computing introduces new challenges, particularly in safeguarding the flow of information within the cloud infrastructure. In this context, the concept of information flow security becomes paramount, encompassing various measures and protocols designed to protect sensitive data as it traverses through the complex web of cloud resources [3,4].

12.1.1.1 Understanding Information Flow Security

Information flow security in cloud computing refers to the set of practices, mechanisms, and policies implemented to control and monitor the movement of data within the cloud ecosystem. The goal is to prevent unauthorized access, leakage, or tampering of sensitive information throughout its lifecycle in the cloud. This encompasses data at rest, in transit, and during processing, ensuring a comprehensive approach to safeguarding valuable assets [5].

DOI: 10.1201/9781003455448-12

12.1.1.2 Key Components of Information Flow Security

Access Controls: Robust access controls play a pivotal role in information flow security. Cloud service providers (CSPs) implement access policies and authentication mechanisms to ensure that only authorized entities can access specific data. This involves user authentication, role-based access control, and encryption to protect data at rest [6,7].

- **Encryption and Decryption:** Data encryption is a fundamental technique employed to secure information as it moves within the cloud. Encryption ensures that even if unauthorized access occurs, the intercepted data remains unreadable without the corresponding decryption keys. This is particularly crucial for protecting sensitive information during transit between the user and the cloud server.
- **Network Security:** Information flow security also involves securing the underlying network infrastructure. Firewalls, intrusion detection/prevention systems, and virtual private networks (VPNs) are deployed to safeguard data as it traverses the network, preventing unauthorized access and potential attacks.
- **Data Loss Prevention (DLP):** DLP solutions are essential in identifying and preventing the unauthorized sharing or leakage of sensitive information. These systems monitor and control data transfers, ensuring compliance with security policies and regulations.
- **Logging and Auditing:** Comprehensive logging and auditing mechanisms are crucial for tracking information flow within the cloud. By maintaining detailed logs of user activities, data access, and system events, organizations can identify and respond to potential security incidents in a timely manner.
- **Identity and Trust Management:** Establishing and managing trust between entities in the cloud environment is vital. Identity and trust management protocols help ensure that entities, whether users or devices, are who they claim to be, thus preventing unauthorized access.

12.1.2 Significance of Secure Data Transmission in Cloud Architectures

In the realm of cloud computing, secure data transmission is not just a feature but a fundamental necessity. As businesses and individuals increasingly rely on cloud architectures for storing, managing, and processing data, the significance of safeguarding data during transmission becomes paramount. This focus on secure data transmission is crucial for maintaining the integrity, confidentiality, and availability of information while mitigating risks associated with cyber threats and unauthorized access [8,9].

12.1.2.1 The Importance of Secure Data Transmission in Cloud Architectures

- **Protection Against Cyber Threats:** One of the primary reasons for ensuring secure data transmission in cloud architectures is the prevalence of cyber threats. As data moves across the internet to and from cloud services, it becomes vulnerable to interception, eavesdropping, and other forms of cyberattacks. Secure transmission protocols encrypt data during transit, making it unintelligible to unauthorized interceptors.

- **Compliance with Regulatory Requirements:** Various industries are governed by stringent data protection regulations (like GDPR, HIPAA, etc.) that mandate the secure handling of sensitive information. Compliance with these regulations often requires the implementation of secure data transmission protocols to prevent data breaches and avoid hefty fines and legal repercussions.
- **Maintaining Data Integrity:** Secure transmission ensures that the data remains unaltered during transit. Any tampering or corruption of data can lead to significant consequences, particularly when dealing with financial transactions, healthcare records, or legal documents. Encryption and secure transmission protocols help in maintaining the integrity of the data from its source to its destination.
- **Building Trust with Customers and Clients:** Customers and clients are increasingly aware of data security issues. Organizations that demonstrate a commitment to secure data transmission in their cloud architectures can build and maintain trust with their clients, assuring them that their sensitive information is handled safely and confidentially.
- **Facilitating Secure Cloud Collaboration:** Cloud computing often involves collaboration across different entities and geographies. Secure data transmission ensures that as data is shared and accessed across various networks and devices, it remains protected, fostering a secure environment for collaboration.

12.1.2.1.1 Key Components of Secure Data Transmission in Cloud Architectures

- **Encryption:** Encryption is the cornerstone of secure data transmission. Techniques like SSL/Transport Layer Security (TLS) encryption are widely used for securing data in transit, ensuring that even if data is intercepted, it remains unreadable to the attacker.
- **Secure Network Channels:** Utilizing VPNs and other secure networking technologies helps in creating encrypted channels for data transmission, adding an additional layer of security, especially for remote access scenarios.
- **Authentication and Authorization Protocols:** Implementing strong authentication mechanisms ensures that only authorized users and systems can access and transmit data, thereby preventing unauthorized data breaches.
- **Continuous Monitoring and Intrusion Detection Systems:** Real-time monitoring of network traffic and the deployment of intrusion detection systems can help in identifying and mitigating suspicious activities during data transmission.
- **Regular Updates and Patch Management:** Keeping software and security protocols up to date is crucial in protecting against known vulnerabilities that could be exploited during data transmission.

12.1.3 Overview of Emerging Encryption Technologies in Cloud Security

As cloud computing continues to evolve, the security of data stored and processed in the cloud remains a top priority. Encryption technologies play a vital role in protecting data confidentiality and integrity. This section explores the latest advancements in encryption technologies that are shaping the future of cloud security, offering enhanced protection against an ever-evolving landscape of cyber threats [10,11].

12.1.3.1 Emerging Encryption Technologies in Cloud Security

- **Homomorphic Encryption:** Homomorphic encryption is a cutting-edge technology that allows data to be processed in its encrypted form, enabling computations on encrypted data without needing to decrypt it first. This form of encryption is particularly valuable for cloud environments where sensitive data is processed by third-party servers. It ensures data privacy even during processing, opening new avenues for secure data analytics and machine learning in the cloud.
- **Quantum Key Distribution:** Quantum key distribution (QKD) leverages the principles of quantum mechanics to secure communication channels. It enables two parties to produce a shared random secret key, which can be used to encrypt and decrypt messages, with the security of the key distribution guaranteed by the laws of quantum physics. In the era of quantum computing, QKD provides a solution to the threat posed by quantum computers to traditional encryption methods. It ensures a future-proof encryption mechanism that cannot be easily compromised by quantum computing.
- **Multiparty Computation:** Multiparty computation (MPC) allows multiple parties to jointly compute a function over their inputs while keeping those inputs private. In cloud environments, MPC can be used for secure data sharing and collaborative computations without exposing individual data sets to other parties, crucial for privacy-preserving collaborations.
- **Attribute-Based Encryption:** Attribute-based encryption (ABE) is a type of public-key encryption where the secret key of a user and the ciphertext are dependent upon attributes (e.g., the user's role). In cloud services, ABE offers fine-grained access control, allowing data owners to define access policies based on user attributes, enhancing the security and flexibility of data sharing in the cloud.
- **Post-Quantum Cryptography:** This refers to cryptographic algorithms that are believed to be secure against an attack by a quantum computer. As the potential of quantum computing grows, post-quantum cryptography is essential for preparing cloud security infrastructures against future threats that traditional algorithms might not withstand.
- **Zero-Knowledge Proofs (ZKP):** ZKPs allow one party to prove to another that a statement is true without conveying any information apart from the fact that the statement is indeed true. ZKPs can be used in cloud environments to authenticate users or verify transactions without revealing any underlying data, thus enhancing both security and privacy.

12.2 DYNAMIC CHALLENGES AND INNOVATIVE SOLUTIONS IN INFORMATION FLOW SECURITY

In the rapidly evolving landscape of information security, staying abreast of current research trends is crucial for safeguarding data in cloud environments. This section delves into the dynamic nature of threats affecting information flow in cloud systems and highlights cutting-edge research advances in secure data transmission mechanisms [12,13].

12.2.1 Dynamic Nature of Threats to Information Flow in Clouds

The dynamic nature of threats to information flow in cloud environments refers to the ever-changing and evolving challenges that arise in securing data within cloud computing systems. As organizations increasingly rely on cloud services for storage, processing, and communication, the threat landscape continually shifts, presenting new risks and vulnerabilities.

These dynamic threats encompass a range of issues, including but not limited to:

- **Cyber Attacks:** Cloud systems are susceptible to a variety of cyber attacks, such as malware, ransomware, and distributed denial-of-service (DDoS) attacks. The methods and techniques employed by malicious actors are constantly evolving, requiring a proactive and adaptive approach to cybersecurity.
- **Data Breaches:** The risk of unauthorized access to sensitive data is heightened in cloud environments. Data breaches can occur due to misconfigurations, insider threats, or targeted attacks, emphasizing the need for robust access controls and encryption mechanisms.
- **Compliance Challenges:** The regulatory landscape governing data protection and privacy is subject to change. CSPs and their clients must stay vigilant to ensure compliance with evolving regulations, adding a layer of complexity to information flow security.
- **Insider Threats:** The dynamic nature of insider threats, where individuals with authorized access misuse their privileges, poses a constant challenge. Organizations must implement monitoring systems and behavioral analytics to detect and mitigate potential insider threats.
- **Zero-Day Vulnerabilities:** Cloud services often rely on various software and applications. The discovery of previously unknown vulnerabilities, known as zero-day vulnerabilities, can expose cloud systems to exploitation. Timely patching and proactive security measures are essential to mitigate these risks.

To address the dynamic nature of these threats, organizations need to adopt a comprehensive and adaptive approach to information flow security in cloud environments. This includes regular security assessments, real-time monitoring, timely updates and patches, employee training, and collaboration with CSPs to stay ahead of emerging risks and ensure the ongoing integrity and confidentiality of data in the cloud.

12.2.2 Research Advances in Secure Data Transmission Mechanisms

Research advances in secure data transmission mechanisms have paved the way for robust and sophisticated solutions to safeguard information during its transit. These innovations are crucial in addressing the evolving landscape of cybersecurity threats and ensuring the confidentiality and integrity of data as it moves across networks. Some key areas of research progress in this domain include [14,15]:

- **Encryption Techniques:** Ongoing research has led to advancements in encryption algorithms, enhancing the protection of data during transmission. Novel encryption methods, including homomorphic encryption and post-quantum cryptography, are being explored to fortify data against emerging computational threats.
- **Quantum Key Distribution:** With the emergence of quantum computing, researchers are delving into quantum-resistant technologies. QKD is one such area, leveraging quantum properties to secure the exchange of cryptographic keys, providing a more resilient foundation for secure data transmission.
- **Blockchain for Secure Transactions:** Blockchain technology is being researched as a means to ensure secure and tamper-resistant data transmission. Its decentralized and distributed ledger architecture adds an additional layer of trust and integrity to the transmitted data.
- **Secure Multiparty Computation (SMPC):** SMPC protocols allow parties to jointly compute a function over their inputs while keeping these inputs private. This research area contributes to secure collaborative data processing, particularly in scenarios where multiple entities need to collectively analyze data without revealing individual inputs.
- **Post-Quantum Cryptography:** As quantum computers pose a potential threat to traditional cryptographic systems, research is focused on developing post-quantum cryptographic algorithms. These algorithms aim to withstand quantum attacks, ensuring the continued security of data transmission in a quantum computing era.
- **Trusted Execution Environments (TEEs):** TEEs, such as Intel SGX and ARM TrustZone, offer secure enclaves for executing sensitive computations. Ongoing research explores the practical implementation and enhancement of TEEs to fortify the security of data transmission processes.
- **Secure Communication Protocols:** Research efforts are directed toward the development of secure communication protocols, with a focus on refining existing standards and introducing new methodologies. Protocols such as TLS and Datagram TLS continue to evolve to address emerging threats.

Example: Utilizing Amazon Web Services (AWS) PrivateLink for Secure and Direct Communication in Machine Learning Workloads

CSPs, such as AWS, play a pivotal role in shaping the future of secure data transmission. AWS PrivateLink emerges as an innovative solution, providing a secure and direct communication channel for machine learning workloads. This research advance leverages the inherent benefits of AWS PrivateLink, allowing organizations to establish private connections between their Virtual Private Clouds (VPCs) and AWS services. By doing so, sensitive data transmission is shielded from the public internet, mitigating the risk of unauthorized access or data interception.

- **Assessing Workload Requirements:** Begin by thoroughly understanding the machine learning workloads and their communication needs within your AWS environment. Identify the specific components and services involved in the workflows to determine the scope and requirements for secure communication.
- **AWS PrivateLink Setup:** Initiate the configuration of AWS PrivateLink by navigating to the AWS Management Console. Access the VPC settings and enable AWS PrivateLink for the desired services associated with the machine learning workloads.
- **VPC Endpoint Creation:** Create VPC endpoints for the selected AWS services to establish a private connection. These endpoints act as entry points for communication, ensuring that the data does not traverse the public internet, enhancing security.
- **Security Group Configuration:** Adjust security group settings to control inbound and outbound traffic between the machine learning components. Define specific rules to restrict access to the necessary entities, thereby fortifying the overall security posture.
- **IAM Role Definition:** Create and configure Identity and Access Management (IAM) roles with the appropriate permissions. Define roles that allow only the necessary actions for the machine learning workloads, adhering to the principle of least privilege.
- **Integration with Machine Learning Frameworks:** Integrate AWS PrivateLink with the machine learning frameworks employed in your workloads. Ensure that the frameworks are configured to utilize the private connection established through the VPC endpoints.
- **Data Encryption Implementation:** Enhance data security by implementing encryption mechanisms. Leverage AWS Key Management Service or other encryption tools to encrypt data in transit, further securing the communication channels between different components.
- **Monitoring and Logging Setup:** Implement robust monitoring and logging practices to track communication patterns and identify any anomalous activities. Utilize AWS CloudWatch or other monitoring tools to gain insights into the performance and security of the machine learning workloads.
- **Testing and Validation:** Conduct thorough testing to validate the effectiveness of the AWS PrivateLink implementation. Test different scenarios and workloads to ensure that the secure communication channels function as intended without compromising performance or data integrity.
- **Documentation and Best Practices:** Document the AWS PrivateLink setup, including configurations, roles, and security measures implemented.

Establish best practices for ongoing maintenance and share this documentation with relevant stakeholders to ensure consistency and compliance.

- **Regular Audits and Updates:** Schedule regular audits of the AWS PrivateLink implementation to identify and address any potential vulnerabilities or changes in the machine learning workloads. Stay informed about updates from AWS and adjust configurations accordingly to maintain a secure communication infrastructure.

12.3 REAL-WORLD CASE STUDIES IN INFORMATION FLOW SECURITY

In this section, we delve into real-world case studies that illustrate effective strategies and technologies employed to secure information flow in diverse computing environments. These case studies offer practical insights into overcoming challenges associated with multicloud environments, cloud-based machine learning, and edge computing scenarios [16,17].

12.3.1 Case Study 1: Secure Information Flow in Multicloud Environments

Example: Google Cloud Platform (GCP) Interconnect for Secure Communication Between Public and Private Clouds

This case study examines the implementation of secure information flow in multicloud environments, addressing the need for seamless and protected communication between public and private clouds. GCP Interconnect emerges as a key solution, enabling organizations to establish dedicated and secure connections between on-premises data centers and GCP.

12.3.1.1 Key Components and Strategies

- **Dedicated Interconnects:** GCP Interconnect facilitates the creation of dedicated, private connections, eliminating the reliance on the public internet for data transmission.
- **Low Latency:** The use of dedicated interconnects ensures low-latency communication, crucial for real-time applications and data-sensitive workloads.
- **Isolation of Traffic:** GCP Interconnect allows organizations to isolate and prioritize traffic, enhancing security and efficiency.
- **Scalability:** The solution scales to accommodate evolving business needs, providing flexibility in managing information flow across multicloud environments.

12.3.2 Case Study 2: Ensuring Privacy in Cloud-based Machine Learning

Case Study: Azure Confidential Computing for Machine Learning Model Encryption and Deployment

This case study explores the challenges of ensuring privacy in cloud-based machine learning and highlights the utilization of Azure Confidential Computing to encrypt machine learning models and secure their deployment.

12.3.2.1 Key Components and Strategies

- **Confidential Containers:** Azure Confidential Computing leverages secure enclaves to ensure that machine learning models run in isolated and protected environments.
- **Model Encryption:** Machine learning models are encrypted during deployment, safeguarding intellectual property and sensitive information.
- **Secure Deployment:** Azure Confidential Computing enables the secure deployment of encrypted models, ensuring that only authorized entities can access and utilize them.
- **Data Privacy Assurance:** The case study emphasizes the assurance of data privacy in cloud-based machine learning workflows, addressing concerns related to confidentiality and compliance.

12.3.3 Case Study 3: Secure Data Transfer in Edge Computing Environments

Example: AWS IoT Greengrass for Encrypted Information Flow in Edge-to-Cloud Communication

This case study delves into the challenges of secure data transfer in edge computing environments and introduces AWS IoT Greengrass as a solution for encrypting information flow in edge-to-cloud communication.

12.3.3.1 Key Components and Strategies

- **Edge Computing Encryption:** AWS IoT Greengrass ensures end-to-end encryption for data transmitted between edge devices and the cloud, mitigating the risk of interception.
- **Local Processing:** The solution supports local processing on edge devices, minimizing the need for continuous data transfer and reducing latency.
- **Secure Device Authentication:** AWS IoT Greengrass employs secure device authentication mechanisms, allowing only authenticated and authorized devices to participate in the information flow.
- **Edge Security Policies:** Organizations can define and enforce security policies at the edge, enhancing control over data transfer and access in edge computing environments.

These case studies collectively demonstrate the practical application of advanced technologies and strategies to address specific challenges in information flow security across multicloud, cloud-based machine learning, and edge computing scenarios. They provide valuable insights for organizations seeking to implement secure and efficient information flow architectures in real-world computing environments.

12.4 MACHINE LEARNING AND DISTRIBUTED LEARNING IN INFORMATION FLOW SECURITY

This section delves into the pivotal role of machine learning and distributed learning in enhancing information flow security. We explore the integration of machine learning for anomaly detection in data transmission and delve into distributed learning approaches, specifically focusing on securing model training across distributed cloud resources.

12.4.1 Integrating Machine Learning for Anomaly Detection in Information Flow

Example: Google Cloud artificial intelligence (AI) Platform's AutoML for Adaptive Anomaly Detection in Data Transmission

This example investigates the incorporation of machine learning, particularly Google Cloud AI Platform's AutoML, to bolster information flow security through adaptive anomaly detection in data transmission.

12.4.1.1 Key Components and Strategies

- **Automated Model Training:** Google Cloud AI Platform's AutoML streamlines the process of developing machine learning models, enabling automated and efficient model training for anomaly detection.
- **Adaptive Anomaly Detection:** The machine learning models, once trained, adapt dynamically to the changing patterns and characteristics of data transmission, enhancing their ability to detect anomalies in real time.
- **Continuous Learning:** AutoML's adaptive capabilities facilitate continuous learning, allowing the models to evolve and improve their anomaly detection accuracy over time.
- **Scalability:** The solution scales seamlessly to handle varying data volumes and complexities, ensuring robust anomaly detection in diverse information flow scenarios.

12.4.2 Distributed Learning Approaches for Secure Model Training and Deployment

Example: AWS SageMaker for Federated Learning in Securing Model Training Across Distributed Cloud Resources.

This example explores the application of distributed learning methodologies, specifically leveraging AWS SageMaker for federated learning, to ensure secure model training and deployment across distributed cloud resources.

12.4.2.1 Key Components and Strategies

- **Federated Learning Framework:** AWS SageMaker's federated learning framework enables model training across distributed nodes without centralizing raw data, preserving data privacy and security.

- **Decentralized Model Updates:** Model updates occur locally on distributed devices, minimizing the need for transferring sensitive data to a central location and reducing privacy risks.
- **Secure Aggregation:** Federated learning incorporates secure aggregation techniques, ensuring that model updates are aggregated in a privacy-preserving manner.
- **Multicloud Compatibility:** AWS SageMaker's federated learning approach is adaptable to multicloud environments, allowing organizations to harness distributed resources securely across various cloud platforms.

These examples collectively underscore the significance of machine learning and distributed learning in fortifying information flow security. By integrating adaptive anomaly detection and distributed learning approaches, organizations can enhance their capabilities to detect and respond to threats in real time while ensuring the confidentiality and privacy of sensitive data. These methodologies contribute to a proactive and resilient information flow security framework, aligning with the dynamic and distributed nature of contemporary computing environments.

12.5 ENCRYPTION TECHNOLOGIES SHAPING INFORMATION FLOW SECURITY

This section explores the pivotal role of encryption technologies in shaping and fortifying information flow security. It delves into specific encryption methodologies, highlighting their applications and real-world case studies [18,19].

12.5.1 Homomorphic Encryption for Secure Data Processing in Clouds

Case Study: Microsoft Azure Homomorphic Encryption Toolkit for Privacy-preserving Cloud Computation.

This segment investigates the utilization of homomorphic encryption, with a focus on the Microsoft Azure Homomorphic Encryption Toolkit, to achieve secure data processing in cloud environments while preserving privacy.

12.5.1.1 Key Components and Strategies

- **Privacy-Preserving Computation:** Homomorphic encryption enables computations on encrypted data without the need for decryption, ensuring that sensitive information remains confidential during processing.
- **Microsoft Azure Toolkit:** The Azure Homomorphic Encryption Toolkit provides a set of tools and libraries for developers to implement homomorphic encryption in cloud applications, allowing for seamless integration into existing workflows.
- **Secure Data Outsourcing:** Organizations can leverage homomorphic encryption to outsource data processing tasks to the cloud securely, mitigating concerns related to data exposure.

12.5.2 QKD for Next-Level Encryption

Example: IBM Quantum Safe Cryptography Suite for Quantum-resistant Encryption in Cloud Environments

This example explores the application of QKD as a next-level encryption technology, with a specific example from the IBM Quantum Safe Cryptography Suite for securing communications in cloud environments against potential quantum threats.

12.5.2.1 Key Components and Strategies

Quantum-Resistant Encryption: QKD ensures the secure distribution of cryptographic keys, protecting data against potential threats posed by quantum computers capable of breaking traditional encryption algorithms.

IBM Quantum Safe Cryptography Suite: This suite provides a comprehensive set of cryptographic algorithms designed to withstand quantum attacks, offering a quantum-resistant layer of security for data transmitted in cloud environments.

Securing Communications: By implementing QKD and quantum safe cryptography, organizations can safeguard their communications against the future threat of quantum-enabled attacks.

12.5.3 Post-Quantum Cryptography Solutions

Example: Azure Quantum for Experimenting with Post-Quantum Cryptography Algorithms

This part focuses on post-quantum cryptography solutions, exemplified by Microsoft's Azure Quantum, which allows organizations to experiment with and prepare for the adoption of algorithms resilient to quantum computing.

12.5.3.1 Key Components and Strategies

Quantum Safe Algorithms: Post-quantum cryptography involves the exploration and development of cryptographic algorithms that remain secure even in the era of quantum computing.

Azure Quantum Platform: Microsoft's Azure Quantum provides a platform for researchers and developers to experiment with post-quantum cryptography algorithms, allowing organizations to stay ahead of potential quantum threats.

Preparedness for Quantum Era: By engaging with post-quantum cryptography solutions, organizations can proactively prepare for the transition to quantum-resistant encryption, ensuring the long-term security of their sensitive information.

From privacy-preserving computation with homomorphic encryption to quantum-resistant solutions and post-quantum cryptography, these technologies contribute to building robust and future-proof security measures for safeguarding information in diverse computing environments. The case studies and examples illustrate practical implementations and highlight the significance of staying ahead of evolving threats in the realm of information security.

12.6 CHALLENGES AND SOLUTIONS IN INFORMATION FLOW SECURITY

This section delves into the challenges encountered in information flow security and presents solutions to address these issues. The topic explores key challenges in cloud encryption, considerations for performance in encrypted information flow, and the crucial aspect of regulatory compliance [20,21].

12.6.1 Addressing Key Management Challenges in Cloud Encryption

Here the focus is on challenges related to key management in cloud encryption and proposes solutions to ensure the secure and effective use of encryption keys.

12.6.1.1 Key Challenges

- **Key Generation and Storage:** Generating and securely storing encryption keys in cloud environments can pose challenges, especially when dealing with large-scale and dynamic workloads.
- **Key Rotation and Revocation:** Managing the periodic rotation of encryption keys and ensuring the secure revocation of compromised keys can be operationally complex.
- **Key Distribution:** Effectively distributing keys to authorized entities while preventing unauthorized access requires robust mechanisms.

12.6.1.2 Solutions

- **Cloud Key Management Services:** Leveraging cloud-based key management services provides centralized control and secure storage of encryption keys.
- **Automated Key Rotation:** Implementing automated processes for key rotation reduces manual intervention, enhancing security.
- **Access Controls:** Strict access controls and authentication mechanisms ensure that only authorized entities have access to encryption keys.

12.6.2 Performance Considerations in Encrypted Information Flow

The performance implications of encrypted information flow require these key considerations:

- **Latency:** Encrypting and decrypting data can introduce latency, impacting the overall performance of applications.
- **Computational Overhead:** The additional computational load required for encryption and decryption processes can affect the efficiency of data transmission.
- **Isolation of Sensitive Workloads:** Ensuring the isolation of sensitive workloads is crucial to prevent interference from other processes or potential security threats.

12.6.2.1 Case Study: AWS Nitro Enclaves

1. **Isolated Execution:** AWS Nitro Enclaves provide isolated and secure environments for executing sensitive workloads, minimizing the risk of interference.
2. **Efficient Resource Allocation:** Nitro Enclaves enable efficient resource allocation, ensuring that encryption processes do not compromise the overall performance of the system.
3. **Enhanced Security:** By dedicating specific hardware resources to sensitive workloads, Nitro Enclaves contribute to both performance optimization and heightened security.

12.6.3 Regulatory Compliance in Encrypted Data Transmission

The challenges associated with regulatory compliance in encrypted data transmission and introducing GCP's External Key Manager as an example solution are:

- **Data Residency Requirements:** Regulatory frameworks may impose restrictions on where certain types of data can be stored or transmitted.
- **Auditability:** Ensuring the ability to audit and prove compliance with regulatory standards regarding data encryption and transmission.
- **Key Lifecycle Management:** Compliance often requires meticulous key lifecycle management practices.

12.6.3.1 Example: GCP External Key Manager

- **Compliance-Aware Key Management:** GCP External Key Manager allows organizations to manage encryption keys in a manner compliant with regulatory requirements.
- **Key Residency Controls:** The solution provides controls over where encryption keys reside, facilitating adherence to data residency regulations.
- **Audit Trails:** GCP External Key Manager offers audit trails and logging features, supporting compliance audits and demonstrating adherence to regulatory standards.

From effective key management and performance considerations to regulatory compliance, the presented solutions aim to foster a secure, efficient, and compliant environment for the seamless flow of information in diverse computing scenarios.

12.7 FUTURE DIRECTIONS AND INNOVATIONS IN INFORMATION FLOW SECURITY

In the dynamic landscape of cybersecurity, 2023 has witnessed the emergence of pivotal trends that are reshaping how organizations approach and implement security measures. These trends, influenced by evolving technological advancements and changing global scenarios, underscore the necessity for agile, sophisticated, and comprehensive security strategies. From the complexities of navigating geopolitical

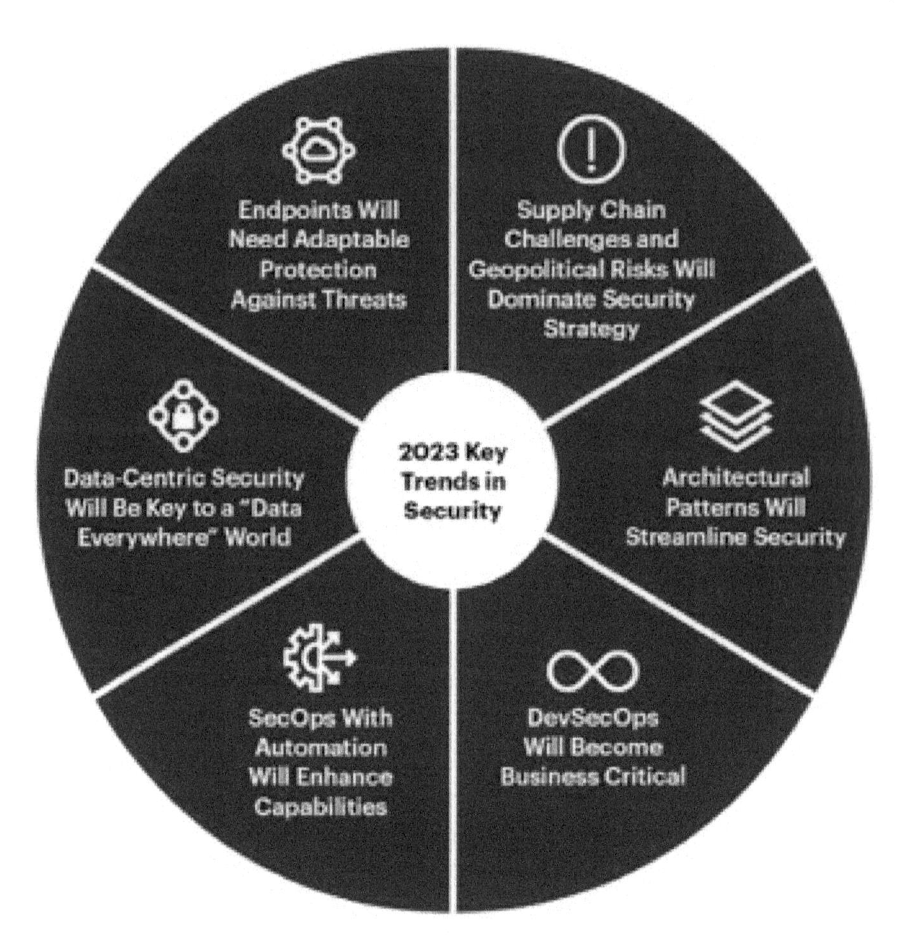

FIGURE 12.1 Key trends of security in 2023.

and supply chain risks to the integration of cutting-edge architectural patterns, these trends highlight the critical areas of focus for Chief Information Security Officers (CISOs) and security teams. As we delve into these key trends, it is imperative to understand their implications, the challenges they pose, and the innovative solutions they demand for ensuring robust and resilient security in today's digitally interconnected world. The overview of the same is given in Figure 12.1 and is explained below in detail [22–25].

12.7.1 Trend 1: Geopolitical and Supply Chain Risks in Security Strategy

In 2023, organizations worldwide are significantly impacted by geopolitical tensions, which are increasingly manifesting as vulnerabilities in supply chains. This scenario heightens the risk of various cyber threats, including malware, cloud infrastructure attacks, DDoS attacks, and data breaches. CISOs are now focusing on mitigating these risks by establishing robust controls in dealings with suppliers. These controls range from basic acceptance criteria for goods to complex measures like granting suppliers access to IT systems and planning joint response activities. Adapting security architecture to address geopolitical risks and ensuring cyber resilience across the supply chain are crucial steps.

12.7.2 Trend 2: Security Through Emerging Architectural Patterns

The complexity of aligning security controls with IT systems is growing. To address this, major security vendors are developing unified cybersecurity platforms and Cybersecurity Mesh Architectures (CSMAs). CISOs should prioritize the implementation of security solutions based on CSMA principles and adopt zero-trust architecture to bolster security. Streamlining security through tool consolidation and using intelligent analytics for decision-making can create more effective risk mitigation strategies.

12.7.3 Trend 3: The Critical Role of DevSecOps

With the expanding attack surface due to diverse APIs and applications, secure development and deployment become business-critical. DevSecOps, which integrates security into the application delivery process, is essential. CISOs should promote a culture where security is an integral part of development and ensure transparency across software delivery, understanding the composition of applications to identify potential vulnerabilities.

12.7.4 Trend 4: Enhanced Security Operations Through Automation

Security monitoring has evolved, but it remains labor-intensive. Integrating automation into security operations, either through existing tools or via Security Orchestration, Automation, and Response tools, can scale up the capabilities of security teams. CISOs should assess automation strategies for their efficiency and cost-effectiveness, ensuring that automated processes genuinely enhance security operations.

12.7.5 Trend 5: Data-Centric Security in a Data-Abundant World

With the explosion of data usage and the rise of AI, tracking and understanding data becomes critical, particularly in identifying lurking data risks. Tools for data discovery, classification, and loss prevention are key to gaining visibility and protecting against breaches. CISOs need to adopt specific strategies for data protection, focusing on discovery and visibility. They should also consider Enterprise Digital Rights Management to secure data beyond corporate boundaries, controlling and tracking data access and usage even after it has been shared.

12.7.6 Trend 6: Adaptable Protection for Endpoints

Endpoints continue to be prime targets for cyberattacks, including ransomware and business email compromise. The challenge is compounded by the growing number of devices, such as IoT and virtual assistants, needing secure network access. CISOs must implement a blend of preventive and detective controls on all endpoints, both physical and cloud-based. A comprehensive endpoint security strategy, including ransomware protection and a solid backup/recovery process, is vital for safeguarding against these evolving threats.

12.7.7 Evolving Landscape of Information Flow Security

The dynamic and evolving nature of information flow security, considering the challenges and opportunities presented by emerging technologies and evolving threat landscapes requires the following considerations:

- **Advanced Threats:** As technology advances, the nature of cybersecurity threats evolves. Future information flow security must adapt to defend against increasingly sophisticated attacks.
- **IoT and Edge Computing:** The proliferation of IoT devices and the growth of edge computing introduce new dimensions to information flow security, requiring innovative strategies to secure data transmission in decentralized environments.
- **5G Networks:** The deployment of 5G networks introduces higher data speeds and increased connectivity, necessitating robust security measures to protect information flow in this accelerated and interconnected environment.

12.7.8 Integration of AI in Encryption Key Management

The integration of AI into encryption key management, emphasizing the role of AI-driven solutions such as Azure Key Vault Managed HSM requires these Key Components and Strategies.

- **Dynamic Key Lifecycle Management:** AI-driven solutions, like Azure Key Vault Managed HSM, employ machine learning algorithms to dynamically manage encryption key lifecycles, adapting to changing security requirements.
- **Predictive Analytics:** AI can analyze historical data and patterns to predict potential security threats, enabling proactive measures in key management.
- **Automation:** AI-driven key management solutions automate tasks such as key rotation, distribution, and access controls, reducing manual intervention and human error.
- **Continuous Learning:** These solutions continually learn from security events and incidents, enhancing their ability to respond effectively to evolving threats.

12.7.9 Anticipated Technological Advancements in Cloud Encryption

The expected technological advancements in cloud encryption, envisioning innovations that will shape the future of securing information flow in cloud environments are:

- **Quantum Safe Encryption:** As the threat of quantum computing grows, the development and adoption of quantum safe encryption algorithms become imperative to ensure the resilience of encrypted data in the future.
- **Homomorphic Encryption Enhancements:** Ongoing research and development in homomorphic encryption are expected to result in more efficient and practical implementations, expanding its applicability in various use cases.
- **Blockchain Integration:** The integration of blockchain technology into cloud encryption holds the potential to enhance the transparency, integrity, and traceability of encrypted data transactions.
- **Zero-Trust Architectures:** The evolution of zero-trust architectures in cloud environments, emphasizing continuous verification and strict access controls, is anticipated to bolster the overall security of information flow.

12.8 RECOMMENDATIONS FOR PRACTITIONERS

The best practices for secure information flow implementation, strategies for adapting to emerging encryption technologies, and ensuring compliance in the face of evolving threats and technologies are:

12.8.1 Best Practices for Implementing Secure Information Flow in Clouds

- **Comprehensive Risk Assessment:** Conduct a thorough risk assessment to identify potential threats, vulnerabilities, and risks specific to the organization's cloud environment.
- **Data Classification:** Classify data based on sensitivity and implement differentiated security measures accordingly. Not all data requires the same level of protection.
- **Strong Access Controls:** Implement robust access controls to ensure that only authorized individuals and systems have access to sensitive data.
- **Encryption Across the Lifecycle:** Apply encryption consistently throughout the data lifecycle, including storage, transmission, and processing, to maintain data confidentiality.
- **Regular Security Audits:** Conduct regular security audits and assessments to identify and remediate vulnerabilities promptly.
- **Employee Training:** Provide comprehensive training for employees to enhance awareness of security best practices, emphasizing their role in maintaining information flow security.
- **Incident Response Planning:** Develop and regularly update incident response plans to ensure a swift and effective response to security incidents.

12.8.2 Strategies for Adapting to Emerging Encryption Technologies

The strategies for practitioners to adapt to and leverage emerging encryption technologies effectively are:

- **Continuous Education and Awareness:** Stay informed about emerging encryption technologies through continuous education and awareness programs. Regularly assess their applicability to your organization's security needs.
- **Pilot Programs:** Consider piloting new encryption technologies in controlled environments to evaluate their performance, interoperability, and impact on existing workflows.
- **Collaboration with Vendors:** Engage with encryption technology vendors and industry experts to understand the latest advancements and potential integrations into your existing infrastructure.
- **Scalable Architectures:** Design and implement scalable architectures that can accommodate the integration of new encryption technologies as they evolve.
- **Community Engagement:** Participate in security communities and forums to exchange insights and experiences with peers regarding the adoption of emerging encryption technologies.

12.8.3 Ensuring Compliance in the Face of Evolving Threats and Technologies

The strategies to ensure compliance with regulatory requirements while navigating evolving threats and technologies are:

- **Continuous Monitoring of Regulatory Changes:** Stay vigilant about changes in data protection and privacy regulations. Regularly monitor updates to ensure ongoing compliance.
- **Frameworks and Standards:** Adopt recognized frameworks and standards for data protection, such as GDPR or HIPAA, to guide compliance efforts.
- **Engagement with Regulatory Bodies:** Establish communication channels with regulatory bodies to seek guidance and stay abreast of evolving compliance requirements.
- **Integrated Compliance Programs:** Integrate compliance into the organization's broader security program. Develop policies, procedures, and controls that align with both security and compliance objectives.
- **Regular Compliance Audits:** Conduct regular compliance audits, involving internal and external assessments, to ensure adherence to regulatory requirements.
- **Flexibility in Security Policies:** Develop flexible security policies that can adapt to changes in technology and regulations while maintaining a strong security posture.

12.9 CONCLUSION

In the ever-expanding realm of digitized data and pervasive cloud computing influence, the imperative of information security stands as a paramount concern. This book chapter delves into the nuanced landscape of cloud security, with a specific focus on securing the flow of information. As organizations increasingly rely on cloud environments to safeguard their critical data, the imperative for robust security measures has led to a dynamic field of exploration and innovation. Commencing with a comprehensive introduction to information flow security in cloud computing, this chapter elucidates its significance and surveys cutting-edge encryption technologies. Current research trends spotlight the dynamic nature of threats and advances in secure data transmission mechanisms, exemplified by the practical application of AWS PrivateLink for secure communication in machine learning workloads. Real-world case studies provide practical insights, covering secure information flow in multicloud environments through GCP Interconnect and ensuring privacy in cloud-based machine learning using Azure Confidential Computing.

The integration of machine learning and distributed learning techniques for anomaly detection and secure model training is explored through platforms like Google Cloud AI Platform's AutoML and AWS SageMaker for federated learning. This chapter investigates encryption technologies that shape information flow security, including homomorphic encryption for secure data processing and QKD, exemplified by the Microsoft Azure Homomorphic Encryption Toolkit and IBM Quantum Safe Cryptography Suite. Addressing challenges such as key management, performance considerations, and regulatory compliance, this chapter features case studies like AWS Nitro Enclaves and GCP External Key Manager. Future directions and innovations, such as the integration of AI in encryption key management through Azure Key Vault Managed HSM, are examined. In its conclusion, this chapter consolidates insights into practical recommendations for practitioners, encapsulating best practices for implementing secure information flow, strategies for adapting to emerging encryption technologies and ensuring compliance in the face of evolving threats and technologies.

REFERENCES

1. Pöyhönen, J., Hummelholm, A., & Lehto, M. (2022, June). Cybersecurity risk assessment subjects in information flows. In *Proceedings of the European Conference on Cyber Warfare and Security*. Academic Conferences International Ltd.
2. Gurav, Y. B., & Patil, B. M. (2023). De-centralized information flow control for cloud virtual machines with hybrid AES-ECC and improved meta-heuristic optimization based optimal key generation. *International Journal of Intelligent Robotics and Applications*, **7**(2), 406–425.
3. Sayeed, A., Verma, C., Kumar, N., Koul, N., & Illés, Z. (2022). Approaches and challenges in Internet of Robotic Things. *Future Internet*, **14**(9), 265.
4. Han, H., Liu, Z., Wang, X., & Li, S. (2021, May). Research of the relations among cloud computing, internet of things, big data, artificial intelligence, block chain and their application in maritime field. *In Journal of Physics*: *Conference Series* (Vol. 1927, No. 1, p. 012026). IOP Publishing.

5. James, E., & Rabbi, F. (2023). Fortifying the IoT landscape: strategies to counter security risks in connected systems. Tensorgate *Journal of Sustainable Technology and Infrastructure for Developing Countries*, **6**(1), 32–46.
6. Zhou, J., Chen, S., Choo, K. K. R., Cao, Z., & Dong, X. (2021). EPNS: efficient privacy-preserving intelligent traffic navigation from multiparty delegated computation in cloud-assisted VANETs. *IEEE Transactions on Mobile Computing*, **22**(3), 1491–1506.
7. Khan, M. J. (2023). Zero trust architecture: Redefining network security paradigms in the digital age. World Journal of Advanced Research and Reviews, **19**(3), 105–116.
8. Dawei Jiang, & Guoquan Shi (2021). [Retracted] Research on data security and privacy protection of wearable equipment in healthcare. *Journal of Healthcare Engineering*, **2021**, Article ID 6656204, 7 pages. https://doi.org/10.1155/2021/6656204.
9. Forti, N., D'Afflisio, E., Braca, P., Millefiori, L. M., Carniel, S., & Willett, P. (2022). Point of view: Next-Gen intelligent situational awareness systems for maritime surveillance and autonomous navigation. *Proceedings of the IEEE*, **110**(10), 0018–9219.
10. Vimal, V., Muruganantham, R., Prabha, R., Arularasan, A. N., Nandal, P., Chanthirasekaran, K., & Reddy Ranabothu, G. (2022). Enhance software-defined network security with IoT for strengthen the encryption of information access control. *Computational Intelligence and Neuroscience*, **2022**, 1–10.
11. Dawood, M., Tu, S., Xiao, C., Alasmary, H., Waqas, M., & Rehman, S. U. (2023). Cyberattacks and security of cloud computing: a complete guideline. *Symmetry*, **15**(11), 1981.
12. You, B., & Xiao, X. (2023). Data encryption technology application in enterprise cost operation management based on cloud computing. *Soft Computing*, 1–13.
13. Mateus-Coelho, N. (2021). A new methodology for the development of secure and Paranoid Operating Systems. *Procedia Computer Science*, **181**, 1207–1215.
14. Keshari, N., Singh, D., & Maurya, A. K. (2022). A survey on vehicular fog computing: Current state-of-the-art and future directions. *Vehicular Communications*, **38**, 100512.
15. Ding, L., Wang, Z., Wang, X., & Wu, D. (2020). Security information transmission algorithms for IoT based on cloud computing. *Computer Communications*, **155**, 32–39.
16. Perwej, Y., Akhtar, N., Kulshrestha, N., & Mishra, P. (2022). A methodical analysis of Medical Internet of Things (MIoT) security and privacy in current and future trends. *Journal of Emerging Technologies and Innovative Research*, **9**(1), d346–d371.
17. Moussaid, N. E., & Azhari, M. E. (2020). Enhance the security properties and information flow control. *International Journal of Electronic Business*, **15**(3), 249–274.
18. Manimuthu, A., Dharshini, V., Zografopoulos, I., Priyan, M. K., & Konstantinou, C. (2021). Contactless technologies for smart cities: big data, IoT, and cloud infrastructures. *SN Computer Science*, **2**(4), 334.
19. Masood, A., Lakew, D. S., & Cho, S. (2020). Security and privacy challenges in connected vehicular cloud computing. *IEEE Communications Surveys & Tutorials*, **22**(4), 2725–2764.
20. Chauhan, M., & Shiaeles, S. (2023). An analysis of cloud security frameworks, problems and proposed solutions. *Network*, **3**(3), 422–450.
21. Mogadem, M. M., Li, Y., & Meheretie, D. L. (2021). A survey on Internet of energy security: related fields, challenges, threats and emerging technologies. *Cluster Computing*, **25**(1), 1–37.
22. Omolara, A. E., Alawida, M., & Abiodun, O. I. (2023). Drone cybersecurity issues, solutions, trend insights and future perspectives: a survey. *Neural Computing and Applications*, **35**(31), 23063–23101.
23. Hataba, M., Sherif, A., Mahmoud, M., Abdallah, M., & Alasmary, W. (2022). Security and privacy issues in autonomous vehicles: a layer-based survey. *IEEE Open Journal of the Communications Society*, **3**, 811–829.

24. Jazyah, Y. H. (2023). 5G security, challenges, solutions, and authentication. *International Journal of Advances in Soft Computing & Its Applications*, **15**(3), 1–10.
25. Nag, A., Hassan, M. M., Das, A., Sinha, A., Chand, N., Kar, A., ... & Alkhayyat, A. (2024). Exploring the applications and security threats of Internet of Thing in the cloud computing paradigm: A comprehensive study on the cloud of things. *Transactions on Emerging Telecommunications Technologies*, **35**(4), e4897.

13 Securing Mobile Workspaces in the Cloud

Navigating Bring Your Own Device Challenges with Cyber Resilience

H. V. Srikrishna and Jamuna S. Murthy

13.1 UNVEILING THE EVOLUTION OF BYOD IN CLOUD WORKSPACES

13.1.1 The Historical Landscape: Evolution of BYOD

The evolution of Bring Your Own Device (BYOD) has been shaped by the emergence of powerful mobile technology, particularly smartphones and tablets, which blurred the lines between personal and professional device usage. As smartphones became ubiquitous, the shift toward flexible work arrangements and remote work contributed to the rise of BYOD. Cloud computing further facilitated remote access to corporate resources, but it also brought about security concerns. IT departments responded by implementing Mobile Device Management (MDM) solutions to enforce security policies and manage personal devices accessing corporate networks. The development of formal BYOD policies, along with advancements in endpoint security, aimed to strike a balance between productivity and data protection. Today, BYOD is a well-established practice, with ongoing trends focusing on integrating artificial intelligence, adopting zero-trust security models, and enhancing user education to address the evolving challenges of personal device usage in professional settings [1,2].

13.1.2 Impactful Dynamics: BYOD's Influence on Modern Workplace Dynamics

The influence of BYOD on modern workplace dynamics is profound, reshaping the way businesses operate and employees engage with their professional responsibilities. The introduction of BYOD has catalyzed a shift toward greater flexibility and mobility, as employees now have the freedom to choose and use their personal devices for work-related tasks. This has resulted in increased employee satisfaction and productivity, as individuals can seamlessly transition between personal and professional activities on a single device [3].

DOI: 10.1201/9781003455448-13

Moreover, BYOD has fostered a more collaborative and interconnected work environment. With employees accessing corporate resources from their own devices, communication and collaboration have become more agile. Cloud-based applications and collaborative tools enable real-time sharing and editing of documents, transcending physical and geographical barriers and fostering a more dynamic and efficient workflow.

However, this paradigm shift is not without challenges. Security concerns have become a central issue, as organizations must navigate the delicate balance between granting employees the flexibility to use their devices and ensuring the protection of sensitive corporate data. The implementation of robust security measures, such as encryption, multifactor authentication (MFA), and MDM solutions, has become imperative to mitigate potential risks associated with BYOD [4].

BYOD has also necessitated the development of clear policies and guidelines governing its use in the workplace. Organizations must establish transparent protocols outlining acceptable use, security standards, and employee responsibilities. This not only helps in maintaining a secure working environment but also sets expectations for both employers and employees regarding the boundaries of personal device usage.

In terms of cost-effectiveness, BYOD has proven advantageous for businesses. Instead of investing in company-owned devices, organizations can leverage the existing technology infrastructure owned by employees, potentially reducing capital expenditures. However, this cost-effectiveness must be weighed against the potential security and support costs associated with a diverse array of personal devices [5,6].

In summary, BYOD's impact on modern workplace dynamics is multifaceted. It has ushered in a new era of flexibility, collaboration, and cost-effectiveness. Yet, organizations must carefully navigate security challenges and establish clear guidelines to harness the full potential of BYOD in shaping a contemporary and adaptive work environment. The ongoing integration of BYOD into workplace dynamics underscores its transformative influence and highlights the need for organizations to continually adapt their strategies to align with the evolving landscape of technology in the professional sphere.

13.1.3 Current Perspectives: Trends and Adoption Rates in Cloud-Driven Environments

In the contemporary technological landscape, cloud-driven environments are witnessing significant trends and adoption rates that reshape the operational dynamics of businesses. One prevalent trend is the rise of multicloud and hybrid cloud architectures, allowing organizations to optimize performance by leveraging various cloud service providers. Serverless computing is gaining traction, simplifying application development and enhancing scalability. The integration of artificial intelligence and machine learning into cloud services is enhancing data analytics and automation. Containerization, particularly with platforms like Kubernetes, is becoming widely adopted for its consistency and portability. While industries such as finance and healthcare increasingly embrace the cloud for operational efficiency, security concerns, and regulatory compliance remain challenges. Nevertheless, the ongoing emphasis on robust cloud security strategies indicates a continued evolution in cloud adoption, with a focus on addressing security challenges and optimizing the integration of emerging technologies [7,8].

13.2 WEIGHING THE RISKS AND REWARDS OF BYOD ADOPTION IN CLOUD ECOSYSTEMS

13.2.1 Probing Security Risks in Cloud-Based BYOD

13.2.1.1 Data Leakage and Unauthorized Access

Examining security risks in cloud-based BYOD environments sheds light on two critical concerns: data leakage and unauthorized access. These risks pose significant threats to the confidentiality and integrity of sensitive information within organizations [9–11].

1. **Data Leakage:** Data leakage in cloud-based BYOD scenarios occurs when sensitive information is unintentionally or maliciously disclosed to unauthorized individuals or entities. This risk arises from the intertwining of personal and professional data on devices, creating potential vulnerabilities. Employees accessing corporate resources on their personal devices may inadvertently share confidential data through unsecured channels or compromised applications. Mitigating data leakage involves implementing robust encryption protocols, monitoring data transfers, and educating users about secure data handling practices.
2. **Unauthorized Access:** Unauthorized access is a grave security risk in cloud-based BYOD environments, where individuals gain illicit entry to corporate systems or data. This could result from compromised user credentials, weak authentication mechanisms, or exploitation of vulnerabilities in device security. Implementing stringent access controls, MFA, and regular security audits are crucial measures to prevent unauthorized access. Additionally, organizations must enforce policies that restrict device access to only those meeting specified security standards.

Addressing these security risks requires a comprehensive approach. Organizations should invest in advanced endpoint protection to secure devices, employ encryption techniques to safeguard data in transit and at rest, and implement robust identity and access management solutions. Regular security awareness training for employees is equally vital to cultivate a security-conscious culture and minimize human-related vulnerabilities.

In summary, probing security risks in cloud-based BYOD environments reveals data leakage and unauthorized access as prominent threats. Safeguarding against these risks demands a combination of technological solutions, policy enforcement, and user education to fortify the overall security posture of organizations embracing BYOD in the cloud.

13.2.1.2 Malware and Endpoint Security Challenges

Exploring security risks in cloud-based BYOD environments unveils two significant challenges: the proliferation of malware and the complexities associated with endpoint security [12].

- **Malware Threats:** One of the foremost concerns in cloud-based BYOD scenarios is the heightened risk of malware infiltration. Personal devices utilized for both professional and personal tasks may inadvertently introduce malware into the corporate network. This can occur through malicious apps, compromised websites, or infected files. Malware, ranging from viruses to ransomware, poses a severe threat to data integrity and system functionality. Mitigating this risk requires a multilayered approach, including regular malware scans, up-to-date antivirus software, and user education on recognizing and avoiding potential threats.
- **Endpoint Security Challenges:** Endpoint security challenges are exacerbated in a cloud-based BYOD environment due to the diverse array of devices accessing corporate networks. Ensuring the security of these endpoints becomes complex as organizations must contend with various operating systems, device types, and security postures. Endpoint security measures, such as firewalls, intrusion detection/prevention systems, and device encryption, are essential. Additionally, organizations should implement MDM and Endpoint Detection and Response solutions to enforce security policies, monitor device activities, and respond swiftly to potential security incidents.

To effectively navigate these challenges, organizations must prioritize continuous monitoring of endpoint devices, regularly update security protocols, and enforce strict access controls. Regular employee training on recognizing phishing attempts, secure browsing practices, and the importance of prompt system updates contributes to a proactive defense against malware and strengthens overall endpoint security.

In conclusion, probing security risks in cloud-based BYOD environments highlights the critical challenges posed by malware threats and endpoint security complexities. A robust defense strategy involves a combination of technological solutions, continuous monitoring, and comprehensive user education to fortify organizations against evolving security threats in the dynamic landscape of BYOD and cloud integration.

13.2.2 Balancing Act: Productivity and Cost Benefits in Cloud-Enabled BYOD

13.2.2.1 Amplifying Employee Satisfaction and Flexibility

Harmonizing productivity and cost efficiency in a cloud-enabled BYOD environment not only optimizes operational processes but also elevates employee satisfaction and flexibility. The intersection of cloud technology with BYOD policies has redefined the workplace paradigm, providing employees with a seamless integration of their personal devices into professional workflows [13].

1. **Amplifying Employee Satisfaction:** The integration of BYOD with cloud services plays a pivotal role in bolstering employee satisfaction. This approach acknowledges the preference for personalized devices, empowering employees with the autonomy to use their chosen tools for work. This familiarity contributes to a positive work experience, fostering a sense of control and comfort. As employees navigate tasks with devices of their choice, job satisfaction is heightened, positively impacting overall morale and engagement.
2. **Enhancing Flexibility:** Cloud-enabled BYOD environments introduce unprecedented flexibility, enabling employees to transcend traditional office constraints. The ability to access work-related data and applications from anywhere facilitates remote work scenarios, offering individuals the flexibility to create personalized workspaces. This adaptability not only increases productivity but also allows employees to strike a harmonious balance between professional responsibilities and personal life commitments.
3. **Operational Cost Benefits:** From an organizational standpoint, the integration of BYOD with cloud services presents tangible cost benefits. Capital expenditures traditionally allocated to hardware provision and maintenance are significantly reduced, as employees utilize their existing devices. Cloud services further contribute to cost efficiency by providing scalable solutions, negating the need for extensive on-premises infrastructure. This strategic allocation of resources allows organizations to redirect funds toward innovation and growth initiatives.
4. **Strategic Balancing Act:** Achieving an effective balance between productivity and cost benefits necessitates a strategic approach. Well-defined BYOD policies, coupled with robust security measures, form the foundation of this balance. Optimizing cloud resources, implementing stringent security protocols to safeguard sensitive data, and continuously educating employees on secure BYOD practices ensure that the advantages of heightened employee satisfaction and flexibility align seamlessly with overarching organizational objectives.

In summary, the integration of cloud technology with BYOD policies creates a symbiotic relationship that not only optimizes productivity and cost efficiency but also enhances employee satisfaction and flexibility. This approach, centered around individual preferences and adaptability, fosters a motivated and engaged workforce, ultimately driving productivity and achieving cost efficiencies in the contemporary landscape of work.

13.2.2.2 Harnessing Cost Reduction and Efficiency Gains

Balancing productivity and cost benefits in a cloud-enabled BYOD environment entails harnessing significant cost reduction and efficiency gains. The fusion of cloud technology with BYOD policies presents an opportunity for organizations to optimize operations and resource allocation strategically [14].

Cost Reduction through BYOD Integration: Integrating BYOD with cloud services allows organizations to capitalize on cost reduction opportunities. Leveraging existing personal devices minimizes the need for substantial investments in hardware, contributing to immediate cost savings. This approach aligns with a cost-effective strategy, as employees utilize their devices for work tasks, alleviating the financial burden associated with company-provided hardware.

Operational Efficiency Gains with Cloud Services: Cloud services play a pivotal role in enhancing operational efficiency. By migrating to the cloud, organizations can streamline processes, reduce maintenance costs, and benefit from scalable solutions that align with fluctuating workloads. Cloud-enabled BYOD environments enable seamless collaboration and data accessibility, eliminating barriers posed by traditional on-premises infrastructure and further contributing to operational efficiency gains [15].

Strategic Resource Allocation: The strategic alignment of BYOD and cloud services facilitates resource allocation that is both efficient and flexible. Organizations can redirect funds previously allocated to hardware provision toward innovative initiatives and growth opportunities. This dynamic resource allocation allows for increased adaptability, enabling organizations to respond effectively to changing market conditions and technological advancements.

Security Measures for Cost-Efficient Protection: While harnessing cost reduction and efficiency gains, it is imperative to implement robust security measures. Ensuring data integrity and safeguarding against potential threats is integral to maintaining a cost-efficient and productive BYOD environment. This includes the implementation of encryption, secure access controls, and regular security audits to mitigate risks associated with diverse personal devices accessing corporate networks [16].

In conclusion, the strategic amalgamation of BYOD and cloud services not only drives cost reduction but also unlocks efficiency gains for organizations. Leveraging personal devices alongside cloud technology enables a more flexible and adaptive work environment, fostering innovation and strategic resource allocation. The balancing act between productivity and cost benefits hinges on careful planning, incorporating security measures, and embracing the transformative potential of cloud-enabled BYOD environments.

13.3 ORCHESTRATING DEVICE MANAGEMENT AND ACCESS CONTROL IN CLOUD BYOD

13.3.1 MDM Solutions in the Cloud

13.3.1.1 Unveiling Features and Capabilities

Exploring the features and capabilities of MDM solutions in the cloud reveals a versatile set of tools designed to efficiently manage and secure mobile devices within an organization.

- **Centralized Device Management:** One of the fundamental features of cloud-based MDM solutions is centralized device management. Administrators can remotely configure, monitor, and manage a diverse range of mobile devices from a unified cloud-based platform. This centralized control enhances operational efficiency and ensures consistency in device settings.
- **Over-the-Air Updates:** Cloud-enabled MDM solutions facilitate Over-the-Air updates, allowing administrators to remotely update device configurations, applications, and operating systems. This feature streamlines the update process, ensuring that devices stay current with the latest security patches and organizational policies without requiring physical interaction.
- **Security Policies and Compliance Management:** MDM solutions in the cloud empower organizations to enforce robust security policies on mobile devices. Administrators can define and implement policies related to data encryption, password requirements, and access controls. These measures contribute to maintaining a secure and compliant mobile device environment.
- **Application Management and Distribution:** Cloud-based MDM solutions offer efficient application management by enabling administrators to distribute, monitor, and update applications on mobile devices. This feature ensures that employees have access to the necessary applications while allowing administrators to control application usage and permissions.
- **Geolocation and Device Tracking:** Enhancing device security, cloud-based MDM solutions often include geolocation and device tracking capabilities. Administrators can track the physical location of mobile devices in real-time, aiding in asset management and providing a valuable tool in case of device loss or theft.
- **User Authentication and Access Control:** MDM solutions play a critical role in user authentication and access control. Cloud-based MDM allows organizations to implement MFA and granular access controls, ensuring that only authorized users with compliant devices can access sensitive data and resources.
- **Real-Time Monitoring and Reporting:** Cloud-enabled MDM solutions provide real-time monitoring and reporting features. Administrators can track device activities, detect anomalies, and generate comprehensive reports. This visibility enhances the organization's ability to respond promptly to security incidents, ensuring a proactive approach to MDM.

In summary, the features and capabilities of cloud-based MDM solutions contribute to a comprehensive and efficient MDM strategy. From centralized control to real-time monitoring, these tools empower organizations to secure, monitor, and manage mobile devices seamlessly, enhancing both security and operational effectiveness in the modern digital landscape.

13.3.1.2 Orchestrating Implementation Best Practices

Implementing MDM solutions in the cloud necessitates a strategic approach based on best practices. Commence with the development of comprehensive policies, outlining security protocols and acceptable use guidelines. Effective user education and communication are paramount to garner user cooperation and compliance. Before a full-scale deployment, conduct pilot programs to test the system, identify potential issues, and refine policies. Scalability planning is crucial to accommodate future growth, and seamless integration with existing systems ensures operational continuity. Prioritize robust security measures, including encryption, access controls, and MFA, to protect sensitive data on mobile devices. Consider privacy concerns and comply with regulations, communicating transparently about data collection. Implement continuous monitoring, regular auditing, and seek employee feedback for ongoing adaptation and improvement. Lastly, stay abreast of compliance requirements to ensure alignment with industry-specific and regional regulations. This orchestrated approach ensures a secure, efficient, and user-friendly environment for managing mobile devices in the cloud.

13.3.2 Mastering Access Control in Cloud-Based BYOD

13.3.2.1 Role-Based Access Control Strategies

In mastering access control within a cloud-based BYOD environment, Role-Based Access Control (RBAC) strategies play a pivotal role in ensuring security, efficiency, and adherence to organizational policies. RBAC is a dynamic framework that assigns specific roles to users based on their responsibilities, allowing for granular control over access permissions.

1. **Role Definition and Mapping:** Initiate RBAC implementation by clearly defining distinct roles within the organization. Roles should align with job responsibilities, ensuring that each user has a specific set of permissions corresponding to their tasks. Map these roles to specific individuals or groups based on their functions within the BYOD ecosystem.
2. **Hierarchical Role Structuring:** Structure roles hierarchically to reflect organizational hierarchies. This enables a more streamlined and efficient management of access control, with higher-level roles inheriting permissions from lower-level roles. This hierarchical approach simplifies administration and ensures that users receive the necessary permissions without unnecessary complexities.
3. **Tailored Permissions and Least Privilege Principle:** Adhere to the principle of least privilege by granting users the minimum level of access required to perform their duties. Tailor permissions within each role to avoid over-privileged access, reducing the risk of security breaches. This ensures that users only have access to the resources essential for their specific roles, enhancing overall security.
4. **Dynamic Role Assignment:** Enable dynamic role assignment to accommodate changes in organizational structure and employee responsibilities. As

roles evolve, RBAC allows for seamless adjustments in access permissions without necessitating a complete overhaul of the access control system. This flexibility is crucial in dynamic BYOD environments where personnel roles may change frequently.

5. **Regular Auditing and Monitoring:** Implement regular auditing and monitoring processes to ensure that RBAC policies are effectively enforced. Regularly review and update role assignments, permissions, and user access logs to identify anomalies or unauthorized access promptly. Continuous monitoring enhances the system's responsiveness to potential security threats.
6. **Integration with Identity Management Systems:** Integrate RBAC strategies with identity management systems for enhanced accuracy and efficiency. Linking RBAC to identity management allows for automated provisioning and de-provisioning of user access based on changes in user roles, ensuring synchronization between user roles and access permissions.
7. **Training and User Awareness:** Conduct training sessions and create awareness among users about the RBAC framework. Ensure that employees understand the roles assigned to them, the associated permissions, and the importance of adhering to access control policies. Educating users fosters a security-conscious culture within the organization.
8. **MFA for Role Changes:** Implement MFA as an additional layer of security, especially when making significant role changes. MFA adds an extra level of verification, reducing the risk of unauthorized access during role modifications and enhancing the overall security posture of the BYOD environment.

In conclusion, mastering access control in a cloud-based BYOD environment through RBAC strategies involves meticulous role definition, hierarchical structuring, and adherence to the least privilege principle. Regular auditing, dynamic role assignment, and integration with identity management systems contribute to an adaptive and secure access control framework. Training and user awareness, coupled with MFA for role changes, ensure a comprehensive and robust RBAC implementation, ultimately enhancing security and efficiency in the management of BYOD access control.

13.3.2.1.1 Navigating Network Segmentation Challenges in Cloud BYOD

Effectively mastering access control in a cloud-based BYOD environment involves addressing challenges associated with network segmentation. One of the primary challenges arises from the heterogeneous nature of personal devices in a BYOD setting, where varying operating systems, security postures, and device capabilities make achieving uniform network segmentation complex. Therefore, implementing a flexible segmentation strategy becomes crucial to accommodate this diversity and ensure effective access control [17].

The dynamic nature of BYOD environments, characterized by frequent device connections and disconnections, poses another challenge to traditional network segmentation approaches. Static policies may struggle to adapt to the fluidity of device connections, necessitating the implementation of dynamic and context-aware segmentation solutions. These solutions allow for real-time adjustments based on device attributes, user roles, and other contextual factors, ensuring the efficacy of access control in a dynamic BYOD landscape.

BYOD users are often mobile, moving between different locations and networks, challenging the effectiveness of traditional network segmentation. To address this, implementing solutions that consider user context, such as location-based policies, ensures consistent access control irrespective of user mobility. Integration with a unified identity management system becomes paramount in overcoming network segmentation challenges, associating user identities with devices, and maintaining a cohesive access control framework.

The complexity of segmentation policies, particularly as the number of devices and user roles increases, is a notable challenge. Striking a balance between granularity in access control and practicality in policy management is essential. Implementing simplified, role-based policies and regularly reviewing and refining these policies helps manage complexity without sacrificing security.

Security risks during transitions between network segments, when users move between them, require careful consideration. Implementing secure transition protocols, such as Virtual Private Networks or encrypted communication channels, ensures that sensitive data remains protected during movement across different segments. Additionally, ensuring compliance with industry regulations and data protection standards poses an ongoing challenge in BYOD network segmentation. Regular audits and assessments are essential to verify that segmentation policies align with compliance requirements [18].

Employee education and awareness are critical components of navigating network segmentation challenges. Educating employees about the importance of adhering to segmentation policies, understanding the implications of device movement between segments, and reporting any unusual network activity fosters a culture of security consciousness among BYOD users. In conclusion, mastering access control in a cloud-based BYOD environment while navigating network segmentation challenges requires a multifaceted approach that adapts to the diversity and dynamics of personal devices, prioritizes context-aware solutions, and integrates identity management seamlessly. Addressing compliance concerns, fostering user education, and striking a balance between security and usability contribute to a comprehensive strategy for effective access control in the evolving landscape of cloud-based BYOD.

13.4 SAFEGUARDING DATA THROUGH ENCRYPTION AND INTEGRITY PROTOCOLS IN CLOUD-BASED BYOD ENVIRONMENTS

13.4.1 Encryption Protocols and Standards for Cloud BYOD

13.4.1.1 Comprehensive Insights into Full Disk Encryption

Examining encryption protocols and standards for Cloud BYOD environments sheds light on the pivotal role played by Full Disk Encryption (FDE) in fortifying comprehensive data security. FDE stands out as a robust encryption method designed to safeguard the entirety of data on a disk or device, including the operating system, applications, and user data. In the context of Cloud BYOD, where personal devices interact with sensitive corporate data, FDE emerges as an indispensable component of a holistic security strategy [19].

At its core, FDE ensures that all contents on a disk or device are encrypted, rendering them inaccessible to unauthorized users. This all-encompassing approach provides a transparent layer of protection, requiring minimal user intervention while delivering robust security against unauthorized access. Its seamless integration with cloud services commonly used in BYOD environments enhances data security both in transit and at rest.

A fundamental strength of FDE lies in its ability to protect data at rest effectively. In scenarios where devices may be lost or stolen, FDE encrypts sensitive information on the device's disk, thwarting attempts to extract meaningful data. This is particularly pertinent in the BYOD context, where the mobility of devices increases the risk of physical loss or theft.

FDE's integration with cloud services further fortifies data security. As BYOD environments often leverage cloud storage platforms and collaboration tools, FDE ensures that data transferred to and from the cloud remains encrypted throughout the process. This seamless integration bolsters the overall security posture of data, aligning with the dynamic nature of BYOD environments.

Crucially, FDE provides protection not only against physical threats but also against cyber threats. In the face of unauthorized access attempts or cyber-attacks, FDE acts as a robust deterrent by encrypting data, making it exceptionally challenging for malicious actors to gain meaningful access to sensitive information [20].

In the realm of regulatory compliance, FDE aligns seamlessly with various standards that mandate the encryption of sensitive information. Organizations operating in regulated industries, such as healthcare and finance, find FDE instrumental in meeting data protection requirements, thereby ensuring adherence to stringent compliance standards.

FDE incorporates user authentication mechanisms, adding an extra layer of protection. Users must provide valid credentials or authentication factors to unlock and decrypt the device, reinforcing access control measures. While FDE offers significant security benefits, organizations should be mindful of potential challenges such as key management and performance impact. Effectively managing encryption keys and assessing performance impact on devices are crucial considerations to strike a balance between security and operational efficiency.

In essence, FDE emerges as a cornerstone in the encryption protocols and standards for Cloud BYOD, providing organizations with comprehensive insights into data security. By safeguarding data at rest, seamlessly integrating with cloud services, protecting against physical and cyber threats, ensuring regulatory compliance, and incorporating user authentication mechanisms, FDE establishes a robust defense against unauthorized access in the dynamic landscape of BYOD within the cloud [21].

13.4.1.2 Application-Level Encryption Strategies

Exploring encryption protocols and standards for Cloud BYOD environments unveils the significance of Application-Level Encryption as a targeted strategy for securing sensitive data. Application-Level Encryption focuses on protecting data at the granular level, specifically within applications and their associated databases. In the dynamic landscape of Cloud BYOD, where personal devices access and interact with corporate applications, Application-Level Encryption stands out as a critical component for ensuring the confidentiality and integrity of sensitive information.

- **Key Characteristics of Application-Level Encryption:** Application-Level Encryption is characterized by its precision in securing data within specific applications, offering a more fine-grained approach compared to broader encryption methods. It encrypts data as it enters an application and decrypts it when needed, ensuring that sensitive information remains protected throughout its lifecycle within the application environment.
- **Granular Protection for Diverse Data Types:** One of the strengths of Application-Level Encryption lies in its ability to provide granular protection for diverse data types handled by applications. Whether it is structured data within databases, unstructured data in documents, or user credentials, this strategy allows organizations to tailor encryption to the specific needs and formats of the data processed by various applications.
- **Dynamic Encryption and Decryption Processes:** Application-Level Encryption employs dynamic encryption and decryption processes, ensuring that data remains encrypted when at rest, in transit, and during processing within the application. This adaptability aligns seamlessly with the dynamic nature of BYOD environments, accommodating the mobility and diverse usage patterns of personal devices.
- **Integration with Cloud Services:** Given the prevalent use of cloud services in BYOD scenarios, Application-Level Encryption can be seamlessly integrated into cloud-based applications. This ensures that data transferred to and from the cloud remains encrypted, maintaining a consistent level of protection regardless of the device accessing the application or the location of data storage.
- **Enhanced Access Controls:** Application-Level Encryption enhances access controls within the context of individual applications. By encrypting data at the application layer, organizations can implement more refined access control mechanisms, restricting access to specific data subsets based on user roles or permissions. This approach contributes to the principle of least privilege and helps prevent unauthorized access.
- **Addressing Data Residency and Compliance:** For organizations navigating data residency requirements and compliance standards, Application-Level Encryption provides a valuable tool. Encrypting data within applications allows for more nuanced control over where sensitive information resides, supporting efforts to comply with regional data protection regulations and industry-specific compliance standards.
- **Challenges and Considerations:** While Application-Level Encryption offers targeted protection, it comes with considerations. Key management becomes crucial for secure and efficient encryption processes. Organizations must implement robust key management practices to ensure that encryption keys are securely stored, rotated, and managed throughout the application lifecycle.

In conclusion, Application-Level Encryption emerges as a strategic approach within encryption protocols and standards for Cloud BYOD environments. By focusing on securing data within specific applications, this strategy provides granular protection, integrates seamlessly with cloud services, enhances access controls, and addresses compliance requirements. As organizations seek to balance the benefits of BYOD with stringent data security mandates, Application-Level Encryption stands as a key enabler for safeguarding sensitive information within the diverse and interconnected landscape of Cloud BYOD.

13.4.2 Upholding Data Integrity in Transit and at Rest in Cloud BYOD

13.4.2.1 Implementing Integrity Checks and Robust Hashing Algorithms

In the realm of Cloud BYOD environments, maintaining data integrity both in transit and at rest is paramount. Implementing integrity checks and robust hashing algorithms emerges as a foundational strategy to ensure the trustworthiness and unaltered state of data, particularly as personal devices interact with sensitive information in cloud-based ecosystems [22].

- **Integrity Checks in Transit:** For data in transit, integrity checks play a crucial role in verifying that information traversing networks remains unchanged and uncorrupted during transmission. Implementing cryptographic protocols, such as Transport Layer Security (TLS) or its predecessor, Secure Sockets Layer, facilitates secure communication channels. These protocols incorporate integrity checks, ensuring that data arriving at its destination is identical to the original content. Regularly updating and patching cryptographic implementations is vital to staying resilient against emerging threats and vulnerabilities.
- **Robust Hashing Algorithms:** Robust hashing algorithms serve as the backbone for verifying data integrity both in transit and at rest. Hash functions, like SHA-256 (Secure Hash Algorithm 256-bit), generate fixed-size hashes unique to specific data sets. By comparing the hash values of transmitted or stored data with the original hash, organizations can quickly detect any alterations. Employing industry-standard and cryptographically secure hashing algorithms strengthens data integrity measures, enhancing resistance against malicious tampering or unauthorized modifications.
- **Ensuring Data Integrity at Rest:** Securing data at rest involves implementing measures to guarantee its integrity when stored on devices or within cloud databases. Employing FDE ensures that data remains encrypted on personal devices, preventing unauthorized modifications. Additionally, cryptographic hashing can be applied to verify the integrity of data stored in the cloud. Periodically recalculating and comparing hash values helps detect any unauthorized changes, providing an additional layer of assurance in upholding data integrity.

- **Challenges and Considerations:** While implementing integrity checks and robust hashing algorithms is instrumental, organizations must be mindful of challenges. Key management becomes a critical consideration to safeguard cryptographic keys used for both encryption and hashing. Regularly updating algorithms and methodologies is essential to adapt to evolving security standards and address vulnerabilities that may emerge over time.
- **User Education and Awareness:** To enhance the effectiveness of data integrity measures, organizations should prioritize user education and awareness. Training users on the importance of data integrity, recognizing potential threats, and reporting any suspicious activities contributes to a culture of security consciousness. Users play a vital role in identifying anomalies that may indicate unauthorized alterations to data.

In conclusion, ensuring data integrity in Cloud BYOD environments necessitates a multifaceted approach that includes implementing integrity checks and robust hashing algorithms. These measures provide a layer of assurance that data remains unaltered during transit and at rest. By combining cryptographic protocols, robust hashing algorithms, and user awareness, organizations can fortify their defense against unauthorized modifications, thereby upholding the integrity of sensitive information in the dynamic landscape of Cloud BYOD.

13.4.2.2 Best Practices for Secure Data Storage in Cloud BYOD

In the complex landscape of Cloud BYOD environments, secure data storage is a critical component for upholding data integrity both in transit and at rest. Implementing best practices ensures that sensitive information remains intact, unaltered, and protected from unauthorized access or tampering [23,24].

1. **Encryption Protocols and FDE:** Leveraging robust encryption protocols, such as TLS for data in transit and FDE for data at rest, forms the foundation of secure data storage. FDE ensures that information stored on personal devices remains encrypted, thwarting unauthorized access in case of device loss or theft. Regularly updating encryption protocols and FDE mechanisms is vital to staying ahead of evolving security threats.
2. **Strong Authentication Mechanisms:** Implementing strong authentication mechanisms, including MFA, adds an extra layer of security to data storage. Authentication controls access to stored data, reducing the risk of unauthorized alterations. By incorporating biometrics, smart cards, or one-time passwords, organizations enhance the integrity of data access in BYOD environments.
3. **Regular Data Backups:** Establishing a routine data backup strategy is crucial for data integrity. Regularly backing up data ensures that even in the event of data corruption or loss, organizations can recover to a trusted state. Cloud-based backup solutions offer scalability and accessibility, providing an added layer of protection against unforeseen incidents.
4. **Secure Hashing Algorithms:** Employing secure hashing algorithms, such as SHA-256, assists in verifying the integrity of stored data. Hash values

generated for data sets act as unique fingerprints, allowing organizations to quickly detect any unauthorized changes. Regularly recalculating and comparing hash values provides ongoing assurance of data integrity.

5. **Data Residency Compliance:** Adhering to data residency regulations and compliance standards is crucial for secure storage. Understanding the legal and regulatory requirements regarding the storage and processing of data ensures that organizations meet specific standards, enhancing both legal compliance and data integrity.
6. **Role-Based Access Controls:** Implementing RBAC is instrumental in managing access permissions to stored data. Assigning roles based on job responsibilities ensures that users have the necessary access privileges without granting unnecessary permissions. RBAC contributes to the principle of least privilege, limiting the potential for unauthorized alterations.
7. **Continuous Monitoring and Auditing:** Implementing continuous monitoring and auditing processes enables organizations to detect and respond to anomalies promptly. Monitoring user activities, access logs, and changes to data storage enhances visibility into potential security incidents. Regular audits contribute to a proactive approach, ensuring data integrity is maintained over time.
8. **User Education and Awareness:** Educating and raising awareness among BYOD users about secure data storage practices is a fundamental aspect of maintaining data integrity. Training users on recognizing potential threats, reporting suspicious activities, and understanding the importance of following security protocols fosters a culture of vigilance and responsibility (Figure 13.1).

FIGURE 13.1 BYOD best practices at the workplace.

13.5 EMPOWERING USERS THROUGH EDUCATION AND AWARENESS PROGRAMS IN THE CLOUD ERA

13.5.1 Significance of User Training in Securing Cloud-Based BYOD

The significance of user training in securing cloud-based BYOD environments is multifaceted and pivotal for ensuring a robust cybersecurity posture. As organizations increasingly embrace cloud computing and adopt BYOD policies, educating users becomes a fundamental strategy to mitigate security risks effectively [25].

A primary focus of user training is to enhance cybersecurity awareness among employees who utilize personal devices in the cloud. By educating users about potential threats, phishing attacks, and the importance of recognizing suspicious activities, organizations cultivate a vigilant user base capable of identifying and mitigating security risks in real time.

Moreover, user training emphasizes the critical aspects of data protection and privacy within the context of BYOD and cloud usage. Through training sessions, users gain insights into handling sensitive information responsibly, adhering to data protection policies, and understanding the potential consequences of data breaches. This knowledge empowers users to actively contribute to data security efforts, fostering a culture of responsibility.

In the realm of cloud services that underpin BYOD ecosystems, user training plays a pivotal role in promoting safe cloud practices. Users are guided on secure file sharing, data access controls, and the responsible use of cloud applications. This proactive approach helps prevent accidental exposure of sensitive data and ensures that users leverage cloud services securely.

Simultaneously, user training delves into device security best practices, providing users with the knowledge to fortify their personal devices against potential threats. This includes implementing strong passwords, enabling device encryption, keeping software and applications updated, and utilizing security features such as biometrics or MFA. Strengthening device security is foundational to securing BYOD in the cloud.

Training sessions serve as a platform for communicating and reinforcing BYOD policies. Users gain insights into acceptable use guidelines, security protocols, and compliance requirements. Understanding and complying with BYOD policies ensures a cohesive and secure environment, where users actively contribute to maintaining a consistent security posture.

Furthermore, user training addresses the prevalent risks associated with phishing and social engineering attacks in cloud-based BYOD scenarios. Users learn to recognize phishing attempts, avoid clicking on suspicious links, and report potential security incidents. Heightened awareness in this regard acts as a frontline defense against cyber threats, reducing the likelihood of successful attacks.

User training extends to incident response preparedness, ensuring that users know the appropriate steps to take in the event of a security incident. This proactive approach minimizes response time, limits the potential impact of security breaches, and facilitates a swift and effective resolution.

Lastly, user training fosters a culture of continuous learning and adaptation. As cyber threats evolve, regular training sessions ensure that users stay informed about emerging risks and changing security landscapes. This ongoing education empowers users to adapt to new cybersecurity challenges, contributing to an organization's overall resilience against evolving threats.

In conclusion, the significance of user training in securing cloud-based BYOD environments lies in its capacity to create informed, vigilant, and proactive users. Through comprehensive education, organizations can empower users to play an active role in fortifying the security foundations of cloud-based BYOD environments.

13.5.2 Crafting Effective Awareness Programs in Cloud BYOD Environments

13.5.2.1 Combating Phishing and Social Engineering: A Cloud Perspective

Combating phishing and social engineering threats in the context of cloud-based BYOD environments is a critical imperative for organizations seeking to uphold security standards. Crafting effective awareness programs tailored to the cloud perspective becomes essential in educating users about these pervasive threats and mitigating potential risks associated with BYOD scenarios.

Understanding Cloud-Specific Threats: In the realm of cloud-based BYOD, where personal devices interact with sensitive corporate data, phishing attacks and social engineering threats take on new dimensions. Adversaries may exploit cloud platforms and collaboration tools, making it imperative for users to discern and respond to malicious attempts within this specific context.

Tailoring Awareness Programs to Cloud Dynamics: Effective awareness programs must be tailored to the unique dynamics of cloud-based BYOD environments. Users need to grasp the intricacies of phishing schemes that leverage cloud services, such as deceptive login pages or fraudulent file-sharing requests. The awareness training should also highlight the social engineering tactics employed in cloud-centric scenarios, emphasizing the importance of verifying requests for sensitive information or access permissions.

Simulated Phishing Exercises: Integrating simulated phishing exercises into awareness programs provides a hands-on approach for users to recognize and respond to phishing attempts. By creating realistic scenarios that mimic cloud-based interactions, organizations can gauge the effectiveness of their training initiatives and empower users to develop a heightened sense of skepticism when navigating cloud platforms.

Cloud-Specific Red Flags: Educating users on cloud-specific red flags associated with phishing and social engineering is pivotal. This includes recognizing unusual login activities, verifying the legitimacy of shared documents or links, and being cautious about unsolicited requests for sensitive information within cloud applications. Training should emphasize the importance of verifying the identity of entities seeking access or information, especially in cloud collaboration scenarios.

MFA Emphasis: Promoting the use of MFA as part of awareness programs adds an extra layer of defense against phishing attacks. Emphasizing the significance of enabling MFA for cloud services reinforces the importance of an additional authentication factor, reducing the likelihood of unauthorized access even if credentials are compromised.

Real-Time Threat Reporting: Encouraging a culture of real-time threat reporting is integral to the success of awareness programs. Users should feel empowered to report suspicious emails, messages, or activities encountered in cloud environments promptly. Establishing clear reporting channels and acknowledging the importance of user vigilance fosters a collaborative approach to combating phishing and social engineering threats.

Continuous Education and Updates: Phishing techniques evolve, and cloud-specific tactics may change over time. Continuous education and regular updates are crucial components of effective awareness programs. Keeping users informed about emerging threats, recent phishing trends, and updates to cloud security protocols ensures that their knowledge remains current and relevant.

Measuring Awareness Program Effectiveness: Implementing metrics to measure the effectiveness of awareness programs is essential. Regular assessments, user feedback, and the analysis of real-world incidents contribute to refining and enhancing the program's impact. Identifying areas of improvement ensures that the awareness initiatives remain adaptive and aligned with the evolving landscape of cloud-based BYOD security.

In conclusion, combating phishing and social engineering threats in cloud-based BYOD environments necessitates a nuanced and cloud-specific approach to awareness programs. By tailoring education initiatives to address cloud dynamics, incorporating simulated phishing exercises, highlighting cloud-specific red flags, emphasizing MFA, promoting real-time threat reporting, ensuring continuous education, and measuring program effectiveness, organizations can empower users to navigate the cloud securely and contribute to a robust defense against evolving cyber threats.

13.5.2.2 Streamlining Reporting Protocols for Security Incidents in Cloud BYOD

Streamlining reporting protocols for security incidents is a critical aspect of crafting effective awareness programs in Cloud BYOD environments. As organizations increasingly rely on cloud-based services and accommodate personal devices within their ecosystems, establishing clear and efficient incident reporting mechanisms becomes pivotal for detecting and mitigating potential security threats.

Promoting a Culture of Vigilance: A central objective of awareness programs is to instill a culture of vigilance among users in cloud-based BYOD environments. Users need to be educated on the importance of recognizing and reporting security incidents promptly. Emphasizing that every individual plays a crucial role in the organization's overall security posture fosters a collective responsibility for incident detection.

Clear and Accessible Reporting Channels: Crafting effective awareness programs involves providing users with clear and accessible reporting channels. Users should be aware of how to report incidents, whether it is a suspicious email, a potential data breach, or any abnormal behavior within cloud applications. These reporting channels could include dedicated email addresses, online forms, or direct communication with IT and security teams.

User-Friendly Incident Reporting Tools: Ensuring that incident reporting tools are user-friendly contributes to the efficiency of reporting protocols. Intuitive interfaces and straightforward procedures simplify the reporting process, encouraging users to report incidents without hesitation. This aspect is particularly crucial in a BYOD context where diverse users with varying technical proficiency are involved.

Training on Identifying Security Incidents: An effective awareness program includes training sessions on identifying security incidents specific to cloud-based BYOD environments. Users should be educated on recognizing signs of unauthorized access, abnormal account activities, or suspicious data transfer within cloud platforms. This proactive education equips users with the knowledge needed to detect potential incidents early.

Encouraging Timely Reporting: Timeliness is of the essence in incident response. Awareness programs should stress the importance of timely reporting—promptly notifying the relevant teams when users identify or suspect a security incident. This urgency allows organizations to initiate swift and targeted responses, minimizing the potential impact of security threats.

Recognition and Acknowledgment: Acknowledging and recognizing users who proactively report security incidents is a positive reinforcement strategy. This recognition can be integrated into the awareness program to motivate users and create a positive feedback loop. Publicizing success stories of incident reporting can encourage others to actively participate in maintaining a secure Cloud BYOD environment.

Education on Incident Response Procedures: Users should be educated not only on incident detection but also on the subsequent steps in the incident response process. Training programs should cover the procedures that follow incident reporting, including communication protocols, collaboration with IT and security teams, and any necessary user actions to contain and remediate incidents.

Continuous Improvement through Feedback: Crafting effective awareness programs involves a commitment to continuous improvement. Encouraging users to provide feedback on the incident reporting process helps organizations refine their protocols. Regularly assessing the effectiveness of reporting channels and incident response procedures ensures that the awareness program evolves to meet the changing dynamics of cloud-based BYOD security.

13.6 CASE STUDIES: NAVIGATING SUCCESSES AND FAILURES IN SECURING BYOD IN THE CLOUD

13.6.1 Real-World Triumphs: Successful Cloud BYOD Implementations

Real-world triumphs in successful Cloud BYOD implementations stand as compelling examples of organizations navigating the dynamic landscape of technology to achieve enhanced flexibility, productivity, and security. These success stories underscore the transformative power of leveraging cloud-based solutions in conjunction with BYOD strategies.

One notable triumph in the corporate realm involves a multinational organization that seamlessly integrated cloud technologies with BYOD policies, revolutionizing their workflow. By adopting cloud collaboration platforms, employees gained the ability to access, edit, and share documents in real time from their personal devices. This not only streamlined collaboration across geographically dispersed teams but also improved overall productivity. The cloud-based infrastructure facilitated a responsive and scalable IT environment, accommodating the diverse array of personal devices while maintaining rigorous security protocols.

In the education sector, a university's successful implementation of Cloud BYOD garnered attention for its innovative approach to enhancing learning experiences. Leveraging cloud-based learning management systems and collaborative tools, students and faculty could access course materials, collaborate on projects, and engage in virtual discussions from their personal devices. This implementation not only catered to the tech-savvy preferences of modern learners but also demonstrated significant cost savings for the institution by reducing the need for extensive hardware investments.

Another triumph emerges from the healthcare industry, where a leading medical facility achieved a seamless and secure Cloud BYOD environment. Through the adoption of cloud-based electronic health record systems and mobile healthcare applications, clinicians could access patient data securely from their personal devices, fostering mobility without compromising data security. This successful implementation not only improved healthcare delivery but also demonstrated the potential for BYOD to enhance efficiency and patient care.

Government agencies have also witnessed triumphs in Cloud BYOD implementations, exemplified by a municipality that embraced cloud-based solutions to modernize its operations. By enabling employees to use their personal devices while accessing cloud-based applications, the municipality achieved significant cost savings and improved responsiveness. The implementation showcased the scalability and adaptability of cloud solutions in a BYOD context, addressing the unique needs of a diverse workforce.

These real-world triumphs highlight the transformative impact of successful Cloud BYOD implementations across various sectors. The key factors contributing to these successes include strategic planning, robust security measures, seamless integration of cloud services, and a user-centric approach that prioritizes flexibility and productivity. As organizations continue to evolve in the digital age, these success stories serve as inspirations for others seeking to harness the full potential of Cloud BYOD strategies to achieve their goals.

13.6.2 Learning from Mistakes: Insights from Cloud BYOD Security Failures

13.6.2.1 Identifying Common Pitfalls and Learning from Mistakes

Identifying common pitfalls and learning from mistakes is a crucial aspect of enhancing Cloud BYOD security, as organizations grapple with the intricacies of managing personal devices in cloud environments. Insights gleaned from past security failures in Cloud BYOD scenarios provide valuable lessons and guidance to fortify future implementations.

1. **Inadequate User Training and Awareness:** One common pitfall is the lack of comprehensive user training and awareness programs. Organizations may overlook the importance of educating users about the unique security

challenges associated with BYOD in the cloud. Learning from mistakes in this area emphasizes the need for ongoing training that covers best practices, security protocols, and the recognition of potential threats specific to cloud-based environments.

2. **Insufficient Access Controls and Monitoring:** Security failures often stem from insufficient access controls and monitoring mechanisms. Organizations may neglect to implement robust RBAC or fail to monitor user activities effectively. Learning from mistakes in this regard underscores the necessity of establishing granular access controls, regularly reviewing permissions, and implementing continuous monitoring to detect and respond to anomalous behavior promptly.
3. **Poorly Defined BYOD Policies:** Ambiguous or poorly defined BYOD policies contribute to security vulnerabilities. Organizations may neglect to articulate clear guidelines on device usage, security configurations, and data handling practices. Learning from mistakes in this area emphasizes the importance of crafting comprehensive BYOD policies that address specific considerations in a cloud environment, ensuring that users understand their responsibilities and comply with security protocols.
4. **Insecure Data Transmission and Storage Practices:** Security failures often arise from insecure data transmission and storage practices. Organizations may overlook the significance of encrypting data in transit and at rest, exposing sensitive information to potential interception or unauthorized access. Learning from these mistakes underscores the importance of implementing robust encryption protocols to safeguard data throughout its lifecycle in the cloud.
5. **Neglecting Regular Security Audits and Updates:** A common pitfall is the neglect of regular security audits and updates. Organizations may fail to conduct timely assessments of their Cloud BYOD security posture, leading to vulnerabilities going unnoticed. Learning from mistakes highlights the necessity of periodic security audits, vulnerability assessments, and prompt application of security updates to address potential weaknesses and stay resilient against emerging threats.
6. **Lack of Contingency Planning and Incident Response:** Insufficient contingency planning and incident response readiness are recurrent pitfalls. Organizations may not have effective strategies in place to respond promptly to security incidents, leading to prolonged exposure and potential data breaches. Learning from these mistakes emphasizes the importance of developing robust incident response plans, conducting simulations, and continually refining strategies to mitigate the impact of security incidents.
7. **Overlooking Data Residency and Compliance:** Security failures may result from overlooking data residency requirements and compliance standards. Organizations may inadvertently violate regulatory frameworks by storing or processing data in non-compliant ways. Learning from these mistakes highlights the necessity of understanding and adhering to regional and industry-specific compliance standards when implementing BYOD in the cloud.

13.6.2.2 Strategic Mitigations for Cloud BYOD Security Failures

In the wake of identified failures in Cloud BYOD security, organizations are strategically mitigating risks to fortify their security postures. Learning from past mistakes, one key mitigation involves prioritizing comprehensive user training and awareness programs. Educating users on the nuances of BYOD security in the cloud, emphasizing best practices, and fostering a culture of cybersecurity awareness are crucial steps. Regular training sessions ensure that users remain informed and vigilant, contributing to a proactive defense against potential threats.

Another strategic mitigation focuses on the implementation of robust access controls and continuous monitoring. By investing in RBAC to restrict permissions based on job roles, organizations can limit the potential impact of security incidents. Continuous monitoring enhances the ability to detect anomalous activities promptly, enabling organizations to respond swiftly to potential breaches and maintain a vigilant security stance.

To address the pitfalls of poorly defined BYOD policies, organizations are prioritizing the establishment of clear and enforceable guidelines. These policies explicitly address device usage, security configurations, data handling practices, and compliance with cloud-specific security measures. Regular reviews and updates are essential to ensure that BYOD policies remain aligned with evolving security requirements and industry standards.

Secure data transmission and storage practices are critical strategic mitigations, involving the enforcement of encryption protocols for data in transit and at rest. Regular audits and assessments confirm the effectiveness of encryption measures, providing organizations with insights into potential vulnerabilities and ensuring the ongoing security of sensitive information in the cloud.

Neglecting regular security audits and updates is mitigated through a proactive security posture. Organizations conduct regular security audits and vulnerability assessments, promptly applying security updates to strengthen defenses against emerging threats. This strategic approach ensures that systems are resilient and adaptable to the evolving threat landscape.

To address the lack of contingency planning and incident response readiness, organizations are developing and testing robust incident response plans. Simulated exercises and drills help teams understand their roles and responsibilities during a security incident. Regular updates and refinements to incident response plans ensure their effectiveness in mitigating the impact of security incidents and minimizing potential damage.

Mitigating compliance and data residency issues involves a proactive approach to understanding and adhering to regulations. Thorough assessments of data residency requirements and compliance standards relevant to the industry help organizations align their Cloud BYOD practices with legal and regulatory expectations. This strategic mitigation ensures that organizations operate within the boundaries of the law while maintaining a secure and compliant environment.

In conclusion, strategic mitigations for Cloud BYOD security failures involve a multifaceted approach that addresses common pitfalls through user education, access controls, policy refinement, secure data practices, regular audits, effective incident response, and compliance measures. By incorporating these strategic elements into their security strategies, organizations can actively learn from past mistakes and cultivate a robust and adaptive security framework for their Cloud BYOD environments.

13.7 CONCLUSION

In conclusion, the strategic mitigations outlined for Cloud BYOD security represent a comprehensive and proactive approach to addressing past failures and strengthening the overall security posture of organizations. By prioritizing user training and awareness, implementing robust access controls and continuous monitoring, refining clear BYOD policies, securing data through encryption, conducting regular security audits, and developing effective incident response plans, organizations are better positioned to navigate the challenges of BYOD in the cloud. The future scope of these efforts lies in the ongoing evolution of security strategies to adapt to emerging technologies and threats. As cloud computing and BYOD continue to advance, organizations will need to stay agile in refining their security frameworks. Continuous advancements in user education and awareness programs will be crucial, considering the evolving nature of cyber threats. Additionally, the integration of artificial intelligence and machine learning into security measures holds promise for enhancing threat detection and response capabilities. These technologies can automate the analysis of user behavior, identify anomalies, and contribute to more robust monitoring in the dynamic landscape of Cloud BYOD. The future will also likely witness increased emphasis on regulatory compliance and data governance, necessitating organizations to stay abreast of evolving legal frameworks. With an ever-expanding threat landscape, collaboration and information sharing among organizations will become pivotal for staying ahead of sophisticated cyber threats. In summary, the future of Cloud BYOD security involves a continual commitment to proactive strategies, embracing technological advancements, and fostering collaboration within the security community. As organizations implement and adapt these strategic mitigations, they will be better equipped to navigate the evolving landscape of cloud-based BYOD security challenges and ensure a resilient and secure digital environment.

REFERENCES

1. Al_Janabi, S., & Hussein, N. Y. (2020). The reality and future of the secure mobile cloud computing (SMCC): survey. In *Big Data and Networks Technologies 3* (pp. 231–261). Springer International Publishing.
2. Sujatha, R., Thomas, S. C., Mathews, A., & Prabhu, S. (2021, December). Secure Cloud-based remote monitoring of environmental factors using Mobile and Web apps for industry automation. In *2021 International Conference on Computational Performance Evaluation (ComPE)* (pp. 282–287). IEEE.
3. Salih, M. M. (2021). A comparative study between Google workspace and Microsoft Office 365 productivity services in Iraqi educational institutions. International Journal of Humanities and Educational Research, **3**(5), 123–135.

4. Chen, K., Hoque, R., Dharmarajan, K., LLontopl, E., Adebola, S., Ichnowski, J., ... & Goldberg, K. (2023, October). FogROS2-SGC: A ROS2 cloud robotics platform for secure global connectivity. In *2023 IEEE/RSJ International Conference on Intelligent Robots and Systems (IROS)* (pp. 1–8). IEEE.
5. Ibrahim, A., Yousef, A. H., & Medhat, W. (2022, May). DevSecOps: A security model for infrastructure as code over the cloud. In *2022 2nd International Mobile, Intelligent, and Ubiquitous Computing Conference (MIUCC)* (pp. 284–288). IEEE.
6. Njuguna, D., & Kanyi, W. (2023). An evaluation of BYOD integration cybersecurity concerns: A case study. Int*ernational Journal of Recent Research in Mathematics Computer Science and* Information *Technol*ogy, **9**, 80–91.
7. Kelly, A. M. (2020). *The Ability to Protect Against Insider Threats Introduced via Bring Your Own Device* (Doctoral dissertation, Capella University).
8. Lanham, T. M. (2023). *Factors Impacting BYOD Mobile Device Security in Nonwork Settings: A Correlational Study* (Doctoral Dissertation, Capella University).
9. Ganiyu, S. O., & Jimoh, R. G. (2021). Extended risk-based context-aware model for dynamic access control in bring your own device strategy. *Machine Learning and Data Mining for Emerging Trend in Cyber Dynamics: Theories and Applications* (pp. 295–315).
10. Perwej, Y., Abbas, S. Q., Dixit, J. P., Akhtar, N., & Jaiswal, A. K. (2021). A systematic literature review on the cyber security. International Journal of Scientific Research and Management, **9**(12), 669–710.
11. Simpson, A. (2020). *The Factors that Impact Generation X to Adopt Bring-Your-Own-Device within the Workplace: A Correlational Study* (Doctoral Dissertation, Capella University).
12. Kholoanyane, M. E. (2020). *Security Awareness and Training Policy Guidelines to Minimise the Risk of BYOD in a South African SME* (Doctoral Dissertation, North-West University (South Africa)).
13. Adame, D. (2021). *Managing and Securing Endpoints: A Solution for a Telework Environment.*
14. Rohan, R., Papasratorn, B., Chutimaskul, W., Hautamäki, J., Funilkul, S., & Pal, D. (2023, December). Enhancing cybersecurity resilience: A comprehensive analysis of human factors and security practices aligned with the NIST cybersecurity framework. In *Proceedings of the 13th International Conference on Advances in Information Technology* (pp. 1–16).
15. Weichbroth, P., & Łysik, Ł. (2020). Mobile security: Threats and best practices. Mobile Information Systems, **2020**, 1–15.
16. Wu, D., Moody, G. D., Zhang, J., & Lowry, P. B. (2020). Effects of the design of mobile security notifications and mobile app usability on users' security perceptions and continued use intention. Information & Management, **57**(5), 103235.
17. Mitrea, T., & Borda, M. (2020). Mobile security threats: a survey on protection and mitigation strategies. In *International Conference Knowledge-Based Organization* (Vol. 26, No. 3, pp. 131–135).
18. Balapour, A., Nikkhah, H. R., & Sabherwal, R. (2020). Mobile application security: Role of perceived privacy as the predictor of security perceptions. International Journal of Information Management, **52**, 102063.
19. Krishnappa, T. (2022). Mobile security threats and a short survey on mobile awareness: a review. *International Journal of Engineering Applied Science Technology*, **7**(8), 83–88.
20. Ahmad, Z., Ong, T. S., Gan, Y. W., Liew, T. H., & Norhashim, M. (2022). Predictors of employees' mobile security practice: an analysis of personal and work-related variables. *Applied Sciences*, **12**(9), 4198.

21. Mensch, S. E., & Wilkie, L. (2021). Smart phone security practices: item analysis of mobile security behaviors of college students. In *Research Anthology on Securing Mobile Technologies and Applications* (pp. 501–516). IGI Global.
22. Russo, E., Verderame, L., & Merlo, A. (2020, December). Enabling next-generation cyber ranges with mobile security components. In *IFIP International Conference on Testing Software and Systems* (pp. 150–165). Cham: Springer International Publishing.
23. Sharma, V., You, I., Andersson, K., Palmieri, F., Rehmani, M. H., & Lim, J. (2020). Security, privacy and trust for smart mobile-Internet of Things (M-IoT): A survey. *IEEE Access*, **8**, 167123–167163.
24. Engel, M. M., Ramadhan, A., Abdurachman, E., & Trisetyarso, A. (2022). Mobile device security: a systematic literature review on research trends, methods and datasets. Journal of System and Management Sciences, **12**(2), 66–78.
25. Ismail, M., El-Rashidy, N., & Moustafa, N. (2021). Mobile cloud database security: problems and solutions. Fusion: Practice and Applications, **7**(1), 15–29.

14 CloudGuardian
Safeguarding the Internet of Things (IoT) – Navigating Security Frontiers in Cloud-Connected Ecosystems

Jahanvi B. Dinesh and Jamuna S. Murthy

14.1 UNDERSTANDING THE LANDSCAPE OF CLOUD-CONNECTED IoT DEVICES

In the contemporary technological landscape, the seamless integration of Internet of Things (IoT) devices with cloud computing has emerged as a transformative force. This synergy not only enhances the capabilities of individual devices but also enables the creation of interconnected ecosystems with unprecedented efficiency and functionality. This exploration delves into the multifaceted landscape of cloud-connected IoT devices, unraveling the intricate relationships, architectures, and dynamics that define this innovative convergence [1,2].

14.1.1 The Convergence of IoT and Cloud Computing

IoT involves connecting physical devices, sensors, and everyday objects to the internet, allowing them to collect and exchange data. Devices in an IoT ecosystem can range from smart thermostats and wearables to industrial sensors and autonomous vehicles. The primary goal of IoT is to enable real-time data monitoring, analysis, and control of connected devices, leading to improved decision-making and operational efficiency [3,4].

Cloud computing involves delivering computing services (such as storage, processing power, and applications) over the internet, rather than relying on local servers or hardware. Cloud services are provided by remote data centers, allowing users to access and utilize computing resources on-demand, often paying for what they consume [5,6].

The convergence of IoT and cloud computing refers to the integration and collaboration between these two technological domains to enhance and optimize various

DOI: 10.1201/9781003455448-14

processes and services. Both IoT and cloud computing play crucial roles in shaping the digital landscape, and their convergence brings about synergies that contribute to the efficiency and scalability of connected systems [7–10].

14.1.2 Cloud-Enabled IoT Architectures

In a cloud-enabled IoT architecture, the system is typically structured into multiple layers, each serving a distinct function in the overall framework as shown in Figure 14.1. This architecture ensures efficient data flow from the physical world to the application interface. Here is an explanation of the key layers [11,12]:

- **Sensing Layer:** Data Sensing and Collection Protocols: This layer is where the physical interaction with the environment takes place. It comprises various sensors and data collection protocols. Sensors could range from temperature sensors in a smart home to moisture sensors in smart agriculture. These devices collect data from their environment, which can be anything from simple measurements like temperature or humidity to more complex data like images or sounds. The collection protocols determine how these sensors operate, how often they collect data, and how this data is initially processed.
- **Network Layer:** IoT Devices Connected to Networks: After the data is collected, it needs to be transmitted to a place where it can be further processed and analyzed. This is where the network layer comes in. It consists of the IoT devices themselves equipped with networking capabilities, allowing them to connect to the internet or other network types (like LAN or WAN). This layer is crucial for ensuring that data collected by sensors is reliably and securely transmitted to cloud services or data centers where further processing can occur. It includes various communication technologies like Wi-Fi, Bluetooth, Zigbee, or cellular networks.

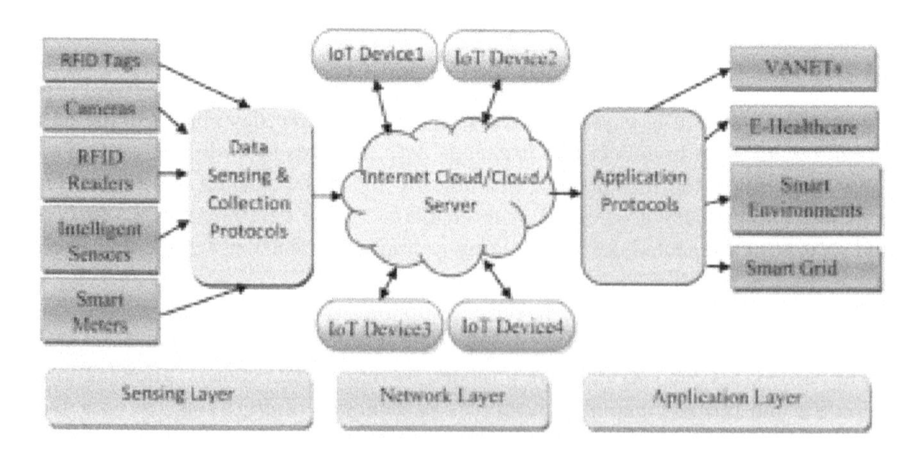

FIGURE 14.1 IoT enabled cloud architecture.

- **Application Layer:** Application Protocols: The final layer is where the processed data is utilized. The application layer consists of the protocols and software that provide the end-user functionality. This could be anything from a mobile app that lets you control your smart home devices to complex analytics software that processes data from industrial IoT sensors for predictive maintenance. Application protocols define how this software communicates with the lower layers and how it presents information to the users or other systems. It is about turning the data into actionable insights or convenient controls for the end-users.

14.1.3 Impact of Cloud Integration on IoT Device Functionality

The integration of IoT and cloud computing brings several benefits [13,14]:

- **Scalability:** Cloud computing provides scalable resources, allowing IoT systems to handle varying workloads and accommodate a growing number of connected devices.
- **Storage and Processing Power:** Cloud platforms offer extensive storage and powerful processing capabilities, enabling the efficient storage, analysis, and management of large volumes of data generated by IoT devices.
- **Real-Time Analytics:** Cloud-based analytics tools can process and analyze IoT-generated data in real-time, providing valuable insights for businesses, organizations, and individuals.
- **Cost Efficiency:** Cloud services often operate on a pay-as-you-go model, allowing organizations to manage costs effectively by paying only for the resources they consume.
- **Remote Management:** Cloud computing facilitates the remote management and monitoring of IoT devices, making it easier to update software, apply security patches, and troubleshoot issues without physical intervention.
- **Interoperability:** The convergence promotes interoperability among different IoT devices and platforms, as cloud services provide a common ground for data exchange and communication.
- **Security and Compliance:** Cloud providers often implement robust security measures, helping ensure the confidentiality, integrity, and availability of IoT data. Compliance with regulations and standards can also be better managed in a cloud environment.

14.2 UNVEILING VULNERABILITIES AND THREATS IN CLOUD-CONNECTED IoT ECOSYSTEMS

In a cloud-connected IoT ecosystem, while the integration of cloud computing with IoT devices offers numerous benefits, it also introduces specific vulnerabilities and threats that must be addressed. Understanding these risks is crucial for ensuring the security and reliability of such systems [15,16].

14.2.1 Common Vulnerabilities in Cloud-Integrated IoT Devices

- **Insecure Communication Channels:** One of the primary vulnerabilities in IoT devices integrated with cloud services is the potential for insecure communication channels. These devices often transmit sensitive data across networks. If these communications are not properly encrypted or secured, they become susceptible to interception and eavesdropping by unauthorized parties. This vulnerability can lead to the exposure of sensitive data, including personal information and proprietary business data [17].
- **Lack of Device Authentication:** Another significant issue is the lack of robust authentication mechanisms for IoT devices. Without proper authentication, unauthorized devices can easily join the network and masquerade as legitimate ones. This lack of authentication can lead to unauthorized access to the network, allowing malicious actors to gain control over IoT devices or access sensitive data [18].

14.2.2 Threats to Cloud-Connected IoT Systems

- **Data Tampering and Manipulation:** In a cloud-connected IoT ecosystem, the integrity of data is of utmost importance. However, these systems are often vulnerable to data tampering and manipulation attacks. In such attacks, unauthorized individuals may alter or manipulate the data being sent from IoT devices to the cloud or vice versa. This can lead to false information being processed, which can have serious consequences, especially in critical applications like healthcare or industrial automation.
- **Denial-of-Service Attacks on Cloud-Connected IoT Platforms:** Denial-of-Service (DoS) attacks are a significant threat to cloud-connected IoT systems. In such attacks, the attacker aims to overwhelm the system with excessive traffic or requests, leading to overloading of the IoT devices or the cloud servers. This can result in legitimate requests being denied, causing disruptions in service. In some cases, Distributed Denial-of-Service (DDoS) attacks may also be employed, where the attack comes from multiple sources, making it more difficult to prevent or mitigate.

14.3 ORCHESTRATING AUTHENTICATION AND AUTHORIZATION IN CLOUD-INTEGRATED IoT ENVIRONMENTS

In cloud-integrated IoT environments, orchestrating robust authentication and authorization mechanisms is crucial for ensuring the security and integrity of the system. This section delves into the importance of these mechanisms and the specific strategies employed to secure IoT ecosystems [19].

14.3.1 Importance of Robust Authentication Mechanisms

- **Multifactor Authentication for IoT Devices:** Multifactor authentication (MFA) adds an extra layer of security beyond just username and password. In the context of IoT, this could mean requiring a combination of credentials, such as a password, a token generated by another device, or even biometric data. Implementing MFA ensures that even if one authentication factor is compromised, unauthorized access to IoT devices remains difficult.
- **Secure Identity Management in Cloud-Connected IoT:** Managing the identities of numerous IoT devices is a complex task. Secure identity management involves ensuring that each device has a unique, verifiable identity and that these identities are managed securely throughout their lifecycle. This includes securely provisioning new devices, managing updates, and safely decommissioning devices. Proper identity management helps prevent impersonation and unauthorized access to the IoT network.

14.3.2 Authorization Protocols for Cloud-Based IoT Systems

- **Role-Based Authorization in Cloud-Connected IoT:** In role-based authorization, access rights and permissions are assigned to roles rather than individual devices. Devices or users are then assigned to these roles, inheriting their permissions. For instance, in a smart home, a 'guest' role might have limited access compared to a 'homeowner' role. This approach simplifies the management of permissions, especially in large-scale IoT deployments, and ensures that devices and users have only the access necessary for their function, reducing the risk of unauthorized or malicious activities.

14.4 SAFEGUARDING DATA THROUGH ENCRYPTION AND PRIVACY MEASURES IN CLOUD-INTEGRATED IoT

In cloud-integrated IoT environments, protecting the confidentiality and integrity of data is of paramount importance. Encryption and privacy measures play a vital role in safeguarding data from unauthorized access and ensuring that user privacy is respected. Let us delve into these aspects in more detail [20]:

14.4.1 Encryption Strategies for Cloud-Based IoT Data

- **End-to-End Encryption for IoT Communication:** End-to-end encryption (E2EE) is a method where data is encrypted on the sender's side and only decrypted by the intended recipient. In the context of IoT, this means that data transmitted from IoT devices to the cloud (or vice versa) is encrypted throughout its journey, preventing any unauthorized access or tampering during transit. This ensures that even if data is intercepted, it remains unreadable and secure.

  Example: Consider a smart home security system that includes cameras and motion sensors. When these devices detect motion or capture video, the data is sent to the cloud for processing and storage. End-to-end encryption ensures that this data, potentially sensitive, is encrypted right from the device and remains encrypted until it reaches the cloud server where it is intended to be processed. This way, even if a hacker intercepts the data mid-transmission, they cannot decipher its content.

- **Securing Data at Rest in Cloud-Connected IoT Platforms:** Apart from securing data in transit, it is equally important to protect data at rest, which refers to data stored on devices or in the cloud. Encrypting stored data ensures that even if physical security measures fail or unauthorized access is gained to storage systems, the data remains protected and inaccessible without the proper decryption keys.

  Scenario: In a smart hospital, patient monitoring devices continuously collect health data and store it in a cloud-based server. This data is encrypted while stored ("at rest") in the cloud. Even if there is a breach in the cloud storage provider's system, the encrypted patient data remains secure and unreadable without the appropriate decryption keys.

14.4.2 Privacy Considerations in Cloud-Enabled IoT

- **User Consent and Data Collection Practices:** In an IoT ecosystem, especially one that interfaces with personal or sensitive user data, it is crucial to obtain user consent for data collection. Transparent data collection practices should be established, informing users about what data is being collected, for what purpose, and how it will be used. Users should have the option to opt in or out of data collection, and their preferences must be respected [21].

  Example: A fitness tracker collects data about a user's physical activities, sleep patterns, and heart rate. The company behind the tracker clearly communicates to users what data is collected and how it will be used – for instance, for personal fitness tracking, improving device functionality, or research purposes. Users are given the option to opt-out of certain types of data collection or to delete their data from the company's servers.
- **Compliance with Data Privacy Regulations in Cloud-Connected IoT:** IoT systems, particularly those integrated with cloud services, must comply with various data privacy regulations. This includes laws like the General Data Protection Regulation (GDPR) in the European Union, which sets stringent guidelines on data protection and privacy. Compliance involves ensuring that data is collected, processed, stored, and shared in accordance with these regulations, and that users' rights to their data are maintained. This may include providing users with access to their data, the ability to correct it, and the option to have it deleted [22].

  Scenario: An IoT-based agricultural technology company operates in multiple countries and uses sensors to collect data on soil conditions, crop health, and weather patterns. The company ensures that its data practices comply with regional data privacy laws such as GDPR in Europe, CCPA in

California, and others. This includes seeking explicit consent from farmers for data collection, allowing them access to their data, and providing options to rectify or delete their data upon request.

14.5 ENSURING IoT DEVICE LIFECYCLE SECURITY IN THE CLOUD

Ensuring IoT device lifecycle security in the cloud is a multifaceted task that involves several practices and strategies. Let us explore this with industry examples and case studies [23,24]:

14.5.1 Secure Device Provisioning and Onboarding

- **Cloud-Driven Provisioning Best Practices:** A key example is Amazon Web Services (AWS) IoT Core, which offers secure device provisioning. AWS IoT Core allows devices to be provisioned in bulk with unique identities, ensuring secure communication with the cloud from the outset.
- **Establishing Trustworthy Device Identity in Cloud-Connected IoT:** An industry case is the use of Trusted Platform Modules (TPM) in devices. For instance, Microsoft Azure Sphere uses TPM for secure hardware-based storage of device credentials and cryptographic keys.

14.5.2 Monitoring and Updating IoT Devices in Cloud Environments

- **Real-Time Monitoring Strategies:** Companies like Cisco employ cloud-based IoT monitoring solutions that provide real-time visibility into IoT operations, helping detect anomalies and potential security breaches.
- **Over-the-Air Updates for Cloud-Integrated IoT Devices:** Tesla's electric vehicles are a classic example. They receive over-the-air (OTA) updates for everything from battery management to enhanced autopilot features, ensuring that the vehicle's software is always up-to-date with the latest security patches and features.

14.6 EXPLORING FUTURE TRENDS AND CHALLENGES IN CLOUD-BASED IoT SECURITY

Exploring future trends and challenges in cloud-based IoT security provides insights into the evolving landscape of IoT security within cloud environments. Here are some key aspects to consider [25]:

1. **Integration of AI and ML in Security Solutions**

    1. **Trend:** The use of Artificial Intelligence (AI) and Machine Learning (ML) for enhancing IoT security is expected to grow. These technologies can analyze large datasets in real-time, identify patterns, and detect anomalies, helping to predict and prevent security threats.

2. **Challenge:** Ensuring the robustness and reliability of AI and ML algorithms is a challenge. Adversarial attacks, where attackers manipulate input data to deceive AI systems, need to be addressed to maintain the effectiveness of these technologies.

2. **Zero Trust Security Architecture**

3. **Trend:** The adoption of a Zero Trust security model, which assumes that no entity, whether inside or outside the network, can be trusted, is gaining prominence. This model ensures continuous verification of device identity and authorization, reducing the risk of unauthorized access.

4. **Challenge:** Implementing and managing Zero Trust architectures can be complex, requiring careful planning and integration with existing systems.

3. **Supply Chain Security**

5. **Trend:** Focus on securing the entire IoT supply chain, from device manufacturing to deployment, is increasing. This involves implementing security measures at each stage to mitigate risks associated with compromised devices.

6. **Challenge:** Coordinating security measures across diverse stakeholders in the supply chain and maintaining visibility into the security practices of each participant can be challenging.

4. **Regulatory Compliance and Privacy Concerns**

7. **Trend:** Growing emphasis on regulatory compliance, especially regarding data privacy laws such as GDPR, is influencing IoT security strategies. Organizations are expected to adhere to strict data protection regulations.

8. **Challenge:** Navigating complex and evolving regulatory landscapes across different regions and ensuring compliance with diverse privacy requirements pose ongoing challenges.

5. **Quantum Computing Threats**

9. **Trend:** With advancements in quantum computing, there is a growing recognition of potential threats to existing cryptographic algorithms. Preparing for post-quantum cryptography is becoming a consideration in IoT security planning.

10. **Challenge:** Developing and implementing quantum-resistant cryptographic solutions that can withstand future quantum attacks is a complex challenge.

6. **Edge Computing Security**

11. **Trend:** The rise of edge computing in IoT introduces new security considerations. Security measures need to be extended to edge devices, where data processing occurs, to ensure the integrity and confidentiality of sensitive information.

12. **Challenge:** Managing security at the edge requires addressing resource constraints, diverse device types, and potential exposure to physical tampering.

7. **Collaborative Security Measures**

13. **Trend:** Increased collaboration between industry stakeholders, including manufacturers, cloud service providers, and cybersecurity firms, is emerging. Shared threat intelligence and standardized security protocols can improve overall IoT security.

14. **Challenge:** Establishing trust and collaboration among diverse entities while maintaining competitive advantages and protecting sensitive information is a challenge.

8. **5G Security Implications**

15. **Trend:** The widespread deployment of 5G networks introduces new capabilities for IoT but also raises security concerns. Ensuring the security of data transmitted over high-speed 5G networks is a key consideration.

16. **Challenge:** Addressing potential vulnerabilities and ensuring the resilience of IoT devices and networks in the context of 5G security challenges.

9. **Device Lifecycle Management**

17. **Trend:** Comprehensive management of the entire lifecycle of IoT devices, including secure provisioning, continuous monitoring, and timely updates, is gaining importance.

18. **Challenge:** Managing a large number of diverse devices, each with its unique characteristics, and ensuring the security of legacy devices pose ongoing challenges.

10. **Ethical Considerations in IoT Security**

19. **Trend:** Increasing awareness of the ethical implications of IoT technologies and the data they collect is influencing security practices. Considerations include user consent, transparent data usage policies, and responsible handling of sensitive information.

20. **Challenge:** Balancing innovation with ethical considerations and addressing potential biases in IoT systems require careful attention and governance.

14.6.1 Emerging Technologies Shaping the Future of Cloud-Connected IoT

1. **5G Networks:** 5G technology offers faster speeds and lower latency, facilitating more efficient and real-time data transfer between IoT devices and the cloud.
2. **Edge Computing:** This involves processing data closer to where it is generated (i.e., near IoT devices), reducing reliance on the cloud for data processing and enabling faster response times.
3. **Artificial Intelligence and Machine Learning:** AI and ML are being integrated into IoT devices for predictive analytics, automated decision-making, and enhanced data processing capabilities.
4. **Blockchain:** Blockchain technology provides a secure and transparent way to handle IoT data transactions, enhancing security and trust in IoT ecosystems.

5. **Quantum Computing:** Though still in early stages, quantum computing promises to revolutionize data processing capabilities, potentially solving complex problems much faster than traditional computers.
6. **Advanced Cybersecurity Technologies:** As IoT devices become more prevalent, advanced security technologies like AI-driven threat detection and automated response systems are becoming essential.
7. **Augmented Reality (AR) and Virtual Reality (VR):** AR and VR technologies are being integrated with IoT to enhance user experiences, especially in industries like retail, education, and healthcare.
8. **Digital Twins:** This technology involves creating digital replicas of physical devices or systems. It is used for simulation, analysis, and to predict performance issues in IoT ecosystems.
9. **Voice and Natural Language Processing (NLP):** Advanced voice recognition and NLP are being integrated into IoT devices, making interactions more intuitive and enhancing user interfaces.
10. **Energy Harvesting Technologies:** These technologies enable IoT devices to gather energy from their environment (e.g., solar, thermal, kinetic), reducing dependency on external power sources and enhancing sustainability.

14.6.2 Anticipating Security Challenges in Evolving Cloud-Enabled IoT Ecosystems

- **Scalability and Interoperability Challenges:** As IoT devices proliferate, managing and securing them at scale becomes challenging. Smart city projects, like those underway in Singapore, face interoperability challenges as they attempt to integrate various IoT devices from different vendors into a cohesive, secure ecosystem.
- **Security Implications of Edge Computing in Cloud-Connected IoT:** With the rise of edge computing, where data processing is done closer to the IoT device, new security challenges emerge. For example, autonomous vehicles operate on edge computing principles, and ensuring the security of these decentralized, high-speed data processes is a significant challenge.

These examples and case studies highlight the critical aspects of ensuring IoT device lifecycle security in the cloud, from provisioning and onboarding to ongoing monitoring and updating, along with adapting to emerging trends and challenges in a rapidly evolving field.

14.7 CONCLUSION

In conclusion, this chapter provides a thorough examination of the intricate and evolving relationship between the IoT and cloud computing, a synergy that has profoundly transformed the technological realm. It offers an insightful exploration into the architectures and functionalities that underpin cloud-enabled IoT systems, highlighting the transformative effects of cloud integration on these devices. A critical analysis of the vulnerabilities and threats facing cloud-connected IoT ecosystems forms a significant part of the discussion, underscoring the urgency for stringent security measures in the face of risks like insecure communication channels, device authentication issues, data tampering, and DoS attacks.

This chapter goes beyond identifying challenges, delving into effective strategies for authentication, authorization, and data protection within cloud-integrated IoT environments. It emphasizes the pivotal role of MFA and secure identity management in reinforcing security, alongside the deployment of sophisticated authorization protocols like role-based authorization. Furthermore, it underscores the importance of data protection, exploring advanced encryption strategies and privacy considerations, including compliance with emerging data privacy regulations.

A comprehensive approach to ensuring the security and integrity of IoT devices throughout their lifecycle in the cloud is also meticulously outlined. This encompasses everything from secure device provisioning and onboarding to the essential practices of real-time monitoring and regular OTA updates, ensuring that IoT devices remain secure and functional in the dynamic cloud environment.

Lastly, this chapter projects into the future, anticipating the trends and challenges that will shape cloud-based IoT security. It highlights the potential impact of burgeoning technologies like edge computing and discusses the implications of scalability and interoperability challenges in this rapidly evolving field. By providing a holistic view of the current state and future direction of cloud-connected IoT security, this chapter serves as a valuable resource for understanding and navigating the complex landscape of IoT and cloud computing integration.

REFERENCES

1. Alam, T. (2021). Cloud-based IoT applications and their roles in smart cities. *Smart Cities*, **4**(3), 1196–1219.
2. Sadeeq, M. M., Abdulkareem, N. M., Zeebaree, S. R., Ahmed, D. M., Sami, A. S., & Zebari, R. R. (2021). IoT and Cloud computing issues, challenges and opportunities: A review. *Qubahan Academic Journal*, **1**(2), 1–7.
3. Ray, P. P., & Kumar, N. (2021). SDN/NFV architectures for edge-cloud oriented IoT: A systematic review. *Computer Communications*, **169**, 129–153.
4. Wazid, M., Das, A. K., Bhat, V., & Vasilakos, A. V. (2020). LAM-CIoT: Lightweight authentication mechanism in cloud-based IoT environment. *Journal of Network and Computer Applications*, **150**, 102496.
5. Akhbarifar, S., Javadi, H. H. S., Rahmani, A. M., & Hosseinzadeh, M. (2023). A secure remote health monitoring model for early disease diagnosis in cloud-based IoT environment. *Personal and Ubiquitous Computing*, **27**(3), 697–713.
6. Sagheer, A., Mohammed, M., Riad, K., & Alhajhoj, M. (2020). A cloud-based IoT platform for precision control of soilless greenhouse cultivation. *Sensors*, **21**(1), 223.
7. Thirumalai, C., Mohan, S., & Srivastava, G. (2020). An efficient public key secure scheme for cloud and IoT security. *Computer Communications*, **150**, 634–643.
8. Alsharif, M., & Rawat, D. B. (2021). Study of machine learning for cloud assisted iot security as a service. *Sensors*, **21**(4), 1034.
9. Deng, H., Qin, Z., Sha, L., & Yin, H. (2020). A flexible privacy-preserving data sharing scheme in cloud-assisted IoT. *IEEE Internet of Things Journal*, **7**(12), 11601–11611.
10. Saunders, T. I. (2021). *Cybersecurity Challenges of the IoT-Enabled Home Automation Technology: A Security by Design Perspective* (Doctoral dissertation, Marymount University).

11. Sharma, V., Tripathi, A. K., & Mittal, H. (2022). Technological revolutions in smart farming: Current trends, challenges & future directions. *Computers and Electronics in Agriculture*, **201**, 107217.
12. Butt, U., Shaheer Gutappa, B., Pendlebury, G., Hassan, B., Butt, W., & Davelis, A. (2023). IoT privacy by design. In *Opportunities and Challenges of Business 5.0 in Emerging Markets* (pp. 270–300). IGI Global.
13. Ahmed Abdulsaheb, J., & Jasim Kadhim, D. (2023). Real-time SLAM mobile robot and navigation based on cloud-based implementation. *Journal of Robotics*, **2023**.
14. Hwang, H., & Joe, I. (2023). Enhancing IoT connectivity and services for worldwide ships through multi-region fog cloud architecture platforms. *Electronics*, **12**(20), 4250.
15. Singh, P. K., Singh, R., & Nandi, S. (2020). V-CARE: A Blockchain Based Framework for Secure Vehicle Health Record System. *arXiv preprint arXiv:2007.13647.*
16. Aluvalu, R., Maheswari, V. U., Mudrakola, S., & Chennam, K. K. (2022). Blockchain and IoT architectures in autonomous vehicles. *International Journal of Vehicle Autonomous Systems*, **16**(2–4), 180–203.
17. Gupta, S., Meissonier, R., Drave, V. A., & Roubaud, D. (2020). Examining the impact of Cloud ERP on sustainable performance: A dynamic capability view. *International Journal of Information Management*, **51**, 102028.
18. de Lima Salgado, A., Singh, B., Hung, P. C., Jiang, A., Liu, Y. H., de Albuquerque Wheler, A. P., & Gaber, H. A. (2020, October). Preliminary tendencies of users' expectations about privacy on connected-autonomous vehicles. In *2020 IEEE International Conference on Systems, Man, and Cybernetics* (*SMC*) (pp. 296–301). IEEE.
19. Li, X., Wang, Q., Lan, X., Chen, X., Zhang, N., & Chen, D. (2019). Enhancing cloud-based IoT security through trustworthy cloud service: An integration of security and reputation approach. *IEEE Access*, **7**, 9368–9383.
20. Kumar, R., Kumar, P., & Singhal, V. (2019, March). A survey: Review of cloud IoT security techniques, issues and challenges. In *Proceedings of 2nd International Conference on Advanced Computing and Software Engineering* (*ICACSE*).
21. Stergiou, C., Psannis, K. E., Kim, B. G., & Gupta, B. (2018). Secure integration of IoT and cloud computing. *Future Generation Computer Systems*, **78**, 964–975.
22. Choudhury, T., Gupta, A., Pradhan, S., Kumar, P., & Rathore, Y. S. (2017, October). Privacy and security of cloud-based internet of things (IoT). In *2017 3rd International Conference on Computational Intelligence and Networks* (*CINE*) (pp. 40–45). IEEE.
23. Almolhis, N., Alashjaee, A. M., Duraibi, S., Alqahtani, F., & Moussa, A. N. (2020, February). The security issues in IoT-cloud: A review. In *2020 16th IEEE International Colloquium on Signal Processing & Its Applications* (*CSPA*) (pp. 191–196). IEEE.
24. Surya, L. (2016). Security challenges and strategies for the IoT in cloud computing. *International Journal of Innovations in Engineering Research and Technology ISSN*, **3**(9), 2394–3696.
25. Alsharif, M., & Rawat, D. B. (2021). Study of machine learning for cloud assisted iot security as a service. *Sensors*, **21**(4), 1034.

15 CloudSec Dynamics
Safeguarding Interconnected Realms – From Cyber-Physical Systems to Vehicular Networks in the Cloud Age

Kedarnath S. Gubbi and Jamuna S. Murthy

15.1 UNDERSTANDING CPS IN THE CLOUD ERA

15.1.1 Overview of Cloud-Connected CPS

In the rapidly evolving landscape of technology, this section provides an in-depth exploration of Cyber-physical systems (CPS) in the context of the cloud era. It examines the fundamental principles of CPS and the pivotal role played by cloud computing in reshaping their architecture and functionality [1,2].

15.1.2 Integration of CPS into Cloud Computing Environments

In the intricate landscape of merging CPS with cloud computing environments, the subsection further navigates the technical complexities inherent in this integration process. Offering a nuanced exploration, it delves into the pivotal aspects that underpin the seamless amalgamation of CPS functionality into the cloud ecosystem [3].

- **Architecture and Protocols:** The integration unfolds within a carefully crafted architectural framework, where considerations extend to communication protocols and standardization. This involves not merely connecting physical and virtual components but architecting interfaces that facilitate efficient data exchange. The chapter meticulously dissects how these architectural elements contribute to the creation of a unified environment, where computational processes harmoniously interact with the intricacies of physical systems. By scrutinizing these details, stakeholders gain insights into the foundational structures that enable the synergy between CPS and cloud computing.
- **Data Transfer and Interoperability:** At the heart of the integration lies the imperative of smooth data transfer between CPS and cloud platforms. This section addresses challenges related to data transfer, placing a significant emphasis on the critical factor of interoperability. The discourse

DOI: 10.1201/9781003455448-15

goes beyond acknowledging the challenges, delving into strategies aimed at mitigating potential bottlenecks and enhancing the overall efficiency of data exchange. As data forms the lifeblood of CPS operations, understanding and optimizing its seamless flow become paramount in ensuring the efficacy of cloud-connected CPS.

- **Security Measures:** Recognizing the inherent sensitivity of data within CPS and cloud environments, the chapter places security at the forefront of the integration process. The exploration transcends a mere acknowledgment of security concerns, delving into the implementation of robust measures. Encryption protocols, secure communication channels, and stringent access controls take center stage as the chapter unfolds strategies to fortify the integrated system against potential cyber threats. This emphasis on security not only safeguards sensitive information but also establishes a foundation of trust among stakeholders, crucial for the successful adoption of cloud-connected CPS.
- **Scalability and Resource Optimization:** Cloud computing environments offer unparalleled advantages in scalability and resource optimization. This facet of the integration process is scrutinized in terms of how CPS can dynamically leverage cloud resources. Understanding the dynamics of scalability ensures that the integrated system is poised to adapt to evolving demands efficiently.

15.1.3 Impact of Cloud Integration on CPS Functionality

The integration of CPS into cloud environments brings about a transformative paradigm shift, reshaping the very fabric of CPS functionality. This section delves into the multifaceted impacts that the amalgamation with cloud systems has on the overall capabilities and dynamics of CPS [4].

1. **Enhanced Scalability and Flexibility:** One of the pivotal impacts of cloud integration on CPS functionality is the unprecedented enhancement of scalability and flexibility. Cloud environments, with their vast computational resources, empower CPS to dynamically scale operations based on demand. This scalability ensures that CPS can seamlessly adapt to varying workloads, whether it is in manufacturing, healthcare, or any other domain. As the computational needs fluctuate, the cloud provides a responsive infrastructure, optimizing resource utilization and bolstering the overall efficiency of CPS functionality.
2. **Real-Time Data Processing and Analysis:** Cloud integration propels CPS into a realm of enhanced real-time data processing and analysis. The cloud's computational prowess enables CPS to handle massive datasets generated by sensors and actuators in real time. This capability is particularly impactful in applications such as smart manufacturing, where instantaneous decision-making based on live data is critical. The cloud's ability to swiftly process and analyze information contributes to the agility of CPS functionality, enabling timely responses to changing conditions and optimizing system performance.

3. **Collaborative and Decentralized Operation:** Cloud-connected CPS introduces a collaborative and decentralized operational paradigm. The cloud acts as a unifying platform where disparate CPS components can seamlessly communicate and share information. This collaboration enhances the overall efficiency of CPS functionality by fostering a cohesive ecosystem where different elements contribute synergistically. Decentralization, facilitated by cloud integration, distributes computational tasks across the network, minimizing bottlenecks and points of failure. This distributed architecture ensures the reliability and resilience of CPS functionality, even in the face of individual component failures.
4. **Cost-Efficiency and Resource Optimization:** The impact of cloud integration extends to cost-efficiency and resource optimization within CPS. By leveraging cloud resources, organizations can optimize their infrastructure costs. Cloud services provide a pay-as-you-go model, allowing CPS to access computational power and storage without the need for substantial upfront investments. This flexibility in resource utilization enhances the economic viability of CPS deployment, making advanced technologies more accessible to a broader range of applications.
5. **Challenges in Latency and Connectivity:** While the impact of cloud integration on CPS functionality is overwhelmingly positive, challenges such as latency and connectivity should be acknowledged. The reliance on cloud services introduces a potential lag in data transmission, which may be critical in applications demanding ultra-low latency, such as autonomous vehicles. Balancing the benefits of cloud integration with the need for minimal latency is an ongoing consideration in optimizing CPS functionality.

In essence, the impact of cloud integration on CPS functionality is profound, ushering in an era of heightened scalability, real-time capabilities, collaborative operation, and cost-efficient resource utilization. As organizations navigate the complexities of this integration, they must strike a delicate balance to harness the benefits while addressing challenges, ensuring that CPS functionality evolves in tandem with the dynamic landscape of cloud technology.

15.2 INFUSING SECURITY INTO CPS DESIGN IN CLOUD ENVIRONMENTS

15.2.1 Strategies for Secure Cloud CPS Integration

This section constitutes a pivotal aspect of this chapter, focusing on the imperative task of infusing security measures into the design of CPS within cloud environments. It delves into nuanced strategies that play a crucial role in ensuring the integrity, confidentiality, and reliability of CPS operations within the dynamic context of cloud integration [5,6].

15.2.1.1 Secure Communication Channels between CPS and Cloud

One of the core strategies explored is the establishment of secure communication channels between CPS and cloud platforms. This involves adopting encryption techniques and secure protocols to safeguard data during transmission.

An effective strategy involves implementing transport layer security (TLS), a cryptographic protocol widely used for securing internet communications. For example, in a smart grid scenario, TLS encrypts data transmitted from sensors to a cloud-based control system. This encryption prevents unauthorized access, ensuring the confidentiality and integrity of sensitive information. TLS also supports mutual authentication, verifying the identity of both CPS and the cloud server, bolstering the overall security of communication channels [7].

15.2.1.2 Ensuring Integrity in Cloud-Connected CPS

Strategies for data integrity encompass techniques that detect and prevent unauthorized modifications or tampering of data during its journey between the physical and digital realms. By employing checksums, digital signatures, and hash functions, CPS can verify the authenticity and integrity of data, mitigating the risk of data corruption.

1. **Checksums and Verification Measures:** Implementing checksums stands out as a fundamental strategy to ensure data integrity in cloud-connected CPS. Checksums are mathematical values calculated from data and transmitted alongside it. Upon reaching the cloud, these checksums are recalculated, and any discrepancy indicates potential tampering. This method acts as a checksum verification measure, adding a layer of assurance that the data transferred is consistent and unmodified.
2. **Digital Signatures for Authentication:** The utilization of digital signatures further reinforces integrity measures. In scenarios where authentication is crucial, digital signatures are applied to data, serving as a cryptographic assurance of its origin and integrity. For instance, in a healthcare CPS where patient data is transmitted to a cloud-based analytics platform, digital signatures can validate the authenticity of the data, ensuring it has not been compromised during transmission.
3. **Hash Functions for Data Verification:** Hash functions play a vital role in ensuring the integrity of cloud-connected CPS data. By generating a fixed-size hash value unique to the data being transferred, any modification to the data will result in a different hash value. This allows for efficient verification upon arrival at the cloud, detecting any alterations and maintaining the overall integrity of the transmitted information.

The goal is to equip practitioners and system architects with a nuanced understanding of the intricacies involved in fortifying CPS designs within the dynamic and distributed environment of cloud computing. By integrating secure communication channels and ensuring data integrity resilient security framework for cloud-connected CPS can be established.

In practical terms, envision a scenario where a smart city's environmental monitoring CPS sends real-time data to a cloud repository for analysis. By employing checksums, digital signatures, or hash functions, the system can systematically verify the integrity of air quality or sensor readings. This proactive approach not only ensures the reliability of the data used for decision-making but also safeguards against potential threats seeking to manipulate critical information.

15.2.2 Cloud-Driven Security Measures in CPS Design

Within the intricate realm of CPS design immersed in cloud environments, the imperative of robust security measures takes center stage. This section serves as a comprehensive exploration of key strategies dedicated to fortifying the security posture of cloud-connected CPS. The focal points of attention encompass authentication, authorization, and encryption protocols, each playing a pivotal role in ensuring the resilience and integrity of the system against potential cyber threats [8].

15.2.2.1 Authentication and Authorization in Cloud-Connected CPS

Authentication and authorization stand as the bedrock of cloud-driven security in CPS design. Authentication ensures the verification of the identities of entities interacting within the system, allowing only legitimate users or devices access. Authorization complements this by defining permissions and actions allowed for authenticated entities.

15.2.2.1.1 Strategies

- **Multi-Factor Authentication (MFA):** Implementing MFA adds an additional layer of security by requiring users to provide multiple forms of identification before granting access. This can include passwords, biometrics, or security tokens.
- **Role-Based Access Control (RBAC):** Utilizing RBAC ensures that access permissions are granted based on the roles and responsibilities of individual entities within the CPS. This granular approach enhances security by limiting access to only necessary functionalities.
- **Token-Based Authorization:** Employing token-based authorization mechanisms where entities are granted access tokens with specific privileges. These tokens expire after a designated period, enhancing security by regularly refreshing access permissions.

15.2.2.2 Encryption Protocols for Cloud CPS Communication

Securing communication channels is pivotal in cloud-connected CPS, and encryption protocols play a central role in achieving this.

15.2.2.2.1 Strategies

- **Transport Layer Security (TLS):** Implementing TLS encrypts data during transit between CPS components and cloud platforms, ensuring the confidentiality and integrity of information. This is particularly crucial in scenarios where real-time data exchange occurs, such as in industrial automation or healthcare systems.

- **End-to-End Encryption:** Employing end-to-end encryption ensures that data remains encrypted throughout its entire journey, from the source to the destination. This is essential in safeguarding against potential interception or tampering, particularly in CPS scenarios involving critical data transfers.
- **Data Encryption at Rest:** Encrypting data at rest within cloud storage or databases adds an extra layer of protection. This ensures that even if unauthorized access occurs, the data remains unreadable without the appropriate decryption keys.

By emphasizing these cloud-driven security measures, the section aims to fortify the foundation of CPS design within cloud environments. Authentication, authorization, and encryption collectively contribute to creating a secure and resilient framework essential for the successful and trustworthy deployment of CPS in cloud environments.

15.3 IDENTIFYING THREATS AND ATTACKS ON CLOUD-CONNECTED CPS

15.3.1 Common Threat Vectors in Cloud-Integrated CPS

This section serves as a critical exploration into the potential risks and vulnerabilities faced by cloud-integrated CPS. By highlighting common threat vectors, it sheds light on the multifaceted challenges that necessitate vigilant security measures [9].

15.3.1.1 Cyber Threats to Physical Infrastructure

In this focused subsection, the spotlight turns toward the realm of cyber threats specifically directed at the physical infrastructure of CPS. The integration of cloud services introduces a new dimension of vulnerability, as attacks on the digital components can potentially manifest as real-world consequences.

15.3.1.1.1 Examples of Cyber Threats

- **Tampering with Industrial Control Systems:** Malicious actors may attempt to manipulate or interfere with the Industrial Control Systems (ICS) that govern physical processes in sectors like manufacturing or energy. Unauthorized access to these systems can lead to disruptions, downtime, or even physical damage to machinery.
- **Compromising Sensor Data:** Sensors play a crucial role in collecting real-time data from the physical environment. Cyber threats may target these sensors, injecting false data or manipulating readings. In a smart city's traffic management CPS, for instance, false sensor data could lead to misinformed traffic control decisions, causing congestion or accidents.
- **Denial-of-Service Attacks Impacting Operations:** Cloud-connected CPS are susceptible to Denial-of-Service (DoS) attacks where the availability of services is disrupted. Such attacks, if successful, can halt critical operations within the CPS. In a healthcare system relying on cloud services for patient monitoring, a DoS attack could jeopardize timely access to vital health data.

To mitigate these threats, implementing robust security measures is imperative. This involves:

1. **Access Control and Authentication Mechanisms:** Restricting access to critical components through stringent access controls and authentication mechanisms.
2. **Intrusion Detection Systems:** Deploying Intrusion Detection Systems (IDS) to detect and respond to anomalous activities in real-time, ensuring timely intervention in the face of potential threats.
3. **Secure Communication Protocols:** Implementing secure communication protocols, such as encrypted channels between physical sensors and cloud platforms, to protect data integrity.

By delving into the specifics of cyber threats to physical infrastructure, this subsection underscores the urgency of comprehensive security strategies. As cloud-connected CPS become integral to various sectors, safeguarding the physical realm from digital threats becomes paramount for ensuring the reliability, safety, and resilience of these interconnected systems.

15.3.1.2 Cloud-Based Attacks on CPS Components

This focused subsection scrutinizes the specific challenges posed by attacks originating from the cloud, emphasizing the need for proactive strategies to detect and mitigate threats targeting various components within CPS architecture [10].

15.3.1.2.1 Types of Cloud-Based Attacks

- **Data Exfiltration:** Malicious actors may attempt to extract sensitive data from CPS components hosted in the cloud. This could include proprietary algorithms, critical configuration data, or personally identifiable information. Robust encryption and access controls are crucial in preventing unauthorized access to sensitive data.
- **Distributed Denial-of-Service (DDoS) from Cloud Resources:** Cloud resources can be leveraged to launch powerful DDoS attacks on CPS components. This could overwhelm the systems, causing disruption in communication and rendering critical services unavailable. Implementing traffic filtering and DDoS mitigation strategies is essential to withstand such attacks.
- **Compromising Cloud Credentials:** Attackers may target weak authentication mechanisms or exploit vulnerabilities in cloud platforms to gain unauthorized access to CPS components. Strengthening authentication processes and regularly updating cloud platform security measures are essential in preventing unauthorized access.

15.3.1.2.2 Detection and Mitigation Strategies

- **Behavioral Analysis:** Implementing behavioral analysis tools can help detect unusual patterns or activities within cloud-based CPS components. Deviations from normal behavior can trigger alerts, allowing for swift response to potential threats.

- **Anomaly Detection Systems:** Utilizing anomaly detection systems to identify irregularities in cloud traffic or activities. These systems can detect patterns that deviate from established norms, helping to identify potential security breaches.
- **Regular Security Audits:** Conducting regular security audits of cloud infrastructure and CPS components hosted in the cloud. This proactive approach ensures that any vulnerabilities are identified and addressed promptly, reducing the risk of exploitation.

As cloud services become integral to CPS functionality, understanding and mitigating risks originating from the cloud itself are paramount for ensuring the overall security and reliability of these interconnected systems.

15.3.2 Real-Time Monitoring for Threat Detection in Cloud CPS Environments

In the ever-evolving landscape of CPS integrated with cloud environments, the critical need for real-time monitoring becomes paramount in ensuring the robust security of these complex systems. This subsection meticulously explores the intricacies of real-time monitoring for threat detection, with a specific focus on the utilization of cloud-powered solutions and the formulation of incident response strategies within the domain of cloud-connected CPS [11,12].

15.3.2.1 Cloud-Powered Monitoring Solutions

At the heart of effective threat detection in cloud-connected CPS environments lies the prowess of cloud-powered monitoring solutions. Leveraging the expansive capabilities of cloud computing, these solutions emerge as proactive guardians, employing sophisticated algorithms and scalable infrastructure. The inherent agility of the cloud allows for the dynamic analysis of voluminous datasets generated by various CPS components. By swiftly identifying anomalies and potential threats in real time, these monitoring solutions play a pivotal role in maintaining the integrity of the system. The adaptability to fluctuating workloads is particularly crucial in the context of CPS, where the nature and volume of data continually evolve. Cloud-powered monitoring not only provides a vigilant eye on the health and interactions within the system but also facilitates timely responses to emerging threats, ensuring the continuous operation of cloud-connected CPS in a secure environment.

15.3.2.2 Incident Response Strategies in Cloud-Connected CPS

Complementary to real-time monitoring is the strategic formulation of incident response plans tailored for the intricacies of cloud-connected CPS. Incident response represents a dynamic set of coordinated actions designed to mitigate the impact of security incidents, ranging from cyber-attacks to potential system breaches. The distributed and interconnected nature of cloud-connected CPS demands a responsive and adaptive incident response approach. This encompasses swift identification of the incident's nature and source, isolation of affected components, and the implementation of corrective measures. The centralized control offered by cloud environments proves invaluable, enabling coordinated incident response activities across the entire CPS ecosystem. Furthermore, cloud services provide essential tools for forensic analysis, facilitating a comprehensive post-incident assessment. This iterative process contributes to refining and enhancing future incident response strategies, ensuring the continual resilience of cloud-connected CPS against emerging security challenges [13].

In summary, the subsection underscores the indispensable role of real-time monitoring and incident response strategies in fortifying the security posture of cloud-connected CPS. Cloud-powered monitoring solutions, with their agility and scalability, serve as vigilant sentinels, while well-crafted incident response plans provide a structured and adaptive framework for addressing security incidents. Together, these elements form a robust security architecture, essential for the sustained integrity and functionality of CPS within the dynamic and interconnected realm of cloud computing.

15.4 ENSURING RESILIENCE AND RECOVERY IN CLOUD-BASED CPS

In the dynamic landscape of CPS operating within cloud environments, ensuring resilience and swift recovery mechanisms is paramount. This section delves into key strategies for cloud-driven resilience and disaster recovery planning, with a focus on redundancy, failover mechanisms, and comprehensive recovery strategies.

15.4.1 Cloud-Driven Resilience Strategies for CPS

Cloud-driven resilience strategies are pivotal in maintaining the continuous operation of CPS, even in the face of disruptions or failures. This subsection explores two critical elements: redundancy and failover mechanisms.

15.4.1.1 Redundancy and Failover in Cloud-Connected CPS

1. **Redundancy Strategies:**
    - **Data Redundancy:** Implementing data redundancy by replicating critical data across multiple cloud servers or regions. This ensures that even if one server or location experiences a failure, data remains accessible, reducing the risk of data loss.
    - **Server Redundancy:** Employing server redundancy by distributing CPS components across multiple servers. In case of a server failure, the workload seamlessly transfers to redundant servers, maintaining continuous operation.
2. **Failover Mechanisms:**
    - **Automated Failover:** Implementing automated failover mechanisms that detect system failures in real time and automatically redirect traffic or workload to healthy components. This minimizes downtime and ensures uninterrupted service.

- **Load Balancing:** Utilizing load balancing techniques to distribute incoming traffic evenly across redundant servers. In the event of a server failure, the load balancer redirects traffic to healthy servers, optimizing resource utilization and maintaining performance.

15.4.1.2 Disaster Recovery Planning for CPS in the Cloud

Disaster recovery planning is a proactive approach to mitigate the impact of unforeseen events on CPS functionality.

15.4.1.2.1 Key Components

- **Regular Backups:** Implementing regular backups of critical data and configurations to facilitate rapid recovery in case of data loss or system failure.
- **Geographically Distributed Backups:** Storing backups in geographically distributed locations to ensure data availability even in the event of a regional disaster or outage.
- **Incident Response Planning:** Developing comprehensive incident response plans that outline clear steps to be taken in the event of a security incident, ensuring a swift and coordinated response.
- **Testing and Simulation:** Regularly testing and simulating disaster scenarios to validate the effectiveness of recovery plans. This iterative process helps identify and address potential weaknesses in the recovery strategy.

By embracing these cloud-driven resilience and disaster recovery strategies, organizations can enhance the reliability and availability of CPS in cloud environments. Redundancy, failover mechanisms, and comprehensive recovery planning collectively contribute to the overall resilience of cloud-connected CPS, ensuring continued functionality and minimizing the impact of disruptions.

15.4.2 Recovering from Incidents in Cloud-Integrated CPS

In the ever-evolving landscape of CPS operating within cloud environments, effective incident recovery strategies are critical. This section delves into cloud-assisted incident recovery and draws insights from historical CPS incidents to inform resilient recovery practices.

15.4.2.1 Cloud-Assisted Incident Recovery

Cloud-assisted incident recovery is a strategic approach that leverages cloud capabilities to expedite and optimize the recovery process following a security incident or system failure.

15.4.2.1.1 Key Strategies

- **Dynamic Resource Scaling:** Utilizing the scalability of cloud resources to dynamically adjust computing capacity based on the demands of incident recovery. This ensures that additional resources are available promptly to expedite recovery processes.

- **Isolation and Quarantine:** Leveraging cloud infrastructure to isolate affected components or systems swiftly. This prevents the spread of incidents and allows for focused recovery efforts without compromising the entire CPS.
- **Backup and Snapshot Restoration:** Taking advantage of cloud-based backups and snapshots to restore systems to a known, stable state before the incident occurred. This accelerates the recovery timeline and minimizes data loss.
- **Automated Incident Response:** Implementing automated incident response mechanisms that can detect, analyze, and respond to incidents in real time. Cloud-assisted automation enhances the efficiency of incident recovery by reducing manual intervention.

15.4.2.2 Lessons from Historical CPS Incidents

Drawing lessons from historical CPS incidents provides invaluable insights into potential vulnerabilities and effective recovery strategies.

15.4.2.2.1 Key Learnings

- **Threat Intelligence Integration:** Integrating threat intelligence gained from historical incidents into incident recovery plans. This proactive approach helps organizations anticipate and mitigate emerging threats more effectively.
- **Human Factors Consideration:** Acknowledging the role of human factors in incidents and recovery efforts. Historical incidents often reveal the importance of training and awareness programs to enhance the human element's response to incidents.
- **Continuous Improvement:** Embracing a culture of continuous improvement based on lessons learned from past incidents. Regularly updating incident response plans and recovery strategies ensures adaptability to evolving threat landscapes.
- **Collaboration and Information Sharing:** Encouraging collaboration and information sharing within the industry. Insights gained from historical incidents not only benefit individual organizations but contribute to collective knowledge that strengthens the overall cybersecurity posture of CPS in the cloud.

By integrating cloud-assisted incident recovery strategies and learning from historical incidents, organizations can bolster their resilience in the face of emerging threats. The combination of cloud capabilities and insights from past experiences forms a robust foundation for proactive incident recovery in cloud-integrated CPS, ensuring rapid response and minimizing the impact of security incidents.

15.5 NAVIGATING REGULATORY AND COMPLIANCE CONSIDERATIONS IN CLOUD CPS SECURITY

In the interconnected realm of CPS operating within cloud environments, adherence to regulatory and compliance frameworks is pivotal for ensuring the security, privacy, and ethical handling of data. This section explores the landscape of compliance considerations, emphasizing industry standards, legal obligations, and ethical considerations in the context of cloud-connected CPS.

15.5.1 Compliance Frameworks for Cloud-Connected CPS

15.5.1.1 Industry Standards and Regulations

Industry standards and regulations provide a structured framework for organizations to align their cloud-connected CPS security practices with accepted norms and legal requirements.

15.5.1.1.1 Key Components

- **ISO/IEC 27001:** Adhering to the ISO/IEC 27001 standard ensures the implementation of an Information Security Management System (ISMS). This framework provides guidelines for establishing, maintaining, and continually improving the information security posture of cloud-connected CPS.
- **NIST Cybersecurity Framework:** Embracing the National Institute of Standards and Technology (NIST) Cybersecurity Framework offers a comprehensive approach to managing and improving cybersecurity risk. It provides a set of standards, guidelines, and best practices, promoting a risk-based approach tailored to the unique challenges of cloud CPS security.
- **GDPR Compliance:** Complying with the General Data Protection Regulation (GDPR) is crucial, especially when dealing with personal data in cloud-connected CPS. Ensuring transparency, consent, and the right to erasure aligns CPS operations with the privacy requirements outlined in GDPR.

15.5.1.2 Legal and Ethical Considerations in Cloud CPS

Navigating the legal and ethical landscape is integral to fostering trust and ensuring responsible use of cloud-connected CPS technologies.

- **Data Ownership and Sovereignty:** Clarifying data ownership and sovereignty issues to align with legal frameworks. Understanding where data resides, who owns it, and ensuring compliance with regional data protection laws is essential.
- **Informed Consent:** Upholding principles of informed consent, especially when dealing with sensitive data in cloud-connected CPS. This involves transparent communication with users about data collection, processing, and the purpose of use.
- **Ethical AI and Algorithmic Transparency:** Integrating ethical considerations into the design and deployment of algorithms in CPS. Ensuring transparency in AI decision-making processes contributes to ethical use and mitigates biases that may arise in cloud-driven CPS applications.
- **Incident Reporting and Accountability:** Establishing protocols for incident reporting and accountability in case of security breaches. Compliance

with legal requirements for reporting incidents and taking responsibility for security lapses is fundamental for maintaining trust in cloud-connected CPS operations.

By meticulously addressing compliance frameworks, legal obligations, and ethical considerations, organizations can navigate the complex landscape of cloud CPS security responsibly. Aligning with industry standards, adhering to regulations, and upholding ethical principles collectively contribute to the establishment of a secure, compliant, and ethically sound environment for cloud-connected CPS.

15.5.2 Adhering to Cloud Security Standards for CPS

In the intricate domain of CPS embedded within cloud environments, adherence to rigorous security standards is imperative. This section delves into the crucial aspects of certification, compliance, and privacy considerations in the integration of CPS with cloud services [14,15].

15.5.2.1 Certification and Compliance in Cloud CPS Integration

15.5.2.1.1 Certification Frameworks

- **FedRAMP (Federal Risk and Authorization Management Program):** For organizations operating in or providing services to the U.S. government, FedRAMP certification is essential. It ensures that cloud service providers meet stringent security standards, fostering a secure environment for CPS integration within government applications.
- **SOC 2 (Service Organization Control 2):** SOC 2 compliance focuses on the security, availability, processing integrity, confidentiality, and privacy of data. Adhering to SOC 2 standards is crucial, particularly when cloud-connected CPS involves the handling of sensitive information, ensuring robust security controls are in place.
- **HIPAA (Health Insurance Portability and Accountability Act):** In healthcare applications, cloud-connected CPS must comply with HIPAA regulations to safeguard the privacy and security of patient data. Certification ensures that the system meets the necessary standards for protecting health information.

15.5.2.1.2 Compliance in Cloud CPS Integration

- **Continuous Monitoring and Auditing:** Implementing continuous monitoring and auditing processes to ensure ongoing compliance with certification standards. This proactive approach helps identify and address potential security gaps in real time.
- **Vendor Assessment and Due Diligence:** Conducting thorough assessments of cloud service providers to ensure they adhere to relevant certification standards. This involves evaluating the provider's security controls, data protection measures, and overall commitment to compliance.

15.5.2.2 Privacy and Data Protection in Cloud-Connected CPS

15.5.2.2.1 Privacy Considerations

- **Data Minimization and Purpose Limitation:** Adhering to the principles of data minimization by only collecting and processing data that is strictly necessary for the intended purpose. Clearly defining the purpose of data collection ensures privacy and aligns with legal requirements.
- **User Consent and Transparency:** Prioritizing user consent and transparency regarding data collection and processing activities. Providing clear and understandable information to users fosters trust and compliance with privacy regulations.
- **Data Encryption and Anonymization:** Implementing robust data encryption and anonymization techniques to protect sensitive information. This is particularly crucial in scenarios where cloud-connected CPS involves the transmission and storage of personal or confidential data.
- **Privacy Impact Assessments (PIA):** Conducting Privacy Impact Assessments to systematically evaluate the potential privacy risks associated with cloud-connected CPS. PIAs guide organizations in identifying and mitigating privacy concerns throughout the system's lifecycle.

By prioritizing certification and compliance frameworks, and integrating privacy-centric practices, organizations can navigate the complex terrain of cloud-connected CPS securely and responsibly. Adherence to standards and privacy considerations not only mitigates risks but also fosters a culture of trust and ethical data handling within the evolving landscape of cloud-based CPS.

15.6 SECURING VEHICULAR AD HOC NETWORKS (VANETS) IN THE CLOUD AGE

In the dynamic intersection of vehicular communication and cloud technology, securing Vehicular Ad Hoc Networks (VANETs) becomes a pivotal challenge. This section unfolds the complexities and strategies involved in ensuring the robust security of VANETs within the evolving landscape of cloud connectivity [16,17].

15.6.1 Introduction to Cloud-Connected Vehicular Ad Hoc Networks

15.6.1.1 Integration of VANETs with Cloud

The introduction of cloud connectivity to Vehicular Ad Hoc Networks (VANETs) marks a transformative era in intelligent transportation systems. Cloud integration enhances the capabilities of VANETs by providing centralized services, real-time data analytics, and improved communication infrastructure as shown in Figure 15.1. Vehicles equipped with sensors and communication devices can seamlessly interact with cloud platforms, enabling advanced applications such as traffic optimization, predictive maintenance, and enhanced safety protocols.

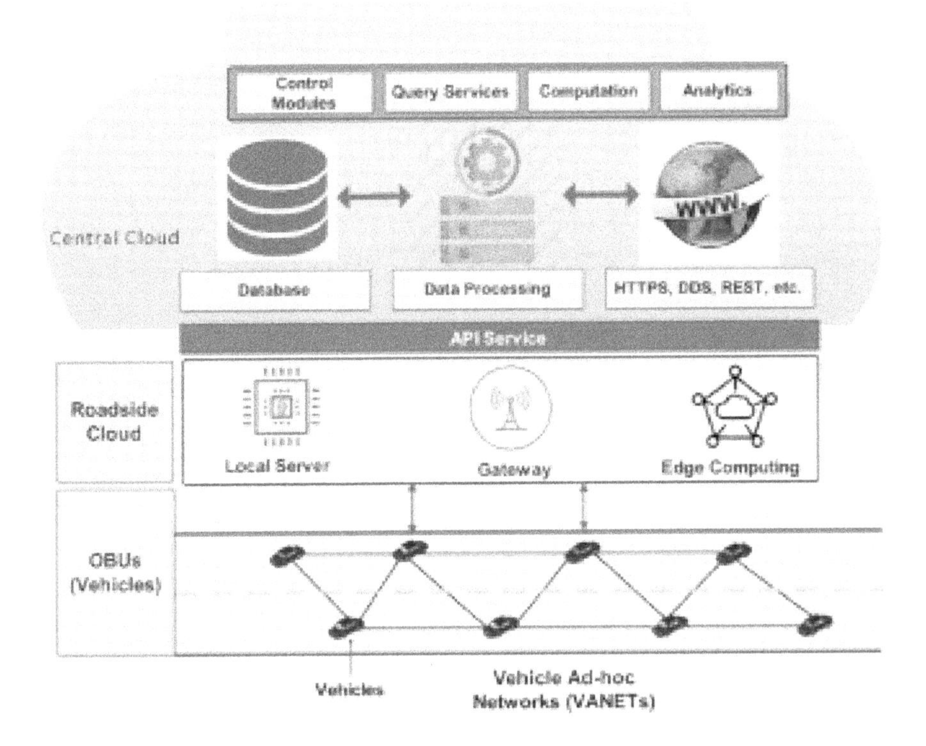

FIGURE 15.1 VANET architecture.

15.6.1.2 Challenges and Opportunities

1. **Scalability:** Cloud integration allows VANETs to scale more effectively, accommodating a growing number of connected vehicles and diverse applications.
2. **Real-Time Analytics:** Cloud-based processing enables real-time analysis of vast datasets generated by vehicles, facilitating timely decision-making for traffic management and safety.
3. **Resource Optimization:** Cloud resources can be leveraged to optimize VANET operations, such as dynamic route planning, efficient traffic flow, and adaptive signal control.

15.6.2 Communication Protocols and Cloud Architecture in VANETs

15.6.2.1 Communication Protocols

1. **Dedicated Short-Range Communication (DSRC):** DSRC remains a fundamental communication protocol in VANETs, facilitating direct vehicle-to-vehicle (V2V) and vehicle-to-infrastructure (V2I) communication.

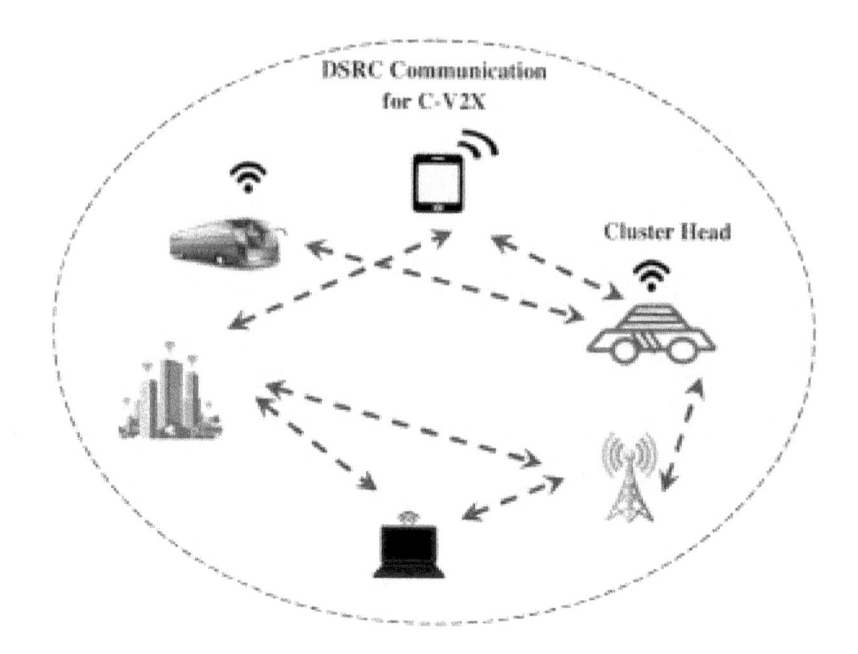

FIGURE 15.2 DRSC communication.

Cloud integration enhances DSRC by enabling extended communication ranges and improved connectivity through cloud relay points as shown in Figure 15.2.

2. **Cellular-V2X (C-V2X):** Cellular networks play a crucial role in VANETs, especially with the advent of 5G. C-V2X leverages cellular infrastructure, enabling seamless communication between vehicles and cloud services. The low latency and high-throughput characteristics of 5G contribute to efficient data exchange in cloud-connected VANETs.
3. **Cloud Architecture in VANETs**

   1. Figure 15.1 depicts the overall VANET architecture with different modules.

   - **Edge Computing for Low Latency:** Edge computing is integrated into VANETs to minimize communication latency. By processing critical data closer to the source, edge computing reduces the time required for data transmission to and from the cloud, enhancing the responsiveness of VANET applications.
   - **Distributed Cloud Services:** VANETs often rely on distributed cloud services to decentralize data processing. This approach ensures that computing tasks are distributed across multiple cloud nodes, preventing a single point of failure and enhancing the overall resilience of the network.
   - **Security in Cloud-Connected VANETs:** Cloud-based security measures are crucial in safeguarding VANETs. Authentication, encryption,

and IDS are deployed in the cloud to secure communication channels and protect sensitive information exchanged between vehicles and cloud platforms.

'Securing VANETs in the cloud age requires a holistic approach that considers communication protocols, cloud architecture, and the unique challenges posed by the vehicular environment. As cloud integration continues to shape the future of intelligent transportation, the security and efficiency of VANETs will be contingent on adaptive strategies that harness the potential of cloud technologies while addressing the specific needs of vehicular communication.

15.6.3 Privacy and Trust Management in Cloud VANETs

- **Privacy Concerns in Cloud VANETs:** Privacy is a paramount concern in the integration of Vehicular Ad Hoc Networks (VANETs) with cloud services. The extensive exchange of sensitive vehicular data in the cloud necessitates robust privacy measures. Trust management mechanisms play a crucial role in establishing a secure and privacy-preserving environment. Techniques such as pseudonymization, where vehicles use temporary identifiers to mask their true identity, contribute to protecting individual privacy. Privacy-preserving data aggregation methods also enable efficient cloud-based analytics without compromising the identity of individual vehicles [18].
- **Trust Management:** Trust in cloud-connected VANETs involves assessing the reliability of information exchanged between vehicles and cloud platforms. Reputation systems can be employed to evaluate the trustworthiness of participating vehicles based on their historical behavior. Secure and transparent protocols for trust establishment and maintenance are essential to foster a collaborative and secure vehicular ecosystem.

15.6.4 Identifying Threats to Vehicular Communication and Data in the Cloud

Identifying and mitigating threats to vehicular communication and data in the cloud is a critical aspect of ensuring the security of VANETs [19,20].

15.6.4.1 Common Threats

- **Data Tampering:** Malicious actors may attempt to alter or manipulate data exchanged between vehicles and the cloud. Robust encryption and integrity verification mechanisms are crucial for detecting and preventing data tampering.
- **Eavesdropping:** Unauthorized interception of communication poses a significant threat. Secure communication protocols, such as end-to-end encryption, are essential to protect against eavesdropping attacks.
- **Denial-of-Service:** Cloud-connected VANETs are susceptible to DoS attacks that can disrupt communication channels. Implementing traffic filtering and anomaly detection can help mitigate the impact of such attacks.

- **Identity Spoofing:** Adversaries may attempt to impersonate legitimate vehicles, leading to trust and security breaches. Strong authentication mechanisms and regular updates of cryptographic keys are vital for preventing identity spoofing.

15.6.5 Cloud-Enabled Security Mechanisms for VANETs

Cloud-enabled security mechanisms play a pivotal role in fortifying VANETs against evolving threats.

- **Cloud-Powered Monitoring Solutions:** Leveraging cloud-based monitoring solutions enhances the capability to detect anomalies and intrusions in real time. The cloud's computational power allows for comprehensive analysis of network behavior and rapid response to security incidents.
- **Incident Response Strategies in Cloud-Connected CPS:** Cloud-assisted incident response strategies contribute to the resilience of VANETs. Automated incident response mechanisms, coupled with cloud resources, enable swift and effective mitigation of security breaches.

15.6.6 Exploring Future Directions in Cloud-Connected Vehicular Network Security

The future of security in cloud-connected vehicular networks envisions several key advancements [21,22].

- **Decentralized Security:** Integrating blockchain technology to establish decentralized security mechanisms. This could involve utilizing blockchain for secure and transparent transaction logs, enhancing trust, and ensuring the integrity of data in cloud VANETs.
- **Predictive Security Measures:** The integration of AI for predictive security measures, enables VANETs to anticipate and proactively addresses security threats. Machine learning algorithms can analyze historical data to identify patterns indicative of potential attacks, enhancing the overall security posture.
- **Quantum-Resistant Encryption:** Implementing quantum-resistant encryption to prepare for the future impact of quantum computing on current cryptographic methods. Quantum-safe cryptography ensures that VANETs remain secure against emerging quantum threats.

As cloud-connected vehicular networks evolve, the focus on privacy, trust management, and advanced security mechanisms becomes increasingly critical. By addressing current challenges and exploring innovative approaches, the security of cloud-connected VANETs can be bolstered, paving the way for safer and more reliable intelligent transportation systems [23–25].

15.7 CONCLUSION

In conclusion, the exploration of "Cloud-Driven Security for Cyber-Physical Systems: Strategies, Threats, and Future Horizons" has unveiled the intricate dynamics of integrating CPS with cloud environments. The chapters delved into foundational aspects such as understanding CPS in the cloud era, emphasizing the overview of cloud-connected CPS, integration strategies, and the subsequent impact on CPS functionality. Strategies for infusing security into CPS design within cloud environments were detailed, including secure communication channels, integrity assurance, and authentication measures. Threat identification in cloud-connected CPS sheds light on common vectors, spanning from cyber threats to physical infrastructure to cloud-based attacks on CPS components. The significance of real-time monitoring and incident response strategies in cloud CPS environments was underscored, emphasizing the need for continuous vigilance and adaptive security measures.

Moreover, resilience and recovery strategies were expounded upon, with a focus on redundancy, failover mechanisms, and comprehensive disaster recovery planning. Navigating regulatory and compliance considerations in cloud CPS security explored industry standards, legal obligations, and ethical considerations, emphasizing the importance of aligning practices with established frameworks. Securing Vehicular Ad Hoc Networks (VANETs) in the cloud age highlighted the transformative integration of cloud services with intelligent transportation systems. The chapters delved into communication protocols, cloud architecture, privacy considerations, trust management, threat identification, and emerging security mechanisms specific to VANETs in the cloud era.

Looking ahead, the future scope lies in the continual evolution of security measures to address emerging challenges. Privacy concerns in CPS and VANETs are likely to persist, necessitating innovative solutions that balance data utilization with individual privacy rights. As quantum computing advancements loom on the horizon, the integration of quantum-resistant encryption becomes imperative to fortify the security of cloud-connected systems. Additionally, the anticipated fusion of artificial intelligence with security measures offers the potential for predictive threat detection and proactive incident response. The ongoing exploration of decentralized technologies like blockchain is poised to reshape security paradigms, ensuring transparency and resilience in the face of evolving cyber threats. As the cloud continues to be a driving force in CPS security, a holistic and adaptive approach will be essential to navigate future challenges and harness the full potential of these interconnected systems securely.

REFERENCES

1. Reine, R., Juwono, F. H., Sim, Z. A., & Wong, W. K. (2021). Cyber-physical-social systems: an overview. *Smart Connected World: Technologies and Applications Shaping the Future*, **1**(1), 25–45.
2. Xie, Y., Zhou, Y., Xu, J., Zhou, J., Chen, X., & Xiao, F. (2021). Cybersecurity protection on in-vehicle networks for distributed automotive cyber-physical systems: state-of-the-art and future challenges. *Software: Practice and Experience*, **51**(11), 2108–2127.

3. Pundir, A., Singh, S., Kumar, M., Bafila, A., & Saxena, G. J. (2022). Cyber-physical systems enabled transport networks in smart cities: Challenges and enabling technologies of the new mobility era. *IEEE Access*, **10**, 16350–16364.
4. Cho, B. M., Jang, M. S., & Park, K. J. (2020). Channel-aware congestion control in vehicular cyber-physical systems. *IEEE Access*, **8**, 73193–73203.
5. Chen, C., Liu, X., Qiu, T., & Sangaiah, A. K. (2020). A short-term traffic prediction model in the vehicular cyber-physical systems. *Future Generation Computer Systems*, **105**, 894–903.
6. Lu, Y., Huang, X., Dai, Y., Maharjan, S., & Zhang, Y. (2020). Federated learning for data privacy preservation in vehicular cyber-physical systems. *IEEE Network*, **34**(3), 50–56.
7. Lu, Y., Huang, X., Dai, Y., Maharjan, S., & Zhang, Y. (2020). Federated learning for data privacy preservation in vehicular cyber-physical systems. *IEEE Network*, **34**(3), 50–56.
8. Alshdadi, A. A. (2021). Cyber-physical system with IoT-based smart vehicles. *Soft Computing*, **25**(18), 12261–12273.
9. Li, C., Zhang, H., Zhang, T., Rao, J., & Yin, G. (2020). Cyber-physical scheduling for predictable reliability of inter-vehicle communications. *IEEE Transactions on Vehicular Technology*, **69**(4), 4192–4206.
10. Zhao, Y., Liu, Z., & Wong, W. S. (2021). Resilient platoon control of vehicular cyber physical systems under DoS attacks and multiple disturbances. *IEEE Transactions on Intelligent Transportation Systems*, **23**(8), 10945–10956.
11. Olowononi, F. O., Rawat, D. B., & Liu, C. (2021, January). Federated learning with differential privacy for resilient vehicular cyber physical systems. In *2021 IEEE 18th Annual Consumer Communications & Networking Conference* (*CCNC*) (pp. 1–5). IEEE.
12. Okafor, K. C., Adebisi, B., Akande, A. O., & Anoh, K. (2024). Agile gravitational search algorithm for cyber-physical path-loss modelling in 5G connected autonomous vehicular network. *Vehicular Communications*, **45**, 100685.
13. Chavhan, S., Dubey, N., Lal, A., Khetan, D., Gupta, D., Khanna, A., ... & Pinheiro, P. R. (2020). Next-generation smart electric vehicles cyber physical system for charging slots booking in charging stations. *IEEE Access*, **8**, 160145–160157.
14. Delicato, F. C., Al-Anbuky, A., Kevin, I., & Wang, K. (2020). Smart cyber-physical systems: toward pervasive intelligence systems. *Future Generation Computer Systems*, **107**, 1134–1139.
15. Kamal, M. A. S., Tan, C. P., Hayakawa, T., Azuma, S. I., & Imura, J. I. (2021). Control of vehicular traffic at an intersection using a cyber-physical multiagent framework. *IEEE Transactions on Industrial Informatics*, **17**(9), 6230–6240.
16. Xie, Y., Zeng, G., Kurachi, R., Xiao, F., & Takada, H. (2021). Optimizing extensibility of CAN FD for automotive cyber-physical systems. *IEEE Transactions on Intelligent Transportation Systems*, **22**(12), 7875–7886.
17. Kavaiya, S., Patel, D. K., Ding, Z., Guan, Y. L., & Sun, S. (2020). Physical layer security in cognitive vehicular networks. *IEEE Transactions on Communications*, **69**(4), 2557–2569.
18. Arooj, A., Farooq, M. S., Umer, T., Rasool, G., & Wang, B. (2020). Cyber physical and social networks in IoV (CPSN-IoV): A multimodal architecture in edge-based networks for optimal route selection using 5G technologies. *IEEE Access*, **8**, 33609–33630.
19. Rathore, M. M., Attique Shah, S., Awad, A., Shukla, D., Vimal, S., & Paul, A. (2021). A cyber-physical system and graph-based approach for transportation management in smart cities. *Sustainability*, **13**(14), 7606.

20. Thiruloga, S. V., Kukkala, V. K., & Pasricha, S. (2022, January). TENET: Temporal CNN with attention for anomaly detection in automotive cyber-physical systems. In *2022 27th Asia and South Pacific Design Automation Conference* (*ASP-DAC*) (pp. 326–331). IEEE.
21. Makarfi, A. U., Rabie, K. M., Kaiwartya, O., Li, X., & Kharel, R. (2020, May). Physical layer security in vehicular networks with reconfigurable intelligent surfaces. In *2020 IEEE 91st Vehicular Technology Conference* (*VTC2020-Spring*) (pp. 1–6). IEEE.
22. Jia, D., Sun, J., Sharma, A., Zheng, Z., & Liu, B. (2021). Integrated simulation platform for conventional, connected and automated driving: A design from cyber-physical systems perspective. *Transportation Research Part C: Emerging Technologies*, **124**, 102984.
23. Ye, J., Guo, L., Yang, B., Li, F., Du, L., Guan, L., & Song, W. (2020). Cyber-physical security of powertrain systems in modern electric vehicles: Vulnerabilities, challenges, and future visions. *IEEE Journal of Emerging and Selected Topics in Power Electronics*, **9**(4), 4639–4657.
24. Mazumder, S. K., Kulkarni, A., Sahoo, S., Blaabjerg, F., Mantooth, H. A., Balda, J. C., ... & De La Fuente, E. P. (2021). A review of current research trends in power-electronic innovations in cyber-physical systems. *IEEE Journal of Emerging and Selected Topics in Power Electronics*, **9**(5), 5146–5163.
25. Jiang, F., Liu, X., & Zhang, L. (2021, July). Event-triggered control for inter-vehicle communications of cyber-physical transportation systems. In *2021 40th Chinese Control Conference* (*CCC*) (pp. 4709–4714). IEEE.

Case Studies

1. Examination of Real-World Case Studies on Successful and Failed Data Sharing
2. Provenance-based Security in a Multicloud Environment
3. Incident Response and Attribution in Cloud-based Systems
4. Successful Implementation of Data Provenance in a Cloud-native Infrastructure
5. Seamless Identity Federation Across Multiple Cloud Providers
6. Challenges and Solutions in Identity Management for Hybrid Clouds
7. Achieving Compliance through Federated Identity Systems
8. Success Stories in Achieving Data Accountability
9. Challenges Encountered and Mitigation Strategies
10. Comparative Analysis of Accountability Practices in Google Cloud and AWS
11. Real-World Implementations and Success Metrics
12. Lessons Learned and Recommendations for Industry Adoption
13. Evaluating the Effectiveness of Privacy-Preserving Techniques in Google Cloud
14. Industry Use Cases with Emphasis on Google Cloud and AWS Deployments
15. Analyzing Security Challenges Faced and Resolutions Achieved
16. Leveraging Azure Blockchain for Enhanced Data Privacy Compliance in a Multinational Cloud Project
17. GCP's Confidential VMs in Securing Sensitive Data in USA-based Financial Cloud Projects
18. AWS Control Tower Implementation for Effective Governance in UK Government Cloud Projects
19. GCP Interconnect for Secure Communication between Public and Private Clouds
20. Azure Confidential Computing for Machine Learning Model Encryption and Deployment
21. Secure Information Flow in Multicloud Environments
22. Ensuring Privacy in Cloud-based Machine Learning
23. Secure Data Transfer in Edge Computing Environments
24. Microsoft Azure Homomorphic Encryption Toolkit for Privacy-preserving Cloud Computation
25. AWS Nitro Enclaves for Efficient and Isolated Execution of Sensitive Workloads
26. Real-World Triumphs: Successful Cloud BYOD Implementations
27. Learning from Mistakes: Insights from Cloud BYOD Security Failures

Index

For Product Safety Concerns and Information please contact our EU representative GPSR@taylorandfrancis.com
Taylor & Francis Verlag GmbH, Kaufingerstraße 24, 80331 München, Germany

www.ingramcontent.com/pod-product-compliance
Ingram Content Group UK Ltd.
Pitfield, Milton Keynes, MK11 3LW, UK
UKHW021117180425
457613UK00005B/122

* 9 7 8 1 0 3 2 5 9 6 1 1 2 *